Introduction

What is an idiom?

The term 'idiom' is not an easily defined one - it can refer to many kinds of words and phrases. The traditional definition of an idiom is 'a group of words which has a different meaning from the sum of its parts'. For example, you can **make someone's blood boil** or say they are **a sight for sore eyes**. Knowing the meanings of all the words in such a phrase will not necessarily help you to understand the meaning of the whole phrase.

This guide is designed to help anyone who wants to know about idioms, including not only what they mean, but also how to use them. It provides an introduction to the most commonly used idioms in British and American English. Each idiom has its own entry with a full-sentence definition. These not only define the idiom but also show it in grammatical context. Further usage information is given in the examples, which have all been based on a corpus. Idioms are clearly labelled to show whether they are common in British or American English and which register or level of language the idiom belongs to. When the idiom has any synonyms or near-synonyms these are also shown.

To make this guide as easy to use as possible, idioms are listed according to a strict ordering system. Under this system, any idiom that you are looking for which contains a noun will be found under the *first noun* that occurs within it. So **make someone's blood boil** will be found under **blood**. If there is no noun in the idiom, look for the *first verb*. For example **not much to look at** will be found under **look**. If there is no noun or verb in the idiom that you are looking for, it will be found at the *first adjective*. An example of this kind of idiom would be **alive and kicking**, which will be found under **alive**. If there is no noun, verb, or adjective, look for the *first adverb*. So **anywhere from**, will be found under **anywhere**.

There is one notable exception to this rule. This is that idioms of the type **happy as a clam**, or **cool as a cucumber**, although they contain a noun, will always be found under the *first adjective*. This is because there are often several possible nouns which can go with the adjective, and so it is more useful to see them grouped together.

This guide also includes Idioms Study panels which present a variety of idioms that can be used in particular situations. Turn to the panel on **anger** and you will find sections called **being angry**, **suddenly becoming angry**, **making someone angry**, and **speaking angrily to someone**. These will help you to express anger in many different ways.

Idioms Study Panels   Page

Contributors

Publishing Manager
Elaine Higgleton

Editors
Kay Cullen
Penny Hands
Una McGovern
John Wright

Organization of entries

books

○ **cook the 'books** (*informal*)

Someone **cooks the books** when they change the numbers in their, or their company's, accounts in order to gain money for themselves or the company: *They are now saying that everyone is cooking the books. If it's true, it's a very serious allegation.*

boom

○ **lower the 'boom on someone** (*AmE; informal*)

When you **lower the boom on someone**, you severely scold or punish them: *If my daughter stays out late again, I'm going to lower the boom on her.*

card

○ **have a 'card up your sleeve** or **keep a 'card up your sleeve**

You **have**, or **are keeping, a card up your sleeve** if other people think that you are in a difficult situation, but you have a secret solution which you plan to surprise them with: *Don't cry. Just wait and see. Your old grandad has still got plenty of cards up his sleeve.*

When people cheat at cards they sometimes hide an extra card up their sleeve.

colour (*AmE* **color**)

○ **add 'colour to something**

Something that **adds colour to something** else brings some energy, interest or variety to that thing: *His enthusiastic lecturing style adds colour to a subject that many people regard as dull.*

day (*see also* **days**)

○ **all in a day's 'work**

You can say that something is **all in a day's work** if it forms part of your everyday activities, and must be accepted as normal, even if you find it unpleasant or difficult in some way: *Controlling a class of excitable seven year olds is all in a day's work if you are a teacher on a placement scheme.* ♦ *see also* **a necessary evil** ▷EVIL

Definitions are written as whole sentences, showing the idiom being used in a natural and grammatically correct way.

Idioms are labelled to show whether they are common in British English (*BrE*) or American English (*AmE*).

Notes of interest (i) explain the history of certain idioms, (ii) define words within idioms and (iii) give variants and information on usage.

The mark ' shows where the main stress occurs in the idiom. If the main stress shifts to another part of the sentence in speech, this is shown in the example.

Cross-references to other headwords help you to find the idiom you are looking for.

Register labels show if an idiom is formal, informal, insulting or vulgar. They will also tell you if the idiom is used humorously, or if it was more commonly used in the past.

Variants are always given in full.

Examples, supported by the British National Corpus, show how the idiom is used.

American spellings are shown in brackets.

Cross-references to other idioms are marked with a diamond and introduced with the words *see also*. These draw your attention to variations and other idioms with similar meanings to help you to expand your knowledge in particular subject areas. The arrow ▷ tells you where to find the idiom.

A

○ **go from A to 'B** or **get from A to 'B**
You **go** or **get from A to B** when you go from one place to another: *How long does it take to get from A to B?*

○ **A to 'Z**
From **A to Z** means from the beginning to the end, or, of a subject, covered thoroughly: *She went through the whole explanation again from A to Z.* □ *an A to Z of London.* [= book of maps showing all the roads in London]

accident

○ **an accident waiting to 'happen**
You can say that someone or something is **an accident waiting to happen** if you feel sure that they are going to be involved in some kind of disaster at some time: *That son of theirs is an accident waiting to happen.*

○ **more by accident than de'sign**
Something desirable that happens **more by accident than design**, happens more through chance than because of anyone's skill or judgement: *He got the job more by accident than design, since it was he who had to take over when his boss first went off sick.*

account

○ **on no ac'count**
1 You say that **on no account** will you do something, or will something happen, when you will not do it, or it will not happen, under any circumstances: *On no account will I ask them for money.*
2 You say that something should **on no account**, or **not on any account**, be done, if it must never be done: *Don't on any account switch off the computer.*

○ **settle an ac'count**
You **settle an account** with someone when you do something to harm them in return for something unpleasant that they have done to you in the past: *It has been suggested that the murder was committed as a way of settling an account between the two gangs.*

ace

○ **have an ace up your 'sleeve** or (*AmE*) **have an ace in the 'hole**
You **have an ace up your sleeve** or **have an ace in the hole** when you have a secret or hidden advantage that you can use against an opponent: *I bet he's got an ace up his sleeve; he wouldn't let anybody beat him that easily.*

act

○ **act of 'God**
An **act of God** is a totally unexpected natural event, such as an earthquake, which you could not have predicted or prevented: *Famine caused by drought is not an unstoppable act of God. It is simply the most dramatic manifestation of soil degradation, caused by poor agricultural techniques.*

> '**Act of God**' is a legal term referring to events for which you cannot expect compensation from insurance.

○ **catch someone in the 'act**
You **catch someone in the act** when you discover them while they are doing something wrong: ♦ *see also* **catch someone red-handed** ▷CATCH

○ **clean up your 'act**
Someone **cleans up their act** when they start complying with general standards of behaviour: *I think it's about time I cleaned up my act and started taking my responsibilities a bit more seriously.*

○ **get in on the 'act**
You **get in on the act** when you get yourself involved in some profitable deal or activity in order to share the benefits: *Everybody's getting in on the act now; the market's totally flooded with computer games of this type.*

○ **get your 'act together**
You **get your act together** when you organize yourself, your time and your work efficiently: *We're going to have to get our act together if we want to finish this job by the end of the month.*

actions

○ **a hard act to 'follow**

You say that someone or something is **a hard act to follow** when they set such a high standard that others will find it difficult or impossible to match them: *It won't be easy taking over from the old managing director; he's quite a hard act to follow.*

> 'Act', here, refers to a performance in the theatre or a cabaret, for example.

○ **put on an 'act**

Someone **puts on an act** when they behave in an elaborately false or artificial way: *The most uncomfortable part now is the interviews, because I can't put on an act, particularly on TV.*

> This expression often occurs in the negative, and is used to talk about not being able to, or not wanting to, change one's natural behaviour.

actions

○ **actions speak louder than 'words**

If you say '**actions speak louder than words**', you mean that what people do is more important and effective than what they say: *Okay, well, since actions speak louder than words, I think we should consider a one-day strike.*

Adam

○ **not know someone from 'Adam**

If you say that you do **not know someone from Adam**, you mean that you do not have any idea who they are: *You can't be suggesting I was with him last night; I don't know him from Adam.*

> According to the Bible, Adam was the first man on earth, and therefore someone you could not possibly know.

age

○ **act your 'age**

If you tell someone to **act their age** you are telling them to stop being childish or silly: *Why don't you just act your age for once?*

○ **come of 'age**

1 You **come of age** when you become legally old enough to have an adult's rights and duties: *I came of age in the '60s, when there were chances, when it*

was all there waiting. **2** Someone or something **comes of age** when they reach a level at which they are recognized as being fully mature, developed, or independent: *The English-language feature film came of age in the 1930s.*

○ **a ripe old 'age or a grand old 'age or the grand old age of 'such-and-such or the ripe old age of 'such-and-such**

Someone who has lived to **a ripe**, or **grand**, **old age**, or to **the ripe**, or **grand**, **old age of** a certain number of years, has lived to a very old age: *She lived to the grand old age of 91.*

agree

○ **agree to 'differ**

Two people **agree to differ** when they decide to stop arguing with each other because neither of them is prepared to change their opinion: *I think we're just going to have to agree to differ, don't you?*

air

○ **clear the 'air**

Something such as a quarrel or argument **clears the air** if it gives people the opportunity to express their opinions frankly, and so reduces tension: *A good argument often clears the air.*

○ **give someone the 'air** (*AmE*)

You **give someone the air** when you reject them as a lover: *He's been depressed since last weekend when she gave him the air.*

○ **into thin 'air**

Someone or something disappears **into thin air** if they disappear suddenly and completely: *My keys seem to have disappeared into thin air.*

○ **out of thin 'air**

Someone or something appears **out of thin air** if they appear suddenly and unexpectedly: *Then suddenly, out of thin air, she appeared in the room.*

○ **walk on 'air**

You **are walking on air** when you are extremely happy: *He's been walking on air ever since he met Julia.* ♦ *see also* **thrilled to bits** ▷BITS; **on cloud nine** ▷CLOUD; **in seventh heaven** ▷HEAVEN; **over the moon** ▷MOON

airs

○ **put on airs and 'graces** (*BrE*) or **put on 'airs** (*AmE*)

Somebody **puts on airs and graces**,

or **puts on airs**, when they behave in a way that suggests that they want people to think that they are more important or sophisticated than they really are: *Bella never put on airs and graces, remaining a real Blackpool girl.*

alarm

○ **alarm bells start to 'ring** or **warning bells start to 'ring**

You say that **alarm bells**, or **warning bells**, **start to ring** when you begin to sense that something is going wrong: *The warning bells started to ring for me when I noticed she seemed to have a lot more money than usual.*

alive

○ **alive and 'kicking**

Someone is **alive and kicking** when they are still alive and in a strong and healthy condition: *No, he's not dead, he's alive and kicking, and living in North London with his family.*

amiss

○ **would not come a'miss** or **would not go a'miss**

You say that something **would not come**, or **go, amiss** when you want it or would welcome it: *A little patience wouldn't come amiss.*

anger *see* **Idioms study** page 4

ants

○ **'ants in your pants**

You say that someone has got **ants in their pants** when they cannot stop moving around or when they are very restless in general: *It rained all day, and by the end of the afternoon we all had ants in our pants.*

anywhere

○ **'anywhere from** (*AmE*)

'**Anywhere from** one thing to another' means between those two things: *I'll be paid anywhere from $5 to $8 for the job.*

appearance *see* **Idioms study** page 5

appearances

○ **keep up ap'pearances**

You **keep up appearances** when you pretend to be cheerful, or in good health, or financially well off, while suffering private misfortunes and worries: *Her deep sense of duty and obli-*

gation impelled her to keep up appearances for the sake of the public.

apple

○ **the apple of someone's 'eye**

If someone is **the apple of your eye**, you love them more than others and you are very proud of them: *Of course he loves all his daughters, but Katy is definitely the apple of his eye.*

> '**Apple**', here, originally referred to the pupil of the eye [= the round, black part]. The person in question was therefore as precious to you as your own eyes.

○ **upset the 'applecart**

Someone **upsets the applecart** when they spoil someone's plans: *He is anxious not to upset the applecart by cutting the lending rate too quickly.*

apron

○ **tied to someone's 'apron strings**

Someone who is **tied to someone's apron strings** is under the control of, or dependent on, a woman, especially their mother: *We have all met adults who are tied to mother's apron strings, often in many subtle ways.*

> An **apron** is a piece of clothing that covers the front of you, which you tie round your waist over your clothes to stop them getting dirty when you are cooking.

ark

○ **like something out of the 'ark** (*BrE*)

You say that a thing is **like something out of the ark** when it is extremely old-fashioned: *Mum was still using that old iron. It's like something out of the ark.*

> The **ark**, here, refers to Noah's ark in the Bible, into which two of every sort of animal went, to shelter from floods. Something out of the ark, therefore, is very old.

arm

○ **chance your 'arm** (*BrE*)

You **chance your arm** when you take a risk: *You'll never get anything done in this life if you don't chance your arm occasionally.*

IDIOMS*study*

anger

The next time you write or talk about **anger** you might try to use some of the following idioms. (Remember you can see how to use each idiom correctly by looking at its entry, which you can find under the word printed in heavy type.)

being angry

up in **arms**
like a **bear** with a sore head
beside yourself

hopping **mad**
foam at the **mouth**
on the **warpath**

suddenly becoming angry

throw up your **arms**
cut up rough
go off the deep **end**
blow a **fuse**
fly off the **handle**
lose your **head**

blow, or flip, your **lid**
do your **nut**
lose your **rag**
fly into a **rage**
see red
go **spare**

blow your **stack**
throw a **tantrum**
lose your **temper**
blow your **top**
throw a **wobbly**

making someone angry

make someone's **blood** boil
get a **rise** out of someone

set someone's **teeth** on edge

speaking angrily to someone

send someone away with a
flea in their ear
give someone **hell**
let fly
take it **out** on someone
give someone a **piece** of your
mind

rant and rave
give someone the rough **side** of
your tongue
cause a **stink**
tear someone off a **strip**
jump down someone's **throat**
have **words** with someone

○ **cost an arm and a 'leg**
Something **costs an arm and a leg** when it is very expensive: *I can't believe these shoes have broken already; they cost an arm and a leg.* ♦ *see also* **a pretty penny** ▷PENNY

○ **give your right 'arm**
You say that you would **give your right arm** for something, or to do

something, if you would like it very much: *I would have given my right arm to be there with a camera.*

○ **put the 'arm on someone** (*AmE*)
You **put the arm on someone** when you put pressure on them for something, especially a loan: *Jeff is putting the arm on his best friend for $200.*

IDIOMS*study*   appearance

The next time you write or talk about **appearance** you might try to use some of the following idioms. (Remember you can see how to use each idiom correctly by looking at its entry, which you can find under the word printed in heavy type.)

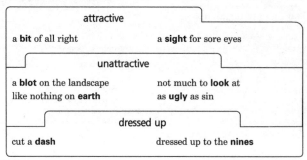

attractive

a **bit** of all right   a **sight** for sore eyes

unattractive

a **blot** on the landscape   not much to **look** at
like nothing on **earth**   as **ugly** as sin

dressed up

cut a **dash**   dressed up to the **nines**

○ **twist someone's 'arm**
You **twist someone's arm** when you try hard to persuade them to do something; people often say, humorously, that someone has twisted their arm if they accept an offer readily: *'Have another drink.' 'Oh go on then, you've twisted my arm.'*

arms

○ **throw up your 'arms**
You say that someone **throws up their arms** when they express a strong emotion such as anger or despair: *She threw up her arms in despair when I told her I'd crashed the car again.*

○ **up in 'arms**
People are **up in arms** when they are very angry, and are protesting about something: *My lads are really up in arms. Nobody believes this story about the sacking incident.*

art

○ **get something down to a fine 'art**
You say you **have got something down to a fine art** if after a lot of practice you have discovered the best way of doing it: *Over the years I've got it down to a fine art. I make lists.*

atmosphere

○ **you could have cut the atmosphere with a 'knife**
You say that **you could have cut the atmosphere with a knife** when you are describing a situation in which you felt that there were very unpleasant or unfriendly feelings between people there: *I think they must have been having a row just before I arrived – you could have cut the atmosphere with a knife in there.*

auction

○ **put something up at 'auction** (*AmE*)
You **put something up at auction** when you offer an item for sale at an auction: *Now I know where my records went. Dad put them up at auction.*

avail

○ **to no a'vail**
You do something **to no avail** when you do not get the desired result: *I have scoured magazines for any information on this subject, but so far to no avail.*

awakening

○ **a rude a'wakening**
You experience **a rude awakening** when you have an unpleasant surprise: *Jones is an idealist, and will probably*

face a rude awakening when confronted with the realities of bureaucracy.

axe (*AmE* **ax**)

○ **have an 'axe to grind**

You **have an axe to grind** when you have a strong belief or desire that something should happen, and you keep telling people about it, and trying to persuade them to see its importance; you **have no axe to grind** if you are not very concerned about a particular matter, or if you do not disapprove of it: *We all have an axe to grind now that our working conditions have become so unbearable.* □ *Mr Doe insists that he is no opponent of privatization as such and has no political axe to grind.*

babe

○ **babe in the 'woods** (*AmE*)

A **babe in the woods** is a person who is innocent and can easily be deceived: *Mary only knew the countryside, and was a babe in the woods when she moved to Miami.*

baby

○ **leave someone holding the 'baby** (*BrE*)

You **leave someone holding the baby** when you stop working on a problem or project, and leave someone else to deal with it on their own; you are **left holding the baby** when you are the person who has to deal with a problem or organize something because everyone else has left you to do it on your own: *I've been left holding the baby; jobless, practically penniless, worrying about how I'm going to pay the rent.* ♦ *see also* **leave someone in the lurch** ▷LURCH

○ **throw the baby out with the 'bathwater**

You **throw the baby out with the bathwater** when you are so enthusiastic about change and getting rid of old ideas that you destroy or dispose of things that remain essential: *The more ambitious supporters of the new method threw the baby out with the bathwater.*

back

○ **the back of be'yond** (*informal*)

A place that is in, or at, **the back of beyond** is a long way from any public facilities or houses: *You feel as if you're in the back of beyond, yet it's only forty-five minutes from London.* ♦ *see also* **in the middle of nowhere** ▷MIDDLE; **out in the sticks** ▷STICKS; **off the beaten track** ▷TRACK; **out of the way** ▷WAY

> This idiom is often used to speak about a place in a critical way.

○ **break the 'back of something**

You say you **have broken the back of something**, such as a task, when you have completed most of it, or the most difficult part of it: *They are confident that they have finally broken the back of the technical problem.*

○ **get off someone's 'back** (*informal*)

If you tell someone to **get off your back** you mean that you want them to stop criticizing and pressurizing you: *If I can just pay this last instalment, the bank manager might get off my back for a while.*

○ **have your back to the 'wall**

You **have your back to the wall** when you are forced into a difficult situation which you feel you cannot escape from: *Of course, if your back is to the wall and you have to fight, then that is also classed as self-defence.*

> This idiom comes from sword fighting, when the person who is losing has walked backwards as far as they can go, and must continue to defend themselves from a fixed position.

○ **put your 'back into something** (*informal*)

You **put your back into something**

when you try hard to do it well: *If he really made an effort and put his back into it, he'd be finished soon.*

○ **put someone's 'back up** (*informal*)
You **put someone's back up** if you annoy them: *I think I put her back up a bit when I remarked on her being late.*

> When a cat is angry, it raises its back into the shape of an arch.

○ **see the 'back of** (*BrE*; *informal*)
You are glad to **see the back of** someone or something unpleasant and annoying if you are relieved to have finished with them: *I bet you'll be glad to see the back of that place when you graduate, won't you?*

> When someone walks away from you, you see their back.

○ **stab someone in the 'back**
Someone **stabs you in the back** if they appear to be friendly when they are with you, but then say unpleasant or harmful things about you when you are not there: *She trusted Robert; he was so unlike Graham, who was probably stabbing her in the back at that very moment.*

○ **you scratch my back and I'll scratch 'yours**
If you say to someone, '**you scratch my back and I'll scratch yours**' you mean that if they do favours for you, you will do favours for them: *After all, you scratch my back and I'll scratch yours; that's what business is about.*

bacon
○ **save someone's 'bacon** (*BrE*; *informal*)
You can say you **have saved someone's bacon** if you have helped them to avoid getting into trouble or if you have helped them out of a dangerous situation: *There is also an 'undo' command which will save your bacon if you have accidentally deleted a file from your disk.*

bad
○ **have got it 'bad** (*informal*)
You say that someone **has got it**

bad if they are so much in love that they act in a way that is not typical of their normal behaviour: *Oh dear, he's got it bad; he's taken to writing poetry now.*

○ **in 'bad with someone** (*AmE*)
You are **in bad with someone** when they are angry with you because of something you have said or done: *Walter took a two-hour lunch and, of course, is now in bad with his boss.*

○ **not 'bad** or **not too 'bad** (*informal*)
You describe something as **not bad**, or **not too bad**, if you think it is fairly good, or if you think it is okay: *That's not a bad drawing.* □ *'How's your sore throat?' 'Not too bad.'*

> 'Not bad' can, in fact, mean anything from 'quite good' to 'not very good at all', depending on the speaker's intonation.

bag
○ **in the 'bag¹** (*informal*)
You say that something is **in the bag** if it is certain to be achieved or obtained: *All they have to do is tell the people what they want to hear; and their re-election's in the bag.*

> A phrase from hunting, where you put what you have shot in your bag.

○ **in the 'bag²** (*AmE*)
Someone is **in the bag** when they are drunk: *When Harold started singing, his wife knew he was in the bag.*

bait
○ **rise to the 'bait** or **take the 'bait**
You **rise to the bait**, or **take the bait**, if you let yourself get annoyed when someone is teasing you and trying to upset you: *Don't rise to the bait; they'll tease you even more.*

> A phrase from fishing, where you put bait on to your hook to attract the fish.

ball
○ **carry the 'ball** (*AmE*)
You **carry the ball** when you take responsibility for something, or make certain that a job is done: *Everyone*

worked hard, but it was Melissa who carried the ball.

> A phrase from American football, where the player who carries the ball is the most important one.

○ **drop the 'ball** (*AmE*)
You **drop the ball** when you make a bad mistake, or when you fail: *Dan was in charge of buying the tickets, but he dropped the ball.*

> A phrase from American football, used when an attacking player loses the ball he is carrying.

○ **the ball is in 'so-and-so's court**
You say that **the ball is in** a certain person's **court** when they are responsible for the next move in a situation: *I told them we were interested in buying, but at a lower price; so the ball's in their court now.*

> In tennis, when the ball is in your court, it is on your side of the net and you must hit it back to the other player.

○ **have a 'ball** (*informal*)
You **are having a ball** if you are having an enjoyable time, usually socially: *Sounds like she's having a ball at that university of hers; I hope she's finding time to get some work done as well.* ♦ *see also* **live it up** ▷LIVE; **have the time of your life** ▷TIME

○ **have something on the 'ball** (*AmE*)
If you say someone **has something on the ball**, you mean they are clever and have ability: *I wouldn't have hired my brother if he didn't have something on the ball.*

○ **on the 'ball** (*informal*)
You are **on the ball 1** if you have all the most recent information about something: *They're very much on the ball in this department where research is concerned.* **2** if you are paying attention to what you are doing: *He wasn't quite on the ball at the meeting this morning.*

○ **set the 'ball rolling or get the 'ball rolling or start the 'ball rolling**
You **set, get,** or **start, the ball rolling** when you cause some activity to begin;

you **keep the ball rolling** when you make sure an activity continues: *To get the ball rolling, here are a few questions I've prepared.*

○ **a whole new 'ball game or a completely different 'ball game or a different ball game alto'gether** (*informal*)
A situation or activity which is **a whole new ball game, a completely different ball game,** or **a different ball game altogether,** is one which you are not used to: *Life's a completely different ball game once you've left home and have to look after yourself.* ♦ *see also* **kettle of fish** ▷KETTLE

> This idiom refers to the fact that every game has its own separate set of rules.

ballistic

○ **go ba'llistic**
You **go ballistic** when you become very angry and shout at people: *When I told him what had happened to the car, he went ballistic.*

balloon

○ **go down like a lead ba'lloon** (*humorous*)
Something such as a suggestion or a performance **goes down like a lead balloon** when it is not well received: *His sexist jokes went down like a lead balloon.* ♦ *see also* **fall flat** ▷FALL

ballpark

○ **in the right 'ballpark, in the wrong 'ballpark** (*informal*)
Something such as an estimate is **in the right ballpark** if it is likely to be more or less correct; an estimate is **in the wrong ballpark** if it is far from being correct: *We exclude those observations where the estimates were clearly in the wrong ballpark.*

> In baseball, the term **in the ballpark** means 'within the limits of the playing area'.

bananas

○ **be ba'nanas** (*informal*)
If you say that someone **is bananas** you mean they are mad or stupid; people **go bananas** when they go mad or get wild with anger: *You paid £6000 for*

that? You must be bananas. ▢ His mum would go bananas if she saw him smoking. ◆ *see also* **off your trolley** ▷TROLLEY; **off your rocker** ▷ROCKER

bandwagon

○ **jump on the 'bandwagon** or **climb on the 'bandwagon**

People **jump**, or **climb, on the bandwagon** when they join in, or show interest in, a popular activity only because it is fashionable, and they hope to gain some advantage or public praise for doing so: *Channel 4's Saturday-night series showing favourite TV shows from the past has been so successful that the BBC have jumped on the bandwagon.*

A **bandwagon** was a large and beautiful vehicle for circus musicians, pulled by a horse in a circus procession.

bane

○ **the bane of your 'life**

Something that is **the bane of your life** causes you constant trouble and problems: *This weight problem has always been the bane of my life.*

bang

○ **bang goes 'such-and-such** (*informal*)

You say **bang goes** a certain thing when the probability of it happening or succeeding suddenly disappears: *Bang go my chances of promotion.*

○ **bang 'on** (*BrE*)

Something is **bang on** when it is exactly right or precise; you are **bang on** something if you are in exactly the right place or situation at the right time: *That's right. You're bang on; how did you know that?* ▢ *The train left bang on 'time for once; just the day that I happened to be late.* ◆ *see also* **spot on** ▷SPOT

○ **go with a 'bang** (*BrE*; *informal*)

Something that **goes with a bang** is a great success: *In the end the evening went with a bang and everyone enjoyed themselves.*

○ **start with a 'bang**

If something **starts with a bang**, it starts with great energy and enthusiasm: *He hired a band to start*

his election campaign with a bang.

bank

○ **I wouldn't 'bank on it** (*informal*)

You say '**I wouldn't bank on it**' if you think that the person you are speaking to is depending on something which in fact may not happen: *'It's okay, Henry will give me a lift to the airport.' 'I wouldn't bank on it, it's his afternoon off.'* ◆ *see also* **don't count your chickens before they are hatched** ▷CHICKENS

bargain

○ **drive a hard 'bargain**

Someone who **drives a hard bargain** negotiates hard to get an agreement that will be of most benefit to themselves: *The new managers were warned that the union chiefs were likely to drive a hard bargain.*

○ **into the 'bargain** (*informal*)

You use '**into the bargain**' when you want to emphasize some additional and rather surprising element in a situation: *They are expected to be exemplary girlfriends, brilliant cooks, and to have a super job into the bargain.*

bargepole

○ **not touch something with a 'bargepole** (*BrE*; *informal*) or **not touch something with a 'ten-foot pole** (*AmE*; *informal*)

If you say that you **wouldn't touch something with a bargepole**, or **with a ten-foot pole**, you mean that you refuse to have anything to do with it, for example, because it is not safe or reliable: *I warned against it at the time, telling investors not to touch it with a bargepole.*

A **bargepole** is a long pole used for moving a barge on a canal.

barrel

○ **have someone over a 'barrel**

Someone **has got you over a barrel** if they are in a position to get whatever they want from you: *If I don't pay now, they'll just keep putting the price up; basically they've got me over a barrel.*

○ **scrape the 'barrel** (*BrE*) or **scrape the bottom of the 'barrel** (*AmE*)

You say you **are scraping the barrel,**

or **scraping the bottom of the barrel**, when you have to use, or take, poor-quality things or people because the best have already been used or taken, or because you can't get anything better: *You're scraping the barrel a bit with those old jokes, aren't you?*

If a barrel is almost empty you may have to scrape inside it to get the last of the contents out.

base

○ **off 'base** (*AmE*; *informal*)
You describe someone as being **off base** when you think they are badly mistaken about something: *If you believe we can afford that, you are way off base.*

In baseball, a runner who is **off base** is in danger of being put out.

bash

○ **have a 'bash** (*BrE*; *informal*)
You **have a bash**, or **have a bash at something**, when you try to do it: *I've never sung a solo in public before but I don't mind having a bash.*

bat

○ **go to 'bat for someone** (*AmE*)
If you **go to bat for someone**, you help, support or defend them: *Everyone blamed Michael, so Jack went to bat for him.*

In baseball, a player bats for another player who is injured or playing poorly.

○ **like a bat out of 'hell**
You go somewhere **like a bat out of hell** when you move at a great speed: *When I saw the headteacher coming I was out of there like a bat out of hell.*

○ **off the 'bat** or **right off the 'bat** (*AmE*)
When you do something **off the bat** or **right off the bat**, you do it immediately: *I said we were in a hurry, so he signed the papers right off the bat.*

○ **off your own 'bat** (*BrE*)
You do something **off your own bat** when you do it without being told to, or without help: *I didn't ask her to prepare a forward plan; she did it off her own bat.*

bath

○ **take a 'bath** (*AmE*)
You **take a bath** when you lose a lot of money in a deal or investment: *The computer shares looked good, but I really took a bath when the market dropped.*

batteries

○ **recharge your 'batteries**
You **recharge your batteries** when you have a rest, for example when you take a holiday, in order to regain your energy and enthusiasm for work: *Don't try to do too much when you're on holiday; this is a good chance for you to recharge your batteries.*

battle

○ **fight a losing 'battle**
You **are fighting a losing battle** if you are trying to do something which is certain to fail: *I'm fighting a losing battle, trying to get Joanne to stay on at school.*

○ **'half the battle**
If you say that something is **half the battle**, you mean that it is an important step towards success: *'They've invited me in for an interview.' 'Oh well, that's half the battle, isn't it?'*

bay

○ **hold at 'bay** or **keep at 'bay** (*formal*)
You **keep**, or **hold**, something or someone unwanted or threatening **at bay** when you keep them at a distance so that they do not harm or affect you: *Concentrating on her guests would keep her worries at bay for a little while.* □ *The best medicine for keeping colds at bay is a dose of your favourite tipple.*

This idiom comes from the French hunting term 'aux abois', describing the stage of the hunt when the animal can neither escape nor attack because it is just about to be caught.

be

○ **the be-all and 'end-all**
The **be-all and end-all** of something is the final aim, or the most important part of that thing: *Don't worry too much; good exam results aren't the be-all and end-all of education.*

This idiom comes from Shakespeare's *Macbeth*.

beans

○ **full of 'beans¹** (*informal*)

You are **full of beans** if you are lively and cheerful: *'You're full of beans this morning.' 'I know; I think it must be the sun.'* ♦ *see also* **bright-eyed and bushy-tailed** ▷BRIGHT

○ **full of beans²** (*AmE*; *informal*)

If you say someone is **full of beans** you believe they are badly mistaken about something: *'You think the Yankees will win the World Series? Boy, are you full of beans.'*

○ **spill the 'beans** (*informal*)

You **spill the beans** about something when you tell people a secret, or when you finally tell them something that you have been keeping to yourself: *'Come on, spill the beans. What's this all about?' 'It's something Mum said.'* ♦ *see also* **let the cat out of the bag** ▷CAT; **give the game away** ▷GAME

bear

○ **like a bear with a sore 'head** (*BrE*)

You describe someone as being **like a bear with a sore head** if they are in a bad mood: *'You're looking thinner.' 'Must be a bug; Luke's got it, too, not to mention behaving like a bear with a sore head when I asked to take an early lunch.'*

beat

○ **beat someone 'hollow** (*BrE*) or **beat someone 'all hollow** (*AmE*)

You **beat someone hollow**, or **all hollow**, when you defeat them easily: *I'd been beaten hollow all year on the squash court, and I was determined to get a bit fitter.* ♦ *see also* **beat someone hands down** ▷HANDS

○ **'beat it** (*informal*)

People **beat it** when they rush away, usually to avoid trouble; if you tell someone to **'beat it!'**, you are telling them, rather rudely, that you want them to go away: *Now beat it, before I call the police.*

○ **if you can't beat 'em, 'join 'em** (*informal*)

If someone says **'if you can't beat 'em, join 'em'** they mean that if you can't persuade people to change their opinions, then the most sensible thing to do is to change your own opinion: *Melanie Simmonite says she started racing 20 years ago – her husband did it so it was a case of if you can't beat 'em join 'em.*

> **'Em**, here, is the short, informal form of the word 'them'.

beauty

○ **beauty is in the eye of the be'holder**

If you say that **beauty is in the eye of the beholder** you mean that things or people that are considered to be beautiful by one person are not necessarily considered beautiful by other people: *In the final analysis, beauty is in the eye of the beholder, and essentially a personal matter. What pleases me may not please you, and my recommendation may disappoint you.*

> This idiom is often adapted to suit the needs of the speaker. You may therefore find expressions like 'perfection is in the eye of the beholder', or 'cleanliness is in the eye of the beholder' [=what is considered perfect, or clean, by one person is not necessarily considered to be so by another].

○ **beauty is only skin 'deep**

If you say that someone's or something's **beauty is only skin deep** you mean that being physically attractive is not necessarily a good guide to a person's character: *Sometimes when you meet a beautiful woman, you know their beauty is more than skin deep, and so it was with Rachel.*

> This idiom is often adapted to the speaker's needs; therefore you may find 'more than skin deep', 'little more than skin deep', or 'that skin-deep quality', for example.

beaver

○ **beaver a'way**

You **are beavering away** at something when you are working very hard at it: *There, beavering away in their individual boxes, were other Eurocrats surrounded by shelves full of files.*

> **Beavers** are animals which are known for working very hard all the time.

○ **eager 'beaver** (*humorous*)
You call someone an **eager beaver** if they are enthusiastic about something, or very hard-working, in rather a child-like way: *The company takes on a new set of young, ambitious eager beavers in September every year.*

> See note at **beaver away.**

beck

○ **at someone's beck and 'call**
You are **at someone's beck and call** if you are always ready to carry out their orders or wishes: *I had to be at his beck and call, night and day. He often got me out of bed at night to run an errand.*

bed

○ **get out of bed on the wrong 'side**
You say that you **have got out of bed on the wrong side** when little things keep going wrong for you; you can also say that someone **got out of bed on the wrong side** when they seem to be in a bad mood: *I must've got out of bed on the wrong side today – that's the second cup of coffee I've spilt.* □ *What's the matter with Alan today? Did he get out of bed on the wrong side?* ♦ *see also* **not be someone's day** ▷DAY; **one of those days** ▷DAYS

○ **in 'bed with** (*informal*)
You say that two or more public figures or groups are **in bed with** each other if they have the same opinions or are helping each other without openly admitting it: *It's supposed to be a self-governing body, but everyone knows they're in bed with the Government.*

○ **no bed of 'roses** or **not a bed of 'roses**
1 If you tell someone that life is **no bed of roses**, or **not a bed of roses**, you mean that things in life are not always pleasant, and that we have to accept the unpleasant moments too. **2** If you say that a certain activity is **no**, or **not a, bed of roses**, you mean that it is unpleasant or difficult: *It's no bed of roses teaching in a secondary school.*

○ **you've made your bed, now you'll have to 'lie in it**
If you say to someone '**you've made your bed, now you'll have to lie in it**', you mean that they will have to suf-

fer the unpleasant side of a situation which they have created themselves: *I'm sorry to sound unsympathetic, but you've made your bed, now you'll have to lie in it.*

bee

○ **a 'bee in your bonnet**
You have **a bee in your bonnet** when you have an idea or belief that has become an obsession: *'Is she still worrying about my diet?' 'You know her – once she gets a bee in her bonnet she won't let the matter rest.'*

○ **think you are the bee's 'knees**
If you say that someone **thinks they are the bee's knees**, you think they have too high an opinion of themselves: *And he thought he was the bee's knees, you see; he thought he knew everything.*
♦ *see also* **think you are the cat's whiskers** ▷CAT

beeline

○ **make a 'beeline for**
You **make a beeline for** a particular place or person when you go towards them quickly and directly: *Victoria made a beeline for the sandwiches.*

> Bees fly in a straight line when they are returning to their hive.

beg

○ **beg to 'differ** (*formal*)
You say that you **beg to differ** with someone on a certain point, when you disagree in a very formal way: *I'm afraid I must beg to differ on this point.*

beggars

○ **beggars can't be 'choosers**
If you say that **beggars can't be choosers**, you mean that people who have a great need for something have to accept whatever is offered: *I didn't really want to take a job like this again, but I suppose now that I'm unemployed – beggars can't be choosers.*

begging

○ **going 'begging** (*informal*)
Something is **going begging** when it does not belong to anyone and is therefore being offered to any person who wants it: *There are a few sandwiches going begging here; has anybody still not had one?*

beginner

○ **beginner's 'luck**

You have **beginner's luck** when you are unexpectedly successful at an early stage of learning something: *Congratulations to our new Assistant Editor, who (thanks to a large slice of beginner's luck!) made accurate predictions for all the World Cup matches.*

behind

○ **right be'hind someone**

You are **right behind someone** when you fully support them: *Don't listen to them – we're right behind you on this.*

belief

○ **beyond be'lief**

Something which is **beyond belief** is incredible: *His rudeness is beyond belief.* ♦ *see also* **have to be seen to be believed** ▷SEEN

bell

○ **ring a 'bell** (*informal*)

You say that something such as a name **rings a bell** if it is familiar or reminds you of something: *His name rings a bell.*

○ **ring the 'bell** (*AmE*)

Something **rings the bell** if it is exactly what is needed: *Lower interest rates will ring the bell for new home-buyers.*

○ **saved by the 'bell**

People sometimes exclaim **'saved by the bell!'** when someone is rescued from an unpleasant or difficult situation by something which brings the situation suddenly to an end.

In boxing, a bell indicates the end of a round and the fight stops.

belt

○ **below the 'belt**

A remark or comment that is **below the belt** is unkind and unfair, or unacceptable: *'Perhaps, Mr Prentice, as you're obviously out of work, you should take a course in housekeeping.' That was below the belt, but she went on.*

In boxing, it is against the rules to hit your opponent below the level of the belt.

○ **tighten your 'belt**

You **tighten your belt** when you have to get used to having less money to spend than usual: *We have to do our best to pull ourselves out of this recession and tighten our belts.*

○ **under your 'belt**

You have something **under your belt** when you have done or achieved it, and will be able to use it to your advantage in the future: *If you have followed our training schedules you will not just turn up on the day, unprepared and with no training under your belt.*

bend

○ **bend over 'backwards**

You **bend over backwards** to help someone when you do everything you can to help them: *They bent over backwards to make sure we were comfortable.* ♦ *see also* **lean over backwards** ▷LEAN

○ **drive someone round the 'bend** (*informal*)

You say that someone or something **is driving you round the bend** if they are annoying you intensely: *That noise outside is driving me round the bend.* ♦ *see also* **get someone's goat** ▷GOAT; **get on someone's nerves** ▷NERVES; **get up someone's nose** ▷NOSE; **rub someone up the wrong way** ▷WAY; **get on someone's wick** ▷WICK

○ **round the 'bend** (*BrE; informal*)

You say that someone is **round the bend** if you think they are mad. ♦ *see also* **round the twist** ▷TWIST

benefit

○ **give someone the benefit of the 'doubt**

You **give someone the benefit of the doubt** when you accept that what they say is true, even though there is no evidence to support it: *I'll give you the benefit of the doubt this time, but you must bring your identification with you.*

bent

○ **bent out of 'shape** (*AmE*)

You are **bent out of shape** if you feel insulted or angry: *Sam has been bent out of shape since we left him off the guest list.*

beside

○ **be'side yourself with something**

You are **beside yourself with** an emotion like worry or anger if that emotion is so strong that you cannot think and behave as you normally do: *He was beside himself with anxiety.*

best

○ **at 'best**

You describe something unsatisfactory as a certain thing **at best** if that is the most optimistic or favourable way you can regard it: *It would be a setback at best if we were denied use of their software.*

○ **make the 'best of something**

People **make the best of** difficult or unpleasant circumstances when they try to accept them as cheerfully as possible: *We were allowed one blanket apiece and had to make the best of it.*

bets

○ **hedge your 'bets**

You **hedge your bets** when you do something to protect yourself from losing something, being criticized, etc: *I suggest you hedge your bets by applying for a university flat, whether you think you want one or not.*

> In gambling, you **hedge your bets** when you make bets on both sides, to make sure that you do not lose any money whatever happens.

better

○ **better late than 'never**

You say **'better late than never' 1** to someone to show that you are not very pleased that they are late. **2** if you think that it is preferable that something should happen late than not at all: *You will have to accept that some permanent damage may already have occurred. Better late than never, though.*

○ **better 'off**

You are **better off 1** if you have more money: *a situation where those who do not work are better off than those who do.* **2** if you are in more satisfactory circumstances: *There are disturbed people in prison who'd be better off in hospital.*

○ **better safe than 'sorry**

You say **'better safe than sorry'** when you want to remind someone that it's worth taking precautions, or to tell them not to be afraid of raising the alarm if they see something suspicious: *You might as well take out holiday insurance; better safe than sorry.*

○ **for better or 'worse**

Something that is the case **for better or worse** is the case whatever you may think of it: *For better or worse, the computer has taken control of our lives.*

○ **get the 'better of someone**

Someone **gets the better of you** when they defeat you, often because they are able to think faster than you; an emotion **gets the better of you** when you fail to control it: *Curiosity eventually got the better of him, and he approached to see what was happening.*

○ **go one 'better**

You **go one better** when you do the same thing as before, or as someone else, only better: *Bernard Tapie will be hoping to go one better than two years ago when they lost to Red Star Belgrade on penalties.* ♦ *see also* **keep up with the Joneses** ▷JONESES

beyond

○ **be'yond you**

Something is **beyond you** if it is too difficult for you to understand: *I can't help him with his homework any more; all that modern stuff is beyond me.* ♦ *see also* **over your head** ▷HEAD

big

○ **make it 'big**

Someone who **has made it big** has become very successful, famous or rich: *I knew from a young age that I wanted to make it big in showbusiness.* ♦ *see also* **make it** ▷MAKE; **make a name for yourself** or **make your name** ▷NAME

bike

○ **on yer 'bike** (*BrE*; *slang*)

People sometimes say **'on yer bike'** as a way of telling someone to go away: *'I'll give you £50 for it.' 'Oh, on yer bike.'*

> **'Yer'**, here, means 'your'.

bill

○ **fit the 'bill** (*informal*)

Something **fits the bill** if it is suitable or what is required: *We need someone with some experience and an ability to mix well with all sorts of people; I think the first candidate fits the bill exactly.*

bird

○ **bird's eye 'view**

You have a **bird's eye view** of something when you are at a point above it from which you can see it very clearly: *I had a bird's eye view of the procession from the top of the lamp post.* **2** You get a **bird's eye view** of a subject when you get a general, but clear, outline of it: *A good selective bibliography gives a bird's eye view of the relevant subject literature.*

○ **a bird in the 'hand is worth two in the 'bush**

People say **'a bird in the hand is worth two in the bush'**, or just **'a bird in the hand'**, when they think that it is not worth giving up something you already have for only the possibility of getting something better.

○ **early 'bird**

An **early bird** is a person who gains some advantage by being early: *If you're an early bird you'll be able to see the sunrise from the top of the mountain.*

This idiom is the shortened form of the saying 'the early bird catches the worm', meaning that people who get up for work early will be successful.

birds

○ **birds of a 'feather**

You say **'birds of a feather'** to mean that people who have the same interests, personalities or backgrounds will often be friendly with each other: *'It's funny how people travel to the other side of the world, and then make friends with people of their own nationality, isn't it?' 'Yes, well, birds of a feather...'*

This idiom is the shortened form of the proverb: 'Birds of a feather flock together'.

○ **kill two birds with one 'stone** (*informal*)

You **kill two birds with one stone** when you manage to achieve two things with a single action: *There are advantages to an apprenticeship. You might as well kill two birds with one stone by doing and learning in parallel.*

biscuit

○ **take the 'biscuit** (*BrE*)

You say that something **takes the biscuit** if it is the best, worst, strangest, etc, of its type that you have experienced: *I've heard a lot of excuses in my time, but this one takes the biscuit.*

This is a British variant of the US form 'take the cake', which probably comes from the giving of cakes as prizes in rural competitions.

bit (*see also* bits)

○ **a bit 'much** (*informal*)

Something such as **a bit much** is unacceptable, unreasonable or unfair: *It's a bit much, her expecting me to wait for her and give her a lift home.*

○ **a bit of all 'right** (*BrE; informal*)

People humorously say that someone is **a bit of all right** if they find them physically attractive: *Who's that guy at the bar? He's a bit of all right, isn't he?*

○ **a bit 'off** (*BrE; informal*)

Something, such as a remark, is **a bit off** when it is rather rude: *'He said he'd give me a lift to the airport, but now at the last minute he says he's meeting a friend.' 'Oh, that's a bit off, isn't it?'*

bite

○ **a bite at the 'cherry** or **a bite of the 'cherry**

You get **a bite at**, or **of, the cherry** when you get a chance to do something: *We had been quite successful on our first visit; now we were returning to have another bite at the cherry.*

Notice that this idiom is always preceded by a word like 'first', 'second', 'last', etc.

○ **bite off more than you can 'chew**

You **have bitten off more than you can chew** if you find that a project or piece of work you have decided to take on is too difficult for you to manage: *I'm going to have to travel up to London every day. I'm beginning to wonder if I've bitten off more than I can chew.*

○ **put the 'bite on someone** (*AmE; informal*)

You **put the bite on someone** when

you try to borrow money from them: *Eddie tried to put the bite on Jack, but he didn't have any money either.*

bits

○ **bits and 'bobs** or **bits and 'pieces** (*informal*)

Bits and bobs, or **bits and pieces**, are small things of various kinds: *There are a few bits and bobs of yours still here; would you like me to send them on to you?*

○ **thrilled to 'bits** (*informal*)

You are **thrilled to bits** if you are surprised and very happy about something: *She looked at the happy faces of her companions, and knew they wanted to be alone.'What marvellous news. I'm thrilled to bits.'* ♦ *see also* **walk on air** ▷AIR; **on cloud nine** ▷CLOUD; **in seventh heaven** ▷HEAVEN; **over the moon** ▷MOON

bitten

○ **once bitten, twice 'shy**

Someone who is **once bitten, twice shy** is afraid to attempt something again because of a previous bad experience: *He hasn't had a girlfriend now for two years; I think it's a case of once bitten, twice shy.*

black

○ **black and 'blue**

You are **black and blue** when you are covered with bruises: *'I couldn't believe it when I saw him. He was black and blue all over; he looked awful.'*

○ **black and 'white**

1 Something which is in **black and white** is written on paper, and therefore definite and cannot be legally stopped: *It sounds like an interesting proposal, but I'd like to see it in black and white before we go any further.* **2** People see something, such as an issue, in **black and white**, when they only look at the two main opposing views, without considering the points in between: *It's a very difficult moral question, and it does no good to talk as if it was a simple black and white issue.*

○ **in the 'black**

You are **in the black** if you do not owe anyone any money: *Business is starting to improve; this is the first time we've been in the black for two years.* ♦ *see also* **in the red** ▷RED

It is customary to use black ink to write entries on the credit side of a ledger.

blank

○ **draw a 'blank**

You **draw a blank** if you get no results, especially if you cannot find the person or thing you are looking for: *The police, who have been trying to track down the missing painting, have drawn a blank.*

This idiom refers to picking a losing ticket in a lottery.

blanket

○ **a wet 'blanket** (*informal*)

A **wet blanket** is someone who does not want to have fun, and spoils other people's enjoyment by being dreary and pessimistic: *'I still think you're mad to embark on something so ambitious.' 'Oh, don't be such a wet blanket.'*

blast

○ **blast from the 'past** (*informal*)

A **blast from the past** is a person or thing from your past that you remember, but had almost forgotten about: *Oh yeah, Alvin Stardust, there's a blast from the past.*

○ **full 'blast** or **at full 'blast**

A machine is on **full blast**, or **at full blast**, when it is producing as much power, heat or sound as it can: *We had the heater on full blast but we were still cold.*

bleed

○ **bleed someone 'dry**

Someone **bleeds you dry** when they use all your money: *If they hadn't bled me dry we could afford a better place.*

blessing

○ **a blessing in dis'guise**

If you describe something as **a blessing in disguise**, you mean that it proved to be the best thing that could have happened, despite having seemed like a disaster at first: *'The accident was probably a blessing in disguise,' admits Barbara.'I had ideas, but no experience. I've had plenty of time to prepare.'*

blessings

○ **a mixed 'blessing**

A situation is **a mixed blessing** if it has both advantages and disadvantages: *Living here is a mixed blessing. Mixed because you can find real solitude in the mountains, but lack of people often means a lack of facilities.*

blessings

○ **count your 'blessings**

You **count your blessings** when you remember what is good in your life instead of complaining: *Count your blessings – you could have ended up in hospital.* ♦ *see also* **thankful for small mercies** ▷MERCIES; **look on the bright side** ▷SIDE

blind

○ **blind as a 'bat** (*informal, humorous*)

Someone who is as **blind as a bat** does not have very good eyesight, or cannot see anything at all: *I am blind as a bat without my glasses.*

○ **the blind leading the 'blind**

A situation may be described as a case of **the blind leading the blind** if the person who is supposed to be teaching or helping others knows little more than, or as little as, those being helped or taught: '*You gave me a lot of help at the beginning, explaining the theory.' 'That was the blind leading the blind. I don't know how I got through the exam myself.'*

blink

○ **in the blink of an 'eye**

Something happens **in the blink of an eye** when it happens very quickly: *He's good at spending a long time doing nothing, then becoming highly active in the blink of an eye.* ♦ *see also* **in the twinkling of an eye** ▷TWINKLING

○ **on the 'blink** (*informal*)

A machine is **on the blink** if it is not working properly: *Oh dear; the telly's on the blink again.*

> This idiom comes from the characteristic flickering of a faulty screen.

block

○ **on the 'block** (*AmE*)

Something that is **on the block** is being sold at an auction: *He had to put his paintings on the block to pay off the taxes he owed.*

blood

○ **blood is thicker than 'water**

When people say that **blood is thicker than water**, they mean that people are generally more loyal to members of their own family than to other people: '*We had a difference of opinion and she left home,' said Mr Harrison. 'But blood is thicker than water and I have been at the hospital waiting to hear how she is.'*

○ **in cold 'blood**

Something is done **in cold blood** when it is done in a deliberately cruel or uncaring way: *At dawn they were shot down in cold blood by a firing squad in the woods behind the camp.*

> This idiom comes from the medieval belief that emotion raised the temperature of the blood.

○ **like getting blood out of a 'stone** or **like trying to get blood out of a 'stone** (*informal*)

You say that obtaining something is **like getting**, or **trying to get**, **blood out of a stone** if it is almost impossible to obtain: *Persuading them to give away any information is like trying to get blood out of a stone.*

○ **make someone's 'blood boil** (*informal*)

Someone or something **makes your blood boil** if they make you very angry: *It makes my blood boil to see how people are ruining the countryside.*

○ **make someone's blood run 'cold**

Something **makes your blood run cold** if it makes you feel very frightened: *Her blood ran cold when she heard that voice on the phone again.*

○ **out for someone's 'blood** or **after someone's 'blood** (*informal*)

You are **out for**, or **after, someone's blood** if you are very angry with them and want to fight them or argue with them: *He's out of prison – says there are people out for his blood.*

○ **sweat 'blood** (*informal*)

You **sweat blood** if you work very hard: *I've sweated blood to get him to agree to see me at all.* ♦ *see also* **work your guts out** ▷GUTS

blot

○ **a blot on the 'landscape** (*BrE*)

Something such as a building can be described as **a blot on the landscape** if it is very ugly and spoils the view: *Yesterday's blot on the landscape is today's tourist curiosity, as lovers of modern architecture will tell you.*

blow

○ **blow someone a'way** (*informal*)

Someone or something **blows you away** if it causes you to feel extremely strong emotions: *'She just blew me away,' he says. 'I was so impressed I asked her if she wanted to do some work immediately.'*

○ **blow-by-'blow**

A **blow-by-blow** account or description of something is a detailed and graphic one: *I didn't feel like hearing a blow-by-blow account of his divorce.*

○ **blow hot and 'cold**

You **blow hot and cold** on someone or something when you keep changing your attitude towards them: *'You don't know where you are with him, do you?' said Dorothy. 'From one week to the next. Blowing hot and cold like that.'*

○ **'blow it** (*informal*)

You **blow it** when you lose your chance of success through your own fault: *'How did your interview go?' 'I blew it.'*

○ **blow 'over**

Bad feelings between people **blow over** when they pass and become forgotten: *I wouldn't worry too much if I were you – it'll all have blown over by Monday.*

○ **blow someone's 'mind**

If you **blow someone's mind**, you amaze or confuse them: *I blew Dad's mind when I told him I was getting married.*

blower

○ **on the 'blower** (*BrE; slang*)

You are **on the blower** if you are on the telephone: *You'd better get on the blower to him now and tell him what's happened.*

blue

○ **out of the 'blue**

Something happens **out of the blue** when it happens without warning: *She appeared again out of the blue after fifteen years' absence.*

> This idiom refers to lightning which strikes out of a clear sky.

blues

○ **got the 'blues** (*informal*)

You say that you've **got the blues** if you are feeling sad or depressed: *Whenever I get the blues I take a long walk in the hills or go for a bike ride.*

bluff

○ **call someone's 'bluff**

You **call someone's bluff** when you are not deceived by another person's attempts to trick you into doing something: *One day, some man is going to call her bluff and she's going to get hurt.*

> In poker, to **bluff** is to pretend to have cards of a greater value than you really have; to **call someone's bluff** is to force them to show their cards.

blushes

○ **spare someone's 'blushes**

You **spare someone's blushes** when you avoid saying something in public which might embarrass them: *We will omit the names to spare the blushes of those who made the biggest mistakes.*

board

○ **go back to the 'drawing board**

You **go back to the drawing board** when you have to abandon something you are working on, and start again at the planning stage: *Radical change can be achieved only by going back to the drawing board, throwing away the previous design and starting again.*

○ **go by the 'board** (*informal*)

An arrangement **goes by the board** if it is ignored or abandoned: *The Government's 'spend less, earn more' policy meant that health, education and other welfare spending went by the board.*

> This was originally a nautical term, meaning 'to disappear over the side of the ship'.

○ **sweep the 'board**

You **sweep the board** in a series of competitions when you win all the prizes: *He swept the board with six wins, winning overall by 26 points.*

This idiom refers to the board used in many games, where one player wins all the pieces or bets.

○ **take something on 'board**

1 You **take something on board** when you make yourself responsible for it: *Try not to take too much on board this year.* **2** You **take** an idea **on board** when you take it into consideration or accept it: *Thank you for your suggestions; we'll definitely take them on board when we start our next project.*

boat

○ **in the same 'boat** (*informal*)

Two or more people who are **in the same boat** are having similar experiences or problems: *By meeting others who are in the same boat, they begin to feel less alone and different.*

○ **miss the 'boat** (*informal*)

You **miss the boat** when you do not get a chance to do or have something because you are too late in arriving or asking for it: *Even if we had celebrated in a small way we would have attracted tourists from all over the world. The council has really missed the boat.*

○ **push the 'boat out** (*BrE*)

If you say that someone has decided to **push the boat out**, you mean that they are going to spend as much money as is necessary, and work as hard as they can to make a particular occasion successful: *When Andy Saville broke his arm after signing two weeks ago, a lot of people thought we would give up, but we pushed the boat out and bought John Thomas.* ♦ *see also* **go to great lengths** ▷LENGTHS; **go to town on something** ▷TOWN; **go out of your way** ▷WAY

○ **rock the 'boat** (*informal*)

Someone **rocks the boat** when they disturb the balance or calmness of a situation, or cause trouble: *I don't want to rock the boat, but don't you think someone should bring this to the attention of the authorities?* ♦ *see also* **make waves** ▷WAVES

body

○ **over my dead 'body** (*informal*)

You respond to some suggested future event with the words '**over my dead body**' to indicate that you are completely opposed to it and will try every means of preventing it: *'Looks like the takeover will be going ahead.' 'Over my dead body.'*

bogged

○ **bogged 'down** (*informal*)

You are **bogged down** if you have too much work to do, or if you are unable to make progress because you are paying too much attention to detail: *I'm not getting anywhere with this essay; I think I'm getting too bogged down in the theoretical side of things.*

This idiom refers to the way in which movement is slowed down by thick mud.

bolt

○ **a bolt from the 'blue**

A **bolt from the blue** is a sudden, unexpected event: *Now, was this forty thousand pounds a bolt from the blue or did you know it was coming to you?*

bone

○ **close to the 'bone** (*informal*)

A remark which is **close to the bone** is one which makes you feel uncomfortable, perhaps because it contains some truth that you would prefer people did not mention: *'Would I be right in saying that we haven't provided you with what you were looking for when you came here?' He was getting a little too close to the bone for my liking.*

○ **have a 'bone to pick with someone** (*informal*)

You say that you **have a bone to pick with someone** if you want to confront them about something they have done which has annoyed you: *I've got a bone to pick with you. Why did you go off and leave me on my own?* ♦ *see also* **have it out with someone** ▷HAVE

boner

○ **pull a 'boner** (*AmE*; *informal*)

If you **pull a boner**, you make a silly mistake: *Ned pulled a boner when he called his girlfriend Sue instead of Alice.*

bones

○ **bare 'bones**

The **bare bones** of something are the

basic or essential parts of it: *The company has worked out the bare bones of the agreement and needs to work on the details now.*

○ **make no 'bones about something**

You **make no bones about something** if you are willing to say it or do it openly: *She made no bones about telling me to take my business elsewhere.*

book

○ **by the 'book**

You do something **by the book** when you do it exactly according to the rules, or in the way you are supposed to do it: *They make us do everything by the book, which doesn't give us much space for creativity.*

○ **throw the 'book at someone**

You **throw the book at someone** when you reprimand or punish them severely, especially for breaking the rules: *We can't do that; they'll just throw the book at us.*

> This idiom refers to the idea of charging someone with all the crimes in 'the book'.

books

○ **cook the 'books** (*informal*)

Someone **cooks the books** when they change the numbers in their, or their company's, accounts in order to gain money for themselves or the company: *They are now saying that everyone is cooking the books. If it's true, it's a very serious allegation.*

○ **one for the 'books**

Something that is **one for the books** is amazing or very unusual: *That sunflower is the tallest I've seen. One for the books, I'd say.*

boom

○ **lower the 'boom on someone** (*AmE*; *informal*)

When you **lower the boom on someone**, you severely scold or punish them: *If my daughter stays out late again, I'm going to lower the boom on her.*

boot

○ **the boot is on the other 'foot** (*BrE*; *informal*) or **the shoe is on the other 'foot** (*AmE*; *informal*)

If you say that **the boot**, or **the shoe**, is on the other foot, you mean that the situation has changed dramatically, and probably that someone or something that was weak has gained power: *In the past, probably because she was four years older, Laura had always seemed the more dominant figure. But now the boot was on the other foot.* ♦ *see also* **turn the tables** ▷ TABLES

○ **give someone the 'boot** (*informal*)

You are **given**, or **get**, **the boot**, when you are dismissed from your job: *'I thought you worked at the insurance company down the road?' 'Well I did, but I got the boot.'* ♦ *see also* **give someone the elbow** ▷ ELBOW; **give someone the push** ▷ PUSH; **give someone the sack** ▷ SACK

boots

○ **lick someone's 'boots** (*informal*)

A person **licks someone's boots** when they flatter them and do everything they want: *I've had enough of licking their boots every time I need something; it's demoralizing and humiliating.*

○ **tough as old 'boots** (*informal*)

1 Someone who is as **tough as old boots** is very strong and not easily hurt, either physically or mentally: *Beneath her frail exterior, she's as tough as old boots.* **2** Food that is **tough as old boots** is difficult to eat because you have to chew it for a long time before you can swallow it: *I'm not going back to that restaurant; the waiters are rude and the steak they serve is tough as old boots.*

bored

○ **bored 'stiff** or **bored to 'death** or **bored to 'tears** (*informal*)

You are **bored stiff**, or **bored to death**, or **bored to tears**, if you are extremely bored: *We were bored stiff by the end of the lecture.*

born

○ **not born 'yesterday** (*informal*)

You say that you were **not born yesterday** if you do not believe what someone has told you, and you think that it is naïve of them to expect you to believe them: *Empty your pockets. Come on. I wasn't born yesterday, you know.*

bottle

○ **bottle 'out** or **lose your 'bottle** (*BrE*; *informal*)

You **bottle out** of something, or you **lose your bottle**, when you decide not to do it because you are afraid: *I was going to do this parachute jump, but I went and bottled out at the last minute.*

○ **hit the 'bottle** (*informal*)

Someone **hits the bottle** when they start to drink too much alcohol, usually because of problems that they are experiencing in their life: *All the pressures she was facing caused her to hit the bottle again.* ♦ *see also* **drown your sorrows** ▷SORROWS

bottom

○ **from the bottom of your 'heart**

You feel something **from the bottom of your heart** if you feel it very deeply and sincerely: *I thank you from the bottom of my heart.*

○ **get to the 'bottom of**

You **get to the bottom of** a mystery, for example, when you find out its cause: *I'll talk to the member of staff concerned and get to the bottom of this.*

bounds

○ **know no 'bounds**

Something which **knows no bounds** seems to be limitless: *His generosity knows no bounds.* [= He is very generous.]

○ **out of 'bounds**

A place is **out of bounds** when people are not allowed to go there: *The playing fields are out of bounds to pupils during the lunch break.*

brains

○ **pick someone's 'brains** (*informal*)

You **pick someone's brains** when you ask them for information about a subject that they have a lot of knowledge and experience of: *Being able to pick your brains on the subject was an immense help.*

○ **rack your 'brains** (*informal*)

You **rack your brains** when you think very hard in order to remember something, or to find a solution to something: *A blonde girl waved at me from across the room. I waved back, racking my brains to remember who she was.*

This idiom refers to the old instrument of torture, the rack, which stretched the body.

---

brass

○ **bold as 'brass** (*informal*)

Someone who is **bold as brass** is very confident and not afraid to ask for things, often to the point of being disrespectful: *She came up to me, bold as brass, and asked me for the car keys.*

brave

○ **brave it 'out** or **put on a brave 'face**

You **brave something out**, or **put on a brave face**, when you do not show any fear about something: *I had to put on a brave face and try not to appear worried, but when I saw him I was shocked at how much he had changed.*

bread

○ **your bread and 'butter**

Your bread and butter is the way you earn your living: *They earn their bread and butter from market research.*

break

○ **break 'even**

A business **breaks even** when it makes as much money as it spends, but does not make a profit: *Although we had broken even, we were unable to go on paying wages.*

○ **give me a 'break** (*very informal, rather offensive*)

You say to someone '**Give me a break!**' if you want them to stop annoying you: *'Come on! Haven't you finished yet?' 'Oh, just give me a break, will you? I'll do it in my own time.'* ♦ *see also* **knock it off** ▷KNOCK; **give it a rest** ▷REST

○ **make a 'break** or **make a clean 'break**

You **make a break**, or **make a clean break**, when you escape from a place or situation, or separate yourself completely from it: *I'll make a clean break from athletics in two years' time and I won't be competing any more.*

♦ *see also* **give someone the slip** ▷SLIP

breakfast

○ **have someone for 'breakfast** or **eat someone for 'breakfast** (*BrE*; *informal*)

You say that someone will **have**, or **eat**,

someone for breakfast if they are
likely to beat them easily in a contest,
or if they easily gain control over people: *Have you seen the size of him? He'll
have our Charlie for breakfast.*

breath

○ **a breath of fresh 'air**

You describe someone or something as
a breath of fresh air if you feel that
they have a fresh and positive influence
on you and people in general: *They remember him as a 'breath of fresh air', as
a manager who rejuvenated the team
with his ability to motivate players.*

○ **catch your 'breath**

You **catch your breath** when you stop
breathing for a moment, because of
fear, amazement or pain, for example:
*A sudden noise made her catch her
breath; but it was only the wind.*

○ **don't hold your 'breath** (*very informal*)

You say to someone '**Don't hold your
breath**' if they are expecting something which you think is unlikely to
happen: *'I'm sure she'll change her mind
when she's thought about it.' 'Don't hold
your breath; she's not known for her flex-
ibility.'*

○ **save your 'breath**

You **save your breath** when you decide
not to bother telling someone something, probably because you know they
won't pay attention: *You might as well
save your breath; whatever you say,
they'll do exactly as they please.*

○ **take someone's 'breath away**

Something **takes your breath away** if
you find it very beautiful, pleasing,
shocking or exciting: *The scenery in
the Alps will take your breath away.*

○ **under your 'breath**

You say something **under your breath**
when you say it quietly or in a whisper:
*'Leave this to me,' she said under her
breath, and winked.*

○ **with bated 'breath**

You wait for something **with bated
breath** when you wait in great antici-
pation: *She waited for a reply to her offer
with bated breath.*

bridge

○ **cross that bridge when you 'come to
it**

If you say that you will **cross that**

bridge when you come to it, you
mean that you are going to deal with a
problem when it arises and not before:
*She lit another cigarette. What would she
do when the secret was out? She would
cross that bridge when she came to it.*

bright

○ **bright-eyed and bushy-'tailed** (*informal*)

You are **bright-eyed and bushy-
tailed** if you are feeling fresh, well-
rested and eager to do something:
*How can you be so bright-eyed and
bushy-tailed on only three hours' sleep?*
♦ *see also* **full of beans** ▷BEANS

broke

○ **go 'broke** (*informal*)

A person or company **goes broke** when
they lose all their money and cannot
continue to work or trade properly.

○ **go for 'broke** (*informal*)

You **go for broke** when you risk everything you have for a chance of being extremely successful: *After winning the
gold in the under 16s' National Cham-
pionships, he decided to go for broke
and turn professional.* ♦ *see also* **stick
your neck out** ▷NECK

○ **stone 'broke** or **stony 'broke** or **flat
'broke** (*informal*)

You are **stone broke**, or **stony broke**,
or **flat broke**, if you have little or no
money left: *Can I pay you next week?
I'm afraid I'm stone broke.*

brows

○ **knit your 'brows**

You **knit your brows** when you bring
your eyebrows together in a frown, because you are thinking, or concentrating very hard: *He knitted his brows as
he tried to remember what she had said.*

brush

○ **tarred with the same 'brush** (*informal*)

Two or more people are **tarred with
the same brush** if they have the same
faults: *You never told me that! Not that
I'm surprised; they're all tarred with the
same brush, that family.* ♦ *see also* **a chip
off the old block** ▷CHIP

buck

○ **pass the 'buck** (*informal*)

You **pass the buck** when you refuse to

accept responsibility for something, especially when you refuse to deal with a problem: *The industrialized nations are the real environmental villains. Shouldn't we now be acknowledging blame rather than passing the buck?*

This idiom comes from the card game, poker, where the **buck** is an object passed to the person who wins, in order to remind them that they must start off the new jackpot.

bucket
○ **kick the 'bucket** (*humorous*)
Someone **kicks the bucket** when they die: *Honestly, I was so ill, I thought I was going to kick the bucket.* ♦ *see also* **cash in your chips** ▷CHIPS; **pop your clogs** ▷CLOGS; **bite the dust** ▷DUST; **give up the ghost** ▷GHOST; **snuff it** ▷SNUFF

bud
○ **nip something in the 'bud** (*informal*)
You **nip something in the bud** when you make it stop at a very early stage: *Her dream of Hollywood stardom was nipped in the bud last night when critics savagely criticized her first big movie.*

bull
○ **like a bull in a 'china shop**
You describe someone as being **like a bull in a china shop 1** if they are very clumsy: *Anthony was always rushing about like a bull in a china shop, knocking things over, and generally causing havoc wherever he went.* **2** if they do not make any effort to be polite and tactful in social situations: *Politically, he often behaved like a bull in a china shop. Privately, he could be a man of great sensitivity.*
○ **shoot the 'bull** (*AmE; informal*)
You **shoot the bull** when you chat with others in an idle way: *I found him in the drugstore shooting the bull with some other salesmen.*
○ **take the bull by the 'horns** (*informal*)
You **take the bull by the horns** when you make a determined decision to do something: *Being the determined woman she was, she decided to take the bull by the horns and organize things for herself.* ♦ *see also* **grasp the nettle** ▷NETTLE; **pull out all the stops** ▷STOPS

bullet
○ **bite the 'bullet** (*informal*)
You **bite the bullet** when you **1** decide to tolerate a situation rather than complain about it, since there is nothing you can do about it: *We have to bite the bullet a little now, but once the ground has been finished, we should start making profits again.* **2** decide that you must do something, even though it will be unpleasant: *Only so much can be done by discussion. Decisions have to be taken, and as director you have got to bite the bullet.*

This idiom refers to the practice used by army doctors of giving patients a bullet to put between their teeth during painful operations.

○ **sweat 'bullets** (*AmE; informal*)
You **sweat bullets** when you are very worried or frightened: *The noise downstairs had me sweating bullets.*

bum
○ **give someone the bum's 'rush** (*AmE*)
You **give someone the bum's rush** when you hurry them out of a place: *The man in the restaurant was drunk, and the manager gave him the bum's rush.*
○ **on the 'bum** (*AmE; informal*)
1 If something is **on the bum** it is not working: *I missed the programme because my radio is on the bum.* **2** Someone is **on the bum** if they are living in an unsettled way like a tramp: *Soon after he lost his job, he was on the bum.* ♦ *see also* **on the fritz** ▷FRITZ

In American English, **bum** is another word for 'tramp'.

bump
○ **like a bump on a 'log** (*AmE*)
If someone is **like a bump on a log**, they sit or stand without moving or responding: *Just give me an answer. Don't sit there like a bump on a log!*

bundle
○ **make a 'bundle** (*informal*)
You **make a bundle** when you make a lot of money: *We made a bundle on that stall at the carnival last year.* ♦ *see also*

coin it or coin it in ▷COIN; make a
killing ▷KILLING; make your pile
▷PILE

> Bundle here refers to banknotes.

○ **not go a 'bundle on something** (*BrE*;
informal)
You **don't go a bundle on something**
when you are not keen on doing it: *They
don't go a bundle on employing married
women in this company.* ♦ *see also* **not
your cup of tea** ▷CUP

> This idiom refers to the money that
> you would not like to bet on something.

bunk

○ **do a 'bunk** (*BrE*; *informal*)
Someone **does a bunk** when they run
away from a place: *Several of the pupils
did a bunk during the morning break.* □
*Two prisoners did a bunk during the
chaos of the riots.*

burner

○ **put something on the back 'burner**
(*informal*)
You **put something on the back burner** when you delay doing it until later:
*The company's activities have been
put on the back burner until production can be resumed abroad with lower
costs.*

> This idiom is an old cooking term.

bursting

○ **bursting to 'do something** (*informal*)
1 You are **bursting to do something**
if you are extremely impatient to do it:
*She met me at the door; there was some-
thing she was bursting to tell me.* **2** '**I'm
bursting**' usually means 'I badly need
to go to the toilet.'

bush

○ **beat about the 'bush**
You tell someone not to **beat about the
bush** when you want them to speak
openly and directly without hiding
anything: *Come on, don't beat about the
bush. What are you trying to say?*

> '**Beating the bush**' is an activity car-
> ried out while hunting birds.

business

○ '**funny business**
Funny business is tricks or dishonest
behaviour: *I think there's some funny
business going on where these accounts
are concerned; something isn't quite
right.* ♦ *see also* **sharp practice**
▷PRACTICE

○ **give someone the 'business** (*AmE*; *informal*)
You **give someone the business** when
you treat them badly: *The new teacher
acted unsure of herself, so the students
really gave her the business.*

○ **go about your 'business**
People **go about their business** when
they attend to their normal everyday
duties: *We watched the small boats going
about their business in the harbour.*

○ **like 'nobody's business** (*informal*)
You do something, or something happens, **like nobody's business** when
you do it very well or fast, or if it happens a lot: *The phone's been ringing like
nobody's business since we put that advert in the newspaper.*

○ **mean 'business** (*informal*)
People **mean business** when they are
seriously determined to do what they
propose: *This time they were not just
threatening; they clearly meant business.*

○ **mind your own 'business** (*informal, offensive*)
1 You say to someone '**Mind your own
business!**' if you think they are being
too curious and inquisitive about your
private affairs: '*How did you vote in the
last election?*' '*Mind your own business.*'
2 You **are minding your own business** when you are concentrating on
matters which concern you, and not
paying attention to, or interfering in,
other people's affairs: *I was so busy
minding my own business that I didn't
notice there was anything wrong.*

○ **none of someone's 'business** or **no
business of 'someone's** (*informal*)
A matter is **none of someone's business**, or **no business of theirs**, if you
think that they are being too curious
about a private matter which does not
concern them: *It's no business of mine
how she gets the money for her foreign
trips.*

butter

○ **butter wouldn't melt in so-and-so's 'mouth**

You say that **butter wouldn't melt in** a certain person's **mouth** when you want to comment that the person looks, or acts, as if they would never do anything wrong, often despite the facts to the contrary: *The boy was first arrested at the age of 10 for giving £1,000 to a drug dealer for heroin. The detective added: 'To look at him you'd think butter wouldn't melt in his mouth.'*

butterflies

○ **have 'butterflies or have 'butterflies in your stomach**

You **have butterflies**, or **have butterflies in your stomach**, if you have a nervous feeling in your stomach: *She's got butterflies about the exam.*

bygones

○ **let bygones be 'bygones**

You say **'let bygones be bygones'** to someone when you agree that you should both forget quarrels or problems from the past: *I expect auntie has told you everything, but please come now. We will let bygones be bygones. Daddy would have wanted it.*

cage

○ **rattle someone's 'cage** (*informal*)

If someone seems unusually cross or unfriendly for no obvious reason, people sometimes ask what has **rattled their cage**: *What rattled his cage this morning? I said he looked well and he told me to mind my own business.* ♦ *see also* **ruffle someone's feathers** ▷FEATHERS

Rattling the cage which an animal or a bird is living in will probably make it upset or angry.

---

cake (*see also* **cakes**)

○ **have your cake and 'eat it**

If someone wants to **have their cake and eat it**, they want to do or have two things which are not usually possible together, instead of making a choice and being happy with just one of those things: *You can't have both. You can't have your cake and eat it.* ♦ *see also* **the grass is always greener on the other side of the fence** ▷GRASS; **the best of both worlds** ▷WORLDS

cakes

○ **sell like 'hot cakes or go like 'hot cakes**

A new product or item which **is selling**, or **going**, **like hot cakes** is so popular that a lot of people are buying it: *Cards depicting Santa are selling like hot cakes.*

call

○ **close 'call**

You have a **close call** when a bad event almost happens, but you manage to avoid it just in time: *Bernadette Devlin had a close call, but she survived the assassination attempt against her.* ♦ *see also* **close shave** ▷SHAVE; **close or near thing** ▷THING

calm

○ **the calm before the 'storm**

The calm before the storm is a time of quiet waiting that comes before a period of great activity or before some unpleasant event occurs: *Those who argue that Scotland is now experiencing the calm before the political storm could well be proved right.*

For a short time before a storm starts, the weather often becomes still.

---

can

○ **can of 'worms**

A situation which is a **can of worms** is full of hidden problems which have been left to get worse, because nobody noticed them or dealt with them while they were developing: *The prosecution could open a can of worms.*

A worm is a long, thin, cylindrical animal, with no backbone or legs, especially one that lives in the soil.

○ **carry the 'can**
You **carry the can** if you take the blame for something: *We were both at fault, but I had to carry the can.*

○ **in the 'can** (*informal*)
If something is **in the can**, it is already done or achieved: *By lunchtime we already had two complete runs of the play in the can.*

candle

○ **burn the candle at both 'ends**
You **are burning the candle at both ends** if you are making yourself tired, probably by going to bed late at night and getting up early in the morning: *This month you are determined to live it up and have a good time, but you must watch your health and try not to burn the candle at both ends.*

cap

○ **cap in 'hand**
You go **cap in hand** to ask for something if you ask for it in a very humble way: *Shouldn't the elderly automatically receive a heating allowance every winter, instead of having to go cap in hand to the government?* ♦ *see also* **on bended knee** ▷KNEE

○ **if the cap fits, 'wear it**
If the cap fits, **wear it**, means 'If you recognize yourself in my description, then let that be the case': *'Are you calling me a traitor?' 'No, but if the cap fits, wear it.'*

card

○ **have a 'card up your sleeve** or **keep a 'card up your sleeve**
You **have**, or **are keeping, a card up your sleeve** if other people think that you are in a difficult situation, but you have a secret solution which you plan to surprise them with: *Don't cry. Just wait and see. Your old grandad has still got plenty of cards up his sleeve.*

When people cheat at cards they sometimes hide an extra card up their sleeve.

cards

○ **the cards are stacked a'gainst someone**
If **the cards are stacked against you**, you are in a situation which gives you very little hope of success: *He's giving his best effort to the election campaign, but the cards are stacked against him.* ♦ *see also* **up against it** ▷UP

○ **have all the 'cards** or **hold all the 'cards**
If you **have**, or **hold, all the cards** you have an advantage which puts you in control of a situation: *They know I hold all the cards, so I'll just wait and see what they do next.*

○ **lay your 'cards on the table** or **put your 'cards on the table**
You **lay**, or **put, your cards on the table** when you make your intentions known, rather than trying to keep them secret: *I'd be glad if you put your cards on the table.* ♦ *see also* **lay it on the line** ▷LINE

○ **play your cards close to your 'chest** or **keep your cards close to your 'chest**
You **are playing**, or **keeping, your cards close to your chest** when you do not give much information to other people about what you are doing: *The League's commercial director is playing his cards close to his chest.*

carpet

○ **roll out the red 'carpet for someone** or **give someone the red-'carpet treatment**
You **roll out the red carpet for someone** who is visiting you, or **give them the red-carpet treatment**, when you make a great effort to welcome them: *What, a cream sponge for dessert? You're giving Gran the red-carpet treatment, aren't you?*

When an important person visits another country, a red carpet is sometimes put on the ground for them to walk on, as a sign of respect.

○ **sweep something under the 'carpet** or **brush something under the 'carpet**
You **sweep**, or **brush**, **something**, such as a problem, **under the carpet** when you ignore it or try to hide it from

other people because you do not want to deal with it: *The row continued last week, despite deliberate efforts in Bonn to brush the affair under the carpet.*

carry

○ **carry it 'off**

You say that you **carried it off** if you know you did something badly, but you think that nobody else noticed your mistakes or weaknesses: *My speech wasn't very well prepared, but I think I carried it off.*

case

○ **make a 'federal case out of something** (*AmE*)

If you say someone is **making a federal case out of something**, you believe they are exaggerating its seriousness or importance: *It was just a simple mistake, but he tried to make a federal case out of it.* ♦ *see also* **make a big deal about something** ▷DEAL

> In the United States, the more serious cases often go to federal courts.

castles

○ **build castles in the 'air**

You **are building castles in the air** when you make plans based on hopes and wishes which will probably never come true: *Unless she knows that she's got the job, all her plans are just castles in the air.* ♦ *see also* **chase rainbows** ▷RAINBOWS

cat

○ **fight like cat and 'dog** (*BrE*) or **fight like cats and dogs** (*AmE*)

Two people **fight like cat and dog**, or **fight like cats and dogs**, when they argue fiercely whenever they are together: *My sister and I get on much better now, but when we were little we used to fight like cat and dog.* ♦ *see also* **at each other's throats** ▷THROATS

○ **let the 'cat out of the bag**

You **let the cat out of the bag** if you accidentally give away information which is supposed to remain a secret: *Mum and Dad found out about the party; someone let the cat out of the bag.* ♦ *see also* **spill the beans** ▷BEANS; **give the game away** ▷GAME

○ **like a cat on hot 'bricks** (*BrE*) or **like a cat on a hot tin 'roof**

If you are so excited or anxious that you cannot sit still or concentrate properly,

○ **you are like a cat on hot bricks** or **a cat on a hot tin roof**: *Ford is hopping like a cat on hot bricks, demanding that something should be done.*

○ **like the cat that got the 'cream**

Someone who looks **like the cat that got the cream** is looking very pleased with themselves: *He was smiling, Mr Barnes, like the cat that got the cream.*

○ **not have a cat in 'hell's chance** or **not stand a cat in 'hell's chance** (*informal*)

You do **not have**, or **stand**, **a cat in hell's chance** if you are extremely unlikely to succeed: *We'd be stupid to climb in this weather. We wouldn't have a cat in hell's chance of reaching the top.* ♦ *see also* **not have a hope in hell** ▷HOPE

○ **play cat-and-'mouse with someone**

If someone **plays cat-and-mouse with** a person less powerful than themselves, they tease them by repeatedly making them afraid and then letting them relax: *The Government is playing cat-and-mouse with political prisoners, releasing and re-imprisoning them.*

> A cat which has caught a mouse often releases it several times to watch it run, before finally killing it.

○ **set the cat among the 'pigeons** or **put the cat among the 'pigeons** (*BrE*)

If someone **has set**, or **put**, **the cat among the pigeons**, they have made a difficult situation even worse: *He said what? That's really set the cat among the pigeons now, hasn't it?*

○ **think you are the cat's 'whiskers** or **the cat's py'jamas** (*insulting*)

If you say that someone **thinks they are the cat's whiskers**, or **the cat's pyjamas**, you think they have too high an opinion of themselves: *She thinks she's the cat's whiskers, but she's no better than anyone else.* ♦ *see also* **think you are the bee's knees** ▷BEE

○ **when the cat's away, the 'mice will play**

If someone says '**when the cat's away,**

the mice will play', they mean that when the person who is normally in authority is absent, people will take advantage of the situation: *The boss is off sick, so we're all going to the pub for the afternoon. When the cat's away ...*

catch

○ **catch someone 'at it** or **catch someone red-'handed** (*informal*)

You **catch someone at it**, or **catch someone red-handed**, when you find them in the act of doing something forbidden: *Night patrols were started in some rural areas, and they sometimes caught cattle thieves red-handed.* ♦ *see also* **catch someone with their trousers down** ▷TROU-SERS

○ **what's the 'catch?**

People ask **'what's the catch?'** if they think there must be a problem with something that seems good, and easy to obtain: *'I'll give it to you completely free of charge.' 'Really? So what's the catch?'*

○ **you won't catch 'so-and-so** or **you won't catch so-and-so 'dead** (*informal*)

You say that **you won't catch so-and-so**, or **you won't catch so-and-so dead**, doing a certain activity, if you are sure that that person would never do, or even consider doing, it: *You won't catch my husband dancing. He says it's naff.*

catch-up

○ **play 'catch-up** or **play 'catch-up ball** (*AmE*; *informal*)

You **play catch-up**, or **play catch-up ball**, when you try harder in order to be as good as someone else: *The Republican gains meant the Democrats would have to play catch-up before the next election.*

caution

○ **throw caution to the 'wind**

When you **throw caution to the wind**, you decide to take a risk, and not to worry about the possible bad result of your actions: *You cannot be tentative or apprehensive in your movements – you have to throw caution to the wind and 'attack' with your objective clearly in mind.*

ceiling

○ **hit the 'ceiling**

You **hit the ceiling** when you become very angry: *When James saw the telephone bill, he hit the ceiling.*

cellar

○ **in the 'cellar** (*AmE*)

If a sports team is **in the cellar**, they are last in their league: *The Chicago Cubs started the season well, but were soon in the cellar.*

cent

○ **not worth a red 'cent** (*AmE*)

If something is **not worth a red cent**, it is not worth anything: *Tom wants me to buy his car, but it's not worth a red cent.*

cents

○ **put your two 'cents in** or **put your two 'cents' worth in** (*AmE*)

1 If you **put your two cents in**, or **put your two cents' worth in**, you take part in a discussion by expressing your opinion: *They criticized my school, but I put my two cents in.* **2** (*informal*) You **put your two cents in**, or **put your two cents' worth in**, when you give unwanted advice: *When it comes to the way we bring up our kids, she always has to put her two cents' worth in.* ♦ *see also* **put your pennyworth in** ▷PEN-NYWORTH

ceremony

○ **stand on 'ceremony**

If you agree not to **stand on ceremony**, you decide with someone that you will ignore certain formalities: *Well bring him in. We don't stand on ceremony in this house.*

chalk

○ **like chalk and 'cheese** (*BrE*)

Two things or people that are **like chalk and cheese** are completely different.

○ **not by a 'long chalk** (*BrE*)

If something is not the case **by a long chalk**, then it is not at all the case: *I'm afraid this essay doesn't deserve a pass mark. Not by a long chalk.*

chance

○ **blow your 'chance** (*informal*)

If someone **has blown their chance**, they have lost an opportunity by mak-

IDIOMS *study*

change

The next time you write or talk about **change** you might try to use some of the following idioms. (Remember you can see how to use each idiom correctly by looking at its entry, which you can find under the word printed in heavy type.)

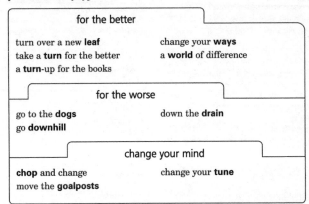

for the better

turn over a new **leaf**
take a **turn** for the better
a **turn**-up for the books

change your **ways**
a **world** of difference

for the worse

go to the **dogs**
go **downhill**

down the **drain**

change your mind

chop and change
move the **goalposts**

change your **tune**

---

ing a mistake or by doing the wrong things: *She'd blown her chance to get close to Guy.*

○ **chance would be a 'fine thing!** (*BrE*; *informal*)
If someone wishes that the thing which has just been mentioned were true, and thinks that it is unlikely that they will be able to do it, they might say '**chance would be a fine thing!**': *How I would have liked to play that, I thought, but chance would be a fine thing!*

○ '**fat chance** (*informal*)
You say there is a **fat chance** or a **fat chance of something** if you are sure that that thing will not happen: *'Please stop loving me,' demands Smith at the album's climax. Fat chance. They'll love him even more.*

○ **a fighting 'chance**
You have **a fighting chance** if you have a small, but real, possibility of success: *If she can get through the first 24 hours, she's got a fighting chance of surviving.*

○ **given half a 'chance**
If you say that a person would do something, especially something considered to be unacceptable, **given half a chance**, you mean that they would do it happily at the slightest opportunity: *That Tom is such a womanizer. He'd be in bed with his own brother's wife, given half a chance.*

○ **in with a 'chance** (*BrE*)
You are **in with a chance** if there is a good possibility that you will succeed or win: *This horse has got to be in with a chance. He has been racing well this season and the going is good.*

○ '**jump at the chance**
If someone says they would **jump at the chance** to do something, they mean they would certainly do it if they could: *I don't understand why you turned down that job. I'd jump at the chance to work abroad.*

○ **not stand a 'chance**
You **do not stand a chance** if you have no hope of succeeding or winning: *I've*

decided not to enter the competition. I don't stand a chance against the other contestants.

○ **on the 'off-chance**

You do something **on the off-chance** when you hope it will be useful or successful but do not expect it to be: *Hi! I'm just calling you on the off-chance that you may be free this afternoon.*

change *see also* **Idioms study** page 29

○ **have a change of 'heart**

When you **have a change of heart**, you decide not to do something which you had intended to do, or you change your opinion about something: *The Government decided that Britain would remain independent, unless there was a change of heart in Washington.*

changes

○ **ring the 'changes**

You **ring the changes**, or **ring the changes on something**, when you change something or do something new for variety: *Why not ring the changes and freshen up your image with some of this season's fantasy jewellery?*

character

○ **in 'character**

A certain action is **in character** for someone if it is what you would expect them to do: *Tony always gets aggressive when he's drunk. I'm afraid he was acting very much in character.*

○ **out of 'character**

A certain action is **out of character** for someone if it is the opposite of what you would expect them to do: *It's very out of character for him to be so quiet. He's usually such a mischievous boy.*

charity

○ **charity begins at 'home**

If someone says '**charity begins at home**', they mean that you should concentrate on helping the people who are close to you instead of making an effort to help people you do not know: *Many believe that charity begins at home and prefer to donate to British, rather than overseas, relief.*

Charley

○ **look a 'Charley** or **feel like a 'Charley** (*BrE*; *old*, *informal*)

You **look**, or **feel like**, **a Charley** if an

embarrassing event or situation makes you appear or feel foolish in public: *I felt a proper Charley when I got to the church and realized I had left the wedding rings at home.*

cheek

○ **cheek by 'jowl**

When two very different things or people are **cheek by jowl**, they are beside each other or sharing the same space: *In Montmartre, you will find painters cheek by jowl with flower sellers.*

A dog's **jowls** are the hanging folds of loose skin which it has instead of cheeks.

○ **turn the other 'cheek**

You **turn the other cheek** when you accept the bad actions or words which someone directs at you without complaining or feeling angry with them: *The British have a reputation for not complaining. Turning the other cheek is the national pastime.*

In the Bible, Jesus instructs his followers to offer the other cheek if someone hits them on one of their cheeks.

cheese

○ **hard 'cheese** (*BrE*; *informal*)

If someone says '**hard cheese**' about another person's misfortune, it is a rude way of saying that that person will just have to accept the situation: *'I don't want to come to the shops with you.' 'Hard cheese, you're coming.'* ♦ *see also* **hard** or **tough luck** ▷LUCK

Cheshire

○ **grin like a Cheshire 'cat**

A person who **is grinning like a Cheshire cat** is smiling widely, in a rather foolish-looking way: *'It's over,' I said out loud. I turned to face Kathleen. She was smiling like a Cheshire cat. 'It's going to be all right now,' I told her.*

The Cheshire Cat is a character in Lewis Carroll's *Alice's Adventures in Wonderland* (1865).

chestnut

○ **an old 'chestnut**

An old chestnut is **1** an old joke which

is no longer funny: *Nigel bent and kissed her hand, murmuring something about pretty, older sisters. Juliet cringed. Not that old chestnut!* **2** a subject that has been debated so much that people have become bored with it: *The subject under discussion is that old chestnut, public or private financing of the arts.*

chicken

○ **the chicken and the 'egg**
People call two things **the chicken and the egg** if they are closely linked, but it is difficult to tell which one causes the other: *Which came first, the chicken or the egg? The existence of a stable political culture in Britain may be due to the effectiveness of government. But what has enabled government to be effective?*

chickens

○ **count your chickens before they are 'hatched**
If someone tells you not to **count your chickens before they are hatched**, they mean that you should not be sure that something good is going to happen until it has actually happened: *I wouldn't count your chickens, Mr Vass. I've agreed to sign the contract, but that's all I've agreed to.* ♦ *see also* **I wouldn't bank on it** ▷BANK

child

○ **'child's play**
Something that is described as **child's play** is so easy that you never worry about it: *It's child's play giving lectures. But I still get nervous when I have to give an after-dinner speech.* ♦ *see also* **easy as ABC** *or* **anything** *or* **falling off a log** *or* **pie** *or* **winking** ▷EASY; **a piece of cake** ▷PIECE; **nothing to it** ▷NOTH-ING

chin

○ **keep your 'chin up**
If you tell someone to **keep their chin up**, you mean that they should try not to be unhappy or afraid: *Come on, keep your chin up. Things are bound to get better soon.*

○ **take it on the 'chin**
If someone accepts something upsetting or discouraging, without complaining, you can say they **are taking**

it on the chin: *See if he ever answers back, or, indeed, reacts in any other way other than to quietly take it on the chin.*

chip

○ **a chip off the old 'block**
You say that someone, especially a man or boy, is **a chip off the old block** if, in behaviour or personality, he reminds you of his father: *From the doorstep she smiled at Jimmy, a chip off the old block with his grey eyes and a bit of his dad's twinkle.* ♦ *see also* **tarred with the same brush** ▷BRUSH

○ **have a 'chip on your shoulder**
Someone who **has a chip on their shoulder**, or **a chip on their shoulder about something**, privately resents something, and gets easily upset or angry when they are reminded of it: *He had a bit of a chip on his shoulder because he felt that other people who were not so talented but who had the right background and connections had got ahead of him and had better career prospects.*

chips

○ **cash in your 'chips** (*informal*)
To **cash in your chips** is to die: *The old man cashed in his chips last week. Funeral's on Friday.* ♦ *see also* **breathe your last** ▷LAST; **kick the bucket** ▷BUCKET; **pop your clogs** ▷CLOGS; **bite the dust** ▷DUST; **give up the ghost** ▷GHOST; **snuff it** ▷SNUFF

> Gamblers usually **cash in their chips** [= exchange them for money], just before they leave the casino.

○ **in the 'chips** (*AmE*; *informal*)
Someone who is **in the chips** is rich: *He could do anything he wanted, because his family was in the chips.*

○ **when the chips are 'down** (*informal*)
A period of time **when the chips are down** is one when you have a particular need, giving you the opportunity to judge the true value of the people or things around you: *It's when the chips are down that you will find out what he's really capable of.* ♦ *see also* **come to the crunch** ▷CRUNCH; **when push comes to shove** ▷PUSH

> In gambling, when the chips are down
> [=on the table], you cannot change
> your bet.

chop

○ **chop and 'change** (*BrE*)

If someone is always **chopping and changing**, they never seem happy with their decisions, and are continually changing them: *Once you've made the choice though, stick to it, don't chop and change from one style to another.*

○ **for the 'chop** (*BrE*; *informal*)

1 Something that is **for the chop** is going to stop existing as the result of official action: *I'm afraid housing benefit is probably next for the chop.* **2** Someone who is **for the chop** is going to lose their job: *We're going to a company meeting today to find out who's for the chop.*

○ **get the 'chop** (*BrE*; *informal*)

1 If something **gets the chop**, it suddenly stops existing as the result of official action: *How will the tourist industry survive if the ferry service gets the chop?* **2** If someone **gets the chop**, they lose their job suddenly: *If Bill gets the chop I'm going to hand in my notice.*

chord

○ **strike a 'chord**

When something **strikes a chord**, or **strikes a chord with someone**, they have an understanding of it, or view it with sympathy, because it relates to something in their own experience: *Our appeal for rights to paternity leave struck a chord with many young fathers on the committee.*

circle

○ **come full 'circle** or **turn full 'circle**

If things **come**, or **turn**, **full circle**, a situation which existed in the past changes and develops, but then returns, probably in a slightly different form, in the present: *Sadly, events have come full circle and those who defended the university then must do so again.*

city hall

○ **fight city 'hall** (*AmE*)

If you **fight city hall**, you fight in a hopeless way against government employees who are more interested in rules than in your problem: *I had a good case but you can't fight city hall.*

clam

○ **shut up like a 'clam** or **clam 'up**

If you **shut up like a clam**, or **clam up**, you refuse to speak about something: *I tried to find out if she knew anything, but she shut up like a clam.*

> A **clam** is a shellfish whose shell is
> made of two halves which it closes together tightly when it senses danger.

clanger

○ **drop a 'clanger**

Someone **has dropped a clanger** if they have accidentally said or done something embarrassing in public: *I think I dropped a clanger when I told her she had lost weight. Was it the wrong thing to say?* ♦ *see also* **put your foot in it** or **in your mouth** ▷FOOT

class

○ **in a class of your 'own**

If you consider that someone or something is **in a class of their own**, you think that they are much better than any other in their area of activity: *Nureyev was in a class of his own. We shall never see a dancer like him again.* ♦ *see also* **a cut above** or **a cut above the rest** ▷CUT; **in a different league** ▷LEAGUE

clean

○ **clean as a 'whistle**

Something that is as **clean as a whistle** is very clean.

○ **come 'clean**

When you **come clean**, you admit that you have done something wrong after telling lies about it for some time: *I may as well come clean. I broke the vase then lied about it to everyone.*

cleaners

○ **take someone to the 'cleaners** (*informal*)

If someone **takes you to the cleaners**, their actions result in your losing or spending all or a lot of your money, or in your complete defeat: *His ex-wife really took him to the cleaners in the divorce settlement.*

clear

○ **clear as a 'bell**

A sound is as **clear as a bell** if you can

hear it very easily: *'Can you hear me?'*
'Yes, you're as clear as a bell.'

○ **clear as 'mud** (*informal*)

You say that something such as an explanation is as **clear as mud** if it is
not very clear at all: *You discover which
bits are clear as daylight and which are
clear as mud.*

○ **in the 'clear**

1 You are **in the clear** if you are no
longer believed to have committed a
crime: *Though it was finally agreed
that I was in the clear, I never got
a formal apology from the police.*
2 You are also **in the clear** if you
no longer have a debt to pay: *If I
watch what I spend for the next fort-
night, I should be in the clear next
month.*

○ **steer 'clear of** or **stay 'clear of**

You **steer 'clear of**, or **stay, clear of** someone or
something when you try to avoid them:
*It was prudent to steer clear of political
debate.* ♦ *see also* **keep your distance**
▷DISTANCE

clever

○ **too clever by 'half** (*insulting*)

If you say that someone is **too clever
by half**, you mean that their confident
behaviour and high opinion of their
own abilities annoys you: *He stood up,
waved at Monica, winked at Paula and
was gone.'That man is too clever by half,'
Paula commented.*

clock

○ **against the 'clock**

When you do something **against the
clock**, you are doing it as fast as you
can and recording how long it takes
you: *It involves an arduous ten kilometre
run preceded by a long assault course,
against the clock.*

clogs

○ **pop your 'clogs** (*BrE*; *informal, humorous*)

To **pop your clogs** is to die: *I've started
thinking about making my will, though
I don't intend to pop my clogs for
a few years yet.* ♦ *see also* **kick the
bucket** ▷BUCKET; **cash in your chips**
▷CHIPS; **bite the dust** ▷DUST; **give
up the ghost** ▷GHOST; **snuff it**
▷SNUFF

close

○ **come to a 'close** or **draw to a 'close**

When something **comes to a close**, it
finishes; if something **is drawing to a
close**, it is about to finish: *The happy
day had come to a close, and everyone
went to bed.*

cloud

○ **cloud 'cuckoo land** (*informal*)

If you say that someone is in **cloud
cuckoo land**, you mean that they are
mad or that their idea of reality is not
accurate: *It's always going to be like that
here, and anyone who thinks differently
is living in cloud cuckoo land.*

○ **every cloud has a silver 'lining**

If you say that **every cloud has a silver lining**, you mean that there is always a positive side to everything,
however bad it may seem: *Now you've
lost your job, at least you'll have more
time for the kids. Every cloud has a silver
lining.*

> Notice how this idiom can be adapted
> to suit the speaker's needs. People also
> sometimes just say **'Every cloud ... '**.

○ **on cloud 'nine**

If you are **on cloud nine**, you are extremely happy: *When I was chosen to
fight my first election in Birmingham, I
was on cloud nine.* ♦ *see also* **walk on
air** ▷AIR; **thrilled to bits** ▷BITS; **in
seventh heaven** ▷HEAVEN; **over the
moon** ▷MOON

○ **under a 'cloud**

If you are **under a cloud**, you are in
trouble for something which you have
done previously and which has caused
strong disapproval: *I don't know the
exact circumstances of her resignation,
but she left under a bit of a cloud.*

clover

○ **in 'clover** (*informal*)

Someone who is **in clover** is living happily and in great comfort: *If Marcos
was cynical, he was no more so than
American foreign policy which kept him
in power and in clover for 20 years.* ♦ *see
also* **in the money** ▷MONEY

club

○ **join the 'club** (*informal*)

You can say **'join the club'** if someone

has just complained about something
and you want to agree with them or to
say that you are affected in the same
way: '*I hate this new pedestrian cross-
ing.*' '*Join the club. It doesn't give you
enough time to get over.*'

clue

○ **not have a 'clue** (*informal*)

1 You say you **do not have a clue** when
you do not know something, or when
you are ignorant about a certain subject: *Sorry, I haven't a clue about cars.* **2**
Someone who **does not have a clue** in
general is unable to do anything properly: *My God! Have you seen what he's
wearing? He just doesn't have a clue,
does he?* ♦ *see also* **not have an earthly**
▷EARTHLY

clued

○ **clued 'up** (*informal*)

When you are **clued up**, you have a lot
of knowledge about a particular thing:
*Choosing the right sparkling wine can be
a minefield if you are not clued up on the
different brands available.*

coals

○ **carry coals to 'Newcastle** or **take
coals to 'Newcastle**

If you **are carrying**, or **taking**, **coals
to Newcastle**, you are taking something to a place where there is plenty
of that thing already: *It was left to Wes-
tern businessmen to manufacture the T-
shirts which ended up on the Soviet
black market, an acute case of carrying
coals to Newcastle.*

> Notice that simply saying '**coals to
> Newcastle**' is often enough.

○ **haul someone over the 'coals**

You **haul someone over the coals**
when you tell them severely that you
disapprove of something they have
done, in order to embarrass them: *I
should have hauled him over the coals
for not surrendering all of his files to
me.* ♦ *see also* **give someone a rap
over the knuckles** ▷RAP

coast

○ **the coast is 'clear**

You say that **the coast is clear** when
you consider that it is safe to do something because a certain person is ab-

sent or is not watching: *Once you're
there, stay absolutely quiet – take slow,
calm, soft breaths and don't move until
you are sure that the coast is clear.*

cobwebs

○ **blow the 'cobwebs away** (*BrE*)

When people say that going outside
will **blow the cobwebs away**, they
mean that it will make you feel better
and more lively: *Why don't you go for a
quick walk? That'll soon blow the cobwebs away.*

> A **cobweb** is a network of threads
> made by a spider. Cobwebs gather in
> places that do not get used, or
> cleaned, very often.

cock

○ **cock-and-'bull story**

If you refer to someone's excuse or explanation as a **cock-and-bull story**,
you mean that you don't believe it: *Last
night, she had returned at some un-
earthly hour with some cock-and-bull
story about having to work late.*

○ **go off at half-'cock** or **go off half-
cocked**

Something which **goes off at half-
cock**, or **goes off half-cocked**, is unsuccessful because of lack of preparation: *My brother tends to rush into
things, so his projects often go off at
half-cock.*

> On old guns, if the firing mechanism
> was **at half-cock** when the gun fired,
> the shot would be wasted.

cockles

○ **warm the cockles of someone's 'heart**
(*old or humorous*)

You say that something **warms the
cockles of your heart** if it makes you
feel happy and sure that the world is
full of good things: *Talk of means-
testing pensions hardly warms the
cockles.*

> Notice that just saying '*such-and-such*
> **warms the cockles**' is often enough.

coin

○ **'coin it** or **'coin it in** (*informal*)

Someone who **is coining it** or **coining**

it in is earning a lot of money: *He figured he could make a lot of money out of this room – he could charge £10 an hour and really coin it in.* ♦ *see also* **make a bundle** ▷BUNDLE; **make a killing** ▷KILLING; **make your pile** ▷PILE

cold

○ **come in from the 'cold**

When someone **comes in from the cold**, they re-enter a group or rejoin an activity after a period of time when they were not permitted to do so: *Allegations of misconduct were dropped and the MP came back in from the cold.*

○ **leave someone 'cold**

If something **leaves you cold**, it has no effect on your emotions: *I'm afraid the film left me cold. I couldn't sympathize with either of the main characters.*

○ **out 'cold**

Someone who is **out cold** is unconscious: *I saw him fall, but when I got to him he was out cold.*

collar

○ **hot under the 'collar**

If you are **hot under the collar**, you feel annoyed and become rather agitated: *There's no need to get so hot under the collar. I'm just slower than you, that's all. Now explain again, slowly.*

colour (*AmE* color)

○ **add 'colour to something**

Something that **adds colour to something** else brings some energy, interest or variety to that thing: *His enthusiastic lecturing style adds colour to a subject that many people regard as dull.*

○ **lend 'colour to something**

Something that **lends colour to** a story or argument, for example, makes it appear more likely, believable or reasonable: *It is essential that nothing is done that might lend colour to the suggestion that they are favouring any one section of the community.*

○ **off-'colour** (*BrE*)

If you are **off-colour**, you are not feeling very well, but you are not really ill either: *I've been feeling a bit off-colour ever since I came back from holiday.* ♦ *see also* **look like death warmed up** ▷DEATH

○ **off-'color** (*AmE*)

If something is **off-color**, it is considered to be rude or in bad taste: *Most of the comedian's stand-up act consisted of off-color jokes.*

○ **see the colour of someone's 'money** (*informal*)

If you say that you want to **see the colour of someone's money**, you mean that you want them to prove that they can be trusted by supporting what they say with money: *He says he'll buy it, but I'll wait to see the colour of his money before I take the advert down.*

colours

○ **someone's true 'colours**

If someone shows **their true colours**, or if **their true colours** are showing, they have stopped pretending to be nicer than they really are, and are starting to show the unpleasant side of their character: *Anyway, she's seen him in his true colours now, and she's lost interest.*

○ **with flying 'colours**

When you do something **with flying colours**, you do it easily and with great success: *She passed her exams with flying colours.*

common

○ **common as 'dirt** or (*BrE*) **common as 'muck** (*informal*)

If someone says that a person is as **common as dirt**, or as **common as muck**, they mean that they do not approve of their badly-educated and unrefined behaviour: *That Sue's as common as dirt.*

○ **common-or-garden** (*BrE*)

A **common-or-garden** person or thing is an ordinary or unexceptional person or thing: *He lived in a normal common-or-garden 'caravan.*

company

○ **two's company, three's a 'crowd**

If someone says '**two's company, three's a crowd**', they mean that, in their opinion, two people are more likely to be happy together than a group of three: *No, sorry, I'd rather you didn't come with us. Two's company.*

> This expression can also refer to a couple of lovers who do not want to be disturbed by another person.

compliment

○ backhanded 'compliment

A **backhanded compliment** is a remark which is intended to be, or seems like, a compliment, but in fact is not: *She said that I was dressed much more tastefully than usual, which was rather a backhanded compliment.*

compliments

○ fish for 'compliments

You **are fishing for compliments** if you try, probably by asking questions, to persuade someone to make a positive comment about you: *'You're pushing me in the direction of flattery again,' he said softly. 'I was not fishing for compliments!'*

concern

○ a going con'cern

Something such as a business is **a going concern** if it is operating successfully and making money: *We will have to increase the profits before we can sell the business as a going concern.*

conclusions

○ jump to con'clusions

You **jump to conclusions** when you form a judgement of a situation without knowing all the facts: *It may just be a coincidence, so let's not jump to any conclusions.*

condition

○ in mint con'dition

Something that is **in mint condition** is in excellent condition, as if it had never been used: *A black and white £5 note, printed between 1920 and 1956, costs from £20. Those in mint condition have doubled in value over the last two years.* ♦ *see also* **sound as a bell** ▷SOUND

confidence

○ in 'confidence

You tell someone something **in confidence** when you instruct them to keep it secret: *Why did you go spreading the things I told you in strictest confidence?*

conscience

○ in all 'conscience *or* in good 'conscience

If you do or say something **in all conscience**, *or* **in good conscience**, you do or say it without feeling guilty:

How, in all conscience, can you continue living with your parents without paying any rent?

○ prick someone's 'conscience

If certain thoughts are **pricking your conscience**, they are preventing you from forgetting guilty feelings: *All the signs which I saw and chose to ignore... they've been pricking my conscience since he died.*

○ with a clear 'conscience

You do something **with a clear conscience** if you are sure that you have no reason to feel ashamed or guilty about doing it: *The clear conscience with which most people here avoid taxes if they can, is to do with their feeling of powerlessness in relation to government.*

considered

○ all things con'sidered

You say that something is the case, **all things considered**, when you are giving a general opinion after thinking about the whole situation: *It rained all the time, but all things considered, we had a good weekend.* ♦ *see also* **at the end of the day** ▷END

consideration

○ take something into conside'ration

You **take something into consideration** if you think about it, and how your actions will affect it, before making a decision: *You've got to take his feelings into consideration.*

○ under conside'ration

Something that is **under consideration** is being considered by someone before they decide whether to accept or reject it: *Proposals for a new visitors' centre are currently under consideration.*

contempt

○ hold in con'tempt

If you **hold** someone or something **in contempt**, you have no respect at all for them: *He holds all violence in the utmost contempt.*

contradiction

○ contradiction in 'terms

If you call a combination of words a **contradiction in terms**, you are saying that it does not make sense because the two elements from which it is formed contradict each other: *The most*

*important instrument is subsidy, even
though subsidy in a free market is a contradiction in terms.*

contrary

○ **'contrary to something**

Something which is **contrary to
something** else is against or opposite
to that thing: *Why do you do things
which are contrary to my wishes?*

○ **on the 'contrary** (*formal*)

You use **'on the contrary'** to tell the
previous speaker that you think what
they have just said is incorrect: *'Anyway, we have no power to change things.'
'On the contrary, I think we have a lot of
power.'*

○ **to the 'contrary** (*formal*)

To the contrary means 'stating or suggesting that the opposite is true': *As
I haven't heard anything to the contrary,
I presume that the work was satisfactory.*

cookie

○ **smart 'cookie** (*AmE; informal*)

If you call someone a **smart cookie**,
you believe that they are clever: *Fred
didn't have a college education, but he
was a smart cookie.*

○ **tough 'cookie** (*informal, insulting*)

If you call someone, usually a woman, a
tough cookie, you mean that they are
hard, independent, and unlikely to
worry about the feelings of others: *She
was winning a reputation as a tough
cookie, a determined career girl refusing
to be deflected from her dreams.*

cookies

○ **toss your 'cookies** (*AmE; informal*)

If you **toss your cookies**, you vomit:
*About an hour after I ate those shrimps
I tossed my cookies.*

cooks

○ **too many cooks spoil the 'broth**

In a situation where so many people
are trying to help with a job that they
are all getting in each other's way, you
can say **'too many cooks spoil the
broth'**: *Thanks for offering, but we've
got lots of volunteers. We don't want a
case of too many cooks.*

> Notice the common short form: 'too
> many cooks'.

cool

○ **cool as a 'cucumber** (*informal*)

Someone who is as **cool as a cucumber** is very calm: *He arrived half an
hour late and cool as a cucumber.*

○ **'cool it** (*informal*)

If you want someone to behave more
calmly, you can tell them to **cool it**: *He
was shouting 'Hey! Cool it! Let's hear
what the preacher has to say.'*

○ **keep your 'cool** (*informal*)

Someone who **is keeping their cool** is
remaining calm in a difficult situation:
*He kept his cool and worked at the lock
until he had finally broken through.*

cop

○ **'cop it** (*BrE; informal*)

To **cop it** is to be punished: *You'll cop it
if your mum finds out.* ♦ *see also* **get it**
▷GET

○ **it's a fair 'cop** (*BrE; informal*)

If a person says **'it's a fair cop'** when
they are accused of doing something
wrong, they are admitting their crime
or error and saying that they are prepared to accept punishment for it; if
other people say **'it's a fair cop'**, they
mean that, in their opinion, the person
has committed a crime or error and
should accept punishment for it: *You've
pleaded guilty to the charge anyhow, it's
a fair cop!*

○ **not much 'cop** (*BrE; informal*)

Something which you describe as **not
much cop** is not very good: *The film
wasn't much cop in the end, so we just
went to bed.*

copybook

○ **blot your 'copybook** (*BrE*)

If you **blot your copybook**, or **blot
your copybook with someone**, you
do something which changes that person's favourable opinion of you: *Lang-
ford made some good tackles, but
then blotted his copybook with a stupid
kick which might have cost his side the
match.*

cork

○ **blow your 'cork** (*AmE; informal*)

You **blow your cork** when you become
very angry: *Roy blew his cork when the
company manager fired him after years
of hard work and dedication.*

corner (*see also* **corners**)

○ **box someone into a 'corner**

You **box someone into a corner** when you force them into a place or a situation where they are no longer in control of things; someone who feels **boxed into a corner** is unable to think of a way out of the difficult situation in which they find themselves: *He had me boxed into a corner, and I knew that if I refused, he would not return my money.*

○ **just round the 'corner** or **just around the 'corner**

An event which is **just round**, or **around**, **the corner** is going to happen very soon: *Spring is just round the corner.*

○ **turn the 'corner**

You say that you **have turned the corner** if the worst part of a bad period is finished and things are starting to get better: *The general message is that Kent have turned the corner and are confident that improvements on the field will be matched by overall prosperity.*

corners

○ **cut 'corners**

You **cut corners** when you try to do something in a way which involves less effort, money or time than if you had used the more usual method, probably giving you a result which is not so good: *Constructing equipment of this nature is a time-consuming occupation although there are a few that try to cut corners to maximize profits.*

costs

○ **at 'all costs**

Something which must happen **at all costs** is so important that everything possible must be done to make sure it happens: *This letter must reach him by this afternoon at all costs.*

couch

○ **couch 'potato** (*informal, insulting*)

If you call someone a **couch potato**, you mean that they are very lazy and never do anything physically active: *Dan had become a couch potato, sitting in front of the television all day.*

count

○ **count me 'in**

If you say to a person or a group of peo-

ple '**count me in**', you mean that you want to be involved in something they are planning: *Count me in for the trip to London next week.*

○ **count me 'out**

If you say to a person or a group of people '**count me out**', you mean that you do not want to be involved in something that they are planning: *You can count me out if this is going to mean doing anything illegal.*

○ **out for the 'count** (*informal*)

Somebody who is **out for the count** is sleeping so deeply that it would be very difficult to wake them up: *I knew the children were tired. Look at them. They're both out for the count.*

> In boxing, **out for the count** refers to a boxer who is lying on the floor and who fails to get up while the referee counts to ten.

counter

○ **under the 'counter**

Something that is sold **under the counter** is sold secretly and illegally: *He used to slip me some cigarettes under the counter for wholesale prices.*

country

○ **go to the 'country** (*BrE*)

The political party in power **goes to the country** when they hold a general election to find out if public opinion supports or rejects their decisions: *The Tories were forced to go to the country over the affair.*

courage

○ **Dutch 'courage**

You get **Dutch courage** when you drink alcohol to make you feel braver than usual: *Then, with slightly more than a little Dutch courage inside him, he suddenly started to sing.*

course

○ **stay the 'course**

If you **stay the course**, you manage to continue with something difficult or challenging until you have achieved your aim: *The question is often asked when a firm is taking people on for training: how many will stay the course?*

○ **steer a middle 'course**

You **steer a middle course** between

two options when you choose to do something which is neither one nor the other, but halfway between them: *Not knowing whether to be gentle or more fierce, I decided to steer a middle course between the two.*

Coventry

○ **send someone to 'Coventry**

If people **send someone to Coventry**, they agree together to ignore and not to speak to that person, as a form of unofficial punishment: *To disregard such a challenge was unthinkable. I would be sent to Coventry and be considered a coward for the rest of my schooldays.*

cover

○ **blow someone's 'cover**

To **blow someone's cover** is to reveal their secret identity: *She was posing as a health visitor, but a complaint to the Department of Health blew her cover.*

cows

○ **till the 'cows come home**

If you say that a certain activity could continue **till the cows come home**, you mean that you think it could go on forever: *People are able to go on reasoning till the cows come home, but nothing ever gets done.*

crack

○ **a fair crack of the 'whip** (*BrE*)

You have had **a fair crack of the whip** if you have had a good length of time doing a certain activity and it is the end of your turn: *Okay, you've had a fair crack of the whip now. Whose turn is it next?*

cracked

○ **not what it's cracked 'up to be** or **not all it's cracked 'up to be** (*informal*)

Something which is **not what**, or **not all, it's cracked up to be** is not as good as its reputation suggests: *Life as a rock star is not all it's cracked up to be. There are many bands who are barely making a living.*

cracking

○ **get 'cracking** (*informal*)

You tell someone to **get cracking** if you want them to start doing something immediately, and as fast as they can: *We'd better get cracking if we want to finish cleaning before your parents ar-*

rive. ♦ *see also* **put your shoulder to the wheel** ▷SHOULDER

cracks

○ **paper over the 'cracks**

Someone who is **papering over the cracks** is trying to hide the fact that they have done a job badly or made a mistake: *That tax policy was a disaster, and the Government have been papering over the cracks ever since.*

crash

○ **crash and 'burn** (*AmE; informal*)

'To **crash and burn**' means 'to fail completely': *Lois was convinced she would crash and burn on her first date.*

creek

○ **up the creek without a 'paddle** or **up the 'creek** (*informal*)

Someone is **up the creek without a paddle**, or **up the creek** if their situation is so bad that they do not know how to get out of it: *We're up the creek because we don't know where to go from here.* ♦ *see also* **out of your depth** ▷DEPTH; **in the soup** ▷SOUP; **in a tight spot** ▷SPOT; **in deep water** ▷WATER; **in hot water** ▷WATER

creeps

○ **give someone the 'creeps**

1 If someone **gives you the creeps**, you have strong negative feelings about them, because they seem strange and possibly dangerous: *Just standing there like big kids. Saying nothing. Great red faces, not smiling. They used to give us the creeps.* **2** A place **gives you the creeps** if it makes you feel strangely uncomfortable or afraid: *I look round uneasily. This place really gives me the creeps. I can't stand the smell.*

crimp

○ **put a 'crimp in something** (*AmE*)

Something that **puts a crimp in something** interferes with its progress: *Losing that money really put a crimp in our holiday plans.*

crocodile

○ **'crocodile tears**

When someone is pretending to cry, or claiming to feel sad, because that is what people expect, or in order to obtain something for themselves, you say they are crying **crocodile tears**: *They*

*weep crocodile tears for the the poor and
disadvantaged, but are basically happy
with things the way they are.*

There are stories which tell of croco-
diles crying, either to attract the attention of their victims, or while eating
them.

cropper

○ come a 'cropper

Somebody **comes a cropper** when,
probably as a result of becoming too
confident, they have a piece of bad
luck: *He came a cropper last night when
he punched that man. It turned out he
was a judo teacher.* ◆ *see also* **come to
grief** ▷GRIEF

In hunting, you **come a cropper** when
you have a serious fall from your
horse.

cross

○ have a 'cross to bear

You **have a cross to bear** if you have a
problem which you must accept: *Look –
you've got your cross to bear, all right,
I've got mine.*

crossfire

○ get caught in the 'crossfire

If two or more people are having a disagreement or a fight and you become
involved without wanting to, you can
say that you **got caught in the crossfire**: *Major sponsors of the Renault-
Williams team, caught in the crossfire of
the battle between the world champion
and his boss, are in a panic.*

crow

○ as the 'crow flies

When you state a distance **as the crow
flies**, you are talking about the distance as a straight line between two
points, not the distance by road: *You
can see the monastery from here. It's
about 12 miles away as the crow flies.*

crunch

○ come to the 'crunch (*informal*)

You say that it **has come to the
crunch** at the moment when an important decision or action is urgently
needed: *If it came to the crunch, how
many of us would sacrifice our lives for*

what we believe? ◆ *see also* **when the
chips are down** ▷CHIPS; **when push
comes to shove** ▷PUSH

crush

○ have a 'crush on someone

Someone who **has a crush on a** certain person, has fallen in love with that
person, who is probably older than
themselves, in a rather childish and
temporary way: *When I was fourteen, I
had this huge crush on my chemistry teacher.* ◆ *see also* **have a soft spot for
someone** ▷SPOT

cry

○ a far cry from

Something which is **a far cry from** another thing is not at all similar to that
thing: *Labour's lead over the SNP was
30 percentage points, a far cry from the
four-point gap which separated them in
'January.*

cuff

○ off the 'cuff

You do something **off the cuff** when
you do it with no previous preparation:
*I wish I could speak off the cuff like he
does.* □ *brilliant off-the-cuff remarks.*

cup

○ not your cup of 'tea

If something is **not your cup of tea**, it
is not the type of thing which interests
you: *No, I'm afraid an Anne Summers
party is not really my cup of tea.* ◆ *see
also* **not go a bundle on something**
▷BUNDLE

curiosity

○ curiosity killed the 'cat

You tell someone that **curiosity killed
the cat** to advise them not to ask any
more questions: *She was curious, but it
would be stupid to forget that curiosity
had killed the cat.*

curtains

○ 'curtains for someone or something

It is **curtains for someone** or **something** if the time of their end or death
has come: *If that happens, it's curtains
for the European organi'zation.*

curve

○ throw someone a 'curve (*AmE*)

If you **throw someone a curve**, you do
something unexpected that confuses
them: *The professor had said the exam*

would be easy, but then he threw us a curve by adding more questions.

> In baseball, if a pitcher throws a good curve (a ball that curves in the air), the ball is difficult to hit.

cut

○ **a cut a'bove** or **a cut above the 'rest**

If you consider that someone or something is **a cut above**, or **a cut above the rest**, you think that they are of a better standard than the average, or than the people or things you are comparing them with: *The Café Noir is a cut above the other restaurants in town.* ♦ *see also* **in a class of your own** ▷CLASS; **in a different league** ▷LEAGUE

○ **cut and 'thrust**

The **cut and thrust** of a certain activity is the fierce competition which it involves: *She enjoys the cut and thrust of international marketing.*

> In sword-fighting, **cut and thrust** describes the motions made with the sword.

○ **cut someone 'dead**

If someone **cuts you dead**, they pretend not to see you, or they refuse to greet you, as a way of showing their dislike or anger towards you: *I knew it was her. 'Sophie,' I said. And she cut me dead. My own child cut me dead.*

○ **cut it 'fine**

You **are cutting it fine** when you give yourself only just enough time to be able to achieve your aim: *He began the two-mile journey at 9.25am. Even with normal traffic, it was cutting it fine.*

○ **cut it 'out**

If you tell someone to '**cut it out**', you are telling them angrily to stop doing something: *Cut it out, I'm warning you.*

○ **cut 'out for something**

Someone who is **cut out for something** is perfectly suited for it: *I tried my best, but I'm afraid I'm just not cut out for teaching.*

○ **cut up 'rough** or **cut up 'nasty**

If someone **cuts up rough**, or **nasty**, they react badly to something, becoming angry or violent: *You can get round him if you go the right way about it. But*

he can cut up rough and turn a bit nasty if he's got a mind to.

daggers

○ **look 'daggers** (*informal*)

You **look daggers** at someone if you look at them in a way that shows that you hate them, or that you are extremely angry with them for something they have done: *'Anyway, it wasn't my fault.' He looked daggers at me.*

daisies

○ **pushing up the 'daisies** (*humorous*)

Someone who is **pushing up the daisies** is dead: *I should think I'll be pushing up the daisies before they decide to do anything about modernizing the computing system in this office.* ♦ *see also* **dead as a doornail** or **dodo** ▷DEAD; **six feet under** ▷FEET

> A **daisy** is a kind of flower that often grows on graves.

damper, dampers

○ **put a 'damper on something** or **put the 'dampers on something**

You **put a damper**, or **the dampers**, **on something** when you do or say something that spoils other people's enjoyment of it: *If you sit there looking miserable all night you'll really put a damper on things.*

> A **damper** is a device which reduces vibrations, for example, in a piano.

dance

○ **lead someone a 'dance** or **lead someone a merry 'dance** (*BrE*)

Someone **leads you a dance**, or a **merry dance**, when they cause problems for you, making you do a lot of unnecessary things: *She could have any man she fancied. None of them seemed to last very long. She led them all a merry dance, including me.*

dark
○ **in the 'dark**

You are **in the dark** about something if you do not know about it: *They've been keeping us in the dark about the plans to restructure the company.*

dash
○ **cut a 'dash**

Someone who **cuts a dash** dresses with style in order to impress others, or acts in a way that suggests that they want to be noticed: *Harvey really cut a dash in his new suit and white silk scarf.*

day *(see also* **days***)*
○ **all in a day's 'work**

You can say that something is **all in a day's work** if it forms part of your everyday activities, and must be accepted as normal, even if you find it unpleasant or difficult in some way: *Controlling a class of excitable seven year olds is all in a day's work if you are a teacher on a placement scheme.* ♦ *see also* **a necessary evil** ▷EVIL

○ **call it a 'day**

You **call it a day** when you decide to stop working on something: *At 11pm we finally decided to call it a day and went home to get some sleep.*

○ **carry the 'day**

Someone or something **carries the day** if they are responsible for an event's success: *Thank you so much for providing the food; it really helped to carry the day.*

This was originally a military expression, which meant 'to win the battle'.

○ **day in day 'out**

Something that happens **day in day out** happens repeatedly and unchangingly: *I couldn't live there; it rained day in day out when I was on holiday.*

Year in year out is also used to describe things that happen unchangingly over very long periods of time.

○ **late in the 'day** *(informal)*

You say that it's a bit **late in the day** to do something if you think it is probably too late for your actions to have a positive effect: *I think it's a bit late in the day to start making fundamental changes to the text; I mean, the project's supposed to be finished by the end of the month.*

○ **make a 'day of it**

You **make a day of it** if you decide to take advantage of a visit or event by spending the whole day in the place: *Well look, if we both have to go over there, why don't we make a day of it and stay for lunch, and maybe a walk in the afternoon?*

○ **make someone's 'day**

You **make someone's day** if you do something which makes them very happy: *The news that they'd decided to come home at last really made my day.*

○ **not be someone's 'day**

It **is not your day** if things seem to be going wrong for you all the time: *Oh no! It's not my day today; what a mess!* ♦ *see also* **get out of bed on the wrong side** ▷BED; **one of those days** ▷DAYS

○ **a rainy 'day**

You save something, for example money, for **a rainy day** if you save it for a time when you might unexpectedly need it: *I spent half the money, and put the rest away for a rainy day.*

○ **save the 'day**

Someone **saves the day** if they do something which makes a disastrous situation successful again: *The concert was quite atrocious, but once again, James saved the day with a beautiful rendition of 'Ave Maria'.*

○ **seize the 'day**

If someone tells you to **seize the day** they mean that you should take every opportunity to learn and experience new things now, rather than waiting until a later date. ♦ *see also* **you're only young once** ▷YOUNG

○ **'that'll be the day**

You can say **'that'll be the day'** if you think that it is very unlikely that something you would like to happen will happen: *'If we can get some more staff* *in, things will be much easier.' 'Huh! that'll be the day.'*

daylights

○ **scare the living 'daylights out of someone** (*informal*)

Something **scares the living daylights out of you** if it terrifies you or makes you jump: *I didn't find the film funny at all. Quite the contrary, it scared the living daylights out of me.*

days

○ **someone's days are 'numbered** or **something's days are 'numbered**

You can say that **someone's**, or **something's**, **days are numbered** if they will soon no longer be useful, successful or alive: *If you ask me, his days are numbered; the company just doesn't need people with his skills any more.* □ *It was when the sales figures dropped below 400 a year that we knew the product's days were numbered.*

○ **have seen better 'days** (*informal*)

Something that **has seen better days** in not in very good condition: *Well, the furniture's nice, but the carpet's seen better days.* ♦ *see also* **the worse for wear** ▷WEAR

○ **one of those days** (*informal*)

You say that it's **one of those days** if everything seems to be going wrong for you on a particular day: *Sorry, I'm afraid it's just one of those days; I think I should go home and start afresh tomorrow.* ♦ *see also* **get out of bed on the wrong side** ▷BED; **not be someone's day** ▷DAY

○ **those were the 'days** (*informal*)

People say '**those were the days!**' when they are thinking about times in the past which were pleasant in some way when compared to the present: *'I remember when a pint of Guinness cost 15p.' 'Mm, those were the days, eh?'*

dead

○ **dead as a 'doornail** or **as dead as a 'dodo** (*informal*)

Someone or something that is as **dead as a doornail** or as **dead as a dodo** is dead without any doubt at all: *It's not surprising he doesn't answer his fans' letters; he's been dead as a doornail for 30 years now.* ♦ *see also* **pushing up**

the daisies ▷DAISIES; **six feet under** ▷FEET

A **dodo** was a large bird, which was unable to fly, and which no longer exists.

---

deal

○ **big 'deal** (*informal*)

You can say '**big deal**' as a way of showing that you are not at all impressed by something that someone has just told you: *'They've finally agreed to give the nurses a 1% pay rise.' 'Big deal.'*

○ **cut a 'deal with someone** (*AmE*; *informal*)

You **cut a deal with someone** when you reach an agreement or make a bargain: *I cut a deal with the Chevrolet salesman that knocked $5,000 off the price.*

○ **make a big 'deal of something**

If someone **makes a big deal of something**, they exaggerate its seriousness or importance: *His mother made a big deal of Jimmy winning the class debating contest.* ♦ *see also* **make a federal case out of something** ▷CASE

○ **a raw 'deal**

You get **a raw deal** if you do not benefit as greatly from a situation as someone else: *They see this as a way of helping to ensure that their employees do not get a raw deal – for example, when candidates for promotion are being compared.*

death

○ **at death's 'door**

Someone who is **at death's door** is very ill and in danger of dying: *Even when he was at death's door he was still cracking the same old jokes.*

○ **catch your 'death** or **catch your death of 'cold**

You can tell someone that they will **catch their death**, or **catch their death of cold**, if they are going outside without enough clothes on: *The grass here is quite damp you know, and in those slippers, you'll catch your death.*

○ **the 'death of someone**

You can say that someone or something **will be the death of you** if they continually cause problems for you: *He* *always said that his job would be the death of him.*

○ **dice with 'death** (*BrE*)

You **are dicing with death** if you are taking a great risk, possibly with your life: *all those youths who might have experimented with the drug, not knowing that they were dicing with death.* ♦ *see also* **risk your neck** ▷NECK

○ **die a 'death** (*BrE*)

Something **dies a death** if it stops being popular or if it stops operating, often because it was not founded on very solid grounds in the first place: *What happened to all his big plans to start up a business? They died a death, didn't they?*

○ **hang on like grim 'death** or **hold on like grim 'death** (*informal*)

You **hang on**, or **hold on** to something **like grim death** if you hold on to it very tightly: *We hung on to the boat like grim death as it rose and then crashed down again into the stormy seas.* ♦ *see also* **for dear life** ▷LIFE

○ **look like death warmed 'up** or **feel like death warmed 'up** (*informal*)

You **look**, or **feel**, **like death warmed up** if you look or feel very tired or ill: *I wish I'd been a bit more sensible last night; I feel like death warmed up.* ♦ *see also* **off-colour** ▷COLOUR

deck

○ **stack the 'deck against someone** (*AmE*)

If you **stack the deck against someone**, you put them at a disadvantage: *Roy could have become manager, but the Board stacked the deck against him by seeking a younger man.*

decks

○ **clear the 'decks** (*informal*)

You **clear the decks** when you tidy up: *We'd better clear the decks a bit before they arrive; the place looks such a mess.*

A **deck** is a flat area for walking on, on a boat. Marines **clear the decks** when they get a ship ready for battle.

dent

○ **make a dent in**

Something **makes a dent in** something else when it has the effect of re-

ducing it: *Getting these repairs done is going to make a huge dent in our 'savings.*

depth

○ **out of your 'depth**

You are **out of your depth** if you are in a situation which is too difficult for you to cope with, or where you do not understand what is happening: *I was completely out of my depth at the dinner; I mean, I know nothing about stocks and shares and futures markets.* ♦ *see also* **up the creek without a paddle** or **up the creek** ▷CREEK; **in the soup** ▷SOUP; **in a tight spot** ▷SPOT; **in deep water** ▷WATER; **in hot water** ▷WATER; **out of your league** ▷LEAGUE

You are **out of your depth** if you are in deep water where you cannot touch the bottom with your feet.

deserts

○ **get your just de'serts**

Someone **gets their just deserts** when they get what they deserve for something bad they have done: *It is like turning to the end of the story before you begin reading it, to find out if the bad guys got their just deserts.*

designs

○ **have de'signs on**

You **have designs on** someone or something when you want them, and you plan to get them: *I know Jeremy has got designs on the car that Roger's selling, but we really can't afford it.*

desired

○ **leave a lot to be de'sired** (*informal*)

Something that **leaves a lot to be desired** is not of a very high quality, or not satisfactory: *It is not user-friendly and leaves a lot to be desired for a software support product.*

devil

○ **be a 'devil** (*informal*)

You might tell someone to **be a devil** if you want to encourage them to do something unusual, daring or indulgent, that they would not normally do: *Go on, be a devil! Nobody's watching.*

○ **better the devil you 'know**

If you say **'better the devil you know'**, you mean that it is preferable to continue in a situation which is not perfect but satisfactory, than it is to take the risk of changing to a new and unknown situation: *Fenton said, 'Better the devil you know, and we know Neil Webb. We had good times when he was here before.'*

> This idiom is the shortened form of the saying 'Better the devil you know than the devil you don't know'.

○ **between the devil and the deep blue 'sea**

You find yourself **between the devil and the deep blue sea** if you have to make a choice between two alternatives, both of which are unpleasant: *On this question regarding EC membership, the Government finds itself between the devil and the deep blue sea.*

○ **the 'devil to pay**

If you say that there'll be **the devil to pay**, you mean that there is going to be a lot of trouble when someone finds out what has happened: *I fell in the muddy water and spoilt my dress, and there was the devil to pay when we got home.*

> In some legends, people bargain with the devil, offering their soul in return for immediate success.

○ **the luck of the 'devil**

Someone who has **the luck of the devil** is very lucky, sometimes when you think they do not necessarily deserve to be: *'He revised only three subjects out of ten and they all came up in the exam.' 'That boy has the luck of the devil.'*

○ **speak of the 'devil** or **talk of the 'devil** (*informal*)

People often say **'speak, or talk, of the devil!'** when they have just been talking about someone and then that person arrives: *'Huh! Talk of the devil.' 'Why? What were you saying about me?'*

> People used to believe that talking about evil gave it power to happen.

devices

○ **leave someone to their own de'vices**

You **leave someone to their own devices** if you let them do as they please, without interfering or trying to help:

Most gliding clubs have a system of re-checking pilots during the first few hours of solo flying, but then pilots are left very much to their own devices.

die

○ **die 'hard**

People's attitudes and habits **die hard** when they do not change over long periods of time: *Old habits die hard, and even the most progressive-thinking members found that it didn't always come naturally to use the new politically correct terms.*

difference

○ **same 'difference** (*informal*)

You say **'same difference'** when you accept a correction that someone has made, but you think that the difference is unimportant: *Two thousand or twenty hundred, same difference.*

○ **with a 'difference** (*informal*)

You describe something as being **with a difference** if it has something unexpected about it that makes it unusual, original or interesting: *Enjoy a holiday with a difference on this 'Action Break' organized by the Scottish Conservation Projects group.*

difficulties *see* **Idioms study** page 46

dime

○ **a dime a 'dozen** (*AmE*; *informal*)

Something that is **a dime a dozen** is very common: *British ski champions are not exactly a dime a dozen, which is why everyone was so amazed at his performance.*

○ **on a 'dime** (*AmE*)

If something, especially a vehicle, stops or turns **on a dime**, it stops or turns in a very limited space: *London taxis are famous for being able to turn on a dime.*

dine

○ **dine 'out on something** (*BrE*; *informal*)

You **dine out on something**, for example, an event, if you repeatedly use a funny or shocking story about something that has happened to you or someone you know, in order to get people's attention in social situations: *Wow, this was an event on which one could dine out for many months back in one's home town!*

IDIOMS*study* difficulties

The next time you write or talk about **difficulties** you might try to use some of the following idioms. (Remember you can see how to use each idiom correctly by looking at its entry, which you can find under the word printed in heavy type.)

being in difficulty

have your **back** to
  the wall
bogged down
up the **creek** without
  a paddle
in at the deep **end**
out of your **depth**

out of the **frying** pan
  into the fire
up a **gum** tree
have a **job**
in the hot **seat**
in the **soup**
in a tight **spot**

on the **spot**
up against it
in deep **water**
in hot **water**
the **cards** are stacked
  against someone

a difficult situation

a **can** of worms
when the **chips** are down
a hard **nut** to crack
no **picnic**

a no-win **situation**
a sticky **situation**
the **bane** of your life

causing difficulties for yourself

bite off more than you can chew
your own worst **enemy**
tie yourself in **knots**

make a **meal** of something
make a **rod** for your own back

causing difficulties for others

set the **cat** among the pigeons
box someone into a **corner**

play merry **hell** with
put a **spanner** in the works

dinners

○ **have had more of something than
someone has had hot 'dinners** (*BrE*;
informal)
If you say that you **have had more of** a
certain thing **than** a particular person
has had hot dinners, you mean that
that person should not question your
knowledge on the subject, because you
have much more experience of it than
they have: *Eddie Futch, 80, who's prob-*
ably seen more fights than even most
men of his age have had hot dinners, ex-
pects it to be one of the best he's been in-
volved with.

dirt

○ **dirt 'cheap** (*informal*)
Something is **dirt cheap** if it is very
cheap: *It keeps the rain out, it lets a cer-*
tain amount of light in and it's dirt cheap.
□ *The food is dirt cheap but always tastes*
delicious.

IDIOMS*study*

dishonesty

The next time you write or talk about **dishonesty** you might try to use some of the following idioms. (Remember you can see how to use each idiom correctly by looking at its entry, which you can find under the word printed in heavy type.)

deceiving someone

feed someone a **line**
pull a fast one
sell someone a **pup**
put one over on someone
take someone for a **ride**

have the **shirt** off someone's back
laugh up your **sleeve**
pull the **wool** over someone's eyes

telling lies

lie through your **teeth**
a **tissue** of lies

spin a **yarn**

behaving dishonestly

cook the **books**
on the **fiddle**
have light **fingers**
up to no **good**
wheel and deal

do something ...
on the **sly**
under the **counter**
under false **pretences**
under the **table**

dishonest activity

funny **business**

sharp **practice**

○ treat like 'dirt or treat like a piece of 'dirt (*informal*)
Someone **treats you like dirt** or like a **piece of dirt** when they treat you badly, and without respect: *He thinks he can treat people like dirt. Well, she'll make him sorry. She'll find a way.*

dishonesty *see* **Idioms study** page 47

distance

○ go the 'distance
Someone or something **goes the distance** when they succeed or prove their worth: *That song had so many different types of music in there, that I didn't think it'd go the distance.*

○ in 'spitting distance or within 'spitting distance (*informal, humorous*)
You are **in**, or **within, spitting distance** of something, or of doing something, if you are very close to it: *There is nothing worse than playing two superb shots to get within spitting distance of the green, then going to pieces on the last putt.* ♦ *see also* on your doorstep ▷DOORSTEP; a stone's throw ▷STONE

Spitting distance means how far you can **spit** [= project the contents of your mouth, especially the saliva].

do

○ **keep your 'distance**

You **keep your distance** when you avoid going too near to someone or something: *Harry was gripped by a sneezing fit which dissolved into painful coughing. 'I really am sorry about this, Alan. You'd better keep your distance.'* ♦ *see also* **steer** *or* **stay clear of** ▷CLEAR

do

○ **do something up 'brown** (*AmE*; *informal*)

You **do something up brown** when you do it in an excellent or complete way: *If you are going to throw a party for her, you might as well do it up brown.*

doctor

○ **just what the doctor 'ordered**

Someone or something that is described as **just what the doctor ordered** is exactly what was required: *A cold beer. Just what the doctor ordered.*

dog (*see also* dogs)

○ **a 'dog's life**

Someone's life is described as **a dog's life** if they have to work very hard in order to survive, and they have very few pleasures: *It's a dog's life, working on those farms up north; no-one around and complete darkness for half a year.*

○ **dog eat 'dog**

A situation is described as a case of **dog eat dog** if everyone is acting in a way that will benefit themselves the most, without worrying about what happens to anyone else: *the dog eat dog brand of free market capitalism.*

○ **give a dog a bad 'name** (*BrE*)

If you say '**give a dog a bad name**', you mean that once someone has had their reputation damaged, it is difficult for them to regain people's respect: *Picking on Woodhouse Close is perhaps predictable (give a dog a bad name, and all that) but Coundon.*

This is a short form of the expression '**give a dog a bad name and hang him**', meaning that if a dog bites, for example, it will have to be killed, because it cannot be trusted.

○ **put on the 'dog** (*AmE*; *informal*, *insulting*)

You **put on the dog** when you try to show, or give the impression, that you are rich or high class: *Since they inherited that money, they've been going around putting on the dog.*

○ **work like a 'dog**

You **work like a dog** when you work very hard: *I've been working like a dog to get this job finished.* ♦ *see also* **work your fingers to the bone** ▷FINGERS

○ **you can't teach an old dog new 'tricks**

If you say '**you can't teach an old dog new tricks**', you mean that it is very difficult to change old people's opinions, habits and behaviour: *It's a nice thing to learn. They say you can't teach an old dog new tricks, but I'm living proof.* ♦ *see also* **a leopard never changes its spots** ▷LEOPARD

doghouse

○ **in the 'doghouse** (*informal*)

You are **in the doghouse** if someone is not pleased with you, and is not being friendly towards you, or not talking to you: *'Oh, what a relief! I was beginning to think I must be in the doghouse for some reason.'*

Doghouse is a less common word for 'kennel'; a small, wooden shelter, where a dog sleeps. This expression suggests that the person in question has been sent outside in disgrace.

dogs

○ **go to the 'dogs** (*informal*)

A person or thing **has gone to the dogs** if they have changed from being respectable to being worthless: *I'm sick of reading the news. The country's going to the dogs – people out of work everywhere – there's no money about.* ♦ *see also* **go downhill** ▷DOWNHILL

Something that you give to the dogs is worthless, and not wanted by anyone.

doldrums

○ **in the 'doldrums**

Someone who is **in the doldrums** is depressed or sad: *I'm feeling a bit in the doldrums today; sorry if I'm rather quiet.* ♦ *see also* **down in the dumps** ▷DUMPS

The **doldrums** is a part of the sea where there is no wind, making it difficult for sailing boats to make progress.

dollar

○ **as sound as a 'dollar** (*AmE*)

1 If you say someone's career or future is **as sound as a dollar**, you mean it is very secure: *His career in banking is as sound as a dollar.* **2** If a structure is **as sound as a dollar**, it is strongly constructed: *The boys built the chicken house, and it's as sound as a dollar.*

○ **bet your bottom 'dollar**

You **bet your bottom dollar** that something is the case if you are certain that it is so: *Michael is looking for ways to make people take out private insurance. Poverty in old age is one target. Health care must be another on his list. You can bet your bottom dollar.*

○ **the almighty 'dollar** (*AmE*)

You describe the dollar as **the almighty dollar** when you are regarding it as a symbol of power and greed: *He said Latin American countries would be able to stand up to the United States if it wasn't for the almighty dollar.*

○ **dollar for 'dollar** (*AmE*)

You use '**dollar for dollar**' when you are considering how well priced something is: *Our microwave was not a bad deal dollar for dollar.*

donkey

○ **the 'donkey work**

The donkey work is the hard, tiring, physical work involved in a task: *The direction of research within a department is under the control of the supervisors in that department, for whom the PhD student does the donkey work.*

The donkey is an animal traditionally used for carrying heavy loads.

○ **'donkey's years**

Donkey's years means 'a very long time': *Chris Hunter, for donkey's years or so it seemed, had a sweet shop between our house and the football ground.*

This is a play on words with 'donkey's ears', which are very long.

doorstep

○ **on your 'doorstep**

Something that is **on your doorstep** is conveniently close to your home: *It's a great little neighbourhood; you've got everything you need on your doorstep.* ◆ *see also* **in** or **within spitting distance** ▷DISTANCE; **a stone's throw** ▷STONE

dose

○ **like a dose of 'salts**

You do something **like a dose of salts** if you do it very quickly. ◆ *see also* **like a shot** ▷SHOT

Salts, here refers to a laxative, which relieves constipation.

doses

○ **in small 'doses**

You say you can tolerate someone or something **in small doses** if you can tolerate them only for short periods of time: *Babies are fine – in small doses.*

dot

○ **dot your i's and cross your 't's**

You **dot your i's and cross your t's** when you pay great attention to small details, especially when you are putting the finishing touches to a piece of work: *'Those conditions still stand,' she told MPs, 'but no one is suggesting that we dot every "i" and cross every "t" before we look at it.'*

downhill

○ **go down'hill**

You say that something **is going**, or **has gone**, **downhill** if it is not as good as it used to be: *The service here has gone downhill since the last time I came.* ◆ *see also* **go to the dogs** ▷DOGS

dozen

○ **six of one and half a dozen of the 'other**

1 If you describe an unfortunate situation as **six of one and half a dozen of the other**, you mean that neither of the two parties mentioned is more to blame for it than the other: *You blame me, I blame you. It was six of one and half a dozen of the other.* **2** You also say '**it's six of one and half a dozen of the other**' if you see no difference between two things or solutions: *'Do you mind if we have our main meal tonight,* *rather than at lunchtime?' 'No – it's six of one and half a dozen of the other for me.'*

drain

○ **down the 'drain** (*informal*)

Something, such as a plan is, or goes, **down the drain** if it is no longer useful or valid, or if it has been wasted: *There are fears of family life going down the drain, as staff may get only two complete weekends off in seven.* ♦ *see also* **down the plughole** ▷PLUGHOLE

draw

○ **beat someone to the 'draw** (*AmE*)

You **beat someone to the draw** when you do something faster than they do: *Charles wanted to pay for the meal, but I beat him to the draw.*

> The term comes from the American wild west, where your life often depended on how fast you could draw your gun from its holster.

dribs

○ **in dribs and 'drabs**

People or things arrive **in dribs and drabs** when they arrive slowly, and in small quantities or numbers, rather than all at the same time: *Up until now they've been let out in dribs and drabs. They're talking here about a kind of mass release aren't they?*

drift

○ **if you catch my 'drift** or **if you get my 'drift** (*informal*)

You add **if you catch**, or **get**, **my drift** to something you have just said, to let the listener know that you are trying to say something indirectly: *The company 'let him go', if you get my drift.*

drop

○ **drop 'dead** (*offensive*)

You tell someone to '**drop dead**' if you are very angry with them, or if you think that what they have said is nonsense: *'Drop dead, yer silly old bugger,' said a woman.*

○ **'drop everything**

You **drop everything** when you stop whatever you are doing in order to do something else which someone considers to be more important: *This very moment is the most important point of my career. I can't just drop everything.*

○ **a drop in the 'ocean**

You describe something as **a drop in the ocean** if it seems a very small amount in relation to something else, or in relation to what is needed: *We munched our way through an average 18 pasta meals per head last year, a drop in the ocean compared to the Italians, who managed to swallow a massive 300 meals each.*

○ **fit to 'drop**

You are **fit to drop** if you are exhausted: *Just when we were fit to drop, they would tell us that we were going to spend the night on a mountainside, keeping watch for 'enemy advances'.*

○ **get the 'drop on someone** or **have the 'drop on someone** (*AmE*)

If you **get the drop on someone**, or **have the drop on someone**, you have an advantage over them: *Ted got the drop on the other fans by waiting outside the ticket office before it opened.*

> This term, from the American wild west, referred to drawing your gun before an opponent, forcing him to drop his gun.

druthers

○ **have your 'druthers** (*AmE*; *informal*, *humorous*)

You **have your druthers** when you have what you want: *If I had my druthers, I'd go home to Alabama but I can't see my family agreeing.*

> The word comes from quickly saying 'I'd rather'.

dues

○ **pay your 'dues** (*AmE*; *informal*)

You **pay your dues** by working hard in order to succeed or have the right to something: *He became a Hollywood star, but he had paid his dues through years of struggling as an unknown actor.*

dumps

○ **down in the 'dumps**

You are feeling **down in the dumps** if you are depressed or sad: *She's a bit down in the dumps today; she didn't get that job she wanted.* ♦ *see also* **in the doldrums** ▷DOLDRUMS

dust

○ **allow the 'dust to settle** or **let the 'dust settle**
You **allow the dust to settle** or **let the dust settle** when you let someone calm down before you try to do anything else about a situation: *If I were you I'd let the dust settle before you go and ask her for your money back.*

○ **bite the 'dust**
Someone or something **bites the dust** when they finish, no longer have any use, or die: *Another coal mine bit the dust today.* ♦ *see also* **kick the bucket** ▷BUCKET; **cash in your chips** ▷CHIPS; **pop your clogs** ▷CLOGS; **give up the ghost** ▷GHOST; **snuff it** ▷SNUFF

> When men are killed in battle, they fall to the ground with their face in the dust.

○ **not see someone for 'dust** (*BrE*)
You **do not see someone for dust** when they leave very quickly: *We're leaving on Friday, from Dover. We're catching the first ferry and you won't see us for dust.*

> When a horse and carriage moved away quickly and suddenly, it would make a cloud of dust behind it.

dying

○ **be 'dying for something** or **be dying to 'do something** (*informal*)
You **are dying for something** if you want or need it badly; you **are dying to do something** if you are very excited about doing it: *I'm dying for a drink.* □ *I'm dying to see you all again this Christmas.*

○ **be 'dying of something** (*informal*)
If you say you **are dying of something**, for example hunger, you mean that the feeling you mention is very strong: *I'm dying of 'thirst; is there any juice in the fridge?*

ear (*see also* **ears**)

○ **bend someone's 'ear** (*informal*)
You **bend someone's ear** when you force them to listen while you talk to them for a long time about something: *Whenever I meet her, she bends my ear about how things have changed since the good old days.*

○ **go in one ear and out the 'other**
When something that you tell someone **goes in one ear and out the other**, they do not listen to it carefully enough to remember it later: *I told her what I thought she should do, but my advice went in one ear and out the other.*

○ **have your 'ear to the ground** or **keep your 'ear to the ground**
You **have**, or **are keeping**, **your ear to the ground** if you are taking care to be well-informed about what is happening around you: *You must keep your ear to the ground and contact me if you discover anything suspicious.*

> Native Americans used the method of listening with an ear next to the ground to help them discover the position of other people or animals.

○ **out on your 'ear** (*informal*)
If you are **out on your ear**, you have been ordered to leave your job or the place where you were living, probably because of your bad behaviour: *We'll give it one more try, but if you come home drunk again, you'll be out on your ear.*

○ **play it by 'ear**
If you deal with a situation in a way which is not fixed, but can change in response to changes and new demands in that situation, you **are playing it by ear**: *I don't know how often we'll want*

you to come into the office. We'll have to play it by ear.

○ **turn a deaf 'ear**

You **turn a deaf ear** to something when you decide to ignore it, and to pretend you cannot hear it: *He refused to promise anything, just as he turned a deaf ear to their demands for his resignation.* ♦ *see also* **turn a blind eye** ▷ EYE

ears

○ **all 'ears** (*informal*)

You say you are **all ears** if you are listening very carefully: *Okay, so tell me what's bothering you. I'm all ears.*

○ **believe your 'ears**

You say that you cannot **believe your ears** if you hear something which is so surprising that it is difficult to believe: *She couldn't believe her ears when the doctor told her she was pregnant.*

○ **so-and-so's 'ears are burning**

You say that a certain person's **ears are,** or **must be, burning** if people are talking about them a lot: *Some people's ears must've been burning yesterday afternoon when that personnel meeting was taking place.*

As long ago as Roman times, people used to say that your ears grew hot when someone was talking about you.

○ **fall on deaf 'ears**

If the things you say **fall on deaf ears,** they are being ignored by the person you are talking to: *She wept and cried, but her protests fell on deaf ears.*

○ **have something coming out of your 'ears** (*informal*)

If you have so much of something that you do not know what to do with it at all, you say you **have it coming out of your ears**: *We've got information coming out of our ears and what we need now is some way to make sense of it.*

○ **keep your 'ears pinned back**

Someone who **is keeping their ears pinned back** is listening carefully and paying attention: *I must watch my step and keep my ears pinned back.*

○ **pin someone's 'ears back** (*AmE; informal*)

If you **pin someone's ears back,** you give them a beating, or defeat them:

He was a tough guy, but I pinned his ears back.

○ **up to your 'ears** (*informal*)

If you have so much of something to deal with that you cannot see how you are going to manage, you say that you are **up to your ears** in it: *I've been up to my ears in work these past few weeks.* ♦ *see also* **up to your eyes** ▷EYES; **up to your eyeballs** ▷EYEBALLS; **up to your neck** ▷NECK

○ **wet behind the 'ears** (*insulting*)

If you say that someone is **wet behind the ears,** you mean that they are not very experienced in life: *Japan's Prime Minister may still be a little wet behind the ears but, not for the first time, he has confounded his more experienced rivals.*

earth

○ **bring someone back down to 'earth**

You **bring someone back down to earth** when you make them understand that they are not thinking or behaving in a realistic way; you **come,** or **are brought, back down to earth** when you understand that you have not been thinking or behaving in a realistic way: *The news brought me back down to earth with a bump.*

○ **cost the 'earth** (*informal*)

You say that something **costs the earth** when you think it is too expensive; you **pay the earth for something** when you pay a lot of money for it: *A good joint of beef costs the earth these days.* ♦ *see also* **cost a packet** ▷PACKET

○ **like nothing on 'earth** (*humorous, informal*)

If you say that you feel or look **like nothing on earth,** you are saying that you feel or look very ill, unattractive or untidy; something that looks, tastes, sounds, etc, **like nothing on earth** is awful: *I wish I hadn't met him after being at the dentist's. I must have looked like nothing on earth.* □ *It looks like smoked salmon and tastes like nothing on earth.*

earthly

○ **not have an 'earthly** or **not stand an 'earthly** or **not have an 'earthly chance** (*informal*)

1 You say you do **not have an earthly**

when you do not know something: *I haven't an earthly where he's gone.* **2** You also say you do **not have**, or **stand**, **an earthly**, or **an earthly chance**, when you do not have even the slightest chance of success: *I haven't an earthly of winning this game.* ♦ *see also* **not have a clue** ▷CLUE

easy

○ **easy as AB'C** or **easy as 'anything** or **easy as falling off a 'log** or **easy as 'pie** or (*BrE*) **easy as 'winking**

Something which is as **easy as ABC**, or **anything**, or **falling off a log**, or **pie**, or **winking**, is very easy: *She patted me on the back. 'Easy as pie, wasn't it?' she said.* ♦ *see also* **child's play** ▷CHILD; **a piece of cake** ▷PIECE; **nothing to it** ▷NOTHING

○ **easy come, easy 'go**

If you say '**easy come, easy go**', you mean that because something was easy to obtain, you are not too bothered about losing it; '**easy come, easy go**' also refers to an easy-going attitude in general, often one that is disapproved of: *But my attitude to money is slightly easy come, easy go. That is to say, I earn a lot, but I also give quite a lot away in different ways.*

○ **go 'easy on someone**

You **go easy on someone** when you do not punish or criticize them as severely as you could do: *I know he was wrong, but go easy on him. He's still very young.*

○ **go 'easy with something** or **go easy on something**

You **go easy with**, or **on**, **something** if you do not take too much of it: *You can take whatever you like for your picnic, but go easy on the pizza. I want some left.*

○ **take it 'easy** or **take things 'easy**

You **are taking it easy** or **taking things easy** if you are relaxing or being careful not to work too hard: *The doctor told me to take it easy for a couple of weeks.* ♦ *see also* **put your feet up** ▷FEET

eating

○ **what's eating 'so-and-so** (*informal*)

If you seem unusually anxious or unhappy, people sometimes ask '**what's eating so-and-so?**': *What's eating him*

this morning? He's usually so bright and cheerful. ♦ *see also* **rattle someone's cage** ▷CAGE

ebb

○ **at a low 'ebb**

You say that someone or something is **at a low ebb** if they are not as strong as usual: *Enthusiasm among the volunteers has been at a low ebb since the funding for the project was cut.*

> When the tide is **at a low ebb**, the level of the sea is very low.

○ **ebb and 'flow**

The **ebb and flow** of something is the pattern of change which affects it all the time: *the ebb and flow of public support for the Prime 'Minister.* ♦ *see also* **ups and downs** ▷UPS

> The **ebb and flow** of the sea describes the way the tides affect it, with the level of the water falling during the ebb tide and rising during the flow.

edge

○ **the cutting 'edge** or **the leading 'edge**

When you talk about **the cutting edge** or **the leading edge**, you mean the most modern and advanced level in the stated activity: *He's at the cutting edge of research into renewable 'energy sources.*

> The **cutting edge** of a blade is the sharp edge which starts the cutting process.

○ **on 'edge**

If you are **on edge** you are in a nervous state, and anything unexpected is likely to give you a shock: *No wonder he had seemed a bit on edge. It must have been a shock, her turning up out of the blue like that.*

○ **take the 'edge off something**

Something that **takes the edge off** a feeling or taste, for example, makes it less harsh: *The sun was warm on my back, but the south-easterly wind took the edge off the stifling heat.*

egg

○ **have 'egg on your face**

You say someone **has egg on their**

face if their unwise actions result in a situation where they look foolish: *I didn't follow his advice, and I ended up with egg on my face.*

○ **lay an 'egg** (*AmE*; *informal*)
When someone, especially an actor or performer, **lays an egg**, they fail completely: *The comedian laid an egg with all those racist jokes.*

eggs

○ **put all your eggs in one 'basket** or **have all your eggs in one 'basket**
People sometimes tell you not to **put**, or **have**, **all your eggs in one basket** if they think that you are in danger of losing everything by depending on just one plan: *City wisdom suggests that you shouldn't put all your eggs in one basket, so for most people, a general distribution of investment is the wiser choice.*

eggshells

○ **walk on 'eggshells** or **tread on 'eggshells**
You **are walking**, or **treading**, **on eggshells** if you are being careful in what you do and say because you are afraid of upsetting someone: *I started to walk on eggshells for fear of setting him off.*

The shells of eggs are so delicate that you would find it difficult to walk on them without breaking them.

elbow

○ **give someone the 'elbow** (*informal*)
If someone **gives you the elbow**, they get rid of you or take away your job; if you **get the elbow**, you are not wanted any more, or you lose your job: *I hear she's given that boyfriend the elbow at last.* ♦ *see also* **give someone the boot** ▷BOOT; **give someone the push** ▷PUSH

element

○ **in your 'element**
You say you are **in your element** if the situation you are in gives you confidence and allows you to perform at your best: *He was in his element here. Every few minutes, it seemed, men came up to him, sometimes just to greet him, often to ask advice.*

According to medieval science, every creature belonged to one of the four elements: earth, fire, air and water. The signs of the Zodiac are still arranged under these elements.

enchilada

○ **the whole enchi'lada** (*AmE*; *informal*, *humorous*)
'**The whole enchilada**' means 'everything': *I said I could pay Jim half of the loan, but he wanted the whole enchilada.*

An **enchilada** is a Mexican tortilla filled with meat.

end (*see also* **ends**)

○ **at the end of the 'day**
At the end of the day means 'when you look at the whole situation': *At the end of the day, it doesn't matter how many hours you work. It's what you get done that counts.* ♦ *see also* **all things considered** ▷CONSIDERED

○ **at the end of your 'tether**
You are **at the end of your tether** if you have been worried or angry for so long that you cannot bear it any more; you are **at the end of your tether** with someone or something if you have lost patience with them: *My moody boss is driving me to the end of my tether. I am fed up with being put down and made to feel stupid by him.* ♦ *see also* **at your wits' end** ▷WITS

An animal kept on a **tether** [= a rope attached to a central post] can only eat the grass growing inside the circle, whose size depends on the length of the rope. When the animal reaches the end of its tether, it is very hungry and trying to reach more grass.

○ **at a loose 'end**
You are **at a loose end** if you have some spare time, but no ideas of what to do with it: *So then, are we to suppose that being at a loose end leads to drunkenness and murder?* ♦ *see also* **twiddle your thumbs** ▷THUMBS

○ **can't see beyond the end of your 'nose** or **can't see past the end of your 'nose** or **can't see further than** the end of your 'nose (*informal, insulting*)

You say that someone **can't see beyond**, or **can't see past**, or **can't see further than**, the end of their nose if they only notice the most obvious things, or the things that they themselves are doing: *If he thinks redundancies will help the business, he obviously can't see beyond the end of his nose.*

○ **don't know one end of a such-and-such from the 'other** or **can't tell one end of a such-and-such from the 'other**

You say that you **don't know**, or **can't tell**, **one end** of a certain thing **from the other** if you have no knowledge about, or skill with, that thing: *Don't ask me if it looks ill. I don't know one end of a horse from the other.*

○ **an end in it'self**

If you describe a certain activity as **an end in itself**, you mean that the process of doing it is at least as satisfying and important as what you will gain from it: *Learning a language not only improves your prospects; the learning process is an end in itself.*

○ **'end it all**

To **end it all** is to kill yourself: *Sometimes things were so bad that I wanted to end it all.*

○ **the end of the 'road** or **the end of the 'line** (*informal*)

You have reached **the end of the road** or **the end of the line** when you realize that you cannot continue or survive any longer: *I told him we had reached the end of the road, and that I wanted a divorce.*

○ **get hold of the wrong end of the 'stick** or **get the wrong end of the 'stick** (*informal*)

When you **get hold of**, or **get**, **the wrong end of the stick**, you misunderstand a situation or the sense of what someone has said: *People who think the song is about ecstasy have got the wrong end of the stick.*

○ **go off the 'deep end** (*informal*)

When someone **goes off the deep end**, they lose their temper: *I knew he'd be angry, but I had no idea he was going to go off the deep end like that.* ♦ *see also*

blow a fuse ▷FUSE; **let fly** ▷LET; **blow** or **flip your lid** ▷LID; **do your nut** ▷NUT; **lose your rag** ▷RAG; **fly into a rage** ▷RAGE; **hit the roof** ▷ ROOF; **blow your stack** ▷STACK; **lose your temper** ▷TEMPER; **blow your top** ▷ TOP; **throw a wobbly** ▷WOBBLY

○ **in at the 'deep end**

When you are thrown **in at the deep end** of a situation, you are given something very difficult to do, with very little help from anyone: *I'd only been there a week when they threw me in at the deep end and asked me to chair a meeting.* ♦ *see also* **sink or swim** ▷SINK

Notice the variant **'into the deep end'**.

○ **no 'end**

No end means 'a lot': *I'm enjoying this TV series no end.*

○ **thin end of the 'wedge**

When you describe something as the **thin end of the wedge**, you mean that it may be the first sign of something bad which is to come in the future: *The new policy is seen by many as the thin end of the wedge, where payment will be demanded for access to land which was previously open to the public.*

A **wedge** is a triangular block of wood which you use for opening a narrow gap. People sometimes put one under a door to hold it open.

ends

○ **make ends 'meet**

You **are making ends meet** if you are managing to survive with very little money: *It was the time of their lives when they found it hardest to make ends meet. It could not have happened unless the Church had helped to pay for the heating.*

○ **play both ends against the 'middle** (*AmE*)

You **play both ends against the middle** when you encourage two people or two groups to fight against each other so that you can gain an advantage: '*I got my parents fighting, so they forgot to yell at me.' 'That's smart. You know how to play both ends against the middle.'*

enemy

○ **wouldn't wish such-and-such on your worst 'enemy**

If you want to express how unpleasant something or someone is, you sometimes say that you **wouldn't wish them on your worst enemy**: *She's treated you badly. I wouldn't wish a friend like that on my worst enemy.*

○ **your own worst 'enemy**

If someone creates severe problems for themselves by the way they behave, you sometimes say they are **their own worst enemy**: *Her problems since then are all of her own making. You could say that she is her own worst enemy.* ♦ *see also* **make a meal out of something** ▷MEAL; **make a rod for your own back** ▷ROD

even

○ **get 'even**

You **get even**, or **get even** with someone, when you do something to hurt or harm them, in return for something they have done to hurt or harm you in the past: *I had been waiting for years to get even with him, and now I saw my chance.* ♦ *see also* **get your own back** ▷OWN

evil

○ **a necessary 'evil**

You say that something unpleasant is **a necessary evil** if you do not like it, but you have to accept it as a normal part of things: *Negotiation is a necessary evil. It is the antithesis of open, honest communication.* ♦ *see also* **all in a day's work** ▷DAY

exception

○ **take ex'ception to something**

When you say that you **take exception to something**, you are expressing your anger at being treated in a certain way: *Mr Jones, 43, who runs the café in Ross-on-Wye, said: 'I took exception to the fact that she was selling teas outside our door without informing me first.'* ♦ *see also* **not take kindly to something** ▷KINDLY

experience

○ **chalk it up to ex'perience** or **put it down to ex'perience**

If you say you **are chalking up**, or

putting down, to experience a mistake you have made, you mean that you have decided to learn a lesson from the experience, rather than complain about it: *And if it ends up being rejected by the board, we simply put it down to experience, and start again.* ♦ *see also* **just one of those things** ▷THINGS

eye (*see also* eyes)

○ **catch someone's 'eye**

When you see something which **catches your eye**, you suddenly notice it for some reason: *I waded out in the direction of the area where I had seen the fish, when a glint of white under the water caught my eye.*

○ **an 'eye for something**

If someone has **an eye for something**, they have a natural appreciation of and ability to use that thing in a skilful way: *Ernest had an eye for detail.*

○ **an eye for an eye and a tooth for a 'tooth**

When people talk about **an eye for an eye and a tooth for a tooth**, they are referring to the idea that, if someone does something bad to you, you have the right to do something equally bad to them: *I'll get my revenge, just wait. An eye for an eye, that's my philosophy.*

> This is a Biblical reference, from Exodus 21:24, often considered to express, in its simplest form, the severe moral teaching of the Old Testament.

○ **go into something with your 'eyes open** or **walk into something with your 'eyes open**

You **go**, or **walk**, **into something with your eyes open** when you put yourself in a certain situation despite knowing the possible dangers which that situation holds: *He has entered into the contract with his eyes open to the true facts; this comes as no surprise to him.*

○ **have your 'eye on**

If you **have your eye on** someone or something, you are interested in them and would like to have them for yourself: *Charlie had his eye on Sonia, a dark, broad-faced girl with Slavic eyes.*

○ **keep an 'eye out for**

You **are keeping an eye out for** someone or something if you are not actively searching for them, but you are watching, in case they appear, while you are doing other things: *According to this we've to keep an eye out for anything – or anybody – suspicious.*

○ **keep an 'eye on**

You **are keeping an eye on** something or someone if you are watching them to make sure they are all right, or that they do not do anything wrong: *I'll keep an eye on the kids if you want to pop out to the shops.*

○ **the naked 'eye**

You talk about **the naked eye** in reference to what you can see without any special equipment, such as a microscope, or a telescope: *The mite is just visible to the naked eye and feeds on honey bees and their grubs by sucking their body fluids.*

○ **not see eye to 'eye**

If you and another person **do not see eye to eye**, you never agree at all; if you **do not see eye to eye** with someone over, or about something, you cannot agree with them on a certain subject: *I'm afraid I can't come to the meeting if Bruce is going to be there. We just don't see eye to eye.*

○ **one in the 'eye for** (*BrE*)

You say a certain action is **one in the eye for** someone or something if it is understood as a direct criticism of that person or thing: *The surprise victory of the Labour candidate at the by-election was one in the eye for the Tories.*

○ **there's more to such-and-such than meets the 'eye**

If you say that **there's more to** a certain thing or person **than meets the eye**, you mean that they are more complicated or interesting than they seemed at first: *I always thought that windsurfing looked easy, but there is more to it than meets the eye.*

○ **turn a blind 'eye**

You **turn a blind eye**, or **turn a blind eye** to something, if you decide to ignore it, or to pretend you cannot see it: *I usually turn a blind eye to staff arriving a couple of minutes late.* ♦ *see also* **turn a deaf ear** ▷EAR

eyeballs

○ **up to your 'eyeballs** or (*AmE*) **up to your 'eyebrows** (*informal*)

If you have so much of something to deal with that you cannot see how you are going to manage, you can say that you are **up to your eyeballs** in it: *I'll come over to see you next week. I'm up to my eyeballs in work till then.* ♦ *see also* **up to your ears** ▷EARS; **up to your eyes** ▷EYES; **up to your neck** ▷NECK

eyelid

○ **not bat an 'eyelid** (*informal*)

You **don't bat an eyelid** when you show no surprise or emotion: *They're quite relaxed about clothes. No-one batted an eyelid when I came into the office wearing jeans.*

> The verb **bat** in this expression is from the Old French 'batre', meaning 'to blink'.

eyes

○ **eyes in the back of so-and-so's 'head**

You say someone has **eyes in the back of their head** if they always notice exactly what is happening, even when they do not seem to be paying much attention: *You need eyes in the back of your head to see what the children are getting up to in the back of the car.*

○ **keep your 'eyes peeled** or **keep your 'eyes skinned** (*informal*)

You **keep your eyes peeled** or **keep your eyes skinned** when you watch for something with all your attention and concentration: *He pedalled along the canal bank quite slowly, keeping his eyes skinned for signs of human activity.*

○ **lay 'eyes on** or **set 'eyes on** or **clap 'eyes on** (*informal*)

When you **lay**, or **set**, or **clap**, **eyes on** someone or something, you see them for the first time: *I don't know who you are, lass, never clapped eyes on you.*

○ **make 'eyes at someone** (*informal*)

You **make eyes at someone** when you look at them with sexual interest, in a way which you hope they will find attractive: *Bodie was making eyes at the girl, and had been for some time.*

○ **open someone's 'eyes**

An event or experience **opens your**

eyes, or **opens your eyes** to something, if it makes you aware of something you did not know before: *This weekend has really opened my eyes. Without knowing it I have been living in poverty for the last 14 years.*

○ **up to your 'eyes** (*BrE*; *informal*)

If you have so much of something to deal with that you cannot see how you are going to manage, you can say that you are **up to your eyes** in it: *I'm up to my eyes in washing just now.* ♦ *see also* **up to your ears** ▷EARS; **up to your eyeballs** ▷EYEBALLS; **up to your neck** ▷NECK

face

○ **your face 'fits** (*BrE*)

If **your face fits**, you look like the right sort of person for a particular job, or to be accepted by a certain group: *It's fine while you're young and attractive, but when your face doesn't fit any more, you have to go.*

○ **fly in the face of 'such-and-such**

You **fly in the face of** an accepted norm or belief when you go against it: *The proposal appeared to fly in the face of all logic.*

○ **in your 'face** (*very informal*)

Someone or something that is described as **in your face** is direct, provocative and very confident: *This band has an in-your-face approach.*

○ **let's 'face it**

You say **'let's face it'** as a way of introducing a fact which describes the reality of a situation, which must be accepted, even if it is not what people would like: *We might as well stop work and go home now; I mean, let's face it,* we're not going to be able to finish it tonight, are we?

○ **lose 'face**

You **lose face** when you lose other people's respect: *If they publicly disagree, they'll lose face as a united party.*

○ **on the 'face of it**

You introduce a statement with **'on the face of it'** when you want to show that what you are going to say describes the way a situation appears, rather than how it really is: *On the face of it, it would seem that unemployment has been greatly reduced; in actual fact, the situation is worse than ever before.*

○ **pull a 'face** (*BrE*) or **make a 'face**

You **pull**, or **make**, **a face** when you **1** make an unusual expression with your face to make people laugh: *He wandered round the room, looking at himself in the mirrors and pulling faces and laughing.* **2** make a disgusted or displeased expression with your face, to show that you do not like something: *She made a face; 'I hate long walks,' she said.* ♦ *see also* **turn your nose up at something** ▷NOSE

○ **put a brave 'face on it** or **put on a brave 'face**

You **put a brave face on it**, or **put on a brave face**, when you try to show courage, even though you are feeling worried or afraid: *There was nothing I could do but put a brave face on it and hope things would work out all right.*

○ **save 'face**

You **save face** when you do something to prevent yourself, or someone else, from being humiliated: *They are trying to save face for the political leaders. Instead, they should be trying to save their nations' economies.*

○ **staring you in the 'face**

Something, such as the answer to a problem, **is staring you in the face** if it should have been obvious to you, but you didn't see it: *It has been staring us in the face for months and we never even realized!*

○ **throw something back in someone's 'face**

Someone **throws something back in your face** when they remember something you told them in confidence, and

IDIOMS*study*

failure

The next time you write or talk about **failure** you might try to use some of the following idioms. (Remember you can see how to use each idiom correctly by looking at its entry, which you can find under the word printed in heavy type.)

failing

go down like a lead **balloon**

draw a **blank**

go a complete **blank**

go off at half-**cock**

come a **cropper**

bite the **dust**

fall flat

come to **grief**

go up in **smoke**

come **unstuck**

go to the **wall**

causing your own failure

miss the **boat**

blow it

blow your **chance**

dig your own **grave**

make a **pig**'s ear of something

being likely to fail

fight a losing **battle**

not have a **cat** in hell's chance

someone's *or* something's **days** are numbered

slip through your **fingers**

not have a **hope** in hell

on the **rocks**

use it against you in an argument: *I told her I was having trouble working to deadlines and she threw it back in my face at the management meeting.*

○ **until you are blue in the 'face** (*informal*)

Someone does something **until**, or **till**, **they are blue in the face** when they keep doing it without being successful: *She realized that she could deny his accusation until she was blue in the face, but he wasn't going to believe her.*

○ **written all over someone's 'face**

Something which is supposed to be a secret is **written all over someone's face** when you can see it, just by looking at them: *He's lying; it's written all over his face.*

failure see **Idioms study** page 59

fair

○ **fair and 'square**

Everything is **fair and square** if you no longer owe someone any money and they no longer owe you any: *Right, I think we're all fair and square now, aren't we?* ♦ see also **be quits with someone** ▷QUITS

○ **fair e'nough** (*informal*)

You say '**fair enough**' if you are prepared to accept what someone has done or said: *All right, fair enough, you've done that, but what about all the other things you were supposed to do?*

○ **fair's 'fair** (*informal*)

Fair's fair means 'let's be fair': *Come on, fair's fair; you've had your turn, now let someone else have a go.*

IDIOMS*study*   fear

The next time you write or talk about **fear** you might try to use some of the following idioms. (Remember you can see how to use each idiom correctly by looking at its entry, which you can find under the word printed in heavy type.)

frightening someone

make someone's **blood** run cold

scare the living **daylights** out of someone

make someone's **hair** stand on end

being frightened

bottle out

have **butterflies**

get cold **feet**

have your **heart** in your mouth

turn to **jelly**

be rooted to the **spot**

get the **wind** up

be scared out of your **wits**

fall

○ fall 'flat

An event **falls flat** when it is not as successful or entertaining as you hoped or expected: *'How was the party?'* *'Well, it fell flat; hardly anyone turned up.'* ♦ *see also* **go down like a lead balloon** ▷BALLOON

family

○ run in the 'family

A characteristic **runs in the family** if it is shared by two or more members of a family: *Baldness runs in the family.*

fancy

○ take your 'fancy or tickle your 'fancy or (*AmE*) strike your 'fancy (*informal*)

Something **takes**, **tickles**, or **strikes your fancy** when you like it a lot: *If you see anything that takes your fancy, I'll treat you.*

fashion

○ after a 'fashion

You do something **after a fashion** if you do it, but not very well: *'Can you speak German?' 'Well, after a fashion.'*

fat

○ chew the 'fat

You **chew the fat** when you talk to

someone in an informal, friendly way: *We were chewing the fat, telling stories about strange things that had happened.*

fault

○ to a 'fault

You describe someone as having a certain characteristic **to a fault** if they have it more than is necessary or expected: *He was scrupulous to a fault.*

favour (*AmE* favor)

○ curry 'favour

You **curry favour** with someone when you win their approval by praise or flattery: *Mr Lamont conceded that the Budget was 'not designed to curry favour or popularity' but was intended to meet the needs of the country.*

fear *see also* **Idioms study** page 60

○ no 'fear (*informal*)

No fear means 'I have absolutely no intention of doing that': *'Are you going to give a paper at the conference?' 'No fear.'*

feather

○ 'feather in your cap

A **feather in your cap** is an achievement that you can be proud of: *Cambridge will be led by John Wilson, who was last year's Oxford chief coach. It will* *be quite a feather in his cap if Cambridge win today.*

Native Americans had a tradition of presenting a feather to someone who had been very brave.

feathers

○ ruffle someone's 'feathers

You **ruffle someone's feathers** when you upset or annoy someone slightly: *She was determined that she would make sure he didn't ruffle her feathers again. She would be distant but polite.* ♦ *see also* **rattle someone's cage** ▷CAGE

feelings

○ no hard 'feelings

You say '**no hard feelings**' to someone who has treated you badly or upset you, when you want them to know that you do not feel angry with them: *I was deeply upset, but not in any resentful way. Once it was done, it was done and there were no hard feelings on my part.*

feet

○ drag your 'feet

You **are dragging your feet** if you are taking an unnecessarily long time over something: *The management have been dragging their feet over this; I think it's about time they made a decision.*

○ fall on your 'feet *or* land on your 'feet

You **fall**, *or* **land**, **on your feet** when you are successful or lucky, especially after a period of bad luck: *I wouldn't worry too much about James; he always falls on his feet.*

○ find your 'feet

You **find your feet** when you start to feel confident and at ease in a new place: *She lacked assertiveness for a while as she found her feet, but she is remembered mainly for her obvious concern to do the best in every situation.*

○ get cold 'feet

You **get cold feet** when you decide not to do something you had planned to do because you suddenly feel afraid: *We were going to take part in the dancing competition, but my partner got cold feet at the last minute.*

○ have your 'feet on the ground

Someone who **has their feet on the ground** is realistic: *In Paula, he's found a woman who helps him keep his feet on the ground. 'Our favourite times are Sunday afternoons, cooking, watching television and going for long walks.'*

○ have itchy 'feet

You **have itchy feet** if you feel that you need a change: *I have permanently itchy feet – an affliction which I attribute to having spent my childhood abroad.*

○ have two left 'feet

Someone who **has two left feet** cannot dance very well: *Perhaps with two left feet I should never have volunteered to take part in the display, but going to the classes has done wonders for me.*

○ put your 'feet up

You **put your feet up** when you sit or lie down and rest for a while: *I'm just going to put my feet up for a bit before I start on the next job.* ♦ *see also* **take it easy** *or* **take things easy** ▷EASY

○ rushed off your 'feet

You are **rushed off your feet** if you are very busy: *We need more staff over the holiday period; we're rushed off our feet the way it is at the moment.*

○ six feet 'under

Someone who is **six feet under** is dead and buried: *I should think I'll be six feet under by the time they finally get a law like that through parliament.* ♦ *see also* **pushing up the daisies** ▷DAISIES

○ stand on your own two 'feet

You **stand on your own two feet** when you are independent, and do not need help from other people: *Yes, we'll encourage people to stand on their own two feet, but we'll also seek to aid those who need a bit of extra help.*

○ sweep someone off their 'feet

Someone **sweeps you off your feet** when they cause you to fall suddenly in love with them: *So when Dawson came on the scene and swept me off my feet, I half jumped into his arms.*

○ think on your 'feet

You **think on your feet** when you have to make quick decisions: *You have to be able to think on your feet if you want to work in stocks and shares.*

○ under someone's 'feet

You are **under someone's feet** if you are in their way all the time, and making demands on them: *They've been terribly nice, and they don't seem to mind having me under their feet all the time.*

fence

○ sit on the 'fence

You **sit on the fence** when you avoid making a decision or committing yourself to something because you understand and have sympathy for both sides of the argument: *Many MPs have certainly supported him in the first round. He is the obvious choice for those who wish to sit on the fence.*

few

○ have 'had a few or have had a few too 'many

Someone who **has had a few**, or **a few too many**, has had too much to drink: *Trouble is, when he's had a few, he starts to get aggressive.* ♦ see also **under the influence** ▷INFLUENCE

fiddle

○ on the 'fiddle (*informal*)

Someone who is **on the fiddle** is trying to get money dishonestly, for example, by falsifying tax declarations: *They knew he was on the fiddle, but they just couldn't catch him at it.*

○ play second 'fiddle

You **play second fiddle** to someone if they are more important than you: *Throughout her married life she had to play second fiddle to the interests of her husband.*

field

○ lead the 'field

Someone who **leads the field** in their subject is the best at it: *We led the field for years, but competition is so fierce now that we're starting to lose our grip.*

○ out in left 'field (*AmE*)

Someone or something that is **out in left field** is unusual or eccentric: *A university course in witchcraft? That's really out in left field.*

> In baseball, batters hit the fewest balls into left field.

○ play the 'field

You **play the field** when you get involved with several people or things at the same time, in order to increase your opportunities: *'And you don't want

to get married?' he asked. 'Only play the field?'*

figure

○ figure of 'fun

A **figure of fun** is someone who people laugh at unkindly: *The real reason was that he felt at ease; he was no longer a figure of fun or an eyesore, he had a place.*

figures

○ that 'figures

You say '**that figures**' when you think that what someone has just said makes sense, based on what you already know.

finger

○ cannot put your 'finger on something

You say that you **cannot put your finger on something** if you have a feeling about something, but you can't say exactly what it is: *There's something strange about her, but I can't quite put my finger on what it is.*

○ a finger in every 'pie

Someone who has **a finger in every pie** is involved in a lot of different activities: *When we started up in business, we had a finger in every pie, but we soon realized we had to narrow things down a bit.* ♦ see also **irons in the fire** ▷IRONS

○ finger on the 'pulse

You have your **finger on the pulse** of something if you are aware of all the new developments in a particular area: *As a doctor, it's very important to have your finger on the pulse of new developments in your field.*

○ not lift a 'finger

Someone who **does not lift a finger** does not make any effort to help: *I couldn't believe it; she could see we were late, and she didn't lift a finger to help.*

○ point the 'finger at someone

You **point the finger at someone** when you blame them for something: *Her devastated husband Robin, an engineer, said: 'If her work was a factor, it was only one among others. I don't want to point the finger at anyone.'*

○ pull your 'finger out or get your 'finger out (*BrE; informal*)

If you tell someone to **pull their finger out**, you mean that they should stop being lazy or slow, and start working harder: *Come on, pull your finger out; I want this work finished.*

○ **wrap someone round your little 'finger**

You **wrap someone round your little finger**, when you cause them to agree to anything you want; you **have someone wrapped round your little finger** when they will do anything to please you: *She wraps him round her little finger; I mean, would you sleep outside rather than ring the bell and wake someone up?* ♦ *see also* **have someone right where you want them** ▷WANT; **have someone eating out of the palm of your hand** ▷PALM; **have someone eating out of your hand** ▷HAND; **have someone in your pocket** ▷POCKET

fingers

○ **all fingers and 'thumbs** (*BrE*) or **all 'thumbs** (*AmE*)

You are **all fingers and thumbs**, or **all thumbs**, if you are using your hands in an awkward or clumsy way: *I can't tie this thing; I'm all fingers and thumbs today.*

○ **fingers 'crossed**

You say **'fingers crossed'** to someone to show them that you are hoping they will be successful.

○ **get your 'fingers burnt**

You **get your fingers burnt** when you suffer from a bad decision or foolish action: *They've had their fingers burnt on a few occasions already this year, and they're not likely to be taking any more risks.*

○ **have light 'fingers**

Someone who is described as **having light fingers** has a tendency to steal things: *I wouldn't like to accuse him of being a criminal, but, well, let's just say he's got light fingers.*

○ **slip through your 'fingers**

Something **slips through your fingers** when you do not quite manage to obtain it or hold on to it: *And that gold medal has slipped through his fingers again!*

○ **work your fingers to the 'bone**

You **work your fingers to the bone** if you work extremely hard over a long period of time: *Granny worked her fingers to the bone to pay for Mum's education.* ♦ *see also* **work like a dog** ▷DOG

fingertips

○ **have something at your 'fingertips**

You have information about something **at your fingertips** if you are able to give people facts easily, without having to refer to books: *The more facts you've got at your fingertips the more easy it is to persuade people.*

fire

○ **fight fire with 'fire**

You **fight fire with fire** when you use the same methods as someone else to defeat them: *Spain, clearly fearing Ireland's physical strength, have decided to fight fire with fire in this match.*

○ **play with 'fire**

You **are playing with fire** if you are doing something very dangerous: *She tried to warn Maurice he was playing with fire. But he wouldn't listen. He didn't take her seriously.*

fish

○ **drink like a 'fish**

Someone who **drinks like a fish** drinks a lot of alcohol.

○ **have bigger fish to 'fry** or **have other fish to 'fry**

If you say that you **have bigger**, or **other**, **fish to fry**, you mean that you have more important things to do: *How come? I thought you'd have bigger fish to fry with clients like Krantz and Marsh and so on.*

○ **like a fish out of 'water**

You are **like a fish out of water** if you feel very uncomfortable or look very unusual because you are in a situation that you are not used to: *'In the city, we were fish out of water,' said one of the villagers. 'It was so good to be back home again'.*

○ **plenty more fish in the 'sea**

You tell someone who has been deserted by a lover that there are **plenty more fish in the sea**, as a way of reassuring them that there are a lot of other people in the world who could make them happy: *Don't dwell on the past. There are plenty more fish in the sea.*

fit

○ **fit as a 'fiddle**

You are as **fit as a fiddle** if you are

strong and very healthy: *The doctor seems to think I'm fit as a fiddle so I suppose there can't be anything wrong with me.* ♦ *see also* **right as rain** ▷RIGHT

fits
○ **in fits and 'starts**
Something that happens **in fits and starts** is irregular or occurs in small groups: *He was only able to sleep in fits and starts, the pain was so bad.*

flash
○ **flash in the 'pan**
You describe something as a **flash in the pan** if it is the object of great popularity or enthusiasm for only a very short period of time: *Everything she does is a flash in the pan; it was golf lessons last month, now it's aerobics.*

flat
○ **that's 'flat** (*BrE*)
You say '**that's flat**' when you have forbidden someone to do something and you want to show that you will not be persuaded to change your mind: *You're not going by yourself and that's flat.* ♦ *see also* **no two ways about it** ▷WAYS; **that's that** ▷THAT

flea
○ **send someone away with a 'flea in their ear**
You **send someone away with a flea in their ear** when you make an angry remark and tell them to go away: *I sent him away with a flea in his ear; I don't think he'll do it again.* ♦ *see also* **give someone hell** ▷HELL; **give someone a piece of your mind** ▷PIECE; **give someone the rough side of your tongue** ▷SIDE; **tear someone off a strip** ▷STRIP

flesh
○ **make someone's 'flesh crawl** or **make someone's 'flesh creep**
Something that **makes your flesh crawl**, or **creep**, disgusts or horrifies you: *I just can't touch it; the thought of it makes my flesh crawl.*

○ **press the 'flesh** (*AmE*)
If someone, especially a politician, **presses the flesh**, they mingle with a lot of people and shake their hands: *Senator Walker has few ideas, but he knows how to press the flesh.*

flies
○ **drop like 'flies**
People **drop like flies** when they fall ill or give in to exhaustion in great numbers: *The heat was unbearable; people were dropping like flies.*

floodgates
○ **open the 'floodgates**
You **open the floodgates** when you remove restrictions or controls that have been repressing thoughts, feelings or actions: *Durkheim opened the floodgates, offering a radically new way of making sense of social institutions.*

Floodgates are barriers that prevent an area from flooding during periods of heavy rain.

floor
○ **wipe the 'floor with** (*informal*)
You **wipe the floor with** someone when you beat them easily in a competition or match: *'Did you win?' 'No way, they wiped the floor with us.'* ♦ *see also* **make mincemeat of** ▷MINCEMEAT

flow
○ **go with the 'flow**
You **go with the flow** when you do the same as everyone else, or accept the opinions held by most people, because it would be more difficult to do something different or to disagree.

○ **in full 'flow**
You are **in full flow** when you are in the middle of explaining or describing something: *It's hard to cut people off when they're in full flow, but we have to respect time constraints.*

fly (*see also* **flies**)
○ **'fly in the ointment**
You describe something as a **fly in the ointment** if it spoils a situation which could otherwise be pleasant: *The only fly in the ointment was that I still had to study for my maths exam, which was to take place after the summer break.*

A **fly** is a kind of insect.

○ **wouldn't harm a 'fly** or **wouldn't hurt a 'fly**
Someone who **wouldn't harm**, or **hurt**, **a fly** is gentle and kind-hearted,

and would not intentionally make anyone suffer: *What? Liam? He wouldn't hurt a fly; no, it can't have been him.*

food

○ **food for 'thought**

Something that provides **food for thought** makes you think because it is particularly important or interesting: *Thanks for your suggestions; they certainly provide food for thought.*

fool

○ **a fool and his money are soon 'parted**

'A **fool and his money are soon parted**' means that you are foolish if you spend money too quickly, rather than saving it.

○ **more fool 'you** (*informal*)

If you say '**more fool you**' to someone, you mean, unkindly, that they were foolish not to take advantage of a situation: *'I decided not to go on that course in the States because it would mean leaving my boyfriend for two months.' 'More fool you.'*

fools

○ **fools rush 'in**

If you say '**fools rush in**', you mean that foolish people attempt to do things that wiser people would avoid: *He offered to take a class of 35 kids camping; talk about fools rush in!*

> This idiom is the shortened form of the saying '**fools rush in where angels fear to tread**'.

○ **not suffer fools 'gladly**

Someone who **does not suffer fools gladly** is impatient and unsympathetic towards foolish people: *She's a good manager, but watch out; she doesn't suffer fools gladly.*

foot (*see also* **feet**)

○ **a foot in both 'camps**

You have **a foot in both camps** if you have links with people in two groups, each with opposing opinions: *It helps to have a foot in both camps if you can; that way you are sure of understanding both sides.*

○ **a 'foot in the door**

You have **a foot in the door** if you have already completed one stage towards achieving an aim, especially one that involves being accepted by a group or organization: *'They've agreed to give me a month's work experience.' 'Great, well that's a foot in the door, isn't it?'*

> If you put your foot in a doorway, the door cannot be shut.

○ **get off on the wrong 'foot**

You **get off on the wrong foot** when you start something badly: *'How did you get on with his parents?' 'Well, I got off on the wrong foot by using their first names.'*

> When soldiers are marching, they all have to start on the same foot.

○ **have one foot in the 'grave** (*informal*)

If you say that someone **has one foot in the grave**, you mean, humorously, that they are very old: *These holidays aren't only for people with one foot in the grave; they can provide a relaxing break for people of any age.*

> A **grave** is a place where a person's body is buried when they are dead.

○ **put a foot 'wrong**

1 You **put a foot wrong** when you make a mistake or do something that someone disapproves of: *I realized that I should not put a foot wrong; if I did, we might never get the offer accepted.* **2** You say that a person **cannot put a foot wrong** if someone likes or loves them so much that they cannot see that person's faults: *I'm sure you cannot put a foot wrong where she's concerned.*

○ **put your 'foot down**

You **put your foot down** when you decide very firmly not to allow something: *You're going to have to put your foot down this time; you can't let the children go out late at night.*

○ **put your 'foot in it** or **put your foot in your 'mouth** (*informal*)

You **put your foot in it** or **put your foot in your mouth** when you unintentionally say something that embarrasses or upsets someone: *Oh no, I really put my foot in it there; why didn't you tell me they'd split up?* ♦ *see also* **drop a clanger** ▷CLANGER

force

○ **a force to be 'reckoned with**
Something that is described as **a force to be reckoned with** is very powerful and has a lot of influence: *Their accumulated experience, together with their local knowledge, means that they are a force to be reckoned with.*

fort

○ **hold the 'fort**
You **hold the fort** when you temporarily take over the running of an organization: *'Where's Mrs McLeod?' 'She's on holiday; I'm holding the fort.'*

friend

○ **fair-weather 'friend**
A **fair-weather friend** is someone who is friendly with you when you are enjoying good times, but who abandons you when you need help: *This is a time when you will find out who your fair-weather friends are.*

fritz

○ **on the 'fritz** (*AmE; informal*)
Something that is **on the fritz** is broken and not working: *I would lend you my calculator, but it's on the fritz.* ♦ *see also* **on the bum** ▷BUM

frog

○ **a 'frog in your throat**
You say you've got **a frog in your throat** if your voice is not clear, and you feel you need to cough: *Excuse me, I've got a bit of a frog in my throat.*

> A **frog** is a small animal that lives in water, and makes a croaking sound.

frying

○ **out of the frying pan into the 'fire**
A situation is described as **out of the frying pan into the fire**, when it gets even more difficult than it was before.

fun

○ **poke 'fun at** or **make 'fun of**
You **poke fun at**, or **make fun of**, someone when you make jokes about their looks or behaviour in public: *comedians who poke fun at politicians.* ♦ *see also* **take the mickey** ▷MICKEY

fuse

○ **blow a 'fuse**
You **blow a fuse** when you become ex-

tremely angry: *When I told her about the car, she blew a fuse.* ♦ *see also* **go off at the deep end** ▷END; **let fly** ▷LET; **blow** or **flip your lid** ▷LID; **do your nut** ▷NUT; **lose your rag** ▷RAG; **fly into a rage** ▷RAGE; **hit the roof** ▷ROOF; **blow your stack** ▷STACK; **lose your temper** ▷TEMPER; **blow your top** ▷TOP; **throw a wobbly** ▷WOBBLY

game

○ **fair 'game**
If you describe someone as **fair game**, you mean that it is reasonable to criticize or attack them in some way: *But when it came to practical jokes, he regarded anybody as fair game, from people he hardly knew to his dearest friends.*

○ **give the 'game away**
You **give the game away** when you reveal a secret: *If I tell you, will you promise not to give the game away?* ♦ *see also* **let the cat out of the bag** ▷CAT; **spill the beans** ▷BEANS

gangbusters

○ **come on like 'gangbusters** (*AmE; humorous*)
Someone who **comes on like gangbusters** is very loud and aggressive: *I thought she would be shy at the party, but she came on like gangbusters.*

> '**Gangbusters**' was an American radio programme that always began with the sound of guns and police sirens.

garden

○ **lead someone up the garden 'path**
You **lead someone up the garden**

path when you deceive them: *The writer of the crime story has to plot carefully to achieve the surprise at the end. The reader has to be led up the garden path.*
♦ *see also* **take someone for a ride**
▷RIDE

gas

○ **cooking on 'gas** (*BrE*; *informal*) or **cooking with 'gas** (*AmE*; *informal*)
If you say that someone is **cooking on gas**, or **cooking with gas**, you mean that they are acting in a way that is likely to lead to success: *You've decided to go back to University to do a Master's Degree? Now you're cooking with gas.*

An American gas advertisement once said cooking would be better with gas.

○ **out of 'gas** (*AmE*)
When you run **out of gas**, you become very tired: *Rick cleaned out the garage and half the barn before he ran out of gas.*

Americans say a car is **out of gas** when it has run out of petrol. In American English 'gasoline' is another word for petrol.

gate

○ **give someone the 'gate** (*AmE*)
You **give someone the gate** when you reject them and send them away: *After Paul insulted my sister, we gave him the gate.*

gauntlet

○ **pick up the 'gauntlet** or **take up the 'gauntlet**
You **pick up**, or **take up**, **the gauntlet** when you agree to fight or compete with someone: *He took up the gauntlet he saw set before him and entered a career in boxing.*

See note at **throw down the gauntlet**.

○ **run the 'gauntlet**
You **run the gauntlet** when you are attacked or criticized by a lot of people together: *Greeted with shouts of 'traitor!' he had to run the gauntlet of 3000 anti-fascists in Gateshead and 5000 in Newcastle.*

This idiom comes from an old Swedish military punishment – running the 'gatlopp', where the person who had done something wrong would have to run between two lines of men who would hit him.

○ **throw down the 'gauntlet**
You **throw down the gauntlet** when you challenge someone to a fight, or to compete with you in some way: *Fresh from their success, they have thrown down the gauntlet to the rest of the group.*

This idiom comes from a medieval tradition where someone would throw down a gauntlet (a long protective glove), as a sign that they wished to fight.

gear

○ **get into high 'gear** or **go into high 'gear** or **move into high 'gear** (*AmE*)
'Get into high gear' or 'go into high gear' or 'move into high gear' means 'to move quickly or become very active': *After the treaty failed, the military moved into high gear.*

get

○ **get 'funny with someone** (*AmE*) (*informal*)
You **get funny with someone** when you behave in a disrespectful or rude way towards them: *'Get out of my way.' 'Hey, don't get funny with me!'*

○ **'get it** (*informal*)
You say that someone will **get it** when you think that they will be punished: *You'll get it when Mum comes home.* ♦ *see also* **cop it** ▷COP

○ **like all 'get out** or **as something as all 'get out** (*AmE*; *informal*)
Something is a certain way **like all get out**, or **as something as all get out**, when it is that way to a great degree: *He saw the snake and ran like all get out.* □ *Today is as hot as all get out.*

ghost

○ **give up the 'ghost** (*informal*)
Someone **gives up the ghost** when they die; a machine **gives up the ghost** when it stops working: *What if she should die before I got home, give up*

the ghost and pass on, alone in the dark?
□ *I'm a bit worried the car's going to give
up the ghost in the middle of nowhere.* ♦
see also **kick the bucket** ▷BUCKET;
cash in your chips ▷CHIPS; **pop your
clogs** ▷CLOGS; **bite the dust** ▷DUST;
snuff it ▷SNUFF

gift

○ **the gift of the 'gab**
Someone who has **the gift of the gab**
is able to manipulate people by talking
to them very confidently and easily:
*Fortunately, one of my friends had the
gift of the gab and was able to defuse the
situation.*

gloves

○ **treat someone with kid 'gloves**
You **treat someone with kid gloves**
when you treat them very gently, being
careful not to do or say anything which
could cause offence: *There was no point
in treating him with kid gloves; he'd have
to know sooner or later.* ♦ *see also* **walk**
or **tread on eggshells** ▷EGGSHELLS

> **Kid gloves** are made from the very
> soft leather of a baby goat's skin.

go

○ **'go for it** (*informal*)
You tell someone to **go for it 1** to encourage them to try something new and
challenging: *'I don't know whether to
take the risk or not.' 'Go for it, I would.'*
2 to encourage them to perform well:
Go for it! We'll be cheering for you!

goalposts

○ **move the 'goalposts**
You **move the goalposts** when you
change the conditions of an agreement:
*He was always moving the goalposts so
that we could never anticipate what he
wanted.*

goat

○ **get someone's 'goat** (*informal*)
Someone **gets your goat** if they annoy
you: *I hope I didn't say anything rude to
Sandy. She gets my goat sometimes with
her self-assertion.* ♦ *see also* **drive
someone round the bend** ▷BEND;
get on someone's nerves ▷NERVES;
get up someone's nose ▷NOSE; **rub
someone up the wrong way** ▷WAY;
get on someone's wick ▷WICK

going

○ **while the going is 'good**
You do something **while the going is
good** when you take advantage of the
circumstances: *Let's get out of here
while the going's good.*

good (*see also* **goods**)

○ **as good as 'gold**
A child who is **as good as gold** is very
well-behaved: *It's no trouble looking
after him; he's as good as gold.*

○ **give as good as you 'get**
You **give as good as you get** when you
fight, argue or joke with other people
as well as they fight, argue or joke with
you: *Don't worry about Kate; she can
give as good as she gets.*

○ **too good to be 'true**
If you say that something is **too good
to be true**, you mean that it is so good
that you can hardly believe it: *It was
like a dream, too good to be true and
never likely to be recaptured.*

○ **up to no 'good**
Someone who is **up to no good** is secretly doing something dishonest or illegal: *If you ask me, he's up to no good.*

goods

○ **come up with the 'goods** or **deliver
the goods**
Someone **comes up with**, or **delivers**,
the goods when they do what they
have promised they will do, or when
they do a job well: *She's got a lot of
qualifications, but do you think she can
deliver the goods?*

goose

○ **cook someone's 'goose**
Something that **cooks your goose**
spoils your chances of success: *This fall
in share prices will cook Arthur's goose.*

○ **wouldn't say boo to a 'goose**
Someone who **wouldn't say boo to a
goose** is reserved or shy, and would
never attack or criticize anyone.

gooseberry

○ **play 'gooseberry** (*BrE*; *informal*)
You **are playing gooseberry** when
you are invading the privacy of a couple
who are romantically involved with
each other: *All right, I'll come, if
you really don't mind my playing gooseberry.*

gospel
○ **take something as 'gospel**
You **take something**, such as a statement, **as gospel**, when you believe it without questioning it: *Rather than taking as gospel what the manufacturers told us, we decided to visit one of their factories ourselves.*

grabs
○ **up for 'grabs** (*informal*)
Something that is **up for grabs** is for sale or available in some way: *The famous Ritz hotel is up for grabs for a mere £1 million.*

grade
○ **make the 'grade**
You **make the grade** when you reach the required standard: *Determination and resilience are two of the most important qualities needed to make the grade as a sportsperson.*

> In the US, a train that could **make the grade** was one that could climb a steep section of the track.

grain
○ **go against the 'grain**
Something **goes against the grain** when you find it difficult to accept, or do, it because it opposes a belief or principle that you hold: *A lie went against the grain, but it was necessary.*

> On a piece of wood, the **grain** is the natural patterns and lines on its surface. It is easier to cut with the grain than against it.

grandmother
○ **teach your grandmother to suck 'eggs** (*BrE*)
You **are teaching your grandmother to suck eggs** if you are trying to give advice to someone who already has a lot of knowledge about the subject: *There's nothing worse than going into the classroom and thinking, 'they may already know this, I might be teaching my grandmother to suck eggs.'*

grapes
○ **sour 'grapes**
Sour grapes means 'jealousy': *It may sound like sour grapes. but I assure you I feel no bitterness, just disappointment.*

> From Aesop's fable about the fox who, being unable to reach a bunch of grapes, went away saying, 'I see they are sour' [= not sweet].

grass
○ **the grass is always greener on the other side of the 'fence**
If you say that **the grass is 'greener**, or **the grass is always 'greener**, or **the grass is always greener on the other side of the 'fence**, you mean that things that you do not, or cannot, have always seem more attractive than the things you do have: *The other man's grass is always greener, and I had the opportunity when I was younger to work abroad.* ♦ *see also* **the best of both worlds** ▷WORLDS; **have your cake and eat it** ▷CAKE

○ **not let the grass grow under your 'feet**
You **don't let the grass grow under your feet** when you do not delay, or waste time: *Get on with it you lot, don't let the grass grow under your feet.*

○ **put someone out to 'grass** or **turn someone out to 'grass** or **send someone out to 'grass** (*BrE*) or **put someone out to 'pasture** (*AmE*)
You **put someone out to grass**, or **put someone out to pasture**, when you cause them to give up work or retire, usually because they are too old to be effective: *At the ripe old age of fifty five I've been turned out to grass, so to speak.*

> Farm animals that are no longer strong enough to work are left out in the fields.

grasshopper
○ **knee-high to a 'grasshopper**
You describe someone as **knee-high to a grasshopper** if they are very small: *My father told me that story when I was knee-high to a grasshopper.*

> A **grasshopper** is a small jumping insect that makes a harsh noise by rubbing its back legs against its wings.

grave

○ **dig your own 'grave**

You **dig your own grave** when you are responsible for harming yourself, or for your own failure: *These are women who dig their own grave by doing all the housework themselves.*

○ **so-and-so must be turning in their 'grave** (*humorous*)

You say that someone who is already dead **must be turning in their grave** if people are doing or saying something that they would not have approved of: *Your poor mother will be turning in her grave to think of you going out on your own like this.*

grief

○ **come to 'grief**

You **come to grief** when you fail, have an accident, or suffer the unpleasant results of something you have been doing: *This was not the first vehicle that had come to grief on that stretch of road.*

♦ *see also* **come a cropper** ▷CROPPER

grin

○ **grin and 'bear it**

You have to **grin and bear it** when you have to tolerate an unpleasant situation because you have no choice: *I'm in a dead-end job, but for the moment I'm just going to have to grin and bear it.*

grips

○ **get to 'grips with**

You **get to grips with** a subject, for example, when you start understanding it: *I've never really been into that kind of poetry; I can't get to grips with it.*

ground

○ **break new 'ground**

You **break new ground** when you discover or invent something new: *Far from breaking new ground, most of the designs bear a strong relation to that which has gone before.*

○ **get something off the 'ground**

You **get something off the ground** when you cause it to start happening or operating; something **gets off the ground** when it starts happening or operating: *The economic recession of that year forced the Conservative Government to change its policies before they had got off the ground.*

○ **hold your 'ground**

You **hold your ground** when you argue for something you believe without being intimidated or easily persuaded by other people's arguments: *But Richard held his ground, his fixed look showing that he would not give way.* ♦ *see also* **stick to your guns** ▷GUNS

○ **suit down to the 'ground** (*BrE*)

Something **suits you down to the ground** when it suits you well, and you are happy with it: *The climate there would suit you down to the ground.*

○ **thin on the 'ground** (*BrE*)

Something that is **thin on the ground** does not exist in large quantities: *Public transport is pretty thin on the ground there, so it's advisable to hire a car.*

guess

○ **your guess is as good as 'mine**

You say **'your guess is as good as mine'** when you have no idea about something: *We sent out a distress signal, but your guess is as good as mine if anyone heard it.*

gum

○ **up a 'gum tree** (*BrE; informal*)

You are **up a gum tree** if you are in a very difficult position: *If all this leaves you up a gum tree, you would be well advised to seek the help of a good lawyer.*

> In Australia, the possum commonly hides up a gum tree when it is being chased.

gun

○ **jump the 'gun**

You **jump the gun** when you try to start something before the time is right: *If we jump the gun and put the blame on Werner, we could get ourselves into trouble later on.*

> In a race, you have to wait for the gun to be fired before you can start running.

guns

○ **go great 'guns**

You **are going great guns** if you are doing something with energy and vigour: *The company is going great guns at the end of its first year.*

guts

○ **stick to your 'guns**
You **stick to your guns** when you hold your position in an argument: *And there was great admiration for his honesty, his modesty, and determination to stick to his guns.* ♦ *see also* **hold your ground** ▷GROUND

> A soldier who **sticks to his guns** continues to fire at the enemy and does not run away.

guts

○ **have someone's guts for 'garters** (*BrE; informal, humorous*)
If you say that you will **have someone's guts for garters**, you mean that you will be very angry with them, or that you will punish them: *If you breathe a word to anyone I'll have your guts for garters.*

○ **have the guts to 'do something**
If you **have the guts to do something**, you are not afraid to do it: *He was the only one who had the guts to say what he really 'thought.*

○ **work your 'guts out** or (*BrE*) **slog your 'guts out** (*informal*)
You **work**, or **slog**, **your guts out** when you work very hard: *I worked my guts out getting my doctorate, and look where it's got me.*

hair (*see also* hairs)

○ **keep your 'hair on**
'**Keep your hair on**' means 'calm down': *All right, all right! Keep your hair on!*

○ **let your 'hair down**
You **let your hair down** when you relax and enjoy yourself without worrying about what other people think about you: *Visitors young and old let their hair down and enjoyed the entertainment.* ♦ *see also* **enter into the spirit** ▷SPIRIT

> In the past, women always used to put their hair up when they went out, only letting it down in private.

○ **make your 'hair curl**
Something that would **make your hair curl** would horrify you: *I could tell you tales about her that would make your hair curl.*

○ **make someone's 'hair stand on end**
Something that **makes your hair stand on end** terrifies or horrifies you: *His language makes my hair stand on end.*

○ **not turn a 'hair**
Someone who does **not turn a hair** is not surprised or shocked: *Nick wouldn't be embarrassed, he could say things like that without turning a hair.*

hairs

○ **split 'hairs**
You **split hairs** when you pay too much attention to small details, or make unnecessary distinctions between things which are basically the same.

half (*see also* halves)

○ **don't know the 'half of it** or **haven't heard the 'half of it**
You tell someone that they **don't know the half of it** or **haven't heard the half of it** if the situation is even worse than they think it is.

○ **how the other half 'lives**
You see **how the other half lives** or **live** when you see how people who are much richer than you or much poorer than you live: *Tomorrow, Katie Wood will be showing us how the other half live when she mixes with guests on a country house weekend in Oxfordshire.*

halves

○ **not do things by 'halves**
Someone who does **not do things by halves** always puts all their energy and enthusiasm into the things they do: *She never did anything by halves. She gave one hundred and one per cent to whatever was important at the time.*

hammer

○ **go at it hammer and 'tongs**

You **go at it hammer and tongs 1** when you do something with a lot of energy: *I always go hammer and tongs at my running.* **2** when you argue or fight violently: *You two fought hammer and tongs to marry her mother.*

hand (*see also* hands)

○ **at first 'hand**

You experience something **at first hand** when you experience it yourself, and in reality, rather than on television, for example: *His organization has, in fact, collected all the information at first hand from the people themselves.*

○ **get out of 'hand**

An activity **gets out of hand** when it becomes uncontrollable: *They never faced the situation realistically; inflation got out of hand and contributed even more to their downfall.*

○ **give a 'hand** or **lend a 'hand**

1 You **give**, or **lend**, **someone a hand** when you help them: *Could you give me a hand with this box, please?* **2** An audience **gives someone a hand**, or **a big hand**, when they clap to show that they appreciate something they have done, or to welcome them on to the stage before a performance: *Let's have a big hand for Oasis!*

○ **give someone a free 'hand**

You **give someone a free hand** when you let them organize something in their own way, rather than supervising them yourself: *They had good reason to fear that Sutton, given a free hand, would get rid of them.*

○ **go hand in 'hand**

Two things **go hand in hand** when they always happen or are always found together: *Youth and experience do not normally go hand in hand.*

○ **hand in 'glove**

You are **hand in glove** with someone when you are closely associated with them: *This cure for inflation went hand in glove with a rise in unemployment.*

○ **hand over 'fist**

You make, or lose, money **hand over fist** when you make, or lose, a lot of money: *Since Martin started up this new business venture, he's been losing money hand over fist.*

○ **have someone eating out of your 'hand**

You **have someone eating out of your hand** if you can persuade them to do anything you want them to do: *I bet you he'll be eating out of your hand by the second beer.* ♦ *see also* **have someone right where you want them** ▷WANT; **have someone eating out of the palm of your hand** ▷PALM; **have someone in your pocket** ▷POCKET

○ **keep your 'hand in**

You do an activity to **keep your hand in** when you do it so that you do not forget how to do it: *He left journalism, but managed to keep his hand in by writing the staff newspaper.*

○ **old 'hand**

You describe someone as an **old hand** at something if they have been doing it for a long time and know how to do it well: *I was becoming an old hand; I wasn't nearly as nervous, even though the audience was twice the size.*

○ **on 'hand**

You have someone **on hand** if they are present in case they are needed: *John is always on hand if you have trouble with your computer.*

○ **on 'one hand ... on the 'other hand**

You use **on (the) one hand ... on the other (hand)** to show two sides of an argument: *Such confusion has, on one hand, led many doctors to reject acupuncture as a superstition, while on the other it has led a large number of people to react by rejecting traditional medicine.*

○ **take someone in 'hand**

You **take someone in hand** when you start trying to restrain and improve their behaviour: *Someone needs to take that child in hand. He's spoilt rotten.*

○ **try your hand at something**

You **try your hand at something** when you do it in order to see if you like it, or to see if you are good at it: *We had run out of bread again, so I tried my hand at 'making some.*

○ **the upper 'hand**

You have **the upper hand** if you are in a more powerful position than someone else; you gain **the upper hand** when you become more powerful than someone else: *The 'just-in-time' manufacturing method quickly led to the Japanese gaining the upper hand.*

handle

○ **fly off the 'handle**
You **fly off the handle** when you suddenly become very angry: *She flies off the handle without any warning.*

○ **get a 'handle on something**
You **get a handle on something** when you become familiar with it so that you can understand it better: *I think I'm starting to get a handle on the situation now, but thanks for your help.*

hands

○ **beat someone hands 'down**
You **beat someone hands down** when you beat them easily. ♦ *see also* **beat someone hollow** ▷BEAT

○ **get into the wrong 'hands** or **fall into the wrong 'hands**
Something that **has got**, or **fallen, into the wrong hands** has been acquired by someone who is dishonest: *A crossed cheque gives some protection against fraud if it falls into the wrong hands.*

○ **have your 'hands full**
You say that you **have your hands full** if you are very busy: *And Mother had her hands full coping with the housework and looking after four old people.*

○ **in safe 'hands**
You say that something is **in safe hands** if it is being looked after by someone who can be trusted: *You can step on board close to home, know your luggage is in safe hands, and travel in carefree comfort to your hotel near Paris.*

○ **wash your hands of**
You say that you have **washed your hands of** someone or something when you no longer want to have anything to do with them: *The Government seems to be washing its hands of all its 'industry, as it hands it over to the free market.*

○ **win hands 'down**
You **win hands down** when you beat someone very easily: *When we had a quiz, Ken always won hands down.*

hang

○ **get the 'hang of**
You **get the hang of** something when

you start understanding how to do it, or how it works: *I think I'm starting to get the hang of this new software at last.*

happiness *see* **Idioms study** page 74

happy

○ **happy as a 'clam** (*AmE*)
You are as **happy as a clam** when you are very happy and contented: *Mary was living on low wages but she was still happy as a clam.*

hardball

○ **play 'hardball** (*AmE*; *informal*)
If someone **plays hardball**, they act in a tough or aggressive manner: *I wanted to compromise, but my lawyer insisted we play hardball.*

In American English, **hardball** is an informal name for a baseball.

hassle

○ **no 'hassle**
You say **'no hassle'** to show that what you are doing for someone is not a problem for you. ♦ *see also* **no problem** ▷PROBLEM

hat

○ **keep something under your 'hat**
You **keep something under your hat** when you do not tell anyone about it: *He said that somebody or other discovered America before Columbus, but decided it was best to keep it under his hat.* ♦ *see also* **keep something to yourself** ▷KEEP

○ **take your 'hat off to so-and-so**
You say that you **take your hat off to** a certain person when you admire something they have done: *I take my hat off to her – she did all that by herself.*

○ **toss your 'hat in the ring** or **throw your 'hat in the ring** (*AmE*)
You **toss your hat in the ring**, or **throw your hat in the ring**, when you announce that you are going to be a candidate for a political office: *We were all surprised when dad said he'd tossed his hat in the ring.*

have

○ **have someone 'on**
You **are having someone on** if you are teasing them by trying to make them believe something that isn't true: *Oh come on, you're having me on.*

IDIOMS*study*

happiness and sadness

The next time you write or talk about **happiness and sadness** you might try to use some of the following idioms. (Remember you can see how to use each idiom correctly by looking at its entry, which you can find under the word printed in heavy type.)

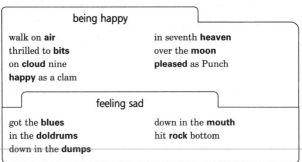

being happy

walk on **air**
thrilled to **bits**
on **cloud** nine
happy as a clam

in seventh **heaven**
over the **moon**
pleased as Punch

feeling sad

got the **blues**
in the **doldrums**
down in the **dumps**

down in the **mouth**
hit **rock** bottom

○ **have it 'out with someone**
You **have it out with someone** when you finally talk to them about something they have done that makes you angry: *I decided to have it out with him; I couldn't bear all that suspicion any longer.*

hay

○ **hit the 'hay**
You **hit the hay** when you go to bed: *Time I hit the hay. Good night everyone.*

> **Hay** is grass that has been cut and dried so that it can be used to feed animals. People sometimes use it for sleeping on outdoors.

○ **make hay while the 'sun shines**
If you tell someone to **make hay while the sun shines**, you mean that they should take advantage of the current favourable circumstances: *The price is right. Make hay while the sun shines, you know.* ♦ *see also* **strike while the iron is hot** ▷IRON

head

○ **bring to a 'head**
You **bring** a situation **to a head** when you feel that it has reached a point

where something must be done about it; a situation **comes to a head** when someone finally does something about a difficult situation: *The strained relationship between staff and management came to a head in the form of widespread industrial action in 1978.*

○ **bury your head in the 'sand**
You **bury your head in the sand** when you try to ignore a problem, in the hope that it will go away: *If you can't afford to repay your debts, don't bury your head in the sand.*

○ **can't get your 'head around something**
You say that you **can't get your head round something**, such as a new concept, when you have tried very hard, but you still can't understand it: *I just can't seem to get my head around this post-modernism stuff.*

○ **can't make head or 'tail of** or (*AmE*) **can't make heads or 'tails of**
You say that you **can't make head or tail of**, or **can't make heads or tails of**, something, such as a piece of information, when you can't understand it: *I can't make head or tail of these instructions.*

○ **go to someone's 'head**
1 Success **goes to your head** if it makes you over-confident: *All the publicity she's been getting has gone to her head.* **2** An alcoholic drink **goes to your head** if it makes you feel drunk: *He was suddenly tired and the beer was going to his head.*

○ **head and shoulders above**
Someone who is **head and shoulders above** everyone else is **1** very tall: *Towering head and shoulders above the 'customs officer, the man strode in, his face as dark as a storm.* **2** much better than them at something: *This success had given him the confidence to stand head and shoulders above the 'rest.*

○ **'head in the clouds**
You have your **head in the clouds** if you do not consider the realities of a situation: *He seemed to have his head in the clouds, to be living in a dream world.*

○ **hold your 'head up high**
You can **hold your head up high** if you do not have any feelings of guilt or shame: *I was told by my mother always to hold my head up high, and remember that I was a MacLeod.*

○ **lose your 'head**
You **lose your head** when you lose control of yourself and do not stay calm: *As soon as I saw the photographers, I lost my temper, lost my head.*

○ **over your 'head**
Something goes **over your head** when you do not pay enough attention to it, or when it is too complicated for you to understand: *Some of what you said went straight over my head, but on the whole it was interesting.* ♦ *see also* **beyond you** ▷BEYOND

○ **take something into your 'head** or **get something into your 'head**
You **take**, or **get**, **something into your head** when you decide that something is the case, and you refuse to change your mind: *For some reason, she's got it into her head that I don't care about her.*

○ **use your 'head**
You say to someone '**use your head**' when you think that thay are not trying hard enough to find a solution to something: *Well why don't you use your*

head and go and do it yourself?

heart

○ **after your own 'heart**
You say that a certain person is a man, woman, etc, **after your own heart** if they appreciate something that you also appreciate very much: *You like good malt whisky? Ah, there's a man after my own heart.*

○ **by 'heart**
You know something **by heart** if you know it so well that you can repeat it from memory with no mistakes: *In his day, he said, students were grounded in spelling and had learned poetry and the Bible by heart.* ♦ *see also* **off pat** ▷PAT

○ **heart 'bleeds for**
You say that your **heart bleeds for** so-and-so when you feel deeply sorry for them; people sometimes use this idiom sarcastically to mean that they have no sympathy for a certain person: *Her heart bled for Cowdrey, for he looked desperate, panic-stricken.*

○ **heart in your 'mouth**
Your **heart is in your mouth** when you feel very nervous or afraid about what is about to happen: *Hesitantly she followed, her heart in her mouth, creeping nervously down the dark pathway.*

○ **'heart in the right place**
You say that someone's **heart is in the right place** when you are recognizing that their intentions are kind, even if the results of their actions do not help anyone: *He's a bit mixed up, but his heart's in the right place.*

○ **your 'heart sinks**
Your **heart sinks** when you are suddenly very disappointed about something: *My heart sank when I saw Richard's car outside the house. I wasn't looking forward to telling him about the secrets I'd been keeping.*

○ **in your heart of 'hearts**
You know, or feel, something **in your heart of hearts** when you know or feel it, even though you do not really want to admit it: *Can you really say, in your heart of hearts, that you are looking forward to old age?*

○ **set your 'heart on something**
You say that someone **has set their heart on something** when they have

decided that they want something very much: *To help him over his ordeal she has bought him the mountain bike he had set his heart on.* ♦ *see also* **set your sights on** ▷SIGHTS

○ **wear your heart on your 'sleeve**
Someone who **wears their heart on their sleeve** does not, or cannot hide their emotions.

heaven

○ **in seventh 'heaven**
You are **in seventh heaven** when you are very happy about something, or enjoying yourself immensely: *Gloria was in seventh heaven as she wandered around the shops knowing she could buy whatever she liked.* ♦ *see also* **walk on air** ▷AIR; **thrilled to bits** ▷BITS; **on cloud nine** ▷CLOUD; **over the moon** ▷MOON

○ **move heaven and 'earth**
You **move heaven and earth** to achieve something when you do everything possible to make sure it happens: *You shake, you sweat, you're pale and weak. We've all experienced it and most of us would move heaven and earth to avoid it.*

heels

○ **close on someone's 'heels** or **hard on someone's 'heels** or **hot on someone's 'heels**
You are **close**, or **hard**, or **hot**, **on someone's heels** if you are chasing them and you have almost caught them: *They're close on our heels now – come on, we must get away.*

○ **dig your 'heels in**
You **dig your heels in** when you stubbornly refuse to change your mind about something: *You can try and persuade her, but she's likely to dig her heels in on this one.*

○ **take to your 'heels**
You **take to your heels** when you start running as fast as you can, usually in order to escape from someone or something: *When she saw him coming she took to her heels.*

hell

○ **all 'hell breaks loose**
All hell breaks loose when people suddenly panic, or when there is sudden great activity and noise: *As the*

news of the President's resignation reached the Stock Exchange, all hell broke loose.

> In some religions, **Hell** is the place where bad people are believed to go after their death. It is imagined as being under the ground and full of flames.

○ **come hell or high 'water**
You say that you will do something **come hell or high water** if you are determined to do it, even if you have to fight for it: *I'll do it tomorrow, I promise. Come hell or high water.*

○ **get the hell 'out of** (*informal*)
You **get the hell out of** a place when you leave it very quickly: *Get the hell out of here!*

○ **give someone 'hell**
You **give someone hell** when you shout at them, criticize them, or cause them pain or suffering: *They've been giving me hell about employing you, but I'm sure I've chosen the right person for the job.* ♦ *see also* **send someone away with a flea in their ear** ▷FLEA; **give someone a piece of your mind** ▷PIECE; **give someone the rough side of your tongue** ▷SIDE; **tear someone off a strip** ▷STRIP

○ **go to 'hell and back**
You say that you **have been to hell and back** when you have been through a period of extreme emotional suffering: *We have been to hell and back, but our love for this little boy has kept us going.*

○ **hell bent on**
You are **hell bent on** doing or achieving something when you are determined to achieve it, and you will not let anyone stop you: *And I was speeding into the darkness with a man who seemed to be hell bent on risking our lives for no apparent 'reason.*

○ **'hell to pay**
You tell someone that there will be **hell to pay** if they do a certain thing, as a warning that someone will be very angry with them if they do it: *There'll be hell to pay when the officers hear about this in the morning.*

○ play 'hell with or (BrE) play merry
'hell with

Someone or something **plays hell**, or
plays merry hell, with something
when they cause confusion: *The band
have been playing merry hell with their
distributors, delaying the launch of their
new album by yet another three months.*

hide

○ not see hide nor 'hair of

You say that you **have not seen hide
nor hair of** someone when you have
not seen them at all: *Nobody has seen
hide nor hair of him since last month.*

high

○ high and 'mighty

A person is described as **high and
mighty** if they act as if they think they
are more important than other people:
*Don't get all high and mighty with me.
Why don't you just admit it?*

hill

○ over the 'hill

Someone who is **over the hill** is considered to be too old to perform a particular activity: *Isn't he a bit over the
hill for a job like that?* ♦ *see also* **past it**
▷PAST; **long in the tooth** ▷TOOTH

hip

○ shoot from the 'hip (AmE; informal)

You **shoot from the hip** when you
speak frankly and often without thinking: *Eddie is often in trouble because he
tends to shoot from the hip.*

hit

○ hit it 'off

You **hit it off** with someone you have
just met when you like each other and
quickly form a good relationship: *She
was a gentle quiet girl, deeply thoughtful,
and we hit it off from the start.*

○ hit-and-'miss (BrE) or hit-or-'miss

A situation that is described as **hit-
and-miss**, or **hit-or-miss**, depends
more on chance than on good planning
or organization: *The system at present is
far too hit-and-miss. Can't we have a
more controlled system of payment?*

hog

○ go hog 'wild (AmE; informal)

You **go hog wild** when you become very
excited: *When Ian won the lottery, he
went hog wild.*

○ go the whole 'hog

You **go the whole hog** when you do
something as completely as possible:
*In the end we decided to go the whole
hog and get a professional photographer
in to do the job.*

○ live high on the 'hog (AmE; informal)

If someone lives **high on the hog**, they
live a rich, easy life: *When Mom became
a lawyer, we began to live high on the hog.*

holds

○ no holds 'barred

'No holds barred' means that nothing
is omitted or forbidden: *He was under
immense pressure to support no holds
barred military action from UN forces.*

hole

○ burn a 'hole in your pocket

Something, especially money, **burns a
hole in your pocket** when you have
the tendency to use it as long as you
have it, rather than saving it: *If you
find that money burns a hole in your
pocket, why not come in and have a chat
with one of our finance advisors?*

○ dig yourself into a 'hole

You **dig yourself into a hole** when you
make a situation even worse for yourself, especially when you are desperately trying to improve it: *Don't try
and make any more excuses; you're just
digging yourself deeper into a hole.*

○ in the 'hole (AmE)

You are **in the hole** when you are in
debt: *That holiday in Spain put us in
the hole.*

holes

○ pick 'holes in

You **pick holes in** someone or something if you criticize them, especially
for insignificant faults: *If you pick too
many holes in your students' work, they
may lose motivation.* ♦ *see also* **tear** or
rip to shreds ▷SHREDS

home

○ be home 'free (AmE)

You **are home free** when you know
that you will soon succeed: *When our
team scored the last goal, I knew we were
home free.*

○ hit 'home

Something **hits home** when you suddenly realize its implications: *Frankly,*

I'm surprised the message hasn't hit home yet; there just isn't adequate medical care in the area.

hook

○ give someone the 'hook (*AmE*; *informal*)

You **give someone the hook** when you dismiss them from employment: *After David failed to interview the winning candidate, the editor gave him the hook.*

○ let someone off the 'hook

You **let someone off the hook** when you decide not to punish them for something wrong they have done: *They will not be let off the hook for this; discrimination will not be tolerated here.*

hooks

○ get your 'hooks into

Someone **has got their hooks into** you if they hold or influence you strongly: *It never makes sense to borrow from backstreet money lenders. Once they've got their hooks into you, they will never let go.*

hooky

○ play 'hooky (*AmE*)

If a student **plays hooky**, they stay away from school without good reason or without permission: *The teacher sent a letter to Becky's parents after she played hooky on Friday.*

hoot

○ not care a 'hoot or not give a 'hoot, or not care two 'hoots or not give two 'hoots

You do **not care** or **give, a hoot**, or **two hoots** if you do not care about something at all: *She doesn't give two hoots about other people, as long as she's okay.* ♦ *see also* **not give a monkey's** ▷MONKEY; **not give** or **care a toss** ▷TOSS; **not care** or **give tuppence** ▷TUPPENCE

hop

○ catch on the 'hop (*BrE*)

You **catch someone on the hop** when they are not ready for, or expecting, you: *British tourists were caught on the hop yesterday as storms spread across southern Europe.*

hope

○ not have a hope in 'hell

Someone who **hasn't got a hope in hell** of achieving something will not be able to achieve it under any circumstances: *They've been training hard all season, but if you ask me, they haven't got a hope in hell against this lot.* ♦ *see also* **not have** or **stand a cat in hell's chance** ▷CAT

hopes

○ pin your 'hopes on

You **pin your hopes on** a particular person or thing when you depend on their success for your own happiness: *'Don't pin your hopes on it,' warned David.'I don't want to see you hurt.'*

horns

○ draw in your 'horns or pull in your 'horns

You **draw**, or **pull, in your horns** when you start spending less money or going out less often than before: *A busy social life could cost a packet, so you might have to pull in your horns a wee bit.*

horse

○ back the wrong 'horse (*AmE*)

You **back the wrong horse** when you support a person or side that will lose: *I backed the wrong horse when I bet on Tiger Woods in the Open.*

○ flog a dead 'horse

You say that you **are flogging a dead horse** if you feel that what you are doing is no longer having any effect: *You'll be flogging a dead horse if you try to make him change his ways.*

○ horse of a different 'color or horse of another 'color (*AmE*)

If you say that something is a **horse of a different color**, or a **horse of another color**, you mean that it is a different matter altogether: *'He's a good politician.' 'Sure, but his private life is a horse of a different color.'*

○ on your high 'horse

Someone who is **on their high horse** is forcefully telling people how they think things should be done: *Well there were one or two who got on their high horse, you know, saying, 'It's disgusting', but I never did because I wouldn't condemn people.*

horses

○ hold your 'horses

You say to someone **'hold your**

horses!' in order to tell them to stop and think before they go ahead and do something: *She could be heard walking to the front door, grumbling to herself, 'Hold your horses, I'm coming.'*

hours

○ **till 'all hours**

You stay out **till all hours** when you come home in the early hours of the morning: *Better not wake her, she worked till all hours last night, she deserves a bit of a lie-in.*

house

○ **get on like a 'house on fire** or (*AmE*) **get on like a 'house afire**

Two or more people **get on like a house on fire**, or **get on like a house afire**, when they greatly enjoy each other's company: *She asked to be seated next to him. They got on like a house on fire and didn't stop talking afterwards.*

○ **set your 'own house in order** or **put your 'own house in order**

You tell someone to **set**, or **put**, their **own house in order** when you think that they should solve their own problems before they start trying to advise you on yours: *The Government would do well to put its own house in order before it starts attacking the Opposition.*

ice

○ **break the 'ice**

You **break the ice** when you do something that makes people feel more at ease with each other, usually at the beginning of a social occasion: *Hudson broke the ice, fixing both girls with his smile, buying them drinks, and listening intently to them.*

○ **cut no 'ice**

You say that someone's behaviour or attitude **cuts no ice** with you if it does not impress you: *So what was this with his new sharp suit? It cut no ice with 'me.*

ideas

○ **get i'deas**

You tell someone not to **get ideas** if you do not want them to start imagining the possibility of having something that they are unlikely to be allowed to, or able to, have: *Don't get ideas. The apartment is exquisite, but small; there's only enough room here for one.*

○ **give someone i'deas** or **put ideas into someone's 'head**

Someone or something **gives you ideas** or **puts ideas into your head 1** when they encourage you to think you can have something that may in fact be very difficult or impossible to acquire. **2** when they make you start thinking about new, possibly radical, concepts: *That new teacher has been putting ideas into your head again.*

ignorance

○ **ignorance is 'bliss**

'**Ignorance is bliss**' means, often ironically, that you will be much happier, at least in the short term, if you are unaware of unpleasant things: *This is the stage where ignorance is bliss, when you don't realize how much there is to it.*

in (*see also* **ins**)

○ **in for 'such-and-such**

You predict that you are **in for** a particular event when you are quite sure that it is going to happen: *Looks like we're in for a storm.*

○ **'in on something**

You are **in on something** if you are one of a number of people carrying out the same activity, or sharing a secret: *Everyone wants to be in on this project now that it looks as if we're going to make some money out of it.*

○ **'in with someone**

You are **in with** a particular famous or influential person if you have some kind of connection with them that can benefit you: *If you're in with the band, you should be able to get in for free.*

○ **what's in it for 'so-and-so?**

You ask '**what's in it for me?**' when

you want to know if there are any advantages for you in a situation.

inch

○ **give 'em an inch and they'll take a 'mile**

'Give 'em an inch and they'll take a mile' means that if you do a small favour for a particular person or group of people, they will take advantage of your kindness and demand more.

○ **not budge an 'inch** or **not give an 'inch** or **not move an 'inch**

1 Something that will **not budge**, or **give**, or **move**, **an inch** cannot be moved at all: *We've been trying to open this old box here, but it won't give an inch.* **2** Someone who will **not budge**, or **give**, **an inch** refuses absolutely to change their mind: *I lay in bed and ranted at Richard; explaining, arguing, weeping. He would not budge an inch.*

influence

○ **under the 'influence**

You are **under the influence** of something, such as alcohol or drugs, if it has some control over you: *In an interview Morgan acknowledged that he had spent years under the influence of cocaine.* ♦ *see also* **have had a few** or **have had a few too many** ▷FEW

innings

○ **have had a good 'innings** (*BrE*)

You say that someone **has had a good innings** if they have had a good and long life: *He's not afraid of dying; says he's had a good innings.*

In cricket, an **innings** is the period of time that a player is batting, before they are out.

inroads

○ **make 'inroads into something**

You **make inroads into** a task, for example, when you do enough work to have a noticeable effect: *All the combined scientific efforts have still only made small inroads into the accumulating list of unsolved questions.*

ins

○ **the ins and 'outs of something**

The **ins and outs** of something are the detailed facts about it: *For the purposes of our argument here, it is not necessary to understand all the ins and outs of these various schemes.*

insult

○ **add insult to 'injury**

Someone or something **adds insult to injury** when they make a bad situation even worse: *The picnic site was plagued by ants. Then, to add insult to injury, it started to rain.*

intelligence *see* **Idioms study** page 81

interest

○ **pay someone back with 'interest**

You **pay someone back with interest** when you react to some harm that someone has done you by doing something even worse to them: *Those who offended the girls in some way were paid back with interest.* ♦ *see also* **give someone a taste of their own medicine** ▷TASTE

iron

○ **a cast iron 'such-and-such**

You have **a cast iron** stomach, or constitution, for example, if that part of you is very strong, and not easily affected by adverse conditions: *You'll need a cast iron stomach to survive one of her curries.*

Iron is a very hard metal.

○ **strike while the iron is 'hot**

You **strike while the iron is hot** when you take advantage of favourable circumstances to get something done. ♦ *see also* **make hay while the sun shines** ▷HAY

An **iron** is an electrical device with a flat metal base. You heat it up and pass it over clothes to remove creases.

irons

○ **irons in the 'fire**

You have several **irons in the fire** when you are involved in several projects at the same time; you have too many **irons in the fire** when you are involved in so many projects that you cannot do any of them successfully: *He did have a few other economic irons in the fire: among them a share in the tobacco monopoly.* ♦ *see also* **a finger in every pie** ▷FINGER

IDIOMS*study* — intelligence and stupidity

The next time you write or talk about **intelligence and stupidity** you might try to use some of the following idioms. (Remember you can see how to use each idiom correctly by looking at its entry, which you can find under the word printed in heavy type.)

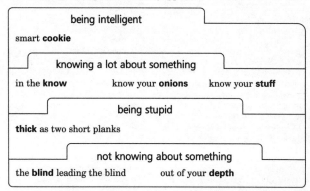

being intelligent

smart **cookie**

knowing a lot about something

in the **know**   know your **onions**   know your **stuff**

being stupid

thick as two short planks

not knowing about something

the **blind** leading the blind   out of your **depth**

issue
○ **cloud the 'issue**
You **cloud the issue** when you give unclear information to support an argument, making people believe something that is not correct: *Our objective is to examine the nature of doubt, clarifying three common misconceptions which cloud the issue today.*

jackpot
○ **hit the 'jackpot**
You say you **have hit the jackpot** when you win or obtain a lot of money or success: *Unemployed roadsweeper Mickey Reid hit the jackpot when his £4 lottery ticket won him £1.8 million.*

jelly
○ **turn to 'jelly**
You say that a part of your body **has turned to jelly** if it feels weak and shaky, usually because you are nervous, afraid, or tired: *She had to lean against him in order to remain upright. Her limbs trembled, the muscles turned to jelly.*

jig
○ **the 'jig is up** (*AmE*; *informal*)
The jig is up when something, especially an illegal activity, is ended or fails: *When the police discovered the stolen goods, Alan knew the jig was up.*

job
○ **do the 'job**
Something, usually an object, that **does the job** solves a practical problem: *It's difficult to get rid of rats, but a good brand of rat poison should probably do the job.* ♦ *see also* **do the trick** ▷TRICK

○ **do a good 'job**
You say that someone **is doing a good job** if they are doing something well: *I'm surprised that you are so critical. I think she's doing a very good job as councillor.*

○ **give something up as a bad 'job**
You **give something up as a bad job** when you decide that there is no point in continuing with it, as there are too many problems involved: *At around six o'clock Pooley gave the whole thing up as a bad job and went home.*

○ **have a 'job** (*informal*)
You **have a job** doing something if it is difficult to do: *You can try and persuade her to come, but you'll have a job.*

○ **it's a good 'job** (*informal*)
You say '**it's a good job**' if you think it is lucky that something is the case: *It's a good job you've come round today, because I'm going on holiday tomorrow.* ♦ *see also* **just as well** ▷ WELL

○ **just the 'job**
Something that is **just the job** is exactly what you need: *This screwdriver with the short handle is just the job for getting into tight little corners.*

○ **make the best of a bad 'job**
You **make the best of a bad job** when you do your best to make an unpleasant situation as pleasant or as tolerable as possible: *Look, why don't we just make the best of a bad job and book into a nice hotel for the night?*

○ **on the 'job**
1 If somebody is doing something which is not permitted while they are supposed to be working, they are doing it **on the job**: *The control room staff were found to be falling asleep on the job.* **2** You learn how to do something **on the job** when you learn it by experiencing the reality of the workplace, rather than through theoretical lessons in a college, for example: *They will be spending 80% of their time in schools learning on the job, instead of listening to lectures on education theory.*

joke
○ **beyond a 'joke**
Something is **beyond a joke** when it has become unacceptable: *The noise coming from the flat next door is getting beyond a joke. What are we going to do about it?*

○ **crack a 'joke**
To **crack a joke** is to make an amusing or witty comment: *All the boys were laughing and cracking jokes.*

○ **no 'joke** (*informal*)
Something that is **no joke** is unpleasant or difficult: *It's no joke getting up at five in the morning if you've had too much to drink the night before.*

○ **see the 'joke**
You **see the joke** when you realize that something, especially an awkward or unpleasant situation that you are in, is quite funny: *The other men laughed too. Plummer didn't see the joke and glanced round irritably, waiting until they calmed down.* ♦ *see also* **see the funny side** ▷ SIDE

○ **take a 'joke**
Someone who can **take a joke** is able to laugh at jokes that other people make about them: *Oh, come on. You know I didn't mean it when I said you were fat. Can't you take a joke?*

joking
○ **joking a'side** or **joking a'part**
If you want to stop being funny and talk about something seriously, you say '**joking aside**', or '**joking apart**': *Yes, I just sit in front of the fire in my rocking chair all day, knitting for my grandchildren! No, joking apart, I have found it hard to adjust to being retired.*

○ **you're 'joking** or **you must be 'joking**
1 '**You're joking**' or '**you must be joking**' are expressions of surprise or disbelief: *'The President died this morning.' 'You're joking.' 'No, really. It's true.'* **2** You also say '**you must be joking**' to someone when you are opposing, or refusing to do, something they have suggested because you consider it to be unreasonable: *'I'll invite them to dinner.' 'You must be joking. They stayed till three in the morning the last time.'* ♦ *see also* **you're kidding** or **you must be kidding** ▷ KIDDING

Joneses
○ **keep up with the 'Joneses**
When people try to **keep up with the Joneses**, their competitive nature makes them try to do the same things

that their neighbours or friends have done, only better: *Poorer families who see the superior goods being consumed by their richer neighbours may attempt to 'keep up with the Joneses'.* ♦ see also **go one better** ▷BETTER

> **The Joneses** here refers to a hypothetical family whose surname is 'Jones'.

joy

○ no 'joy (*BrE*)
You say '**no joy**' to report that you have not had the luck, news or information which you were hoping for: *'Did you find one?' 'No joy. Everything's closed.'*

juice

○ stew in your own 'juice
A person who **is stewing in their own juice** is being forced to spend some time alone, giving them an opportunity to realize that their bad situation is the result of their own actions: *She was still standing there now, waiting impatiently. She suspected he was enjoying letting her stew in her own juice.*

jump

○ for the 'high jump
You say that someone is **for the high jump** if they are going to be punished or get into serious trouble for something they have done: *You'll be for the high jump when mum finds out.*

○ get the 'jump on someone or have the 'jump on someone (*AmE*; *informal*)
You **get**, or **have**, **the jump on someone** when you have an advantage over them because you began before they did: *We left at four o'clock to get the jump on the commuters.*

○ 'jump to it
If you tell someone to **jump to it**, you are ordering them to hurry up and do what they have been told: *Come on, lads, jump to it. We don't have time to sit about chatting all day.*

○ on the 'jump (*AmE*)
If you are **on the jump**, you are moving about in a quick and busy manner: *When the governor visited, we were on the jump all day.*

○ take a running 'jump or take a running jump in the 'lake (*AmE*) (*offensive*)
If you tell someone to **take a running jump**, or **take a running jump in the lake**, you are telling them rudely to go away and leave you alone: *'Can you be quiet?' 'Oh, take a running jump.'*

just

○ just a'bout
You use '**just about**' when the state or level of something is almost exactly that mentioned: *Okay, everyone, don't give up. We're just about there now.*

○ just 'so
1 You have everything **just so** when you have arranged everything exactly as you want it: *He's such a neat and tidy person. Everything has to be just so.* **2** (*formal, old*) You say '**just so**' if you want to express your agreement with the thing that someone has just said: *'In my opinion, there is no advantage to be gained from rushing into a decision.' 'Just so, just so.'* ♦ see also **that's just it** ▷JUST; **too right** ▷RIGHT

○ that's just 'it
You say '**that's just it**' when someone makes a statement which you **1** agree with completely: *'She's growing up.' 'That's just it. She's much more mature.'* **2** disagree with completely: *'I understand what you're going through.' 'That's just it. You don't understand.'* ♦ see also **just so** ▷JUST; **too right** ▷RIGHT

keel

○ on an even 'keel
Someone or something is **on an even keel** if they are in a normal, calm state: *The right politician must be put in charge of the Treasury to bring the economy back to an even keel.*

When the **keel** of a boat is even, it is level or horizontal in the water, allowing the boat to move forward in a steady way.

keep

○ **keep a'breast of something**
You **keep abreast of** a situation which is changing if you keep yourself properly informed of any developments in that situation: *Representative staff will keep abreast of national developments by attending conferences and by visiting other schools.*

○ **keep 'at it**
You **keep at it** if you continue doing something, especially working at something, until you finish the activity or succeed: *Even if it sometimes seems you are getting nowhere with this treatment, you should keep at it.* ♦ *see also* **never say die** ▷SAY

○ **keep it 'up**
You **are keeping it up** if you manage to continue doing something at the same speed or as regularly as you are doing it at present: *This exercise will help if you do it regularly and keep it up for several months.*

○ **keep to your'self** or **keep yourself to your'self**
You **keep to yourself**, or **keep yourself to yourself**, when you avoid other people and spend most of your time alone: *He was a studious boy, with no friends, who kept himself to himself.*

○ **keep something to your'self**
You **keep something to yourself** when you do not tell anyone about it: *Even if you are sure you are pregnant, you should try to keep it to yourself for the first month.* ♦ *see also* **keep it under your hat** ▷HAT

kettle

○ **kettle of 'fish**
1 A pretty, or a fine, **kettle of fish** is a complicated and awkward situation: *As if to herself, she added: 'This is a fine kettle of fish.' And turning back to me: 'You'll do something, eh? Arrange something?'* **2** If you say 'that's a different **kettle of fish**', you mean 'that changes the situation completely'; a person who

is described as a different **kettle of fish** is very different from others, or from someone else who they are being compared to: *But Kate, she was a different kettle of fish altogether. They discussed everything under the sun.* ♦ *see also* **a whole new** or **a completely different ball game** or **a different ball game altogether** ▷BALL

keyed

○ **keyed 'up**
You say someone **is keyed up** if they are excited and nervous: *He had been keyed up, expecting just such a confrontation.*

kick

○ **for a 'kick-off** (*BrE; informal*)
You say '**for a kick-off**' to emphasize that what you are saying is just the first in a list of arguments or complaints: *'What's wrong?' 'Well, I don't feel great for a kick-off ... and I had a bit of bad news this morning.'* ♦ *see also* **for starters** ▷STARTERS

○ **kick-'start something**
An action or event **kick-starts something** if it suddenly gives that thing extra energy to help it recover from certain problems: *The Chancellor's new policy was designed to kick-start the economy.*

You **kick-start** a motorbike by jumping with a lot of force on a pedal which starts the motor.

○ **'kick yourself**
You say you **are kicking yourself** if you are annoyed with yourself for making a mistake or doing something stupid: *I'm never careful enough about the details, and then I end up kicking myself.*

kid (*see also* **kidding**)

○ **I kid you 'not**
You say '**I kid you not**' when you want to emphasize that what you are telling someone is true, even though it may be difficult to believe: *She always sent me Californian poppy bath salts for Christmas. I kid you not, each year.*

kidding

○ **no 'kidding?**
You say '**no kidding?**' to someone when they have just said something

surprising, and you are checking that it is true: *'My dad knew Elvis Presley before he was famous.' 'No kidding?'*

○ you're 'kidding or you must be 'kidding

1 You say '**you're kidding**' or '**you must be kidding**' to someone when they have just said something surprising: *'Gerry told me last night he wants a divorce.' 'You're kidding.' 'No. He says he's met someone else.'* **2** You say '**you must be kidding**' to someone when you are opposing, or refusing to do, the thing which they suggest because you consider it to be unreasonable: *'Get on my back and I'll carry you across.' 'You've got to be kidding. I'd rather get wet feet, thanks.'* ♦ *see also* **you're joking** or **you must be joking** ▷ JOKING

killing

○ make a 'killing

You **make a killing** when you make a lot of money quickly: *We can make an absolute killing by taking a percentage of the profits, and charging them rent.* ♦ *see also* **make a bundle** ▷ BUNDLE; **make your pile** ▷ PILE

kind

○ in 'kind

1 If you pay someone **in kind**, you give them something other than money in exchange for their goods or services: *Will you accept rent-free accommodation as payment in kind for the work you do?* **2** You repay someone who has treated you badly **in kind** if you react by treating them badly too.

○ 'kind of (*informal*)

1 '**Kind of**' (or **kinda**) means 'rather' or 'a bit': *I'd like to come, but I feel kind of tired tonight.* **2** You use '**a kind of**' when giving a rough description or idea of something: *The pudding was a kind of cheesecakey thing, but without a cheesecake base.* ♦ *see also* **sort of** ▷ SORT

○ nothing of the 'kind

'**Nothing of the kind**' means 'not at all the thing just mentioned': *'You said you would be willing to stand down as Prime Minister.' 'I said nothing of the kind.'* ♦ *see also* **nothing of the sort** ▷ SORT

○ of a 'kind

1 You say that a small number of people

or objects are two, three, etc, **of a kind** if they are the same as, or similar to, one another: *In the card game cribbage, three of a kind (three kings, for example) gives you six points.* **2** Something described as a thing **of a kind** is not a very good one: *The Prime Minister has given us a statement of a kind, but he still hasn't answered our questions.*

kindly

○ not take 'kindly to something

When you say that you **do not take kindly to something**, you are saying that you find that thing hard to accept because you dislike or feel insulted by it: *He doesn't take kindly to being told he's put on weight.* ♦ *see also* **take exception to something** ▷ EXCEPTION

kingdom

○ till kingdom 'come

You are doing something **till kingdom come** if you continue with it for a long time without getting the results you hope for: *At this rate we could be waiting till kingdom come for a pay rise.*

> In the Lord's Prayer, Christians look forward to the future with the words '**thy kingdom come**'.

○ to kingdom 'come

Someone goes, or is sent, **to kingdom come** if they are killed violently, especially by an explosion of some kind: *He'd started to forget things, see. Left the gas on, things like that. He nearly blew us all to kingdom come once.*

kiss

○ kiss good'bye to something or kiss something good'bye

To **kiss goodbye to something**, or **kiss something goodbye**, is to accept that a change in the situation means you can no longer have or do something which you had been hoping for: *With this latest scandal, he can kiss goodbye to his chances of taking power.*

○ the kiss of 'death

The **kiss of death** is an action which is meant to be helpful to someone, but which in fact does them a lot of harm: *A reference from your boss would be the kiss of death. I mean it. Everyone in the business hates him.*

kit

○ **the whole kit and ca'boodle** (*informal*)

'The whole kit and caboodle' means everyone or everything: *When Uncle Andy died, he left the whole kit and caboodle to me.*

kite

○ **go fly a 'kite** (*AmE*) (*insulting*)

If you tell someone to **go fly a kite**, you are telling them to go away and stop bothering you: *'Hey, Jimmy, what can we do now?' 'I know what you can do. You can go fly a kite.'*

knee

○ **on bended 'knee** or **on your bended 'knee**

You ask for something **on**, or **on your**, **bended knee** if you ask for it in a humble way: *I beg you, on bended knee, to forgive me.* ♦ *see also* **cap in hand** ▷CAP

The past participle of the verb 'bend' is normally 'bent', not 'bended'. '**Bended**' is an old form.

---

knees

○ **bring someone to their 'knees**

A situation **brings someone to their knees** if it weakens, defeats or destroys them: *The loss of its biggest contract brought the company to its knees.*

○ **on your 'knees**

You are **on your knees** when you are kneeling, or when you are desperately asking someone to do something: *I fell on my knees and asked them not to punish the child any more. They seemed to understand.*

knickers

○ **get your 'knickers in a twist** (*BrE*)

You **get your knickers in a twist** when you are unable to relax and behave in a sensible way because you are so worried or upset: *I've been getting my knickers in a twist about work. It's stupid of me, because it's not that important.*

knife

○ **have your knife into someone**

Someone who **has got their knife into you** is always trying to harm or upset you: *The only reason she's got her knife into 'me is because she's so jealous.*

○ **under the 'knife**

You say that someone is going **under the knife** when they are going to have an operation: *'I go into hospital on Monday, and under the knife on Friday.'*

knight

○ **knight in shining 'armour** (*humorous*)

Your **knight in shining armour** is someone who saves you from a situation which you had thought was hopeless: *The police became knights in shining armour yesterday as they went to the rescue of a young German woman injured on a mountain top.*

In traditional folk tales, handsome knights saved young women from terrible and dangerous situations.

---

knock

○ **knock 'em 'dead** (*informal*)

You say '**knock 'em dead!**' to someone who is about to give a performance, as a way of encouraging them to perform as well as possible.

○ **knock someone for 'six** (*BrE*)

Something which **knocks you for six** surprises or shocks you so much that you are unable to think clearly: *It knocked me for six when she told me she was pregnant. I didn't know what to say.*

○ **knock it 'off** (*informal*)

You say '**knock it off!**' to someone if you want them to stop doing something which is annoying you: *Knock it off, will you? Some people are trying to sleep round here.* ♦ *see also* **give me a break** ▷BREAK; **give it a rest** ▷REST

knot (*see also* knots)

○ **tie the 'knot**

You say you **are tying the knot** when you get married: *We met four years ago, and we tied the knot last June.*

knots

○ **tie yourself in 'knots**

You **are tying yourself in knots** when the harder you try to express yourself, the more difficult it becomes to do so: *He's been tying himself in knots all day, working out how he would tell you about the accident.*

know

○ **before you know where you 'are**

Something happens **before you know**

where you are if it happens so quickly that you do not have time to understand the problem or situation properly: *Imagine you won the national lottery. Suddenly, before you knew where you were, you'd be rich.*

○ **in the 'know**
A person who is **in the know** about something is one of the few people who have information about it: *Those in the know say that she had good reasons for resigning.*

○ **know something 'backwards**
You **know something backwards** when you know it well and in great detail: *We'd studied the novel till we knew it backwards.*

> In American English you can also say **know something backwards and forwards** or **know something backward and forward.**

○ **know 'better**
1 You **know better**, or **know better than to do something** if you realize you should not do it: *He knows better than to allow a confrontation to develop between himself and his predecessor.* **2** Someone who **knows better** than others has information that they do not have, and therefore can judge the situation better: *Everyone else thought he was ill in bed, but I knew better.*

○ **not know whether you are coming or 'going**
You say you **do not know whether you are coming or going** when you are feeling completely confused.

○ **you never 'know**
1 You say **'you never know'** if you are acting to avoid a possible danger or problem: *I always use condoms. Well, you never know, do you?* **2** You say **'you never know'** if you consider that the event just mentioned is not impossible: *'Will you have time to visit us this summer?' 'I might just manage, you never know.'* ♦ *see also* **better safe than sorry** ▷BETTER

knowledge

○ **have a 'working knowledge of something**
You **have a working knowledge of**

something if you know enough about it to be able to use it, without being an expert on it: *I have a working knowledge of several wordprocessing packages.*

○ **to the best of your 'knowledge**
You say that something is true **to the best of your knowledge** if you are almost but not completely sure that it is true: *These facts were, to the best of my knowledge, true when I made the speech a week ago.*

laid

○ **get 'laid** (*vulgar*)
Someone **gets laid** when they have sex with someone with whom they are not already in an established relationship.

lam

○ **on the 'lam** (*AmE*; *informal*)
Someone who is **on the lam** has run away, usually from the police: *They knew who had stolen the car, but he had been on the lam for a week.*

○ **take it on the 'lam** (*AmE*; *informal*)
If someone has **taken it on the lam**, they have escaped from someone who is looking for them, especially the police: *Two patrol cars went to the suspect's house, but he had taken it on the lam.*

land

○ **land someone 'in it**
You **land someone in it** when you reveal something about them that was supposed to be kept a secret, or if you get them into a difficult situation: *Why did you go and land me in it? I'll never be able to get myself out of this one.*

○ **the land of the 'living**
You are in **the land of the living** if you are alive, when you may be expected to

be otherwise: *Only the odd bouts of involuntary twitching in his sleep reassured his owner that Jess was still safe and sound in the land of the living.*

lane
○ 'land someone one

You **land someone one** when you hit them: *Mark landed John one right in the face.*

lane
○ the 'fast lane

Someone who lives their life in **the fast lane** has a very busy, competitive and risky lifestyle: *His face was beginning to show the strain of a life in the fast lane.*

> On a motorway, **the fast lane** is the section of the road designated for fast drivers.

language
○ speak the same 'language or **talk the same 'language**

Two people **speak**, or **talk**, **the same language** when they understand and relate to each other very well: *Like any hobby it's vital that we speak the same language, understand the same terms.*

lap
○ drop into someone's 'lap

Something **drops into your lap** when it comes to you or arrives without you having to make any effort to get it: *This chance of a lifetime, he appreciated, had dropped miraculously into his lap.*

> Your **lap** is formed by the upper parts of your legs which are horizontal when you are sitting on a chair.

○ in the lap of the 'gods

You say that the result of a particular situation is **in the lap of the gods** if it depends on luck, or on circumstances outside your control: *The result of tomorrow's match is in the lap of the gods.*

○ in the lap of 'luxury

You live **in the lap of luxury** if you live in great comfort, especially when it is provided by expensive, beautiful surroundings and objects: *There will always be a need for socialism, so long as there are millionaires living in the lap of luxury and other people living in cardboard boxes.*

large
○ at 'large

A dangerous person or animal that is **at large** has escaped from prison or captivity and has not yet been recaptured: *'You don't think that fellow Burrows could have done it?' asked Frobisher. 'From what I gather, he's still at large.'*

○ by and 'large

Something that is so **by and large** is so in a general way: *By and large we don't have too many problems with absence in our office.*

last
○ last but not 'least

Last but not least is used before mentioning a person or thing that is last in a list, in order to emphasize that they are as important as those mentioned before: *Manifestos and artists' statements, interviews, catalogues, biographies, chronologies, memoirs, and, last but not least, exhibition catalogues and survey books abound.*

○ too good to 'last

You say that a favourable situation is **too good to last** when you feel, pessimistically, that it cannot continue because someone will want to spoil it: *She wept and said she had always known it was too good to last, and went off back home to her mother.*

laugh
○ for a 'laugh

You do something **for a laugh** when you do it for fun or as a joke: *When asked their reasons for stealing the car, the boys said they just did it for a laugh.*

○ have the last 'laugh

You **have the last laugh** when you are finally proved right or succeed in the end: *Yet women drivers have the last laugh. They get cheaper insurance rates because their accident records are better.*

laurels
○ look to your 'laurels

If you tell someone to **look to their laurels**, you mean that they should be careful not to lose a position or reputation because of better performances by others: *I feel sure their new white wines* *will soon be making the French look to their laurels.*

In ancient Greece the winner of a competition received a crown made of laurel leaves.

○ **rest on your 'laurels**
Someone who has been successful is said to **be resting on their laurels** if they are relying on their reputation rather than trying to progress further: *In her famed speech on election night 1987, she encouraged her party troops not to rest on their laurels, but to continue the fight.*

law

○ **a law unto your'self**
Someone who is described as **a law unto themselves** does not follow conventional rules and ways of behaving: *Conventions didn't exist for her. She was a law unto herself and did what she wanted to do.*

○ **lay down the 'law**
Someone **lays down the law** when they state something in a way that indicates that they expect their opinion and orders to be accepted without argument: *I am not attempting to lay down the law, but simply wish to voice my opinion that ethics should be the first guideline of those dealing with public resources.*

○ **take the law into your own 'hands**
Someone **takes the law into their own hands** when they decide to punish someone themselves, rather than following official legal procedures: *Donna, you can't take the law into your own hands. This isn't some bloody film.*

lay

○ **lay it on 'thick**
You **lay it on thick** when you **1** try to gain people's sympathy by exaggerating your misfortune. **2** praise someone or something highly in order to obtain something from them: *'How well you look!' she exclaimed, determined to lay it on thick to please him.*

○ **lay someone 'low**
An illness **lays someone low** when it stops them from being able to do what they usually do: *Gooch had his infa-*

mous encounter with a poisonous prawn that laid him low for several days.

○ **lay someone 'open to something**
A circumstance **lays you open to** criticism or attack if it puts you in danger of being criticized or attacked: *This decision would lay him open to accusations of favouritism or vindictiveness.*

lead¹

○ **lead a'stray**
You **lead someone astray** when you teach them bad habits, or are responsible for making them do something wrong: *Teenagers are fiercely independent, but the risks of being led astray are also much greater at this age.*

lead²

○ **swing the 'lead**
Someone **swings the lead** when they try to avoid working, or invent excuses to hide the fact that they have neglected their work: *I'm not swinging the lead, my doctor sent me here. He says that there is something wrong with me.*

leaf

○ **take a leaf out of 'so-and-so's book**
You **take a leaf out of** a certain person's **book** when you use them as a good example, and try to copy something that they do: *Take a leaf out of my book. Give up smoking.* ♦ *see also* **follow suit** ▷SUIT

Leaf is an old-fashioned word for a page.

○ **turn over a new 'leaf**
You **turn over a new leaf** when you begin a new and better way of behaving or working: *Seems he's decided to turn over a new leaf – let's hope it lasts.* ♦ *see also* **change your ways** ▷WAYS

league

○ **in a different 'league** or **not in the same 'league as someone**
Someone or something that is **in a different league from**, or **not in the same league as**, someone or something else, does not reach that thing's or person's standard: *Their clothes are cheaper, but then they're not in the same league as Armani.* ♦ *see also* **in a class of your own** ▷CLASS; **a cut above** or **a cut above the rest** ▷CUT

○ **out of your 'league** (*AmE*)

You are **out of your league** when you cannot handle a situation, especially because you lack the experience or skills necessary: *They promoted Rick to vice president, but he was out of his league.* ♦ *see also* **out of your depth** ▷DEPTH

leagues

○ **play in the 'big leagues** (*AmE*)

If you **play in the big leagues**, you are part of an important organization or activity: *You need to meet the right people if you want to play in the big leagues.*

> In American baseball, the major leagues are informally called '**the big leagues**'.

lean

○ **lean over 'backwards** or (*AmE*) **lean over 'backward**

You **lean over backwards**, or **lean over backward**, to help someone, when you do everything you can to help them: *We had support, people helping us and advising us; they leant over backwards to help us.* ♦ *see also* **bend over backwards** ▷BEND

leaps

○ **in leaps and 'bounds** (*BrE*) or **by leaps and 'bounds**

Someone or something progresses **in**, or **by**, **leaps and bounds**, when they move forward quickly and successfully: *It was a great learning experience, but I wasn't moving in leaps and bounds; I wanted to really progress.*

lease

○ **a new lease of 'life**

You get **a new lease of life** when you suddenly feel energetic or enthusiastic again after a period of tiredness or boredom: *Ironically, since the accident, their marriage has gained a new lease of life.*

least

○ **in the 'least**

You use '**in the least**' to emphasize a statement in the negative: *She wasn't in the least surprised to hear the news.*

○ **least of 'all**

Least of all emphasizes a particular person or thing to which a negative statement applies: *'You see dears,' said the old lady, 'no-one, least of all a great detective, believes what they read in the newspapers.'*

○ **to say the 'least**

If something is so **to say the least**, the situation is actually more extreme than that: *The instructions are confusing, to say the least.*

leave

○ **leave 'be** or **leave well a'lone** or (*AmE*) **leave well enough a'lone**

1 You **leave** someone or something **be**, or **leave** them **well alone**, when you do not get involved with them, or allow the situation to remain as it is, so as not to make it worse: *'Leave him be, for the moment,' Madeleine advised, 'and he'll be all right.'* **2** You **leave** something **well enough alone** when you do not get involved with it: *Leave that wasp nest well enough alone and you won't get stung.*

○ **leave a lot to be de'sired** or **leave something to be de'sired**

Something that **leaves a lot**, or **something, to be desired** does not reach the standard you would like or expect it to reach: *He explained they had all been up late the night before and that their performance might leave something to be desired. It did.*

○ **leave someone 'standing** (*BrE*)

You **leave someone standing** when you are much better than them at something.

○ **take leave of your 'senses**

You say that someone **has taken leave of their senses** if they have done something which makes you think they must have gone mad: *Her daughter had taken leave of her senses and her husband was never at home when he was needed. The world had gone mad.*

leg (*see also* legs)

○ **give someone a 'leg-up**

You **give someone a leg-up** when you **1** help them to climb over something. **2** help them to improve their situation at work, for example: *This offers the opportunity to develop new skills, as well as giving some a leg-up into an acting career.*

○ **not have a leg to 'stand on**
You say that someone **does not have a leg to stand on** if you think that their behaviour or opinions cannot be supported by facts or evidence.

○ **pull someone's 'leg**
You **pull someone's leg** when you try to make them believe something which is not true, as a joke: *'You're pulling my leg!' Did he really expect her to believe such nonsense?*

○ **shake a 'leg**
You tell someone to **shake a leg** when you want them to hurry up.

○ **talk the hind leg off a 'donkey**
Someone who can, could, or would, **talk the hind leg off a donkey** talks a lot: *That man would talk the hind leg off a donkey, does he never stop?*

legs

○ **be on your last 'legs**
You are **on your last legs** when you are so tired or old that you can hardly continue what you are doing: *Anyone reading the papers would think I was on my last legs. Where did these journalists get their information?*

○ **stretch your 'legs**
You **stretch your legs** when you walk around and get some exercise and fresh air after having spent a long time in the same position: *We pulled over at a roadside café to have a cup of coffee and to stretch our legs.*

lend

○ **'lend itself to**
Something **lends itself to** being used or dealt with in a particular way if it can easily be used or dealt with in that way: *Negotiating is an art, not a science. But it does lend itself to careful analysis and preparation too.*

lengths

○ **go to great 'lengths** or **go to any 'lengths**
You **go to great lengths** to do or achieve something when you take a lot of trouble over it; someone who is prepared to **go to any lengths** to achieve something is determined to achieve it by whatever means may be necessary: *To fulfil his ambition he was prepared to go to any lengths, no matter how underhand or devious they might be.* ♦ *see also*

push the boat out ▷BOAT; **go to town on something** ▷TOWN; **go out of your way** ▷WAY

leopard

○ **a leopard never changes its 'spots**
'A leopard never changes its spots' means that people's characters are unlikely to change: *'A leopard can't change his spots' and other maxims take an essentially pessimistic view about people's ability to change their behaviour.* ♦ *see also* **you can't teach an old dog new tricks** ▷DOG

less

○ **no 'less**
You add '**no less**' after mentioning someone or something in order to emphasize their importance: *When you get to my age, you get a telegram from the Queen, no less.*

This expression is often used ironically, for humorous effect.

lesson

○ **learn your 'lesson**
You **learn your lesson** when you realize that you should not have done something, probably because it has harmed you or someone else, and you decide not to do it again: *I've learnt my lesson. I realize what a fool I was, throwing myself at you the way I did.*

○ **teach someone a 'lesson**
You **teach someone a lesson** when you try to make sure they will not do something bad or wrong again by punishing them: *She had let me down one too many times, and I decided to teach her a lesson.*

let

○ **let 'fly**
You **let fly** at someone when you suddenly become very angry with them: *He had a tendency to let fly for seemingly no reason at all.* ♦ *see also* **go off at the deep end** ▷END; **blow a fuse** ▷FUSE; **blow** or **flip your lid** ▷LID; **do your nut** ▷NUT; **lose your rag** ▷RAG; **fly into a rage** ▷RAGE; **hit the roof** ▷ ROOF; **blow your stack** ▷STACK; **lose your temper** ▷TEMPER; **blow your top** ▷ TOP; **throw a wobbly** ▷WOBBLY

○ **let it 'drop**
You **let it drop** when you stop talking about something because it is not having any effect: *But don't think I'm going to let it drop. I'll find out your reasons, one way or another.*

○ **let 'rip**
You **let rip** when you do something as loudly or as fast as possible: *She turned to the keyboard and let rip: the noise nearly blew me off the balcony.*

○ **let's 'see** or **let me 'see**
You say **'let's see'** or **'let me see'** when you are thinking or trying to remember something: *There must have been, let me see, at least 200 people there.*

○ **let something 'slide**
You **let something slide** when you neglect it and cause its standard to drop: *I noticed he's been letting things slide, but I didn't realize he was so depressed.*

○ **let something 'slip**
If you **let** a piece of secret information **slip**, you tell someone about it unintentionally: *Try not to let it slip that we're organizing something – I'd really like it to be a surprise.*

letter

○ **the letter of the 'law**
If you follow **the letter of the law**, you act according to its exact words, rather than its general meaning: *What the Leeds manager appeared to be saying was that he was glad to see a referee not sticking rigidly to the letter of the law.*

○ **to the 'letter**
You follow instructions, for example, **to the letter** when you follow them exactly, paying attention to every detail: *I don't understand it – I followed your guidelines to the letter, and it still doesn't work.*

level

○ **on the 'level** (*informal*)
Someone or something that is **on the level** is honest or genuine: *Are you sure this deal is on the level? I don't know if I can trust Holt.*

○ **sink to 'such-and-such a level**
Someone **sinks to** a certain **level** when they do something shameful: *Don't sink to their level. If that's the way they behave, it doesn't mean you have to do the same.*

liberties

○ **take 'liberties**
Someone who **takes liberties** expects too much freedom, or does not treat other people or their possessions with enough respect: *I didn't mind at first, but he's started taking liberties now that he knows I'm easy-going.*

lid

○ **blow the 'lid off something** or **take the 'lid off something**
You **blow**, or **take**, **the lid off** a scandal, for example, when you expose it to the public.

○ **blow your 'lid** or **flip your 'lid**
You **blow**, or **flip**, **your lid** when you suddenly become very angry: *This was his moment of weakness, the point at which he'd flipped his lid for the first and last time in his career.* ♦ *see also* **go off at the deep end** ▷END; **blow a fuse** ▷FUSE; **let fly** ▷LET; **do your nut** ▷NUT; **lose your rag** ▷RAG; **fly into a rage** ▷RAGE; **hit the roof** ▷ ROOF; **blow your stack** ▷STACK; **lose your temper** ▷TEMPER; **blow your top** ▷ TOP; **throw a wobbly** ▷WOBBLY

○ **keep the 'lid on something**
You **keep the lid on something** when you try to ensure that people do not find out about it or that they do not do something undesirable: *In 1989, the Government had to appoint a special minister to keep the lid on the transport scandal.*

lie

○ **I tell a 'lie** (*informal*)
You say **'I tell a lie'** when you are about to correct something you have just said: *I got home at 6 o'clock, no, I tell a lie, 7 o'clock.*

○ **lie 'low**
You **lie low** when you hide from someone in order to avoid getting caught: *At the time of the murder he appears to have been lying low in a barn near Leeds.*

○ **the lie of the 'land** or (*AmE*) **the lay of the 'land**
You investigate **the lie of the land**, or **the lay of the land**, when you try to find out the details of a situation before taking action.

○ **live a 'lie**
Someone who **is living a lie** is deceiv-

ing everyone about who they are or what they are doing: *It was the guilt of living a lie for 50 years that forced moral adviser Marje Proops into confessing her secret love affair.*

life

○ **breathe 'life into something** or **bring something to 'life**

Someone **breathes life into something**, or **brings something to life**, when they make it more lively, interesting or attractive; something **comes to life** when it is caused to become more lively, interesting or attractive: *Bogart was just the type of actor needed to breathe life into this kind of story.* ◻ *The road was screened by another brick wall, topped with trellis, brought to life by a mass of climbers and a large purple flowered lilac.*

○ **can't do such-and-such to save your 'life**

You say that you **can't do such-and-such to save your life** if you cannot do it at all, or if you do it very badly: *I can't sing to save my life.*

○ **for dear 'life**

You do something **for dear life** when you do it as forcefully or as firmly as you can: *In the mountains of Greece the passengers cling on for dear life and make the sign of the cross at every bend in the road.* ♦ *see also* **hang** or **hold on like grim death** ▷DEATH

○ **for the 'life of me**

You say you cannot remember, or understand, something **for the life of you** to emphasize the difficulty you are having remembering, or understanding, it: *To that vile city of yours! I can't for the life of me understand what it is you see in it. It's filthy!*

○ **get a 'life** (*informal*)

If you tell someone to **'get a life'**, you mean that they should stop behaving in a ridiculous, pathetic or foolish way, because you have no respect for, or patience with, them.

○ **give your 'life for** or **lay down your 'life for**

A person **gives**, or **lays down**, their **life for** something when they die for something they believe in very strongly: *I mean to lay down my life that*

men like you can live in freedom to fight for what is right in the world.

○ **larger than 'life**

You describe someone as **larger than life** if they have a strong, vibrant personality; something that is **larger than life** makes a very strong impression on you: *She was larger than life, she was game for anything, she was jolly and vibrant, spoke her mind; all in all, she was fun to be with.*

○ **the life and 'soul**

You describe someone as **the life and soul** of a party, for example, if they are the most lively and enthusiastic person there, and their good mood makes other people feel the same way: *She appeared laughing with the other women, toasting Alex in lemonade, her eyes glinting, the life and soul of the party.*

○ **'low life**

'Low life' refers to the lives of people who exist through crime, possibly take drugs, and generally live in a way that other people disapprove of: *Then comes the train journey to Chicago, the low life amid the bright lights.*

○ **not on your 'life**

'Not on your life' means 'certainly not': *No! I ain't going there. Not on your life.*

○ **take your life in your 'hands** or **take your life into your own 'hands**

You **take your life in your hands**, or **take your life into your own hands**, when you take the risk of being killed or attacked: *I knew every driver in that race was taking his life in his hands to the most ludicrous degree.*

○ **there's life in the old dog 'yet** (*humorous*)

You say **'there's life in the old dog yet'** to express surprise that although someone or something is old, they still have a lot of energy or strength left in them; old people sometimes say it about themselves when other people doubt their abilities: *In Britain, Italy and Greece, the left tops the opinion polls. There's life in the old dog yet.*

○ **true to 'life**

Something such as a painting or story that is described as **true to life** closely resembles reality: *These portraits ap-*

pear to modern eyes reassuringly true to life and easy to understand.

light (*see also* **lights**)

○ **bring something to 'light**
If facts **are brought to light**, or if they **come to light**, they become known: *Part of the scandal only came to light when an observant bank clerk spotted changes made to the information on an authorized cheque.*

○ **cast 'light on something** or **shed 'light on something** or **throw 'light on something**
Someone or something that **casts**, or **sheds**, or **throws**, **light on** a situation provides information which makes it easier to understand: *Are there elements in your upbringing which help to explain or cast light on who you are and how you behave and respond?*

○ **first 'light**
First light is the time in the morning when the sun has just come up: *In the first light of morning he had got up to see what the village might have looked like before.*

○ **give the green 'light to**
You **give the green light to** someone when you allow them to do something: *At this Annual General Meeting in May 1983, the green light for change was finally given.*

○ **go out like a 'light**
You **go out like a light** when you go to sleep as soon as you get into bed: *Either it was the brandy or it was the heat, but she went out like a light.*

○ **hide your light under a 'bushel**
Someone who **hides their light under a bushel** does not reveal their talents to other people because they are modest: *And how has she achieved all this? 'Joan hides her light under a bushel' says one who knows her well.*

○ **in a bad 'light**
A report or story about someone or something shows them **in a bad light** if it gives the impression that they are bad.

○ **in the cold light of 'day**
You consider something **in the cold light of day** when you consider it calmly and logically, especially after having first considered it while in a

state of excitement: *In the cold light of day it seems incredible that I fell to my knees in such a manner.*

○ **in a good 'light**
Someone or something is seen **in a good light** if their good qualities are made to be particularly evident.

○ **in the light of 'such-and-such**
You make a decision **in the light of** a particular fact, when you base your decision on that knowledge: *In the light of what we have just heard, I think it would be wise to reassess our decision.*

○ **leading 'light**
A **leading light** is an important or respected member of a group: *The leading light of the animal welfare revival was Jeremy Bentham.*

○ **the light at the end of the 'tunnel**
Someone who is carrying out a long or difficult task can see **the light at the end of the tunnel** when they start to see the possibility of success, or of an end to their suffering: *This is definitely the worst recession I have seen. Few see light at the end of the tunnel, whatever the election result.*

○ **the light of someone's 'life** (*humorous*)
If you describe someone as **the light of your life**, you mean, humorously, that they are the person you love and care for most: *Oh yes, he was the light of my life, Walter Machin. I used to watch his every movement.*

○ **make 'light of something**
You **make light of** a problem or a mistake that someone has made when you show, or give the impression, that you do not think it is important: *But Kendall's men made light of any suggestion of a crisis with an irresistible first-half display.*

○ **see the 'light**
You **see the light 1** when you suddenly understand or accept something: *It took him a while, but he's finally seen the light and started doing some work.* **2** when you suddenly change your beliefs as a result of a religious experience: *She told me she saw the light after the tragic death of her husband.*

lightning

○ **like greased 'lightning**
You move **like greased lightning**

IDIOMS *study*   liking and not liking

The next time you write or talk about **liking and not liking** you might try to use some of the following idioms. (Remember you can see how to use each idiom correctly by looking at its entry, which you can find under the word printed in heavy type.)

liking someone /something a great deal

take a **shine** to someone
after your own **heart**
get on like a **house** on fire
the **apple** of someone's eye

sing the **praises** of
the best **thing** since sliced bread
take someone's **breath** away
have a **thing** about

being pleasantly suitable

up someone's **street**
be **taken** with

suit down to the **ground**

not liking someone /something strongly

a dead **loss**
hold in **contempt**
have no **time** for

take **exception** to something
make someone's **flesh** crawl

not keen on someone /something

not much **cop**
not what it's **cracked** up to be
not your **cup** of tea
not go a **bundle** on something

not take **kindly** to something
turn your **nose** up at something
leave a lot to be **desired**
pull a **face**

when you move very fast: *He leaped over the tailboard of the lorry like greased lightning, and he was gone.*

lights
○ **the bright 'lights**
If you refer to the city, as opposed to the countryside, as **the bright lights**, you are considering it as a centre of excitement and entertainment: *As soon as you have had enough take a return flight to the bright lights of Reykjavik.*

like
○ **like it or 'lump it** or **if you don't like it you can 'lump it** (*informal*)
If you tell someone that they can **like it**

or **lump it**, or say that **if they don't like it they can lump it**, you mean that they will have to accept what has been offered to them, because they have no choice: *They've been told: take the lower interest rate – or lump it.*

liking *see* **Idioms study** page 95

lily
○ **gild the 'lily**
If you **gild the lily**, you add unnecessary decoration or exaggeration to something: *Councillor Arthur Collinge condemned the 'competitive status seeking' of colleges that are seeking to gild the lily by changing their names.*

○ **'lily-livered**

Someone who is described as **lily-livered** is not courageous: *If any were against the proposal, they must have been too lily-livered to protest.*

limb

○ **out on a 'limb**

Someone who is **out on a limb** is in a dangerous and isolated position, usually because they have ideas or opinions that are not accepted by other people.

limit

○ **the 'limit**

You say that someone or something is **the limit** when you are annoyed with them: *He really is the limit, isn't he. What on earth will he do next?*

line (*see also* **lines**)

○ **the bottom 'line**

The bottom line is the final result, or the most important consideration of a situation, activity or discussion: *Okay, enough of all that; what's the bottom line?*

○ **draw the line at 'such-and-such**

You **draw the line at** something when you refuse to do or accept it: *'Anyway,' said Graham, 'I do draw the line at being described as 'militant'.'*

○ **drop someone a 'line**

You **drop someone a line** when you write them a letter: *I'll drop him a line and tell him we're coming over to Oxford.*

○ **feed someone a 'line** or **shoot someone a 'line**

If you **feed**, or **shoot**, **someone a line**, you give them a false explanation or tell a lie: *He fed me some line about the bus breaking down.*

○ **get out of 'line** or **step out of 'line**

You **get**, or **step**, **out of line** when you start behaving in a way that is not allowed or expected of you: *You'd better not step out of line for a while – we need them on our side at the moment.*

○ **hold the 'line**

You ask someone, on the telephone, to **hold the line** when you want them to wait while you try to find the person they want to speak to: *Hold the line please, I'll put you through.*

○ **a 'hotline**

A **hotline** is a line of quick communication between people, especially for use in emergencies: *Phone our 24-hour hotline for all emergency electrical work.*

○ **in the 'firing line**

You are **in the firing line** if you are in a position where you are most likely to be affected by attack or criticism: *Cities are likely to find themselves very much in the firing line, as a series of radical measures are implemented concerning local taxation.*

○ **in the front 'line**

Someone who is **in the front line** is in a position where they can have direct experience of, or influence on, an activity: *organizations like ACET, who are in the front line giving practical care and support to AIDS sufferers.*

○ **in line for 'such-and-such**

You are **in line for something** if you are likely to get it: *I'd stay there if I were you – I think you're in line for promotion.*

○ **keep someone in 'line**

You **keep someone in line** when you make them behave as they ought to: *He had a middle-aged secretary who used to follow him about with his diary and try to keep him in line.*

○ **lay it on the 'line**

You **lay it on the line** when you say very clearly that something is the case: *But soon – perhaps very soon – I am going to have to lay it on the line, tell them what really has been happening.*

○ **on the 'line**

Something such as your job or reputation is **on the line** if you are in danger of losing it.

○ **'somewhere along the line**

'Somewhere along the line' means 'at some point in a procedure': *I realized then that somewhere along the line I must have gone wrong.*

○ **take a hard 'line**

You **take a hard line** when you take strong actions, or hold firmly to decisions or policies that have been made: *The Government has decided to take a hard line on Europe in the period leading up to the election.*

○ **toe the 'line**

You **toe the line** when you behave as you ought to: *On the one hand, they are being urged to make decisions about their future while, on the other, they are* *expected to toe the line both at home and at school.*

linen

○ **wash your dirty linen in 'public** or **air your dirty linen in 'public**

You **are washing your dirty linen in public**, or **airing your dirty linen in public** if you are having an argument about something private, while in the company of others: *They are concerned it should stay in the community. You shouldn't wash dirty linen in public.*

Linen is a formal or old-fashioned word for underwear.

lines

○ **get your 'lines crossed** (*BrE*)

Two people **get their lines crossed** when they misunderstand each other: *I think we got our lines crossed – I thought we were invited for the weekend, but in fact it was just for dinner.*

○ **on the lines of 'such-and-such** or **along the lines of 'such-and-such**

You describe something as being **on**, or **along, the lines of** something else if that is what it is roughly like: *We would then organize the party along the lines of other large events such as pop concerts.*

○ **read between the 'lines**

You **read between the lines** when you understand what is implied by what someone says, although they do not express it openly: *Those who took time to read between the lines would have realized that things were not going as well as they may have first appeared.*

lion

○ **the 'lion's share**

The **lion's share** is the largest part of something: *The dozen strong mixed team also secured the lion's share of individual medals.*

lip

○ **give someone 'lip** (*informal*)

If you **give someone lip**, you are rude and disrespectful towards them: *Don't you give me that lip, boy.*

○ **pay 'lip service to something**

Someone who **pays lip service to** an idea or principle pretends to support or uphold it without really doing so: *The Government pays lip-service to the*

official declarations that no such deals should be made, but in reality they seem to be inevitable.

○ **a stiff upper 'lip**

You keep **a stiff upper lip** if you hide your feelings when you are upset or worried: *The message being sent to the hostages was that they had to keep a stiff upper lip and hope that, one day, the kidnappers might let them go.*

lips

○ **my lips are 'sealed**

If you say that **your lips are sealed**, you mean that you will not reveal a secret that someone has told you: *'You can keep a secret?' Benjamin asked sharply. The fellow nodded, round-eyed. 'Of course. My lips are sealed.'*

little

○ **make 'little of something**

You **make little of something** when you treat it as unimportant: *Subsequent generations made little of their royal connection.*

live

○ **live it 'up**

You **live it up** when you have an enjoyable time, especially with an exciting social life: *He was an individualist who liked to do things his own way, like living it up at night clubs until the early hours.*

♦ *see also* **have a ball** ▷BALL; **have the time of your life** ▷TIME

lo

○ **lo and be'hold**

You say '**lo and behold**' when telling a story, to dramatically introduce the unexpected appearance of someone, or an unexpected occurrence: *And lo and behold, who should walk in the door but Bill, the man himself!*

load

○ **get a load of 'this** (*slang*)

You say '**get a load of this**' in order to get someone's attention when you are about to tell them something interesting or scandalous.

○ **lighten someone's 'load**

Something that **lightens your load** makes a difficult situation easier to manage: *Ironing is one of the least favourite household chores so lighten the load with one of the latest irons.*

loaf

○ **a load of 'rubbish** (*BrE*)

Something that is described as **a load of rubbish** is worthless, untrue or nonsensical: *'These reports are a load of rubbish,' she said. 'I have no idea where the journalists got this information.'*

○ **a load off your 'mind**

You say that something is **a load off your mind** if it makes you feel relieved after a period of worry: *Providing the income you will need after you stop work can take a load off your mind.* ♦ *see also* **a weight off your mind** ▷WEIGHT

loaf

○ **use your 'loaf** (*BrE*)

'**Use your loaf**' means 'use your intelligence'.

> **Loaf of bread** is Cockney rhyming slang for 'head'.

lock

○ **lock, stock and 'barrel**

If you win or lose something **lock, stock and barrel**, you win or lose all of it: *He may even try to buy the club lock, stock and barrel.*

> A **lock**, a **stock**, and a **barrel** are the three main parts of a gun.

log

○ **sleep like a 'log**

You **sleep like a log** when you sleep very deeply: *He won't have heard anything, he sleeps like a log.* ♦ *see also* **sleep like a top** ▷TOP

loggerheads

○ **at 'loggerheads**

You are **at loggerheads** with someone if you disagree with them violently: *For Mrs Thatcher, at loggerheads with many of her own party over European issues, this summit was crucial.*

> A **loggerhead** was a long iron bar with a ball at the end, used, when heated, for melting tar [= a thick, black, sticky substance, used in making roads]. It probably served as a weapon among workers who used it.

long

○ **at long 'last**

You say **at long last** when something

you have been waiting for finally happens: *'I've passed my driving test!' 'At long last!'*

○ **the long and the 'short of it** (*informal*)

You say '**the long and the short of it**' when you are summarizing a story in a few words: *She hadn't known what to expect. She'd expected too much: that was the long and the short of it.*

○ **long as your 'arm**

A list that is as **long as your arm** is a very long list: *I have a list of vices as long as your arm but I am not mean.*

look

○ **a black 'look**

If someone gives you **a black look**, they look at you angrily, without speaking to you: *I gave him such a black look, however, that the smile froze on his face.*

○ **a dirty 'look**

If someone gives you **a dirty look**, they look at you in a way that shows that they disapprove of, or are angry with, you.

○ **look before you 'leap**

If someone tells you to **look before you leap**, they mean that you should consider something more carefully before deciding to do it: *Each was given a free booklet called 'Look Before You Leap', an introduction to time management for the professional photographer.*

○ **look 'lively!** or **look 'sharp!** or **look 'snappy!** (*informal*)

If you tell someone to **look lively!** or **look sharp!** or **look snappy!** you mean that they should hurry up: *'You boys are supposed to be helping with the washing up,' said Mrs Crumwallis. 'Look lively. Bring me those saucers there.'*

○ **look 'small**

If someone makes you **look small**, they humiliate you: *He had never quite forgiven her for making him look small in front of his colleagues.*

○ **not much to 'look at**

Someone or something that is **not much to look at** is not particularly attractive: *You should see the garden, although it's not much to look at at this time of the year.*

lord

○ **'lord it over someone**

Someone **lords it over you** when they

behave towards you as if they were more important than you: *The officer's clerk sat drinking tea and lording it over the candidates.*

lorry

○ **fall off a 'lorry** or **be off the back of a 'lorry** (*BrE*)

If you say that something **fell off a lorry**, or that it's **off the back of a lorry**, you mean that it was stolen: *It's a lovely present, but I can't help wondering if it fell off the back of a lorry.*

lose

○ **have nothing to 'lose**

You **have nothing to lose** by acting in a certain way if it cannot harm you to do so: *You've got nothing to lose. They can only say no if they don't want you.*

○ **'lose it**

Someone who **is losing it** is losing control of themselves or of their surroundings, and allowing the quality of their work to deteriorate.

loss

○ **at a 'loss**

You are **at a loss** when you are puzzled or shocked and do not know what to do or say: *I'm at a loss for words.*

○ **a dead 'loss**

You describe someone or something as **a dead loss** if you think they are hopelessly bad, boring or ineffective: *That course is a dead loss – not worth the money at all.*

lost

○ **get 'lost** (*offensive*)

If you tell someone to **get lost**, you mean, rudely, that you want them to go away.

○ **'lost on someone**

You say that something is **lost on someone** when they do not use, appreciate or understand it properly: *Her ironic tone seemed lost on him.*

love

○ **love is 'blind**

If you say **'love is blind'**, you mean that when someone is in love they do not always see the faults of the person whom they love: *I don't know why they say that love is blind – I was always very aware of all your father's little defects.*

○ **make 'love**

When two people **make love** they have sex: *They have such small beds here to stop undergraduates making love.*

○ **no 'love lost between**

If you say that there is **no love lost between** two people you mean that they dislike each other.

○ **not for love nor 'money**

If you say that you will **not** do something **for love nor money**, you mean that you absolutely refuse to do it: *You wouldn't find me in a place like that for love nor money. Why don't you get respectable premises somewhere else?*

luck

○ **hard 'luck** or **tough 'luck**

You say **'hard luck'** or **'tough luck'** to someone when something unfortunate has happened to them, either to show sympathy, or ironically, as a way of saying that the person will have to accept the situation: *'We lost.' 'Hard luck.'* ♦ *see also* **hard cheese** ▷CHEESE

○ **be down on your 'luck**

If you **are down on your luck**, you are having problems and things are not going well for you: *I met her in Paris three years ago, a bit down on my luck because I'd lost my job.*

○ **a hard-'luck story**

A **hard-luck story** is a story of someone's bad luck or suffering which they tell you because they want your sympathy or your money, for example: *He went on looking at me sympathetically as if I'd been telling him a hard-luck story.*

○ **just so-and-so's 'luck**

You say that something which has happened is **just your luck** if it is typically bad luck: *No tickets left – just my luck.*

○ **the luck of the 'devil** or **the luck of the 'Irish**

Someone who has **the luck of the devil** or **the luck of the Irish** enjoys more than a reasonable or usual amount of good luck: *It was the luck of the Irish that saved him. Martin survived an unsurvivable accident.*

○ **the luck of the 'draw**

You describe something that happens as **the luck of the draw** if it depends purely on chance, rather than on any kind of planning or skill: *It's the luck* *of the draw whether you get a nice room or not – they all cost the same.*

A **draw** is a kind of competition where you buy a ticket with a number on it. If your number is chosen, you win a prize.

○ **push your 'luck** or (*AmE*) **crowd your 'luck**

Someone **is pushing their luck,** or **crowding their luck,** if they are risking disappointment or failure by trying to gain too much: *Trying to fit the walk into a two-week holiday is pushing your luck – you must make allowances for delays.*

○ **worse 'luck**

'**Worse luck**' means 'unfortunately': *'Have you got any homework for tonight?' 'Yes, worse luck.'*

lumbered

○ **be lumbered with** or **get lumbered with** (*BrE*)

You **are,** or you **get, lumbered with** a job or task, when you are given one you do not want: *Why do I always get lumbered with 'organizing these things?*

lump

○ **have a 'lump in your throat**

If you **have a lump in your throat,** you are emotionally moved, you get a tightening feeling in your throat, and feel as if you are going to cry: *I hate it when people cry – it makes me want to do the same thing. I get this lump in my throat and then my eyes start to sting.*

○ **'lump it** (*informal*)

You say that someone will have to **lump it** if they must accept a bad situation without complaining: *If I were you I'd tell them if they don't like it, lump it.*

lunch

○ **out to 'lunch** (*informal*)

Someone who is **out to lunch** is crazy: *He looked out to lunch – his deep-set eyes flashed about behind the long, sweaty strands of hair.* ♦ *see also* **have a screw loose** ▷SCREW

lurch

○ **leave someone in the 'lurch** (*informal*)

You **leave someone in the lurch** if you withdraw your help or support and

leave them in a difficult situation: *TV fashion queen Selina Scott has left BBC bosses in the lurch by quitting 'The Clothes Show' days before a new series.* ♦ *see also* **leave someone holding the baby** ▷BABY

lying

○ **take something lying 'down**

You **take something lying down** if you accept something which is unfair, without complaining or protesting: *Don't take it lying down. Fight to the end.*

mad

○ **barking 'mad** (*BrE*)

If you describe someone as **barking mad** you mean they are completely mad: *There are so many visuals, wild lights and other bizarre things grabbing your attention, it's enough to drive you barking mad.*

○ **hopping 'mad**

Someone who is **hopping mad** is very angry: *That really infuriated Henry! Good Lord, he was hopping mad!*

○ **like 'mad**

You are doing something **like mad** if you are doing it with great energy or enthusiasm: *I've been working like mad to get this stuff finished.*

made

○ **'made for someone**

You say that a person or thing was **made for someone** if it fits or suits them perfectly: *John and Sue are so happy. I think they were made for each other.*

magic

○ **work like 'magic**

If something **works like magic,** it

works effectively and fast: *I got this new carpet cleaner from Tesco's – look, it works like magic.*

make (see also made and making)

○ **make 'do**

You **make do**, or **make do with something**, when you accept it or make the best use of it, even though it is not exactly what you wanted, because nothing better is available: *If we can't get butter, we'll just make do with margarine.*

○ **'make it**

You **make it** when **1** you are successful in doing or being something: *I never hear from him any more, now that he's made it as a pop singer.* **2** you manage to come out of a dangerous situation alive: *My climbing partner broke his leg, and I began to wonder if we'd make it.* **3** you manage to reach a place: *Even if you drive at top speed, we'll never make it in time.* **4** you manage to be present at an event that you have been invited to: *I'd like to come, but I'm not sure if I can make it.* ♦ *see also* **make it big** ▷BIG; **make a name for yourself** or **make your name** ▷NAME

○ **make it 'up**

You **make it up** to someone you have disappointed when you do something for them as a way of apologizing: *I can't be home for your birthday, but I'll make it up to you. I promise.*

○ **on the 'make** (*informal*)

1 You say that someone is **on the make** if you are suspicious of them because you think that they are only concerned with getting money: *He's always on the make, and he doesn't care what rubbish he sells you.* **2** You also say that someone is **on the make** if they are obviously flirting with people and encouraging their sexual interest: *She looks like she's on the make this evening.*

○ **put the 'make on someone** (*AmE; informal*)

If you **put the make on someone**, you make sexual advances towards them: *I couldn't believe it when Dennis put the make on my sister.*

making

○ **in the 'making**

'**In the making**' describes a person or thing that is developing into something: *Here is a talented musician in the making.*

○ **of someone's own 'making**

Something, especially a problem or failure, is **of your own making** if you have caused it by your own actions: *I have no sympathy for her. Any problems she has are of her own making.*

makings

○ **have the 'makings of something**

A person or thing that **has the makings of something** has the qualities or abilities needed to develop into that thing: *This boy has the makings of a world-class yachtsman.*

man (see also men)

○ **be your own 'man**

A man who **is his own man** is independent in his thinking and behaviour and does not have to obey any other person: *If you run your own cab, you're your own man, you can choose your own hours, plan your holidays.*

○ **hit a man when he is 'down** or **kick a man when he is 'down**

You say that someone **is hitting**, or **kicking, a man when he is down** if they are attacking a person who has already been put in a weak position: *The 'don't kick a man when he is down' doctrine meant nothing to Wigg – he believed in gaining the upper hand and keeping it.*

○ **the 'man** (*AmE*)

The man is a person, such as a boss or police officer, who has authority or power: *Paul may think that he's very important, but he still has to answer to the man.*

> **The man** was first used by African Americans to mean 'the white man'.

○ **one man's meat is another man's 'poison**

If someone says '**one man's meat is another man's poison**', they mean that, just because one person likes something, it is not certain that everyone will like it: *If you don't like it, just say. Don't be afraid. One man's meat is another man's poison, as they say.*

○ **to a 'man**
When a group of people do something **to a man**, they all do that thing: *They all agreed to a man that the mission should be abandoned.*

○ **you can't keep a good man 'down**
If someone says '**you can't keep a good man down**', they mean that it is impossible to defeat or discourage the person they are referring to for long, because that person has so much strength and determination: *He's back playing rugby, after being told he might never walk again. You can't keep a good man down.*

manner

○ **by 'no manner of means** or **not by 'any manner of means**
'**By no manner of means**' and '**not by any manner of means**' both mean 'not at all': *We have all worked hard, but by no manner of means can we afford to sit back and relax yet.*

○ **in a manner of 'speaking** or **as a manner of 'speaking**
You add '**in a manner of speaking**' to what you are saying to show that a word or phrase you have used gives a good description of what you mean, but is not intended to be exact or accurate; you say something **as a manner of speaking** if the words you say are not intended to be exact or accurate, only to express some basic idea: *'And I, in a manner of speaking, am a plane without a pilot,' Dwayne says.* □ *He later admitted that he had merely said between seventeen and eighteen as a manner of speaking.*

○ **to the manner 'born**
You say that someone is **to the manner born** if they seem comfortable and natural doing something, as if they have been doing it since the day they were born: *McGrath's companion is also a welcome guest at the dinner, and sits on a chair as if to the manner born with a serviette tucked into his collar.*

> This expression often refers to accomplished social behaviour by someone who is not experienced in such matters.

map

○ **put such-and-such on the 'map**
If something **puts** a certain place **on the map**, it causes that place to be important: *Spielberg using this village in a movie has really put the place on the map.*

marbles

○ **go for all the 'marbles** (*AmE*; *informal*)
You **go for all the marbles** when you try to make a big gain, often at a risk: *They offered me 40% of the company, but I decided to go for all the marbles.*

○ **lose your 'marbles**
If you say that someone **is losing their marbles**, you mean that they are going mad, or becoming forgetful and confused: *As one of her oldest friends affectionately put it to me on her 100th birthday, she has lost her marbles.*

march

○ **steal a 'march on someone**
If you **steal a march on someone**, you secretly gain an advantage, especially an advantage in time, over them: *We tried to steal a march on the other teams by setting off a day early.*

> This is a military term, meaning 'to move an army unexpectedly while the enemy is resting'.

mark

○ **close to the 'mark** or **near to the 'mark**
If something such as a guess is **close**, or **near, to the mark**, it is nearly correct or accurate, and sometimes closer to the truth than some people would like: *I think she was pretty near to the mark when she said the whole thing was a publicity stunt.*

> In archery, the **mark** was an old name for the target which you try to hit with your arrows.

○ **hit the 'mark**
Something which you attempt **hits the mark** if it achieves what it is intended to achieve: *It was a guess, though scarcely a wild one, and Cunningham's reaction confirmed it had hit the mark.*

> See note at **close** or **near to the mark**.

○ **leave your 'mark**
You **leave your mark** if you are re-membered for the influence you have had on something: *She died many years ago, but the words she said have left their mark on me.*

○ **make your 'mark**
You **make your mark** when you first become successful or influential in a particular field: *As a poet, he made his mark first in 1712 with the publication of 'Nereides'.*

○ **off the 'mark** or **wide of the 'mark**
A guess is **off**, or **wide of**, **the mark** if it is not at all correct or accurate: *We can't give a pass to an exam paper like that. He's way off the mark with over half his answers.*

> See note at **close** or **near to the mark**.

○ **overstep the 'mark**
A person **oversteps the mark** when they go beyond what are accepted as the permitted limits: *The regulators ob-viously feel that he has overstepped the mark with his comments this time.*

○ **quick off the 'mark** (*BrE*)
You are **quick off the mark** if your mind works quickly or you have quick reactions in a situation: *Michael was very good at improvising. He was very bright and quick off the mark.*

> In track athletics, the **mark** is the line from which a race starts.

○ **slow off the 'mark**
You are **slow off the mark** if your mind does not work quickly or you have slow reactions in a situation: *You can't accuse her of being slow off the mark. She's a mathematical genius.*

> See note at **quick off the mark**.

marrow

○ **chilled to the 'marrow** or **frozen to the 'marrow**
You are **chilled**, or **frozen, to the marrow**, if you are very cold.

> **The marrow** is the soft substance in the centre of your bones.

mask

○ **someone's 'mask has slipped** (*BrE*)
You say that **someone's mask has slipped** if they have been unable to continue with their false behaviour, and have started doing things which show who they really are, or what they are really like: *Recently the movement's mask has begun to slip as they become more desperate for political success.*

> If a mask which you are wearing to hide your face slips down, your face will no longer be covered and people will see what you really look like.

masses

○ **'masses of something** (*BrE*)
Masses of something is a large quan-tity of it: *There's masses of time before the concert starts.*

match

○ **meet your 'match**
You say that someone **has met their match** when they meet someone who is their equal in some skill or quality: *He finally met his match in one Major Faulks in 1905 who stayed with the firm as a consultant until 1965 when he final-ly retired – at the age of 90.*

○ **no 'match for**
Someone or something is **no match for** another person or thing if they can-not equal that person or thing in some skill or quality: *In the final analysis stu-dents do not have power and are no match for the military.*

matter

○ **as a matter of 'course**
Something which happens **as a mat-ter of course** happens automatically without any need for special instruc-tions or arrangements: *Do I have to re-apply for funding every year? I thought I would get it as a matter of course.*

○ **as a matter of 'fact**
You use the phrase **as a matter of fact** to introduce an unexpected piece of in-formation related to what has just been said, or to correct somebody when you think they have got the wrong impres-sion about something: *'You don't mind my smoking, do you?' 'As a matter of fact, I do.'*

○ **for 'that matter**

'**For that matter**' draws attention to a second statement, usually a short one, which extends the first: *My wife didn't enjoy the film much. For that matter, neither did I. Too much sex and violence.*

matters

○ **to make matters 'worse**

If you are talking about a bad situation and you want to mention something which makes that situation even worse, you can introduce it with the expression '**to make matters worse**': *I've got a horribly busy weekend, and to make matters worse, the car's out of action.* ♦ *see also* **to top it all** ▷TOP; **what is more** ▷WHAT

meal

○ **make a 'meal of something** (*BrE*)

You say that someone **is making a meal of something** if they are taking more than the necessary amount of time or trouble over it, or making it seem more complicated than it really is: *Get it done as quickly as you can – don't make a meal of it.* ♦ *see also* **make a rod for your own back** ▷ROD; **your own worst enemy** ▷ENEMY

○ **a 'meal ticket**

You say that someone treats a person or organization as **a meal ticket** if they seem happy to take all the support or help that that person or organization offers, without showing any gratitude or offering anything in return: *There were times when he suspected he was just a meal ticket to his wife.*

mean

○ **no mean 'such-and-such** (*informal*)

1 You describe a person as **no mean such-and-such** if they have a particular ability in the activity you are referring to: *No mean performer on the rugby field, he has now developed a taste for academia.* **2** You describe something as **no mean such-and such** if it is impressive: *an estate, which, although small, was of no mean value.*

means

○ **beyond your 'means**

A price to be paid for something is **beyond your means** if you do not have enough money to pay it; someone is liv-ing **beyond their means** if they spend more money than they earn: *Credit cards just encourage people to live beyond their means.*

○ **by 'all means**

You say '**by all means**' as a polite way of giving permission: *'May I look at your garden?' 'By all means.'*

○ **by 'no means** or **not by 'any means**

'**By no means**' and '**not by any means**' mean 'not at all': *She has given me a bit of money back, but by no means all that she owed me.*

○ **a means to an 'end**

Something that is **a means to an end** is something that people do not for enjoyment but to achieve something: *Think of discipline as a means to an end, not an end in itself.*

○ **within your 'means**

A price to be paid for something is **within your means** if you have enough money to buy it; someone is living **within their means** if they do not spend more money than they earn: *It's hard to live within your means when the only money you have coming in is Income Support.*

measure

○ **for good 'measure**

You do or have something extra **for good measure** when you do or have it, even though it may not really be necessary, in order to make sure that the situation is complete: *I filled the cake with cream, and dolloped some more round the sides for good measure.*

○ **have the 'measure of someone** or **take the 'measure of someone** or **get the 'measure of someone**

You **have the measure of** a person or animal if you understand them and are able to deal with them effectively; you **take the measure**, or **get the measure, of** them when you start to understand them and to deal with them effectively: *You should have made sure you had the measure of your horse before riding on the roads.* ◻ *It's taken me months, but I think I've finally got the measure of that boy in my class.*

meat

○ **meat and 'drink to someone** (*BrE*)

Something such as a favourite activity

is **meat and drink to someone** if it gives that person so much pleasure that you wonder if they could manage without it: *These corporate executives are people to whom the Conservative party is meat and drink.*

> In the past, **meat** meant 'food' in general.

medium
○ **happy 'medium**

A **happy medium** is a way of dealing with a situation which comes between two extreme methods: '*You have to strike a happy medium between looking like royalty and looking like a housewife,*' *Mrs Tony Newton, wife of the Leader of the Commons, explained.*

meet
○ **meet someone half'way**

You **meet someone halfway** if you refuse to do exactly what they want, but agree to change some of your plans or demands to fit in with theirs: *We'll never find a solution unless the unions are willing to meet us halfway.*

melon
○ **cut the 'melon** (*AmE*; *informal*)

You **cut the melon** when you divide up something such as profits or political favours: *When our syndicate won the lottery, I immediately worked out how we could cut the melon.*

memory
○ **commit something to 'memory**

You **commit something to memory** when you make a mental note of that thing with the intention of remembering it: *I committed the number to memory and threw the paper slip on to the fire.*

○ **down memory 'lane**

A person goes **down memory lane** when they remind themselves of a time when they were younger, by doing or experiencing again the things they used to do in the past: *And at six o'clock on BBC1, there's a trip down memory lane with some of your old favourites in 'Those Were the Days'.*

○ **a memory like an 'elephant** or **the memory of an 'elephant**

You say that someone has **a memory like**, or **the memory of, an elephant** if they have an excellent memory: *If you want to know about the day the Government was elected, speak to Anne. She's got the memory of an elephant.*

> People say that elephants have good memories, although there is no evidence for this.

○ **a memory like a 'sieve**

You say that someone has **a memory like a sieve** if they forget things easily: *Oh dear. Now where did I put my glasses? I've got a memory like a sieve.*

> A **sieve** is a piece of kitchen equipment with a lot of small holes in it to let liquid and small particles through. The idea is that a bad memory lets information escape from it in the same way.

men
○ **men in grey 'suits**

The **men in grey suits** are the powerful businessmen and officials who make the most important decisions in politics and business, although the public are often not aware of their existence: *The Beatles had to start taking responsibility for their world instead of being acted upon by a panoply of 'men in grey suits'.*

○ **the men in white 'coats** (*humorous*)

If people talk about **the men in white coats**, they mean doctors, especially doctors who treat mental illnesses: *You'll have the men in white coats coming to get you if you carry on talking to yourself like that.*

○ **separate the men from the 'boys** or (*BrE*) **sort out the men from the 'boys**

You say that a certain activity **will separate**, or **sort out, the men from the boys** if it will allow people to see who is really able to excel under tough conditions: *John McEnroe goes into today's US Open final with world No.1 Jim Courier insisting: 'This will separate the men from the boys. It will be an unbelievably tough match.'* ♦ *see also* **separate** or **sort out the wheat from the chaff** ▷ WHEAT

mention

○ **not to 'mention**

People say '**not to mention**' before they add something else to what they have already said: *They've got everything in that house. Fitted kitchen, new carpets. Not to mention the spa bath.*

mercies

○ **thankful for small 'mercies** (*BrE*)

If you say that someone should be **thankful for small mercies**, you are remarking that they should take courage from the few positive things which make their situation less difficult: *She died suddenly, so at least she didn't suffer. I suppose we should be thankful for small mercies.* ♦ *see also* **count your blessings** ▷BLESSINGS; **look on the bright side** ▷SIDE

mercy

○ **at the 'mercy of**

If you are **at the mercy of** someone or something, they have complete control over you and can treat you as badly or unfairly as they wish: *You camp if you want, but I don't fancy a night outside at the mercy of the elements.*

merrier

○ **the more the 'merrier**

If someone says '**the more the merrier**', they mean that the more people or things there are, the better: *'Have you got room in the car for us?' 'Pile in. The more the merrier.'*

method

○ **there is method in so-and-so's 'madness**

You say that **there is method in** a certain person's **madness** if, although that person seems to be doing things in the wrong way, they do in fact have a purpose in doing them that way: *We have imagined him as absolutely, and monstrously, evil. But is he a primitive and irrational alien? Might there not be method in his madness?*

In Shakespeare's *Hamlet*, II ii, Polonius realizes that Hamlet's words make some kind of sense although he seems to be mad, and makes the remark 'Though this be madness, yet there is method in it'.

mettle

○ **put someone on their 'mettle**

If something **puts someone on their mettle**, it makes them anxious to do their best and perform well: *Her near defeat in the first set has put the defending champion on her mettle, and she's fighting hard.*

Mexican

○ **a Mexican 'standoff** (*AmE*)

When two opposing groups have a **Mexican standoff**, they face each other for a long time, because neither has an advantage: *The marches stopped where the police blocked the road, and a Mexican standoff took place.*

mickey

○ **take the 'mickey** (*BrE*)

You **take the mickey** when you make jokes or try to play tricks on someone; you **take the mickey**, or **take the mickey out of** something or someone, when you make fun of them: *'I found a puppy in the street, so I brought it home.' 'Are you taking the mickey?'* □ *When other people are taking the mickey out of someone else, try to imagine how they feel about it. Don't join in if it is getting hurtful.* ♦ *see also* **make fun of** or **poke fun at** ▷FUN

middle

○ **in the middle of 'nowhere**

You are **in the middle of nowhere** if you are in a place which is a long distance from any towns and houses, often with a feeling of being lost: *Eventually, we stopped. We were in the middle of nowhere, and it was beginning to get dark.* ♦ *see also* **the back of beyond** ▷BACK; **out in the sticks** ▷STICKS; **off the beaten track** ▷TRACK; **out of the way** ▷WAY

○ **middle-of-the-'road**

You describe something as '**middle-of-the-road**' if it does not involve extreme ideas, tries to be reasonable in all ways, and so appeals to popular taste: *Many people shy away from voting Lib Dem because it seems to be a middle-of-the-road option.*

○ **in mid'stream**

You stop **in midstream** when you suddenly pause while doing something busily, especially talking: *'Will,' he said breathlessly, and stopped in midstream. 'What's going on here? Is this a party?'*

mildly

○ **to put it 'mildly**

You use **'to put it mildly'** to show that you are not expressing yourself as strongly as you could do, considering the situation: *I was a bit annoyed, to put it mildly.*

mile

○ **run a 'mile**

You say that a certain situation would make someone **run a mile** if you think that person would be afraid of, and try to escape from, it: *Oh, I think she likes me. But she'd run a mile if I suggested we got married.*

○ **see something a 'mile off** or **spot something a 'mile off**

You say that you can **see**, or **spot**, **something a mile off** if you notice it easily: *You mean you didn't even notice she'd been crying? But you could spot it a mile off.*

○ **stand out a 'mile** or **stick out a 'mile**

You say that something **stands**, or **sticks**, **out a mile** if you think it is obvious: *Oh, come on. You can tell how posh he is from his accent. It sticks out a mile.*

miles

○ **'miles away**

You say that someone is **miles away** when they are having such deep thoughts about something else that they are not aware of what is happening around them or what someone is saying to them: *'Carrie,' I said. She looked up dreamily. 'Sorry, I was miles away.'*

milk

○ **cry over spilt 'milk**

Someone who **is crying over spilt milk** is regretting something which cannot be changed: *Nora Simpson didn't believe in crying over spilt milk. What had happened had happened, and there was nothing she could do about it.*

mill

○ **go through the 'mill** or **be put through the 'mill**

You say that someone **has gone**, or **been put**, **through the mill** when they

have undergone a series of difficult tests or experiences: *You poor thing. Sounds like you were put through the mill at your interview, then?*

millstone

○ **a millstone round someone's 'neck**

You describe an unpleasant duty or responsibility that prevents you from doing what you would like as **a millstone round your neck**: *Mr Smith said that unemployment at this 'tragic level' was an economic millstone round the country's neck costing £27 billion a year.*

mincemeat

○ **make 'mincemeat of someone**

To **make mincemeat of someone** is to defeat them completely: *We got through to the final round of the quiz, but the champions made mincemeat of us.* ♦ *see also* **wipe the floor with** ▷FLOOR

mind *(see also* **minds**)

○ **all in the 'mind**

You say that a situation is **all in the mind** if you consider it to be wholly produced by your attitudes towards something: *If you believe you're beautiful, you'll look beautiful. It's all in the mind.*

○ **bear something in 'mind** or **keep something in 'mind**

You **bear**, or **keep**, **something in mind** when you remember it or take it into consideration: *Bear in mind that it could rain every day, even in the middle of the summer.*

○ **blow someone's 'mind** *(informal)*

Something which **blows someone's mind** surprises or excites them greatly: *It blows your mind to think that people built these monuments over five thousand years ago.*

> This expression was originally used to describe the effect of mind-altering drugs such as LSD.

○ **cast your 'mind back**

You **cast your mind back** to a certain period or event when you try to remember it: *Cast your mind back to the first time you drove a car. Remember how difficult it seemed?*

○ **change your 'mind**

You **change your mind** when you change your opinion, or change a decision or choice that you have made: *I thought she was quite nice at first, but I've changed my mind about her.*

○ **come to 'mind** or **spring to 'mind**

An idea or memory **comes**, or **springs, to mind** when you suddenly think of it: *'What shall I make for dessert? Something light and not too expensive.' 'Fruit salad springs to mind.'*

○ **cross someone's 'mind**

If a thought **crosses your mind**, you think about it for a moment: *It crossed my mind recently that I hadn't heard from her for some time.*

○ **do you 'mind?** or **do you mind 'not...?**

You say '**do you mind?**' or '**do you mind 'not...?**' to someone to express annoyance at what they are doing: *Do you mind? It's very rude to interrupt when two people are having a conversation.* □ *Hey! Do you mind not making so much noise? People are trying to get some sleep round here.*

○ **go out of your 'mind**

Someone who **is out of their mind** is mad; you say that someone **is going out of their mind** if they are behaving irrationally, often because they are worried or upset: *You gave the police a false name and address? You must be out of your mind.* □ *And what time do you call this to be coming home? Your mother was going out of her mind.*

○ **have something in 'mind**

If you **have something in mind**, you want or intend to have or do that thing: *'What exactly did you have in mind?' 'Something nice. It's for my girlfriend.'*

○ **have a mind of your 'own**

1 You talk about a person or animal **having a mind of their own** if they are able to think for themselves, and do not accept other people's instructions or opinions without question: *Their baby is only six months old, but she's already got a mind of her own.* **2** You say that an object **has a mind of its own** if it behaves in a way that suggests it is thinking and making its own decisions, although you know this is not really the case: *I can't make your*

bike go in a straight line. It's got a mind of its own.

○ **have your 'mind on something**

You **have your mind on something** when you are thinking about it or paying attention to it: *It's difficult to work when you've got your mind on other things.*

○ **have a 'mind to** or **have a good 'mind to** or **have half a 'mind to**

You say you **have a mind to**, or **have a good mind to**, or **have half a mind to**, do something if you are seriously considering doing it, especially if you think it should be done and you think no-one else is going to do it: *He's been putting poisonous chemicals down the drains. I've a good mind to report him to the 'council.*

○ **in your mind's 'eye**

You see something **in your mind's eye** when you have a mental picture of it: *I wondered what his girlfriend was like. In my mind's eye, she was tall, with long, dark hair.*

○ **in your right 'mind**

A person is **in their right mind** if they are in their normal mental state: *I know she said some terrible things, but she wasn't in her right mind. She was ill.*

> This expression is most often used in the negative and interrogative forms.

○ **keep your 'mind on something**

If you **are keeping your mind on something** which you are doing, you are giving all your attention to it: *If you keep your mind on the job you won't have time to speculate about me and my problems.*

○ **keep an open 'mind**

You **keep an open mind** about something if you are willing to consider new ideas about it and change your own: *So now three people believed in the ghost. Noreen said she was keeping an open mind on the subject.*

○ **make up your 'mind**

You **make up your mind** when you make a decision or form an opinion: *I'd like to come, but I may not have time. Can I phone you back when I've made up my mind?*

○ **the mind 'boggles**
If you say 'the mind boggles', you
mean that you find it difficult or impossible to imagine the thing that is being
discussed, because it is so surprising
or ridiculous: *British international
players should soon be able to charge
£1,500 for a solitary interview. The mind
boggles.*

○ **mind over 'matter**
If people talk about **mind over matter**, they mean the power that determination can give you to succeed in
something which you may have thought
you were physically unable to do: *It was
just a question of mind over matter, I
thought, and tried to prepare myself for
the physical effects of a rough ride.*

○ **mind 'you**
People say 'mind you' as a way of emphasizing a point, especially a new
point which has not previously or recently been mentioned: *The food at the
café is very good. Mind you, it isn't
cheap.*

○ **never 'mind**
You say 'never mind' to someone **1** to
comfort them when they are unhappy
or disappointed: *Never mind. You can
have a party when you get better.* **2** to
say that you have forgiven them for
something: *Never mind. I probably deserved half the things you said.* **3** to tell
them not to do something, either because it is unnecessary, or because you
intend to do it yourself: *'I thought you
wanted me to do the washing up?' 'Oh,
never mind. I'll do it myself.'*

○ **prey on someone's 'mind**
A worry **is preying on your mind** if it
remains in your mind, however hard
you try to forget it: *I wish I hadn't gone
to that fortune-teller. Those things she
said have been preying on my mind.*

○ **put someone's 'mind at rest** or **set
someone's 'mind at rest**
If something **puts**, or **sets, your mind
at rest**, it releases you from anxiety or
worry: *Phone the hospital if you're worried. It'll put your mind at rest.*

○ **put your 'mind to something**
You **put your mind to something**, or
to doing something, when you deter-
minedly start deciding how you are

going to do it: *You can do anything if
you put your mind to it.*

○ **slip someone's 'mind**
Something **slips your mind** when you
forget to do it, or forget to deal with it:
*'Have you phoned the bank yet?' 'Oh, I'm
sorry. It completely slipped my mind.'*

○ **speak your 'mind**
You **speak your mind** when you say
what you really think: *I'm going to tell
that nasty little man exactly what I think
of him. I'm not afraid to speak my mind.*

○ **take your 'mind off something**
Something that **takes your mind off
something** such as your problems
makes you relax and forget them temporarily: *If your job is stressful, it's good
to do something in the evenings to take
your mind off your work.*

minds

○ **great minds think a'like** (*humorous*)
If someone says 'great minds think
alike', they mean that clever people
usually have the same ideas and opinions: *'I was just about to say that myself.'
'Great minds think alike, eh?'*

> People usually say this when they dis-
> cover that someone else shares their
> own ideas or opinions, as a way of flat-
> tering themselves and the other per-
> son. '**Fools seldom differ**' is a
> common reply which you can use as a
> humorous way of denying that these
> two people are as clever as they are
> suggesting.

○ **in two 'minds** (*BrE*) or **of two 'minds**
(*AmE*)
You say you are **in two minds**, or **of
two minds**, about something when
you cannot decide whether or not you
want it or want to do it: *I have been offered a place on a business course, but
I'm in two minds whether to take it or
not.* ♦ *see also* **in a cleft stick** ▷STICK

mischief

○ **do someone a 'mischief** or **do yourself
a 'mischief** (*BrE; humorous*)
If you **do someone**, or **do yourself, a
mischief**, you hurt that person or
yourself, particularly on a part of your
body that you are embarrassed to mention: *He had always used a lady's bike be-*

cause he thought the middle bar on a man's one might do him a mischief if he cocked his leg over it carelessly.

miss

○ **give something a 'miss** (*BrE*)

You **give something a miss** when you decide not to do it, have it, or be present at it: *'Are you coming to the party?' 'No, I think I'll give it a miss.'*

moment

○ **at the 'moment**

You use **'at the moment'** when you are referring to the situation as it is, as opposed to how it was in the past or will be later: *I've got my mum staying with me at the moment.*

○ **for the 'moment**

You use **'for the moment'** when referring to the situation as it is, and is likely to remain for some time, as opposed to how it will be later: *We've got all the volunteers we need for the moment, but I'll take your name and address anyway.*

○ **the moment of 'truth**

The moment of truth is a time when you finally hear a piece of information that you have been anxiously waiting for, usually regarding success or failure: *The finalists were now gripped with the tension of the approaching moment of truth, like expectant fathers at a birth.*

This expression comes from the Spanish 'el momento de la verdad', which is the moment at the end of a bullfight when the matador kills the bull.

○ **not a moment to 'lose** or **not one moment to 'lose**

You say that there is **not a**, or **not one**, **moment to lose** when the situation is so urgent that you will have to act immediately and as fast as possible: *Don't move an inch. There's not a moment to lose. I'm going to spell out a warning to the pilot.*

moments

○ **have its 'moments** or **have your 'moments** (*BrE*)

1 You say that someone or something **has their moments** if they have been successful or interesting on a few occa-

sions at least: *'How did you enjoy your day in London?' 'It had its moments,' said Helen evasively.* **2** You say that someone, especially a small child, **has their moments** if they occasionally lose their temper or behave badly: *'I can see your father having his hard side, but your mum's too nice.' 'She has her moments. She's not as soft as you might think.'*

money   *see also* **Idioms study** page 112

○ **for 'my money**

'For my money' means 'in my opinion' or 'if I were to choose': *For my money, I'd say you'd be better going for a reliable man than a good-looking one.*

○ **get your 'money's worth**

You **get your money's worth** if you get good use out of something, or full value for the money which you have spent: *If you're saving all year for your holidays, you want to get your money's worth when you're there.*

○ **have money to 'burn**

You say that someone **has money to burn** if they have enough money to be able to spend it in ways that you think are foolish: *Unless you've got money to burn these expensive guitars are probably not the instruments to get you started.* ♦ *see also* **spend money like water** ▷MONEY; **throw money around** ▷MONEY

○ **in the 'money**

If you say that someone is **in the money**, you mean that they have got a lot of money, especially at the moment, rather than all the time: *It looks as if we're in the money – I just got a bonus at work!* ♦ *see also* **in clover** ▷CLOVER

○ **money doesn't grow on 'trees**

If someone says **'money doesn't grow on trees'**, they are reminding the person they are talking to that money is difficult to obtain or earn, especially if that person seems not to understand this fact: *Sayings of Dorothy's came to mind: 'It doesn't grow on trees, you know.' 'You've got to learn the value of money.'* ♦ *see also* **not made of money** ▷MONEY

○ **money is no 'object**

If you say that **money is no object**, you mean that you do not consider money to be important in the decision which you are about to make, as you can afford to spend whatever amount is necessary to obtain what you want: *She flitted from country to country as if money was no object, which, knowing Lori, it probably wasn't.*

○ money '**talks**

If someone says '**money talks**', they mean that people are more likely to be persuaded to do something if you can offer them money for doing it: *'Our star players are simply not for sale.' But usually money talks in football, no matter what the club, and if United do raise their bid, a sale might still be likely.*

○ not '**made of money**

You tell someone that you are **not made of money** when you want them to realize that you have a limited amount of money to spend: *Stop asking for sweets, because you're not getting any. I'm not made of money, you know.* ♦ *see also* **money doesn't grow on trees** ▷MONEY

○ put your money where your '**mouth is**

If you say that a person or organization should **put their money where their mouth is**, you are telling them to supply money for a purpose which they claim to support: *We want the Government to put their money where their mouth is and fund this project.*

○ spend money like '**water** or spend money like it was going out of '**fashion**

You say that someone **spends money like water**, or **spends money like it was going out of fashion**, if they spend a lot of money all the time: *No wonder she's always short of cash. She spends money like water.* ♦ *see also* **have money to burn** ▷MONEY; **throw money around** ▷MONEY

○ throw good money after '**bad**

A person or organization **is throwing good money after bad** if they are spending money in an unsuccessful attempt to get back money they have already lost: *The company has decided to stop throwing good money after bad and cease using it until it either improves or disappears.*

○ throw '**money around**

You say that someone **is throwing money around** if they are spending money in an obvious way, in order to show people that they are rich: *Mum and Dad started to throw money around like water. Mum went around the shops buying clothes, and Dad ordered the drink.* ♦ *see also* **have money to burn** ▷MONEY; **spend money like water** ▷MONEY

○ throw '**money at something**

A person or organization **is throwing money at something** such as a project if they are providing a large amount of money for it, especially if they are doing so without considering carefully whether that thing is worth the money they are spending: *Investment in transport is scheduled to exceed $7 billion. However, throwing money at problems does not in itself bring solutions.*

monkey

○ not give a '**monkey's** (*BrE*; *informal*)

If someone says that they do **not give a monkey's** about something, they mean that they do not care at all about it: *Quite frankly, I don't give a monkey's what anyone else thinks.* ♦ *see also* **not care** or **give a hoot** or **two hoots** ▷HOOT; **not give** or **care a toss** ▷TOSS; **not care** or **give tuppence** ▷TUPPENCE

month

○ a month of '**Sundays**

If you talk about **a month of Sundays**, you mean a period that is so long that it seems to go on for ever; '**never in a month of Sundays**' emphasizes the speaker's feeling that something in particular will never happen: *It'll never get done in a month of Sundays if I wait for you to do it.*

moon

○ once in a blue '**moon**

You do something **once in a blue moon** if you almost never do it: *We never go out for a meal, and it's only once in a blue moon that we go to the cinema.*

On rare occasions, the moon seems to be slightly blue in colour.

IDIOMS*study*   money

The next time you write or talk about **money** you might try to use some of the following idioms. (Remember you can see how to use each idiom correctly by looking at its entry, which you can find under the word printed in heavy type.)

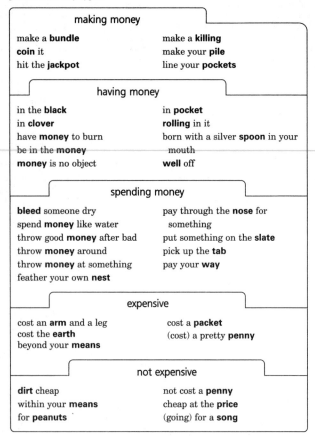

making money

make a **bundle**
coin it
hit the **jackpot**

make a **killing**
make your **pile**
line your **pockets**

having money

in the **black**
in **clover**
have **money** to burn
be in the **money**
money is no object

in **pocket**
rolling in it
born with a silver **spoon** in your mouth
well off

spending money

bleed someone dry
spend **money** like water
throw good **money** after bad
throw **money** around
throw **money** at something
feather your own **nest**

pay through the **nose** for something
put something on the **slate**
pick up the **tab**
pay your **way**

expensive

cost an **arm** and a leg
cost the **earth**
beyond your **means**

cost a **packet**
(cost) a pretty **penny**

not expensive

dirt cheap
within your **means**
for **peanuts**

not cost a **penny**
cheap at the **price**
(going) for a **song**

○ **over the 'moon** (*BrE*)
You say that you are **over the moon** if you are delighted about something: *She's over the moon to be pregnant at last.* ♦ *see also* **walk on air** ▷AIR; **thrilled to bits** ▷BITS; **on cloud nine** ▷CLOUD; **in seventh heaven** ▷HEAVEN

more
○ **more or 'less**
'**More or less**' means **1** 'almost': *I've
more or less finished now.* **2** 'about' or
'approximately': *It was more or less this
time last year that I met you.*

○ **what is 'more**
'**What is more**' is used to introduce a
second statement relating or adding to
the first: *I've had enough of this stupid
work, and what is more, I've had quite
enough of you.*

most
○ **make the 'most of something**
You are **making the most of something** such as an advantageous position when you use it to get as much
benefit as possible from the situation:
*Make the most of your holidays when
you are a student. You'll never have so
much free time again.*

motions
○ **go through the 'motions**
You say that someone **is going
through the motions** when they are
pretending to do something, or they
are doing it without sincerity or enthusiasm: *We don't believe in marriage, but
we're going to go through the motions to
keep the parents happy.*

mould (*AmE* mold)
○ **break the 'mould**
Something which **breaks the mould**
is new and different from previous
things of the same type: *Classical vio-
linists had never appealed much to teen-
age audiences until he came along and
broke the mould.*

> You can use a **mould** if you want to
> make a number of objects, all of ex-
> actly the same shape and size.

mountain (*see also* mountains)
○ **make a mountain out of a 'molehill**
You say that someone **is making a
mountain out of a molehill** if they
are treating something silly and unimportant as if it were serious or important: *People will often agree to
principles because they are too embarrassed to argue or don't want to make a
mountain out of a molehill.* ♦ *see also* **a
storm in a teacup** ▷STORM

mountains
○ **move 'mountains**
You **move mountains** when you cause
something to happen that people think
is impossible or nearly impossible: *I'm
not conceited enough to think that I can
move mountains in the year ahead, but I
promise you I will not let you down.*

mouth
○ **down in the 'mouth**
Someone who is **down in the mouth** is
feeling sad: *He had never seen Karr
looking so down in the mouth. 'Cheer
up,' he said. 'It can't be that bad.'*

○ **foam at the 'mouth**
You say that someone **is foaming at
the mouth** if they are mad with anger:
*He scares me when he gets annoyed. One
minute he's foaming at the mouth and the
next he's laughing and joking.*

> It is said that dogs which have rabies
> **foam at the mouth**.

○ **hush my 'mouth**
You say '**hush my mouth**' if you have
just said something you shouldn't,
especially if you did so intentionally.

○ **shoot your 'mouth off** (*informal*)
A person who **is shooting their
mouth off** is saying things proudly or
in a loud voice, which they will probably regret later: *So you can't shoot your
mouth off. You cannot say that you object,
because you still have to get on with them
at work.*

○ **shut your 'mouth** (*offensive*)
If you say '**shut your mouth**' to someone, you are telling them rudely to stop
talking: *'What time do you call this?
Mmm?' 'Oh shut your mouth. I don't
need you to tell me what to do.'* ♦ *see also*
shut it or **shut up** ▷SHUT

move
○ **someone's every 'move**
A person is watching **your every
move** if they are watching everything
you do: *It's difficult to behave normally
when someone is watching your every
move.*

○ **get a 'move on**
If someone tells you to **get a move on**,
they want you to hurry up: *Get a move
on or you'll be late for school.*

make a 'move

1 Someone **makes a move** when they do something as a clear signal of their intentions: *Women often expect men to make the first move.* **2** If you say it is time you **made a move**, you mean that it is time for you to go where you have to go, or for you to do what you have to do: *Right, we'd better make a move, or we'll be here all night.*

In chess, each player **makes a move** and then has to wait and see how the opposing player will react.

---

muchness

much of a 'muchness (*BrE*)

You say that two or more things are **much of a muchness** if they are all of roughly the same quality: *I don't bother buying expensive film for my camera. They're all much of a muchness anyway.*

mud

sling 'mud or throw 'mud

When one person or group **slings mud**, or **throws mud**, they say things in public which they hope will damage an opposing person's or group's reputation: *'They are trying to sling mud at me to cover up the defeat by Peru.'*

murder

get away with 'murder

Someone who **gets away with murder** is allowed to behave badly without being punished: *She lets her servants get away with murder, too. Look at the dust on that photograph frame.*

I could murder a 'such-and-such

If you say '**I could murder** a certain thing', you mean that you would love to eat or drink that thing: *I could murder a cup of tea.*

scream blue 'murder or shout blue 'murder (*BrE*) or cry blue murder or cry bloody murder (*AmE*)

Someone who **is screaming, shouting,** or **crying blue murder**, or **bloody murder**, is screaming or shouting very loudly: *The frustration she felt at the moment was enough to make her want to scream blue murder.*

muscles

flex your 'muscles

You say that a powerful person or or-ganization is just **flexing their muscles** if you believe that they are doing certain small things at the moment in preparation for the big things they plan to do later: *The rebel forces may just have been flexing their muscles.*

music

face the 'music

You **face the music** when you put your-self into an unpleasant situation invol-ving strong criticism of your past actions, where you will have to either admit that you were wrong or defend what you have done: *Candidates must stand and face the music as the returning officer reads out the results.*

music to someone's 'ears

If it gives you great pleasure to hear something, you can say that that thing is **music to your ears**: *'I'll do the wash-ing-up, shall I?' 'Ah, music to my ears.'*

muster

pass 'muster

A person or thing that **passes muster** is of an acceptable standard: *Critically surveying her reflection, she told herself she would pass muster.*

mutton

mutton dressed as 'lamb (*BrE*)

People describe an older woman as **mutton dressed as lamb** if they think she is trying without success to look much younger than she really is: *'All leather and denim. She looks older than my mother.' 'Awful. Sounds a bit like mutton dressed as lamb.'*

nail

hit the nail on the 'head

You say that someone **has hit the nail on the head** if they have described or identified something precisely or accurately: *The moment she said it she knew she had hit the nail on the head. It was there in his expression.*

○ **'nail-biting**

You describe a story, film, or competition as **nail-biting** if it makes you feel very excited or nervous because you do not know what is going to happen: *Her nail-biting drama about a woman CID officer tracking a serial killer later won a British Academy Award.*

People sometimes **bite their nails** when they feel anxious.

○ **a nail in the 'coffin of**

You describe an event as **a nail in the coffin of** something, or the **nail in** such-and-such's **coffin**, if it helps to contribute to the thing's failure: *His best-selling book 'Diana: Her True Story', is believed to have been the nail in the coffin of the royal marriage.*

A **coffin** is a wooden box that a dead person is buried or cremated in.

○ **on the 'nail**

You pay for something **on the nail** when you pay for it immediately: *Not paying on the nail could be extremely expensive, since interest rates were high.*

The pillars outside the Corn Exchange are called **nails**, and merchants used to complete their financial deals on them before the Exchange was built.

name

○ **clear someone's 'name**

You **clear someone's name** when you prove that they are not guilty of doing something which people suspected them of having done: *I do not doubt your innocence but you must clear your name.*

○ **give a bad 'name**

You **give** someone or something **a bad name** when you harm their reputation by behaving badly: *the sort of man-hating bitterness that has given feminism such a bad name.*

○ **make a 'name for yourself** or **make your 'name**

You **make a name for yourself**, or **make your name**, when you become famous or get a good reputation: *He made a name for himself by touring the clubs, and doing Christmas shows.*
♦ *see also* **make it big** ▷BIG; **make it** ▷MAKE

○ **so-and-so's name is 'mud**

You say that a certain person's **name is mud** if people are very angry with them because of something they have done.

○ **the name of the 'game**

The **name of the game** is the central or most important aspect of a certain activity: *Quality and value for money is the name of the game here!*

○ **take someone's name in 'vain**

You **take someone's**, especially God's, **name in vain** when you use their name without showing proper respect for them: *'You dare to take God's name in vain?' His voice had an underlying note of hysteria.*

○ **you 'name it**

'**You name it**' means 'whatever you can think of or mention': *You name it, he's got it: courage, skill, pace, the lot.*

nature

○ **back to 'nature**

You go **back to nature** when you behave or live in a simple and inexpensive, but healthy way: *So get back to nature, try alternatives to conventional toiletries and techniques.*

near

○ **near as 'dammit** or **near e'nough** (*BrE*; *informal*)

'**Near as dammit**' or '**near enough**' means so near in colour, quality, etc, to something, that it can be considered the same: *The new paint may not be a perfect match but it's as near as dammit.*

nearest

○ **your nearest and 'dearest**

Your nearest and dearest are your closest family and friends: *By making a proper will, you will save your nearest and dearest from paying an unnecessary amount of inheritance tax.*

neck

○ **breathe down someone's 'neck**

Someone who **is breathing down your neck** is annoying you by watching you very carefully in case you make a mistake: *Decisions obviously have to go through the Director, but I don't have accountants breathing down my neck.*

○ **get it in the 'neck**

You **get it in the neck** when you are punished or told off for doing something wrong: *I'd say that if we don't co-operate, we could all get it in the neck.*

○ **risk your 'neck**

You **risk your neck** when what you do exposes you to some kind of danger: *It was interesting. It is years since I risked my neck. I am wet but utterly unharmed.* ♦ *see also* **dice with death** ▷DEATH

○ **save your 'neck**

You **save your neck** when you get out of a difficult or dangerous situation: *Don't use my name to save your neck!*

○ **stick your 'neck out**

You **stick your neck out** when what you do puts you in a situation where you might fail, or might be criticized or attacked: *I wondered gloomily why I'd already stuck my neck out to protect Jett. He wasn't a friend.* ♦ *see also* **go for broke** ▷BROKE

○ **up to your 'neck**

You are **up to your neck** when you are very busy with something or deeply involved in something: *I'm up to my neck in work at the moment – can we make it next week?* ♦ *see also* **up to your ears** ▷ EARS; **up to your eyes** ▷EYES; **up to your eyeballs** ▷EYEBALLS

need

○ **if need 'be** or (*BrE*) **if needs 'be**

If need, or **needs**, **be** means if it is necessary: *Seek professional advice if needs be, rather than make a valiant attempt yourself and then regret it.*

○ **that's 'all I need**

'**That's all I need**' means 'I have too many problems already without having to cope with this one': *Kelly winced. 'That's all I need. Another big bill.'*

needle

○ **like looking for a needle in a 'haystack**

If you are looking for something so small or insignificant, that the search is likely to be hopeless, you can say that it's **like looking for a needle in a haystack**: *I think you're wasting your time. It will be like looking for a needle in a haystack. Far too many young people arrive from England every day.*

needs

○ **needs must when the devil 'drives** (*BrE*)

If you say '**needs must when the devil drives**', you mean that it is necessary to act because action cannot be avoided, however unpleasant the task is: *Fred groaned and put his boots on again. 'Needs must when the old devil drives.'*

nerve

○ **get on someone's 'nerves**

Someone or something that **gets on your nerves** annoys or irritates you: *That dripping tap is getting on my nerves.* ♦ *see also* **drive someone round the bend** ▷BEND; **get someone's goat** ▷GOAT; **get up someone's nose** ▷NOSE; **rub someone up the wrong way** ▷WAY; **get on someone's wick** ▷WICK

nest

○ **feather your own 'nest**

You **feather your own nest** when you gain money for yourself, or make yourself rich, especially at other people's expense: *Two of the others, including the chairman, were using their positions to feather their own nests.* ♦ *see also* **line your pockets** ▷POCKETS

net

○ **cast your net 'wide**

You **cast your net wide** when you make sure that you will not miss any likely opportunity or benefit by covering as wide an area as possible in your search for something you want: *Casting the net wide, he pursued all branches of the creative arts, coming finally to music.*

> In fishing, the wider you cast your net, the more fish you are likely to catch.

○ **surf the 'net**

You **surf the net** when you use a computer to obtain information, using the electronic worldwide communication system called the Internet: *If you too are hooked on surfing the net, you'll know what a wealth of knowledge can be obtained from it.*

When you surf on the sea, you follow the waves and the currents of the water, while standing on a surfboard. When you **surf the net**, you follow the information route that interests you, moving through the network by means of 'links'.

nettle

○ **grasp the 'nettle**

You **grasp the nettle** when you begin an unpleasant or difficult task in a firm, determined way: *However, the Council made it clear that it had no intention of grasping the nettle itself, and taking any decision.*

Nettles are less likely to sting you if you grasp them firmly.

nevermind

○ **pay someone** or **something no 'nevermind** (*AmE*) (*very informal*)

You **pay someone** or **something no nevermind** when you ignore them: *If he gets angry, just pay him no nevermind.*

new

○ **a new one on 'you** (*informal*)

You say '**that's a new one on me**' when you have just been told something that you didn't know before, and which you perhaps find difficult to believe: *However, what the honourable gentleman says is a new one on me, if I may put it as basically as that.* ♦ *see also* **that's news to me** ▷NEWS

news

○ **bad 'news** (*informal*)

If you describe someone as **bad news**, you mean that they should be avoided: *Don't get involved with him; he's bad news, from what I've heard.*

○ **no news is 'good news**

No news is good news means that if you haven't heard from someone, it probably means that everything is all right, and that there is no need to worry: *It really is a case of no news is good*

news. *There is no point in proceeding any further with your plans until you have proper confirmation.*

○ **that's news to 'me**

You say '**that's news to me**', or that a certain thing **is news to** you, when someone tells you something you didn't know, especially something very surprising, or something you think others should have told you earlier: *British Waterways officer John Ellis said: 'The pollution is news to me. I shall have to investigate the matter further'.* ♦ *see also* **a new one on me** ▷NEW

nick

○ **in the nick of 'time**

You do something **in the nick of time** when you only just manage to do it before it is too late: *She was only just rescued in the nick of time.*

'**Nick**', here, refers to a notch on a stick, formerly used as a measurement of time.

nickel

○ **nickel and 'dime it** (*AmE*)

You **nickel and dime it** when you live cheaply: *We did go to Paris, but we had to nickel and dime it.*

○ **nickel and 'dime someone** or **nickel and 'dime someone to death** (*AmE*)

If you **nickel and dime someone**, or **nickel and dime someone to death**, you keep charging them small amounts: *It's cheap to enter the theme park, but then they nickel and dime you for everything.*

○ **not worth a plugged 'nickel** (*AmE*)

Something that is **not worth a plugged nickel** is worthless: *He told us it was an antique, but it turns out that it's not worth a plugged nickel.*

Criminals used to counterfeit coins by plugging the insides with an inferior metal.

night

○ **one-night 'stand**

A **one-night stand** is a sexual relationship that begins and ends on the same evening: *A 17-year-old pupil of* *mine got pregnant last year, the result of a one-night stand.*

○ turn night into 'day

You **turn night into day** when you stay up late, or all night: *The old man was demented, turning night into day, and persistently interrupting the sleep of neighbours.*

nines

○ dressed up to the 'nines or dolled up to the 'nines (*BrE*) or dressed to the nines (*AmE*)

Someone who is **dressed, dressed up,** or **dolled up, to the nines** is dressed in a very glamorous way, sometimes more so than necessary: *There I was, dressed up to the nines, trying to change the wheel of my car at the side of the motorway.*

nip

○ a 'nip in the air

If you say that there is **a nip in the air,** you mean that the weather is a bit cold: *There was a keen nip in the air; winter was only just round the corner.*

○ nip and 'tuck

If a competition is described as **nip and tuck,** it is so close that you do not know who will win: *As the horses rounded the last bend, it was still nip and tuck.*

nitty-gritty

○ get down to the nitty-'gritty

You **get down to the nitty-gritty** when you consider the basic facts of a situation: *There's an introductory talk; then we get down to the real nitty-gritty on Friday morning.*

nod

○ get the 'nod¹ (*BrE*)

You **get the nod** from someone when you get permission from them to do something: *There shouldn't be a problem if you need to leave early for a dental appointment, but I suggest you get the nod from your manager first.*

○ get the 'nod² (*AmE*)

If someone **gets the nod,** they are chosen for a job or other position: *All the applicants were qualified, but Peter got the nod.*

You nod your head [= move it up and down] when you agree to something.

none

○ none other than 'so-and-so

You use **none other than** when telling a story, for example, to dramatize a surprising piece of information about a particular person's or thing's presence: *The engine of the Royal Train failed near Cambridge. Inside was none other than the Queen.*

○ none too 'such-and-such

None too is used before adjectives and adverbs to mean their opposites: *The look in his eyes was none too friendly.*

nook

○ every nook and 'cranny

Every nook and cranny refers to every part of a place: *The full survey will ensure every nook and cranny is inspected. The surveyor will pull up carpets and crawl into the loft.*

Nook is an old word for 'corner' and **cranny** is an old word for 'crack'.

nose

○ cut off your nose to spite your 'face

You **cut off your nose to spite your face** when you do something because of pride or anger, in order to harm someone else, but which in fact harms your own interests: *The charity's director says that by reducing Third World aid to reduce public spending, the Government would be cutting off its nose to spite its face.*

○ follow your 'nose

You **follow your nose** when you **1** go straight on: *You follow your nose down to the bottom of there. Then you turn left.* **2** act according to your natural tendency: *You are on the right track so follow your nose.*

○ get up someone's 'nose (*informal*)

Someone or something **gets up your nose** when they annoy or irritate you: *That fellow's arrogance gets up my nose.*

♦ *see also* **drive someone round the bend** ▷BEND; **get someone's goat** ▷GOAT; **get on someone's nerves** ▷NERVES; **rub someone up the wrong way** ▷WAY; **get on someone's wick** ▷WICK

○ keep your 'nose clean

You **keep your nose clean** when you

behave well in order to avoid trouble from people in authority: *He could've got out of prison in a couple of months if he'd kept his nose clean.*

○ **keep your nose to the 'grindstone** or **have your nose to the 'grindstone** or **put your nose to the 'grindstone**
You **keep, have,** or **put, your nose to the grindstone** when you work hard, without a rest: *He keeps his nose to the grindstone and thinks everyone else should.*

A **grindstone** is a large round stone that is turned by a machine, and is used for making tools sharper.

○ **on the 'nose** (*informal*)
1 You get it, or hit it, **on the nose,** when you state something very precisely: *When Mack said you lied, he hit it right on the nose.* **2** (*AmE*) **'On the nose'** means 'at the right time' or 'in the right amount': *They were able to finish the project on the nose.* □ *He said I owed him $87 on the nose.*

The term comes from horse racing where a bet is placed **on the nose** of a specific horse.

○ **pay through the 'nose for something**
You **pay through the nose for something** when you pay an unreasonably high price for it: *I am surprised that they continue to insist that we return to a system in which single people have to pay through the nose.*

○ **poke your 'nose into something** or **stick your 'nose into something**
You **poke,** or **stick, your nose into something** when you interfere with other people's business: *She didn't want this man poking his nose into her affairs.*

○ **powder your 'nose**
Women sometimes say that they are going to **powder their nose** when they are going to the toilet. ♦ *see also* **spend a penny** ▷PENNY

○ **put someone's 'nose out of joint**
You **put someone's nose out of joint** when you offend them or hurt their pride: *'I'm afraid their noses are a little out of joint,' said Mrs Hollidaye. 'Never mind. They'll just have to learn.'*

○ **rub someone's 'nose in it**
You **rub someone's nose in it** when you constantly remind them of something they have done wrong: *'It's deliberate, isn't it?' Peter had said. 'Just rubbing my nose in it. As if I didn't feel bad enough already.'*

From a frequently recommended way of house-training animals.

○ **thumb your 'nose at someone**
You **thumb your nose at someone** when you refuse to obey them, or show that you have no respect for them: *The band, in a further attempt to thumb their nose at the establishment, wrote lyrics which they knew the radio stations would never broadcast.*

Putting your thumb on your nose with the rest of your fingers outstretched is a disrespectful (or humorous) gesture.

○ **turn your 'nose up at something**
If you **turn your nose up** at something, you are showing, rather rudely, that you do not like it, or that you think that it is not good enough for you: *Models now don't turn their noses up at a job for a lesser magazine if their last assignment was for 'Elle', for example.* ♦ *see also* **pull** or **make a face** ▷FACE

○ **under someone's 'nose**
Something happens **under your nose** when it happens in front of you or very close to you, so that you should notice it: *What I can't understand is how this all went on under my nose, without my noticing anything.*

note

○ **strike the right 'note**
You **strike the right note** when you do or say something that pleases people, or that they find appropriate: *Professor Noel Dilly struck precisely the right note of scepticism, receptivity and curiosity.*

○ **take 'note**
If you **take note** of something, you pay special attention to it: *Each month we take note of your comments and try to redress the balance, hoping that over the year we get it just about right.*

nothing

○ **in nothing 'flat** (*AmE*)
When something happens **in nothing flat**, it happens immediately, or without delay: *When we called the ambulance, they were there in nothing flat.*

○ **make 'nothing of**
1 You **make nothing of** something such as an achievement when you try to give the impression that it is not important or worth being proud of: *I think she got the highest score in the whole country in that exam, but she makes nothing of it.* **2** You **make nothing of** something bad which has happened when you treat it as if it were not important or worth worrying about: *I told her I would pay for the vase I broke, but she made nothing of it.*

○ **next to 'nothing**
Next to nothing means almost nothing: *She came to the door wearing next to nothing.*

○ **nothing 'doing**
Nothing doing means that nothing is happening, or can be done; **nothing doing** is also a rude refusal to consider a request: *Yeah, but she's not working at the moment. She says that there's absolutely nothing doing.*

○ **nothing 'for it** (*BrE*)
If you say that **there's nothing for it** but to do a particular thing, you mean that it is the only possible thing to do, even though you would rather not do it: *There was nothing for it but to try to make their way on foot out of the town.*

○ **nothing if not 'such-and-such**
You use '**nothing if not**' to emphasize a description: *The farmhouse was nothing if not practical.*

○ **nothing 'in it**
1 If you say, in reference to a story or report, that there's **nothing in it**, you mean that it isn't true. **2** You also say that there's **nothing in it** when there is no difference between two things.

○ **nothing short of**
You use '**nothing short of** a certain thing', as a way of emphasizing that thing: *His behaviour has been nothing short of des'picable.*

○ **nothing 'to it**
If you say, when referring to a task, that

there's **nothing to it**, you mean that it is very easy: *'Both of us have done this kind of thing before. There's really nothing to it.'*

notice

○ **sit up and take 'notice** or **sit up and take 'note**
Someone or something that makes you **sit up and take notice**, or **note**, forces you to pay attention to something you paid little or no attention to before: *Campaigners have drawn our attention to the world's diminishing rainforests and are making the guilty West sit up and take note.*

now

○ **as of 'now**
As of now means 'starting from now': *As of now all purchases must be paid for immediately.*

○ **now and 'then** or **now and a'gain** or **every now and 'then** or **every now and a'gain**
Something that happens **now and then**, or **now and again**, or **every now and then**, or **every now and again** happens occasionally: *We would stop every now and then to sit on our rucksacks and gaze in awe at the beauty of the scene.*

number

○ **your number is 'up**
If you say that someone's **number is up**, you mean that they are about to die, or suffer something unpleasant: *That's what we used to say during the war. If your number was up there was nothing you could do about it.*

○ **number 'one**
1 Number one describes what is best, most important, or most popular: *He was number one in the world for longer than any other tennis player.* **2** If you say that you are looking after **number one**, you mean that you are concerned with making sure that you get what you want, rather than helping or sharing with others: *The prevailing attitude to life in the '80s seemed to be to look after number one, to get on, to make money, and not to bother about anyone else.*

○ **someone's opposite 'number**
Your **opposite number** is someone who does the same job as you, but in a

different place or organization: *Nor was the speech by his Labour opposite number that much more uplifting.*

> In team sports, a member of one team has the same number on their back as the person on the opposing team who has the same role.

numbers

○ **the 'numbers** or **the 'numbers game** or **the 'numbers racket** (*AmE*)
The numbers or **the numbers game** or **the numbers racket** is an illegal lottery: *Nearly a fifth of his salary was spent on the numbers.*

nut

○ **do your 'nut** (*BrE; informal*)
You **do your nut** when you get very angry: *Your mum will do her nut! Look at your coat!* ♦ *see also* **go off at the deep end** ▷END; **blow a fuse** ▷FUSE; **let fly** ▷LET; **blow** or **flip your lid** ▷LID; **lose your rag** ▷RAG; **fly into a rage** ▷RAGE; **hit the roof** ♦ ROOF; **blow your stack** ▷STACK; **lose your temper** ▷TEMPER; **blow your top** ▷TOP; **throw a wobbly** ▷WOBBLY

○ **a hard nut to 'crack** or **a tough nut to 'crack**
If you describe a problem as **a hard**, or **a tough, nut to crack**, you mean that it is difficult to solve: *The enemy were determined to hold on to this position. It was a tough nut to crack.*

nuts

○ **nuts about** (*informal*)
If you are **nuts about** someone, you love them madly; if you are **nuts about** something, you are very enthusiastic about it: *I seek an Irish male, 19-25, as a penpal. I'm nuts about 'Ireland and everything to do with it.*

○ **nuts and 'bolts**
The **nuts and bolts** of a thing or situation are the basic facts or important practical details about it: *Whenever he had a promotional tour he would take Leonard along, acquaint him with the nuts and bolts of the business.*

nutshell

○ **in a 'nutshell**
You say '**in a nutshell**', when you are about to describe a situation very briefly, concentrating on the most important point: *'Were relations between himself and the ANC warm?' 'In a nutshell: Yes. But not only with the ANC.'*

oar

○ **put your 'oar in** or **shove your 'oar in** or **stick your 'oar in**
If you say that someone **puts, shoves**, or **sticks, their oar in**, you mean that they are trying to affect a situation, especially by offering their opinion, when their presence or ideas are not wanted: *We were sorting it out quite nicely until you stuck your oar in.*

oats

○ **sow your wild 'oats**
You say that a person, usually a young man, **is sowing his wild oats** if he is living a life of wild enjoyment, especially involving numerous romantic affairs and sexual experiences, before settling down to a quieter, more serious and respectable life: *The sowing of wild oats is not as threatening to the reputation of a man as it is to that of a woman.*

object

○ **the object of the 'exercise**
The object of the exercise is the aim of the activity you are referring to: *The management of properties will be reviewed. The object of the exercise is to ensure the efficient use of natural resources throughout the Trust.*

odd

○ **odd one 'out**
Someone or something that is the **odd one out** in any group is the one that is noticeably different from the rest: *Look at these objects and tell me which is the odd one out.*

odds

○ **against all the 'odds** or **against all 'odds**

Something happens or is done **against all the odds**, or **against all odds**, when it happens or is done despite great difficulty or disadvantage: *Against all odds, Greenpeace has brought the plight of the natural world to the attention of caring people.*

○ **at 'odds with**

You are **at odds with** someone when you are in disagreement with or in opposition to them; something, such as an idea or policy, is **at odds with** something else, such as a person's actions, when they do not correspond to, or match, each other: *How can we ever agree when his views are at odds with everything I believe in?*

○ **make no 'odds** (*BrE*)

You say it **makes no odds** when you want to make it clear that a fact or action will make no difference to a particular situation: *One three times a day, for seven days. You can take it with food, after food, between meals, makes no odds.*

○ **over the 'odds** (*BrE*)

Over the odds means more than is necessary or expected, especially with regard to money: *While a collector may be happy to pay over the odds for such interesting issues, an investor would have to be confident of gold prices to show a profit on resale.*

off

○ **off and 'on**

Something that is the case **off and on** is the case sometimes, but not all the time: *It's been raining off and on all day.*

often

○ **every so 'often**

Something that happens **every so often** happens sometimes, but not frequently: *Every so often, he would come home with a bunch of flowers.*

○ **often as 'not**

Something that happens as **often as not** happens on at least half of the occasions, or in at least half of the cases, that you are referring to; something that happens **more often than not** happens on most of the occasions, or in most of the cases, that you are referring to: *As often as not, if you apologize, people will forgive you and forget the whole thing.* □ *More often than not, lumps in the breast turn out to be harmless fibroids rather than cancers.*

oil

○ **burn the midnight 'oil**

You **burn the midnight oil** if you work or study until late at night: *Having only two weeks to complete the work, they burned the midnight oil to finish it in time.*

○ **pour oil on troubled 'waters**

A person who **is pouring oil on troubled waters** is trying to calm a person or improve a difficult situation: *Ronnie smiled a light smile, seeking to pour oil on troubled waters. 'Please don't worry on my account. It doesn't matter.'*

old

○ **any old 'such-and-such** (*informal*)

Any old means 'any' or 'no matter what', emphasizing that the quality of the thing in question is not important, or not very good: *For her, the real issue is the second generation's right to education, but not any old education.*

○ **'any old how**

You do something **any old how** if you do it without taking any special care: *Could you fold the clothes properly, please? Don't shove them in any old how.*

omelette

○ **you can't make an omelette without breaking 'eggs**

If someone says '**you can't make an omelette without breaking eggs**', they mean that it is often impossible to achieve a desirable aim without doing some kind of damage or harming someone in the process: *I take the view that one cannot make omelettes without breaking eggs. It is almost impossible to forge any sort of career in public life where you do not yourself become the object of hostility in some quarter.*

on

○ **get 'on to someone**

If you **get on to someone**, you contact them: *Get on to your local Councillor if you are unhappy about the new parking restrictions.*

one

○ **on and 'off**

Something that is the case **on and off** is the case sometimes, but not all the time: *They've been seeing each other on and off since Christmas.*

○ **'on to something**

If you say you are **on to something**, especially something wrong or illegal, you mean that you have become aware of it or have discovered it: *I'm on to your little game, and if you try it again I'll call the police.*

one

○ **all 'one**

If, after considering two or more possibilities, you say that it is **all one** to you, you mean that you do not care which thing happens: *'So there are your options. What do you want to do?' 'Oh, you choose. It's all one to me.'*

○ **at 'one**

You are **at one** with someone or something if you are in agreement, or living harmoniously, with them: *It's unusual to meet a couple who are so happy, so utterly at one with each other.* □ *Is it possible for mankind to be at one with nature?*

○ **one or 'two**

One or two means 'a few': *I made one or two mistakes, but I think I did all right.*

onions

○ **know your 'onions**

If you say that someone **knows their onions**, you mean that they know their subject well or do their job well: *I agree that he knows his onions, but that doesn't mean he'll be a good teacher.* ♦ *see also* **know your stuff** ▷STUFF

open

○ **in the 'open** or **out in the 'open**

1 Something that is **in the open**, or **out in the open**, is out of doors, not inside a building: *Horses, like all animals, love to get out in the open.* **2** If something, especially something which might make you ashamed or upset, is **out in the open**, it is not hidden, ignored, or kept secret: *If you think he's seeing another woman, why not mention it? It's better to have it out in the open.*

option

○ **the soft 'option** (*BrE*)

A person who has to decide between a number of possible actions takes **the soft option** when they choose the one which is easiest or involves the least effort: *Whoever thinks staying at home to look after the kids is a soft option should try it for themselves.* ♦ *see also* **take the easy way out** ▷WAY

options

○ **keep your 'options open** or **leave your 'options open**

If you **keep**, or **leave**, **your options open**, you avoid making a choice or decision now, so that you are free to do so at a later time when you have more information, or when you are forced to make a choice: *You need to keep your options open in order to be able to change courses at a moment's notice.*

order

○ **in order to**

You do something **in order to** achieve some result when you do it with that purpose: *I am phoning in order to a'pologize.*

○ **keep 'order**

You **are keeping order** when you are keeping control of a situation: *I am not strong on discipline, and find it difficult to keep order in the classroom.*

○ **the order of the 'day**

You say that something is **the order of the day** if it is considered to be necessary, normal, common or particularly fashionable at a certain time, or in a certain situation: *For Japan's high-tech industries, the order of the day is to maintain quality and cut prices.*

> In a political or formal meeting, **the order of the day** is the list of subjects which must be discussed.

○ **out of 'order**

1 Things are **out of order** if they are **a** not working properly: *Photocopier out of order. Please use photocopier in Finance Department.* **b** not arranged according to the correct system: *There is a file for each year. Don't let them get out of order.* **2** (*informal*) People are **out of order** if they are not behaving according to the rules of a certain situation: *He was right out of order last night, bossing everyone around like that.*

○ **a tall 'order**

You call something that you are expected to do **a tall order** if it seems rather unreasonable, probably because it is too difficult: *They need to force both inflation and interest rates down in time for the next election – a tall order to say the least.*

○ **to 'order**

Something that is made **to order** is only prepared if someone asks for it, taking into account any particular requests they may have: *You can have a sofa made to order in a choice of over 40 fabrics.*

out

○ **have it 'out with someone**

You **have it out with someone** when you have a discussion, usually an angry one, about something they have been doing which annoys you: *Her face registered gathering anger. 'I've a good mind to go and have it out with him here and now. I know where to find him.'*

○ **out and a'bout**

You get **out and about** when you are able to leave your home and lead a sociable life, for example after being ill: *It's great to see him out and about again.*

○ **out-and-out**

Out-and-out is used to describe someone or something that is an extreme or complete example of that thing: *If she told you that, then she's an out-and-out liar.*

○ **'out for something**

You are **out for something** if your intention is to get it: *She's out for all she can 'get.*

○ **'out of it**

1 You feel **out of it** when you feel that you are unable to join in with other people's activities: *I still like the dancing, but I've been feeling a bit out of it since I've stopped going every week.* **2** (*informal*) You say that a person is **out of it** if they are not aware of what is happening around them, because they are tired, or as the result of drinking too much alcohol or taking drugs: *That guy is out of it. He can hardly stand up.*

○ **out to 'do something**

If you are **out to do something**, it is your aim to do it: *He's out to make money, and he doesn't care how he does it.*

○ **'out with it**

If you say **'out with it'** to someone, you mean that you want to hear what they have to say: *He was gripping her shoulder, saying, 'Where is she? Come on, out with it! Where is she?'*

○ **take it 'out of someone**

If something such as work **takes it out of you**, it makes you tired: *Even if I'm asleep for the whole journey, I still find that travelling takes it out of me.*

○ **take it 'out on someone**

A person who is worried or upset **is taking it out on you** when they are unkind to you, not because of anything that you have done, but just because of the unhappy feelings which they are having: *I know you're disappointed, but there's no need to take it out on me.*

outs

○ **on the 'outs with someone** (*AmE*)

If you are **on the outs with someone**, you have had a dispute with them and are on bad terms as a result, or you are unfriendly towards them: *How can you be on the outs with your own brother?*

outside

○ **at the out'side**

If you are guessing how much something will be, and you say that it is a certain number **at the outside**, you mean that it cannot be more than that, and may be less: *It can't be more than three hours' drive at the very outside.*

over

○ **all 'over someone**

Someone is **all over you** if they are being too friendly or trying hard to please you, usually so that you will do something that they want: *She found them too friendly and too knowing. 'They were all over me,' she told her friends.*

○ **over and a'bove**

Things or amounts **over and above** something are in addition to it: *Remember, there will be insurance to pay, over and above the price of the car itself.*

overboard

○ **go 'overboard for** or **go 'overboard about** (*informal*)

You **go overboard for**, or **go over-**

board about, someone or something when you show a lot of, or too much, enthusiasm for that person or thing: *Avoid sexist language – learn to use 'he or she', rather than the male form of the pronoun, but don't go overboard – 'manpower' is still manpower.*

own

○ **come into your 'own**

You **come into your own** when you get the chance to show your good qualities, abilities, or intelligence: *She has always been a bit shy and nervous, but she comes into her own when she works with kids.*

○ **get your 'own back**

You **get your own back**, or **get your own back on someone** who has done you harm or played a trick on you, when you do something to harm or trick them in return: *She made you look a bit of a fool. Didn't it make you angry? Wouldn't you have liked to get your own back?* ♦ *see also* **get even** ▷EVEN

p

○ **mind your p's and 'q's**

When someone tells you to **mind your p's and q's**, they are telling you to take care to behave properly in a certain situation: *Three months' trial period, eh? You'd better mind your p's and q's.*

paces

○ **put someone through their 'paces** or **put something through its 'paces**

You **put someone**, or **something**, **through their paces** when you give them certain things to do, to test their abilities: *After this morning's written test, we'll be putting you through your paces in a real business situation.*

Horses have four paces: 'walk', 'trot', 'canter' and 'gallop'. Someone who is deciding whether to buy a horse puts it through all its paces, observing how it moves at different speeds.

packet

○ **cost a 'packet** (*BrE*)

You can say something **costs a packet** if it is expensive: *'I want an underwater camera.' 'Oh, that'll cost you a packet.'* ♦ *see also* **cost the earth** ▷EARTH

pain

○ **on pain of 'something** or **under pain of 'something**

If you give someone an order **on**, or **under**, **pain of something**, you are threatening them with that thing as a punishment if they fail to do what you ask: *The dissidents were ordered to cease their activities immediately, under pain of imprisonment.* ◻ *I've told her to be back by midnight, under pain of death.*

This use of the word **pain** comes from the French 'peine', meaning 'punishment' or 'penalty'. The expression 'under pain of death' is more often used in a humorous, rather than literal, way, as in the second example.

pains

○ **be at 'pains** or **take 'pains**

If you **are at pains** or **taking pains** to do something, you are making a lot of effort to do it as well as possible: *I never felt at home with the host family, although they were at pains to make me comfortable.*

○ **for someone's 'pains**

If someone says they got something, or got nothing, **for their pains**, they mean that they got, or did not get, a reward or thanks for the effort they made or the work they did: *I expect to be promptly and generously reimbursed for my pains.* ◻ *She worked a full day cleaning that house, and what did she get for her pains? Not even a thankyou.* ♦ *see also* **worth someone's while** ▷WHILE

pair

○ **have only one pair of 'hands**

You say you **have only got one pair of**

hands if you are trying, or someone is asking you, to do more things at once than you consider to be possible: *You can't expect me to do the ironing as well as everything else. I've only got one pair of hands you know.*

○ **show a clean pair of 'heels** (*BrE*)

You say that a person or thing **shows a clean pair of heels** if they run away, or if they move a long way ahead of their competitors: *He showed the other runners a clean pair of heels with an astounding sprint to the finish.* ◻ *With such adventurous marketing, the company is showing the rest of the industry a clean pair of heels.*

pale

○ **beyond the 'pale**

You say that behaviour or a certain action is **beyond the pale** if you think it is so bad that it is unacceptable: *I like to think I am broad-minded, but the language my father used was beyond the pale.*

palm

○ **grease someone's 'palm** (*informal*)

If you **grease someone's palm**, you give them money as a bribe to persuade them to do something for you: *He can tell you where they are hiding, but you'll have to grease his palm first.*

○ **have someone in the palm of your 'hand** or **have someone eating out of the palm of your 'hand**

You **have someone in**, or **eating out of, the palm of your hand** if you have so much influence over that person that you can get them to do anything you want: *They won't do anything without his permission. He's got all his employees in the palm of his hand.* ◆ *see also* **have someone wrapped round your little finger** ▷FINGER; **have someone eating out of your hand** ▷HAND; **have someone right where you want them** ▷ WANT; **have someone in your pocket** ▷POCKET

pan

○ **out of the frying-pan into the 'fire**

You say **'out of the frying-pan into the fire'** when you have just escaped from a difficult or dangerous situation, only to find yourself in a situation which is even worse: *To me they sound as if they're very similar – so be warned. Marry Doreen and you'll be stepping out of the frying pan into the fire.*

paper

○ **on 'paper**

1 When you talk about something as it appears **on paper**, you are talking about the information you get from official documents: *He looked so good on paper, but he performed very badly at the interview.* **2** You get your thoughts or ideas down **on paper** when you write them down: *If you have a complaint, it is important to get it down on paper and send it to the manager.*

par

○ **below 'par** or **not up to 'par**

1 Someone or something that is **below par** or **not up to par** does not perform as usual, or does not come up to the standard required: *Oh yes, he's still playing good tennis. But I still think he was not quite up to par this year.* ◻ *His eyesight was below par, which disqualified him from being a pilot.* **2** If you are feeling **below par**, you are not feeling as well as you usually do: *You might feel below par, your resistance to infection could well be affected; you will not have the zest for life that you should have.* ◆ *see also* **out of sorts** ▷SORTS; **under the weather** ▷WEATHER

○ **on a 'par with something**

You describe two things as being **on a par with each other** if you consider them to be approximately equivalent in terms of degree or achievement: *For a canoeist, the challenge of paddling to the Pharoes is on a par with climbing Everest.*

parrot

○ **'parrot-fashion** (*BrE*)

You learn something **parrot-fashion** if you learn it by memory, without making any attempt to understand it: *Some students were reduced to learning their work parrot-fashion, while lacking any real understanding of what they were taught.*

Parrots can learn to speak, but they just copy the sounds that they hear, without understanding them.

part

○ **the best part of 'such-and-such**

The best part of a certain quantity is almost all of it: *He just disappeared, leaving behind him the best part of a million pounds' worth of unpaid 'debts.*

○ **for 'my part**

For my part means 'if you want to know my preference': *Some people like the city, and others the country. For my part, I prefer the country.*

○ **for the 'most part**

If you make a statement and say that it is true **for the most part**, you mean that there may be a few exceptions, but that, as a general statement, it is true: *The children were very well-behaved, at least for the most part. Tom could have been less noisy.*

○ **have no 'part in something** or **take no 'part in something**

You decide to **have**, or **take**, **no part in something** if you decide not to get involved in that thing, probably because you do not approve of it: *He believed social segregation in education to be totally wrong and he could have no part in perpetuating it.*

○ **part and 'parcel**

Something is **part and parcel** of a certain situation or procedure if it is a necessary, and perhaps rather unpleasant, part: *Infuriating it may be, but you may as well accept that these things are part and parcel of travel overseas.*

○ **part of the 'furniture**

You say that someone or something is like **part of the furniture** if you are used to them, and even feel some affection for them, just because they have been present for such a long time: *He was a drunken old fool, but we'll miss him here at the pub. He was like part of the furniture.*

○ **play a 'part**

A person or thing **plays a part** when they help to cause a certain event: *By donating as little as £3, you can be sure that you have played a part in improving a child's life.* □ *Falling petrol sales certainly played a part in Shell's decision.*

○ **take something in good 'part** (*BrE*)

You **take something**, such as a criti-cism directed at you, **in good part** if you are able to accept it with good humour and not get upset about it: *I thought he took all those jokes about the Irish in remarkably good part.*

○ **take 'part**

You **are taking part**, or **taking part in something**, if you are doing an activity together with a number of other people: *I love silly party games, but my boyfriend always refuses to take part.*

○ **take someone's 'part**

When you **take someone's part**, you support them or their opinion against other people: *I thought I could at least rely on family members to take my part.*

party

○ **be 'party to something**

A person **is party to something** if they participate in it: *Just how that's going to be accomplished we don't know – we're not party to the discussions.*

pass

○ **come to a 'pass** or **come to a pretty 'pass**

You say that things have **come to a pass** or **come to a pretty pass** if you feel shocked by how bad the situation has become: *Things have come to a pretty pass if we can't afford to feed a few visitors! It's disgraceful!*

○ **make a 'pass at someone**

If you **make a pass at someone** you find sexually attractive, you do or say something which makes your attraction obvious, to see whether they are interested in you too: *'My tutor made a pass at me today.' 'I would report it to the students' council if I were you.'*

past

○ **'past it** (*informal, insulting*)

You say someone is **past it** if you consider that they are old, or too old to do certain things: *Don't you think he's getting a bit past it to be going on a skiing holiday?* ♦ *see also* **over the hill** ▷HILL; **long in the tooth** ▷TOOTH

pasture

○ **put someone out to pasture** *see* **put someone out to grass** ▷GRASS

pat

○ **off 'pat** (*BrE*) or **down 'pat**

You know, or have, something **off pat**, or **down pat** if you know it so well that you can repeat it from memory with no mistakes: *I haven't got all the lines off pat yet, but I should be all right in time for the dress rehearsal.* ♦ *see also* **by heart** ▷HEART

○ **a pat on the 'back**

If you are praising someone for doing something well, you can say that they should give themselves, or that they deserve, **a pat on the back**: *First of all, you deserve a pat on the back for successfully completing the first four weeks of the diet.*

patch

○ **go through a 'bad patch**

You **are going through a bad patch** when you are having a lot of problems at a particular time in your life; a marriage or relationship **is going through a bad patch** if the two people involved are not getting on very well with each other: *When I was five my father hit a bad patch and he sold the house.* □ *'Tim and I,' said Louise heavily, 'are going through a bad patch. We get on each other's nerves, to put it bluntly.'*

○ **not a 'patch on** (*BrE*)

You say that something or someone is **not a patch on** the thing or person you are comparing them with if they are much less good than that thing or person: *The barbecue was good, but it wasn't a patch on last year's.* ♦ *see also* **in a class of your own** ▷CLASS; **a cut above** or **a cut above the rest** ▷CUT; **in a different league** ▷LEAGUE

path

○ **cross someone's 'path**

You **cross someone's path** when you meet that person or your life briefly becomes linked with theirs in some way, usually by chance: *She went away with a look on her face which boded ill for anyone who crossed her path that day.*

patter

○ **the patter of tiny 'feet**

If people talk about **the patter of tiny feet**, they are referring to the birth of children: *I'm not saying it's going to be easy, giving all this up, but I quite fancy hearing the patter of tiny feet.*

pavement

○ **pound the 'pavement** (*AmE*; *informal*)

You **pound the pavement** when you walk from place to place seeking a job: *'How can you lie there on the couch?' she said. 'You should be out pounding the pavement.'*

peanuts

○ **for 'peanuts**

1 If you do some work **for peanuts**, you are badly paid for it: *But I mean you don't want to start working in the mines for peanuts or anything, you want a good job.* **2** You say you can't do something **for peanuts** if you can't do it very well, or at all: *I can't dance for peanuts.*

pedestal

○ **put someone on a 'pedestal**

You **are putting someone on a pedestal** if your great admiration for them makes you imagine that they have no faults or weaknesses: *In the courtly love tradition, the woman was put on a pedestal – objectified.*

peg

○ **bring someone 'down a peg or two** or **take someone 'down a peg or two**

If you think that someone is too sure of themselves, and you do or say something to reduce their confidence, you say you **are bringing**, or **taking**, **them down a peg or two**: *It would serve him right. Dared she? He deserved to be taken down a peg or two.*

○ **off the 'peg** (*BrE*)

Clothes which are sold **off the peg** are in a shop, ready to be bought and worn, and there is no need to order them in advance: *He wore a jacket and cream linen trousers that were definitely not off the peg.*

pegging

○ **level 'pegging** (*BrE*)

When two or more competitors have an equal number of points, you say that they are **level pegging**: *The match looked set to be a close affair when the two neighbours were level pegging after three heats.*

pennies

○ **look after** or **take care of the pennies and the pounds will take care of them'selves** (*BrE*)

If someone says 'look after, or take care of, the pennies and the pounds will take care of themselves' they mean that if you make a habit of saving small amounts of money, these small amounts will soon add up to larger amounts: *It's only a bit cheaper, but if you look after the pennies, the pounds will look after themselves.*

penny (*see also* pennies)

○ **in for a penny, in for a 'pound**

You say '**in for a penny, in for a pound**' if, after having taken a small risk, you decide to take a bigger one as well: *'Let's live together,' I said. In for a penny, in for a pound, I thought, and added, 'Will you marry me?'*

○ **not cost a 'penny**

Something which does **not cost a penny** costs nothing: *As an introductory offer, your first year of banking with us won't cost you a penny.*

○ **not have a penny to your 'name**

If you do **not have a penny to your name**, you have no money or financial stability: *And look here, how do you think you're going to pay for it? You haven't a penny to your name.*

○ **the penny 'dropped** or **the penny has 'dropped** (*BrE*)

You say '**the penny dropped**' or '**the penny has dropped**' to refer to the moment when someone understood or realized something that they had not understood or realized before: *She could only stare at him, completely at a loss as to what he meant. Then the penny dropped, and her eyes widened in horrified shock.*

○ **a penny for your 'thoughts** or (*BrE*) **a 'penny for them**

You say '**a penny for your thoughts**', or '**a penny for them**', to someone if they seem to be thinking about something, and you want them to tell you what that thing is: *'A penny for them, Karen.' 'What?' 'A penny for your thoughts. You've gone all dreamy again.'*

○ **'penny-pinching** (*insulting*)

You describe someone as **penny-pinching** if you think they are never willing to spend their money: *People might describe my mother as penny-pinching, but I prefer to say she is frugal.*

○ **penny wise and pound 'foolish**

You say someone is **penny wise, pound foolish** if they are careful with small amounts of money, but they have a tendency to buy large, expensive things which they may not really need: *He told the conference that the health service was being penny wise, pound foolish in the use of medicines. Those in use may be cheap, but the side effects cause greater problems in the long term.*

○ **a pretty 'penny**

You say that something cost **a pretty penny** if it cost a large sum of money: *'That must have cost a pretty penny,' he declared, not really expecting to be told the price.* ♦ *see also* **an arm and a leg** ▷ARM

○ **spend a 'penny** (*BrE*)

If someone says they are going to **spend a penny**, they are saying, in rather an old-fashioned way, that they are going to the toilet: *Can you wait while I go and spend a penny? I won't be a moment.* ♦ *see also* **powder your nose** ▷NOSE

> In the past, the doors on public toilets had a lock on them which only opened when you put a penny in.

○ **turn up like a bad 'penny**

You say that someone or something **turns up like a bad penny** if they often arrive when they are not wanted: *'She's always turning up. Like a bad penny,' Constance thought viciously, saying nothing.*

> This expression comes from the idea that if you try to get rid of a false coin by spending it, that same coin may return to you some day, after passing through the hands of many people who all get rid of it in the same way.

○ **two a 'penny** or **ten a 'penny** (*BrE*)

You say that things are **two**, or **ten**, **a penny** if they are common or easy to obtain: *Müllers are ten a penny in Germany, but it might be the same one.*

pennyworth

○ put your 'pennyworth in

When you **put your pennyworth in**, you take part in a discussion by expressing your opinion: *The National Farmers' Union put its pennyworth in when the milk committee convener said the union expected a reasoned decision.* ♦ *see also* **put your two cents in** ▷CENT

people

○ people who live in glass houses shouldn't throw 'stones

If someone says '**people who live in glass houses shouldn't throw stones**', they mean that a person who can be easily harmed or criticized should not criticize other people or draw attention to themselves: *One would have thought that the principle of people living in glass houses not throwing stones would have warned Ivan off a career as a journalist and gossip.*

perspective

○ in per'spective

When someone sees something **in perspective**, they understand its real importance in relation to other things; when someone gets something **into perspective**, they begin to do this after a period of not doing so: *Outside advice is very important in helping you to see yourself in perspective.* ▫ *Okay, so it's a shame you failed your exams. But try to get it into perspective.*

○ out of per'spective

You say someone is getting something **out of perspective** if you think they are making it seem much more important than it really is: *The election results have been disappointing, but we must not get them out of perspective.* ♦ *see also* **out of proportion** ▷PROPORTION

petard

○ be hoist with your own pe'tard

You say that a person **is hoist with their own petard** if their actions have had the opposite result from that which they had intended, and they themselves end up in difficulty because of their actions: *She found herself hoist with her own petard when the lie she had told turned out to be true.*

Peter

○ rob Peter to pay 'Paul

You say that someone **is robbing Peter to pay Paul** when they obtain the money they need by taking it from an area where it is needed just as much: *Britain's biggest bank has been robbing Peter to pay Paul through the recession. The cash it has taken from the public has gone to cover its losses caused by firms closing down because of the slump.*

phoenix

○ rise like a phoenix from the 'ashes

Someone or something **rises like a phoenix from the ashes** if they become stronger or more admirable than ever before, after and maybe even as a result of having been almost completely destroyed: *Becker, after near defeat in the third set, rose like a phoenix from the ashes and triumphed in five sets.*

phrase

○ to coin a 'phrase

You say '**to coin a phrase**' if you know that you are about to use, or have just used, either **1** a common phrase because you could not think of any better way of expressing your thoughts: *I had to find out the hard way – to coin a phrase.* **2** a new expression which you have just invented: *If the wearing of seat belts reduces accidents, it is also likely to reduce the number of kidneys available for transplant. It is an odd sidelight, to coin a phrase, on road accidents.*

picnic

○ no 'picnic

You say that something is **no picnic** if it involves a lot of problems and difficulty: *It's no picnic, trying to bring up a family on Income Support.*

picture

○ get the 'picture

You say that you **get the picture** to a person who has been describing or explaining something, to show that you understand or can see what they mean: *Fernie looked even more puzzled but Pascoe could see from Alice's face that she was beginning to get the picture.*

○ in the 'picture

1 You put someone **in the picture** when you give them enough information for them to know what is happening: *I'm not really supposed to tell anyone, but I thought I'd better put you in the picture.* **2** If you say that someone is **in the picture**, you mean that they are involved in the situation that you are discussing: *Are ICI still in the picture, or have they pulled out of the project now?*

○ **out of the 'picture**

If you say that someone is **out of the picture**, you mean that they are no longer involved in the situation that you are discussing: *Are you still seeing Jeremy, or is he out of the picture altogether now?*

pie

○ **eat humble 'pie**

If someone **eats humble pie**, they admit that they were wrong about something: *It could easily have been done after all. But they refused to eat humble pie, so we're stuck with the thing until the end of the next century.*

○ **pie in the 'sky**

A promise, plan or hope for the future is **pie in the sky** if it is almost certainly never going to happen: *Some argue that while a coherent system may be desirable, it is not possible; it is pie in the sky, since it ignores reality.*

piece

○ **give someone a piece of your 'mind**

You **give someone a piece of your mind** when you tell them severely how much you disapprove of something they have done: *'He's treated his poor wife disgracefully.' 'I know. I'll give him a piece of my mind when I see him.'* ♦ *see also* **send someone away with a flea in their ear** ▷FLEA; **give someone hell** ▷HELL; **give someone the rough side of your tongue** ▷SIDE; **tear someone off a strip** ▷STRIP

○ **a nasty piece of 'work** (*BrE*)

If you say that someone is **a nasty piece of work**, you mean that they are an unpleasant, and possibly dangerous, person: *You'd best steer clear of him, Manderley, he's a nasty piece of work. Don't want you falling in with the wrong types, do we?*

○ **a piece of the 'action**

Someone who wants **a piece of the**

action wants a share of another person's good luck, especially if this good luck is financial: *American firms are desperate to get a piece of the action but Japanese contractors prefer to do business with their neighbours.* ♦ *see also* **a slice of the action** ▷SLICE; **a slice of the cake** ▷SLICE

○ **a piece of 'cake**

Something which is **a piece of cake** is easy to do or to learn: *All you do is put some cement on the trowel and then throw it like this. It's a piece of cake.* ♦ *see also* **child's play** ▷CHILD; **easy as ABC** or **anything** or **falling off a log** or **pie** or **winking** ▷EASY; **nothing to it** ▷NOTHING

pieces

○ **go to 'pieces**

You **go to pieces** when you get so anxious or upset that you completely lose your ability to deal with things, or to perform as you usually do: *He had been managing well till then, but he went to pieces when someone mentioned his wife.*

○ **pick up the 'pieces**

You **pick up the pieces** when you try to get the situation back to normal again after something bad has happened, leaving everyone shocked and upset: *I just don't want you to get hurt, that's all. And if you do, it'll be me who has to pick up all the pieces.*

pig (*see also* **pigs**)

○ **make a pig's 'ear of something** (*BrE*)

You say that someone **has made a pig's ear of something** if they have done it badly: *I'm afraid I'll have to unpick this sewing and start again. I've made a pig's ear of it.*

○ **a pig in a 'poke**

If someone tells you not to buy **a pig in a poke**, they mean that you should be careful to examine something properly before deciding to buy it: *Can you get your money back if the business you buy turns out to be a pig in a poke?*

> In the past, people were occasionally tricked into buying a poke [= a bag] with what they thought was a piglet inside, when in fact it was a cat.

pigs

○ **pigs might 'fly** (*BrE*)

If someone replies '**pigs might fly**', when you suggest that a certain event is just possible, though unlikely, that person is saying they do not believe it will happen: '*Someone who's not from the area could have been driving through and seen something.*' '*Yeah, and pigs might fly.*'

pile

○ **make your 'pile**

You **make your pile** when you earn a large amount of money: *Mr Cliburn, who was born in Shreveport, Louisiana, into a family that made its pile from oil, has been able to retire to a vast mansion.*

♦ *see also* **make a bundle** ▷BUNDLE; **coin it** or **coin it in** ▷COIN; **make a killing** ▷KILLING

○ **pile it on 'thick**

You say that a person **is piling it on thick** if they are expressing their feelings in such a strong way that you find it difficult to believe and slightly amusing: *Did you see that tribute to Margaret Thatcher on the telly? The guy was piling it on thick, wasn't he?*

pill

○ **a bitter pill to 'swallow**

You say that a fact is **a bitter pill to swallow** for someone if it is something that they do not want to know or believe, but which they have to accept: *To his surprise he found out that his friend had broken the agreement. It was a bit of a blow, a bitter pill to swallow. But I guess that's life!*

pillar

○ **from pillar to 'post**

You go, or are sent, **from pillar to post** when you go or are sent from one place to another without receiving the help you need at any one of them: *These migrants were pushed from pillar to post from the moment they left their homes in Europe.*

pin

○ **you could hear a 'pin drop**

You say that **you could hear a pin drop** if no-one is making a sound and there is complete silence; you also say that **you could have heard a pin**

drop when people are so shocked by something that no-one speaks for a moment: *I still think the great moments in acting are when you could hear a pin drop because you've got them totally captivated in the drama.* □ *Suddenly it was announced that the King had died. You could have heard a pin drop. I can still remember the feeling of intense shock.*

pinch

○ **feel the 'pinch**

Someone who **is feeling the pinch** is having problems because of lack of money: *We've had VAT on domestic fuel for a while, but we will only feel the pinch with the first cold winter.*

○ **take something with a pinch of 'salt**

You **take something with a pinch of salt** when you do not take it too seriously: *Moira always has had a vivid imagination, you have to take what she says with a pinch of salt.*

pinch-hit

○ **pinch-'hit for someone** (*AmE*)

If you **pinch-hit for someone**, you temporarily take their place: *When the speaker became ill, they asked me to pinch-hit for him.*

> In baseball, a player pinch-hits for another when he substitutes for him.

pipe (*see also* piping)

○ **put 'that in your pipe and smoke it**

After insulting someone, or saying something that you know they are not going to like, you can add '**put that in your pipe and smoke it!**' to tell them rudely that you do not care how they feel about it: *I'm going to the party whether you like it or not, so put that in your pipe and smoke it!*

pipeline

○ **in the 'pipeline**

You say that something is **in the pipeline** when it is being planned or prepared: *There are big changes in the pipeline, but no-one knows quite what they are yet.*

piping

○ **piping 'hot**

Food or water that is **piping hot** is very hot: *Be careful not to burn your tongue. The soup is piping hot.*

pit (*see also* **pits**)

○ **a bottomless 'pit**

If you describe something as **a bottomless pit**, you mean that it can never be filled or will never run out: *But there is no bottomless pit of money, so certain players may end up being sold.*

pitch

○ **make a 'pitch for** (*AmE*; *informal*)

If you **make a pitch for** someone or something, you support or promote them: *The actor's first job was in a commercial making a pitch for toothpaste.* ▫ *When the job became available, I went to the boss and made a pitch for Jeffrey.*

○ **queer the 'pitch** or **queer someone's 'pitch** (*BrE*)

You **queer the pitch** or **queer someone's pitch** if you do something which makes the situation difficult for others: *I know you better than to think you'd try to queer my pitch.*

pitching

○ **in there 'pitching** (*AmE*; *informal*)

Someone is **in there pitching** when they are trying hard: *The sales rose because we were all in there pitching.*

> The baseball player who must work the hardest physically is the pitcher.

pits

○ **the 'pits** (*informal*)

When you say someone's behaviour, or a situation, is **the pits**, you are emphasizing that it is the worst possible behaviour or situation: *Mugging people is bad enough, but mugging defenceless old ladies? That's the pits.*

pity

○ **more's the 'pity**

More's the pity means the same as 'I'm sorry to say', and you usually add it just after stating a fact which makes you unhappy: *They don't make cars like that any more – more's the pity.*

place (*see also* **places**)

○ **fall into 'place**

1 Things **fall into place** when you begin to understand a particular situation: *I read the letter again, and then things started to fall into place.* **2** Things **fall into place** when your plans suddenly start to work after a time when

things seemed uncertain: *Don't worry. Now that the church and the reception are booked, everything else will fall into place.*

○ **know your 'place**

You say a person **knows their place** if they accept the authority that certain people have over them: *These upstarts, they don't know their place – they think they can tell me what to do.*

○ **out of 'place**

1 Something that is **out of place** is not in its correct position: *He is always smartly dressed, with never a hair out of place.* **2** A person or thing seems **out of place** if they seem not to belong in a particular situation: *I must say, I felt a bit out of place in among all those military men and their wives.*

○ **put someone in their 'place**

You **put someone in their place** when you make them realize that they are not as important as they think they are, or that they cannot do everything they want: *If you don't put that kid in his place soon, he is going to become totally unmanageable.*

○ **put yourself in such-and-such's 'place**

1 You **are putting yourself in** a certain person's **place** when you think about how it must feel to be in the situation that they are in: *I know she is acting stupidly, but put yourself in her place. What would you do?* **2** You say '**in your place**' before giving someone your advice: *Do you know what I would do in your place? I would go to the police and admit everything.* ♦ *see also* **put yourself in such-and-such's shoes** ▷SHOES

○ **take 'place**

Something **takes place** when it happens: *A motorbike scrambling competition is to take place at Westness Farm next Sunday.*

○ **take the 'place of** or **take someone's 'place**

A person or thing that **takes the place of** another person or thing, does something, or is provided, instead of them: *There are plenty of people who would be happy to take her place if she got the sack.*

places

○ **take second 'place**

One person or thing has to **take second place** to another if they are treated as less important than the other: *She soon realized she would have to take second place to her mother-in-law in her husband's affections.*

places

○ **'go places**

When you say that someone **is going places**, you mean that they are having a lot of success, especially in their job: *She's twenty-four, independent, and with a fairly flourishing career. In fact, she's a girl who's going places.*

plague

○ **avoid like the 'plague**

If you **are avoiding** someone or something **like the plague**, you are doing your best not to come into contact with or be involved with that person or thing: *That woman is poison. I'd avoid her like the plague if I were you.*

plain

○ **plain as a 'pikestaff** (*BrE*) or **plain as the nose on your 'face**

Something which is as **plain as a pikestaff**, or as **plain as the nose on your face**, is very obvious: *None of us ever knew the whole story, even though it was as plain as a pikestaff he had made some unforgivable mistake.*

plate

○ **hand something to someone on a 'plate**

Something **is handed to you on a plate** when you obtain it easily, without making much effort or doing anything special: *It was a win handed to him on a plate when rivals Prost and Schumacher were forced out of the race.*

play

○ **come into 'play** or **be brought into 'play**

Something **comes**, or **is brought**, **into play** when it is introduced into a situation: *It is now that the side reins may be brought into play, encouraging your horse to lower his head.*

○ **make a 'play for**

When you **make a play for** something or someone, you try to get them: *His eyes lingered on Lesley-Jane Decker.*

'Who's that? Has Micky made a play for her yet?'

○ **play 'fair**

Someone **is playing fair** when they behave honestly or do not cheat: *No one who witnessed these debates has ever suggested that Lewis played fair.*

○ **play hard to 'get**

Someone who **is playing hard to get** is trying to avoid someone else, or to avoid accepting an offer or invitation, often with the purpose of making themselves more desirable or wanted: *The key to striking a good bargain is never to seem too eager. Play hard to get.*

○ **play it 'cool**

You say that someone **is playing it cool** when they deal with a situation or problem in a calm way: *If things go wrong, don't panic. Just play it cool and keep going.*

○ **play it 'cozy** (*AmE; informal*)

If you **play it cozy**, you act cautiously in order to avoid a risk: *Thanks for the invitation to follow the tornado, but I think I'll play it cozy at home.*

○ **a play on 'words**

A **play on words** is a joke made by playing with language, or a clever saying, based on similarities between words: *The play on words must now be obvious. Not only does it refer to developing in a photographic sense, but to the development of a group of young people.*

○ **play 'safe** or **play it 'safe**

You **are playing safe**, or **playing it safe**, when you are not taking any risks: *Carry cash in a money-belt, and play it safe by leaving your passport at the hotel reception.*

plea

○ **cop a 'plea** (*AmE; informal*)

Someone who is accused of a crime **cops a plea** when they plead guilty in the hope of getting a lighter sentence: *Jack knew they had the evidence, so he copped a plea.*

pleased

○ **pleased as 'Punch**

Someone who is as **pleased as Punch** is very happy or pleased. ♦ *see also* **happy as a clam** ▷HAPPY

In Punch and Judy puppet shows, Punch (or Mr Punch) always seems to be pleased and excited, especially when he is doing something cruel to the other characters.

plot

○ **the plot 'thickens**

You say '**the plot thickens**', often in a humorous way, to show that the strange combination of recent events makes you suspect that something strange or mysterious is going on: '*The night I noticed my spectacles were missing, I found this note in my pocket.*' '*Hmm. The plot thickens. What does it say?*'

plug

○ **pull the 'plug on something**

You **pull the plug on something** when you suddenly make it impossible for that thing to continue or succeed: *The project was almost finished when the Government pulled the plug on it by withdrawing funding.*

plughole

○ **down the 'plughole** (*BrE*)

Something, usually a plan or an organization, which goes **down the plughole** fails completely and ceases to exist: '*Bars all over the world acquired a fair percentage of my money,*' Jimmy regrets. '*And the rest went down the plughole with various business ventures.*' ♦ *see also* **down the drain** ▷DRAIN

plumb

○ **plumb the 'depths of something**

If you say that someone or something **plumbs the depths of something** such as an unpleasant feeling or bad behaviour, you mean that they reach the lowest point of that feeling or behaviour: *All in the course of one day, I tasted glory, and then plumbed the depths of despair.*

plunge

○ **take the 'plunge**

When you **take the plunge**, you make a difficult decision, especially after you have thought about the decision for a long time: '*I am very pleased I finally took the plunge and started my own business,*' he said.

pocket

○ **in 'pocket** (*BrE*)

You say you are **in pocket** if you have gained money as a result of something such as a business deal: *I was extremely lucky with the house sale, and ended up about ten thousand pounds in pocket.*

○ **have someone in your 'pocket** or (*AmE*) **have someone in your 'hip pocket**

If you **have someone in your pocket**, or **have someone in your hip pocket**, you have complete power or influence over them, and you can make them do what you want: *During the years of the 'special relationship', critics claim Thatcher had Reagan in her pocket.* ♦ *see also* **have someone wrapped round your little finger** ▷FINGER; **have someone eating out of your hand** ▷HAND; **have someone right where you want them** ▷ WANT; **have someone in the palm of your hand** or **eating out of the palm of your hand** ▷PALM

○ **out of 'pocket**

You say you are **out of pocket** if you have lost money as a result of something, especially when you consider the situation to be unfair in some way: *If he stays in the house, he'll have to pay for the electricity. I don't want to end up out of pocket.*

○ **pay out of 'pocket** (*AmE*)

When you **pay out of pocket**, you pay for something using money you have with you: *Alice wanted to use the credit card, but I just paid out of pocket.*

○ **pick someone's 'pocket**

If someone **picks your pocket**, they steal something from the pocket of the clothes you are wearing: *A number of my friends have had their pockets picked on the Paris Metro.*

pockets

○ **be in each other's 'pockets**

If you say that two people **are in each other's pockets**, you mean that they are together too much: *I know they're best friends, but it doesn't mean they have to live in each other's pockets.*

○ **line your 'pockets** or **line someone's 'pockets**

Someone who is **lining their pockets**

is making money dishonestly from their job; you **line someone's pockets** when the money you spend goes to someone dishonest, who is not providing the service you would expect: *It makes me mad to think of a man like him, lining his pockets from people's pension payments.* □ *They would do better to collaborate with the council to ensure the scheme's success, rather than lining the pockets of these so-called consultants.* ♦ *see also* **feather your own nest** ▷NEST

point (*see also* **points**)

○ **beside the 'point**

Something that someone says during a discussion is **beside the point** if it does not bear much or any relation to the main subject being discussed: *Whether he did it or not is beside the point. My question is, who is going to pay for the damage?*

○ **come to the 'point** or **get to the 'point**

1 You **come**, or **get**, **to the point** of what you are saying when, following some vague or general remarks, you finally make the comment or statement which is the main part of your message: *Could you stop wasting time and get to the point, please?* **2** If you say that someone is not able to do something when it **comes**, or **gets**, **to the point**, you mean that they cannot do it when the right time comes: *He had spent days rehearsing what he would say, but when it came to the point, he couldn't tell her.*

○ **in point of 'fact** (*formal*)

You use the phrase **in point of fact** to emphasize the truth or accuracy of what you are reporting, or to correct somebody when you think they have got the wrong idea about something: *Despite being branded a Eurosceptic, I am, in point of fact, more pro-European than my colleagues.* ♦ *see also* **as a matter of fact** ▷ MATTER

○ **I take your 'point** (*rather formal*) or **point 'taken**

If you say '**I take your point**', or '**point taken**' to someone you are discussing something with, you mean that you accept the fairness and truth of what they are saying: *I take your point, Mr Blair, but surely you agree that a mini-*

mum wage will mean fewer jobs? □ *'The problems experienced in the past won't recur.' 'Point taken, but are there no lessons to be learned?'*

○ **make a 'point of** or **make it a 'point to**

You **make a point of** doing something, or **make it a point to** do something, when you make a special effort to do it: *That woman is very kind. She made a special point of coming over to offer me her sympathy.*

○ **not to put too fine a 'point on it**

You say '**not to put too fine a point on it**' to show someone that you are speaking honestly, and without trying to avoid shocking or upsetting the listener: *'Not to put too fine a point on it, your Emily is a liar,' said Chase.*

○ **on the 'point of**

You are **on the point of** doing something when you are just going to do it: *I was on the point of apologizing when she started insulting me again.*

○ **the point of no re'turn**

You reach **the point of no return** in some activity when you have to continue with it because it is too late to stop or give up: *Having reached the point of no return, the Government had no choice but to support the decision.*

○ **score a 'point against someone**

In a competitive situation, you try to **score a point against another person** when you attack them with a detail in the hope of establishing your own position of power, or impressing the other people who are present: *I can discuss things constructively with Phil, but Dean is always out to score a point against me.* ♦ *see also* **score points** ▷POINTS

○ **a sore 'point**

Something that is, or touches, **a sore point** with someone is a subject which you should not raise when they are present, because, as a result of arguments they have had or criticism they have received about it in the past, they get easily upset or angry when people mention it: *It is still a sore point with both grandparents that neither Alice nor Henry have been baptized.*

○ **to the 'point**

Something such as a statement or a

question that is **to the point** contains only the details which are useful and important: *A good interviewer will ask questions which are brief and to the point.*

○ up to a 'point

Something that is the case **up to a point** is partly the case: *I certainly agree with socialist doctrine up to a point, but I would never call myself a communist.* □ *We can blame it on negligence up to a point, but other factors did play a part.*

○ what's the 'point?

You ask '**what's the point?**' when you believe that the action which you are considering is not worth doing, as it cannot have a useful result: *'You should write to your MP.' 'What's the point? He's already aware of the problem.'*

○ when it comes to the 'point

You say '**when it comes to the point**' when you are inviting the person you are speaking with to think again about the thing you are discussing: *When it comes to the point, one of the clearest rights of a Prime Minister is that of choosing the date of an election.*

points

○ score 'points

In a competitive situation, you try to **score points**, or **score points off** another person, when you attack them with details in the hope of establishing your own position of power, or impressing the other people who are present: *Prime Minister's Question Time is dominated by MPs determined to score points off one another.* ♦ see also **score a point against someone** ▷POINT

poles

○ 'poles apart

If you say that people or their opinions are **poles apart**, you mean that they are as different or as far apart as is possible: *We get on OK, but have always been poles apart in matters of taste.* ♦ see also **worlds apart** ▷WORLDS

port

○ any port in a 'storm

If someone says '**any port in a storm**', they mean that, if you are having difficulties, you will or should accept any possible solution or help which is available: *It may not be a very nice flat but I have to live somewhere. Any port in a storm.*

pose

○ strike a 'pose

If you **strike a pose**, you take up a particular position which you hope will make people notice you and admire you: *She struck a dramatic pose and waited for the click of the camera.*

position

○ jockey for po'sition

When a number of people or organizations **are jockeying for position**, each one is trying to push their way into an advantageous position: *The knowledge that a general election was imminent saw all political parties jockeying for position.*

possessed

○ what pos'sessed so-and-so?

When you ask **what possessed someone** to do a certain bad or stupid thing, you are saying that you cannot understand why they did that thing: *Whatever possessed you to say that?*

post

○ pip someone at the 'post (*BrE*)

You **pip someone at the post** when you move ahead and beat them in the last stages of a competition; you **are pipped at the post** when you are beaten in this way: *She planned to launch her own designer clothes label but her younger sister pipped her at the post.* □ *And commiserations to our runner-up, who was just pipped at the post in the last round.*

In horse-racing, the horse that passes the winning-post first wins the race. In the past, the word 'pipped' meant 'defeated', and came from a system of voting in which votes were made by placing either a white ball (for) or a black ball (against) inside a box. The image of the pip comes from the black ball.

posted

○ keep someone 'posted

If you **keep someone posted**, you keep them informed about a situation by giving them the latest news or details of any developments: *Just to let you know, there is about to be a bit of a reshuffle in the department. Anyway, I'll keep you posted.*

pot

○ go to 'pot

If you say that something or someone **has gone to pot**, you mean that they have been spoiled or ruined: *That used to be the best farm in the county, but since he started drinking, he's let it all go to pot.*

> To **go to pot** originally meant 'to be made into a stew'.

○ the pot calling the kettle 'black

If someone criticizes you for some fault or bad characteristic which they also possess, you can say it is a case of **the pot calling the kettle black**: *Both partners in the marriage consistently blame the other in the fights which ensue, the pot calls the kettle black.*

> In the past, when cooking was done over a fire, pots, kettles and everything else which hung over the fire all got as black as one another.

○ take pot 'luck

You **are taking pot luck** when you choose something from among a group of similar things without making a careful decision or worrying about getting the best one: *On the odd occasion when I bet on horses, I never bother with the racing tips. I just take pot luck.*

> To **take pot luck**, in its original sense, means 'to accept whatever is served to you from the cooking pot'.

○ a watched pot never 'boils

If you say 'a watched pot never boils' to someone who is waiting anxiously for something, you mean that the more they wait for it to happen, the longer it will seem before it happens: *Go and do something else to occupy yourself – a watched pot...*

> This expression is often shortened to **'a watched pot'**, as in the example.

potato

○ a hot po'tato

A **hot potato** is a subject, or occasionally a person, that is difficult and dangerous to deal with: *The subject was dropped like a hot potato when they realized the amount of money involved.*

> If you try to hold a hot potato, you will burn your hands.

potshot

○ take a 'potshot at someone (*AmE; informal*)

You **take a potshot at someone** when you make a critical remark about them: *Debbie had gained weight, and Anne couldn't help taking a potshot at her about it.*

pound

○ get your pound of 'flesh or have your pound of 'flesh

You say that someone **has got**, or **has had, their pound of flesh** if they have finally obtained something which is rightfully theirs, especially if this causes difficulties or unhappiness for another person: *The rail workers, determined to get their pound of flesh, have turned down the six per cent pay rise.*

> In Shakespeare's *The Merchant of Venice*, Shylock insists that Antonio give him a pound of his own flesh in exchange for a debt which he cannot repay, according to the terms of an agreement which they made earlier in the play.

power

○ more power to so-and-so's 'elbow (*BrE*)

If you say '**more power to** a certain person's **elbow**', you mean that you wish them good luck: *If she could earn a few more pounds and give everyone a bit of fun, then more power to her elbow.*

powers

○ the powers that 'be

The **powers that be** are the people who have control or authority, for example the government of a country or the management of a business: *Research funding bodies are largely under*

the control of the powers that be in the
medical profession.

practice

○ in 'practice

1 What happens **in practice** is what
happens in reality, as opposed to what
ought to happen in theory, or according
to the rules: *While the system works in*
theory, in practice there are a number of
other factors to be considered. **2** If you
keep **in practice**, you spend a lot of
time practising an activity so that you
maintain a certain level of skill at it: *I*
should play at least three games a week if
I want to be in practice for the tourna-
ment this summer.

○ out of 'practice

If you are **out of practice**, you cannot
do an activity as well as you used to because you have not spent time practising it: *I used to be very good at this, but*
I'm a bit out of practice now.

○ practice makes 'perfect

If someone says '**practice makes per-**
fect', they mean that the only way to
develop a particular skill is by practising it: *Writing articles is a game, another*
area where practice makes perfect. The
skills come through doing it again and
again.

○ put something into 'practice

You **put something** such as ideas or
knowledge **into practice** when you
use them to guide your actions in a real
situation: *Now was the moment to put*
what she had learned in the class into
practice.

○ sharp 'practice

If a person or business regularly deals
with people in a dishonourable and underhand way, you say that they are
using **sharp practice**: *Any kind of*
sharp practice or dishonest dealing will
ruin his career. ♦ *see also* **funny busi-**
ness ▷BUSINESS

practise (*AmE* practice)

○ practise what you 'preach

If you **practise what you preach**, you
never give advice to other people without following that advice yourself:
Practise what you preach: after all
there's no logic in you telling her not to
hit people if that's exactly what you're
doing by smacking the child.

praises

○ sing the 'praises of

If you **sing the praises of** someone or
something, you praise them enthusiastically: *I think I might try this new stain*
remover. My mum's always singing its
praises.

preach

○ preach to the 'converted

Someone who **is preaching to the**
converted is wasting time and energy
by speaking in a persuasive way to people who already agree with the things
they are saying: *You're preaching to the*
converted with us, but you've got to con-
vince everyone else too.

precious

○ precious 'few

Precious few means 'very few': *There*
are precious few beautiful places left in
Europe still unspoilt by tourism.

○ precious 'little

Precious little means 'very little': *Un-*
fortunately, there is precious little evi-
dence that the government is trying to
understand the protestors.

pressed

○ hard 'pressed

You say you would be **hard pressed** to
do something if you would find it difficult or impossible to do: *'Well?' she de-*
manded as he put the phone down. She
was hard pressed to conceal her anxiety.

○ 'pressed for something

You **are pressed for something** such
as time or money if you do not have enough of it: *It's good to see you, but I'm a*
bit pressed for time just now. Can we
meet for coffee tomorrow?

pressure

○ bring 'pressure to bear

You **bring pressure to bear** when you
try to persuade someone to do what you
want, in a forceful way: *Workers have*
their own organizations which can bring
pressure to bear on governments and
make demands on the state.

pretences

○ under false pre'tences

You are doing something **under false**
pretences if you have told lies, or allowed people to believe something
which is not the case, in order to do it:

Is it morally permissible for a social scientist to get information under false pretences?

pretty

○ pretty 'much *(informal)* or pretty 'well *(informal)* or pretty 'nearly *(informal)*
Pretty much, pretty well and **pretty nearly** all mean 'almost': *I think everything's under control now ... or pretty much, anyway.* □ *When we got there, it was past midnight and the party was pretty well over.* □ *'Have you finished yet?' 'Pretty nearly.'*

prey

○ fall 'prey to or be 'prey to
If you **fall**, or **are**, **prey to** something or someone, you put yourself in a position where they harm or destroy you: *He said he suspected the birds had fallen prey to the same disease which hit the colony before.*

> The **prey** of an animal which hunts for its food are the creatures it kills and eats.

price

○ the 'asking price
The asking price of an item that is for sale is the price that the seller says they want for it: *It's been sold. It seems someone's offered more than the asking price and they've accepted it.*

○ at a 'price
1 Something which can be obtained **at a price** is very expensive: *The breast meat of the Muscovy duck comes at a price, but it is well worth the extra you pay.* **2** You achieve something **at a price** if you suffer while, or as a result of, achieving it: *Success in business often comes at a personal price, and family life often suffers as a result.*

○ at 'any price
A person who wants or demands something **at any price** is so determined to get it that they ignore the problems or the expense involved: *This man is out to win, and he'll do it at any price.* ♦ *see also* **stop at nothing** ▷STOP

○ beyond 'price
You say that something is **beyond price** if you consider that it has more value than anything that you could

buy: *We had forty-eight days together in which he was happy and free from pain, which I regard as beyond price.*

○ 'cheap at the price or cheap at 'half the price
You say that something is **cheap at the price**, or **cheap at half the price**, if you think that it is not expensive, considering its quality: *I'll tell you, this is a quality car. It's a bargain, cheap at half the price.*

○ pay the 'price for something
You **pay the price for something**, such as a mistake or a crime, if you suffer or are punished for it: *She didn't do much work at school, and she's paying the price now.*

○ put a 'price on something
You **put a price on something** when you say how much it is worth in money: *It certainly is a beautiful painting, but I wouldn't like to put a price on it.*

○ what price 'such-and-such?
1 You ask '**what price** a certain thing?' to show that you think the person you are speaking about has forgotten the good values which used to be important to them: *You invest your extra cash in cigarette companies? What price ethics, then?* **2** You ask '**what price** a certain thing?' when you are expressing an idea or a possibility and asking what someone thinks of it: *What price a back-to-back victory for Nick Price?*

> This expression in its base sense means 'what price would you be willing to give if you were buying, or betting on, the thing in question?'

pride

○ pride comes before a 'fall or pride goes before a 'fall
If someone says '**pride comes before a fall**', they are warning that a person who is too sure of themselves is likely to have some kind of failure or accident: *'She's convinced she's going to win.' 'I hate to say it, but pride often comes before a fall, you know.'*

○ pride of 'place
You give **pride of place** to something when the way you treat it shows that it is the most important thing in a group

or collection: *But pride of place among their unique collection goes to the magnificent silver swan, which graces the entrance hall.*

○ **swallow your 'pride**

You **swallow your pride** when you do something which you know you must do, but that makes you feel ashamed: *If you're not very good at this sort of thing, swallow your pride and get somebody in to do it for you.*

prime

○ **be cut off in your 'prime**

A person **is cut off in their prime** if they die when they are still young, or during the most successful period of their life: *It's a tragedy that such a talented young man was cut off in his prime.*

principle

○ **in 'principle**

You agree with something **in principle** if you agree with it in general but not with all of its details: *I agree with the idea in principle, but I don't think it will be very easy to apply.*

○ **on 'principle**

You do something **on principle** if you have a particular religious or moral belief which causes you to do that thing: *I never eat veal on principle.*

probability

○ **in all proba'bility**

If you say that, **in all probability**, something is the case or is going to happen, you mean that it is very likely to be the case or to happen: *In all probability, the Government will try to lower taxes again before the next election.*

problem

○ **no 'problem** (*informal*)

1 You say something is **no problem** if you can do it easily: *'Can you lend me your computer for a couple of days?' 'Yeah, no problem.'* **2** You say something was **no problem** as a way of accepting a person's thanks for doing it: *'How much do I owe you?' 'It was no problem, honestly. Buy me a drink sometime.'* ♦ see also **no hassle** ▷HASSLE

○ **what's your 'problem?**

When you ask someone **'what's your problem?'** you are saying rudely that

you think they are behaving in a way which is unreasonable: *Erlich did not understand the hostility of this man. 'What's your problem?' 'My problem? By Christ, I'll tell you what my problem is.'*

profile

○ **keep a low 'profile**

You **are keeping a low profile** when you are behaving in such a way that people do not notice you: *He seems to have been keeping rather a low profile in political debates recently.*

proof

○ **living 'proof of something**

Someone or something is **living proof of** a particular theory if their existence, or the state they are in, gives support to, or proves, that theory: *Fairport Convention – living proof that middle-age doesn't mean you're past it.*

○ **the proof of the pudding is in the 'eating** or **the proof of the 'pudding**

If someone says **'the proof of the pudding is in the eating'**, or **'the proof of the pudding'**, they mean that, even if something seems to be good, you can only judge how good it really is when you see how it performs: *Arguments of this kind are easy to invent, but difficult to settle. In the end, the proof of the pudding will be in the eating.*

> The only way of testing whether a pudding is as delicious as it looks is to taste it.

proportion

○ **in pro'portion**

1 Something is **in proportion** if the relationship between its separate parts is correct: *The model ship was skilfully made, with every detail in perfect proportion.* **2** One thing is small or large **in proportion to** another if it is small or large in relation to the second thing: *I hated my nose when I was a teenager. It seemed huge in proportion to the rest of my face.* **3** One thing grows **in proportion to** another if it grows at the same rate as the second thing: *The satisfaction you get from a hobby grows in proportion to the amount of effort you put in.*

○ **out of pro'portion**

You are letting things get **out of pro-**

portion if you spend more time thinking or worrying about them than is necessary; one thing is **out of all proportion to** another if it seems larger, more important, or more serious than it needs to be, when you consider it in relation to the second thing: *I know money is important, but don't let it get out of proportion.* □ *Even if Cantona was provoked, his reaction was out of all proportion to the provocation.* ♦ see also **out of perspective** ▷PERSPECTIVE

protest
○ **under 'protest**

You do something **under protest** if you do it unwillingly: *Eventually she agreed, under protest, to see a marriage guidance councillor.*

proud
○ **do someone 'proud**

When someone has given you excellent service or entertainment, you say they **have done you proud**: *And special thanks to the catering staff who, once again, have done us proud.*

providence
○ **tempt 'providence**

If you say that someone **is tempting providence**, you mean that they are taking a big risk, or, superstitiously, that they are encouraging something bad to happen by being over-optimistic: *John, having loved and lost, felt he would be tempting providence to allow himself to love again.* ♦ see also **speak too soon** ▷SPEAK

prowl
○ **on the 'prowl**

A person is **on the prowl** if they are moving about and looking for something in a threatening way: *We'd better get a licence for our TV. The detector vans are on the prowl again.*

An animal is **on the prowl** if it is hunting.

pull
○ **pull a 'fast one**

You say that someone **has pulled a fast one**, or **pulled a fast one** on you, if they have tricked or deceived you: *'You're trying to pull a fast one, aren't you? You've been playing around somewhere!' 'We haven't! It was the train, truly it was!'* ♦ see also **sell someone a pup** ▷PUP; **put one over on someone** ▷PUT; **take someone for a ride** ▷RIDE; **lie through your teeth** ▷TEETH

○ **pull the 'other one** (*BrE*)

If you say '**pull the other one**' to someone, you are telling them that you do not believe what they say: *'I spend most of my evenings at home.' Jake laughed. 'Pull the other one! Don't tell me you've lost your taste for nightclubs.'*

A longer and more humorous version of this expression is: 'pull the other one, it's got bells on'. Both versions refer to the core expression 'pull someone's leg'.

○ **pull yourself to'gether**

If you say to someone '**pull yourself together**', you mean that they should take control of themselves and stop behaving foolishly: *If it had been any other soldier, he would have told him sternly to pull himself together and be a man.* ♦ see also **snap out of it** ▷SNAP

punch
○ **pack a 'punch**

You say that someone or something **packs a punch** if they have a powerful effect or impact: *Though the hurricane packed a stronger punch in the north-eastern states, it wreaked greater havoc in the south.*

In its original meaning, **to pack a punch** means 'to hit hard or powerfully with the fist'.

punches
○ **pull your 'punches**

Someone who **pulls their punches** is using less force in attacking than they are really capable of; someone who **does not pull any punches** does not try to reduce the strength of what they are saying or doing: *Telling the man the simple truth could reduce him to a wreck, so on the whole, she pulled her punches and held her tongue.*

In boxing, a boxer **is pulling his punches** if he is not using his full strength to hit with.

pup

○ **sell someone a 'pup** (*BrE*)

If you have been **sold a pup**, someone has cheated you: *They've been sold a pup with these amendments.* ♦ *see also* **pull a fast one** ▷PULL; **put one over on someone** ▷PUT; **take someone for a ride** ▷RIDE; **lie through your teeth** ▷TEETH

pure

○ **pure as the driven 'snow**

Someone, usually a young woman, who is described as **pure as the driven snow** has no evil thoughts, and probably not much sexual experience: *Brown claimed that Charlie was 'pure as the driven snow'. An audible ripple of laughter went round the court room.*

> People often use this expression sarcastically, meaning the exact opposite of the above definition.

purpose

○ **serve a 'purpose**

Something or someone **serves a purpose** if it is useful; something **serves its purpose** if it does the thing it is designed to do: *Nobody likes traffic wardens, but they certainly serve a purpose.* □ *It's quite an ugly walking-stick, but it serves its purpose.*

○ **to good 'purpose**

You use something **to good purpose** if you find a good use for it: *I would leave him all my money if I thought he would use it to good purpose.*

purse

○ **you can't make a silk purse out of a sow's 'ear**

If someone says **'you can't make a silk purse out of a sow's ear'**, they mean that, if the materials you are working with are bad, no amount of hard work will make a good quality final product: *It's a true case of trying to make an agricultural silk purse out of a sow's ear. If land is not suitable for efficient farming, the land should be used for more profitable purposes.*

> Certain types of pig have large ears which are similar in shape to purses, but everyone knows you cannot make a beautiful purse out of a sow's (= a female pig's) ear.

pursuit

○ **in hot pur'suit**

You are **in hot pursuit**, or **in hot pursuit of** someone or something, when you are chasing them and are determined to catch them: *The three killer dogs burst from the trees in hot pursuit, their gleaming fangs bared for the attack.*

push

○ **at a 'push** (*BrE*)

You say that something is possible **at a push** if you consider it to be just possible, although a lot of extra effort would be needed to do it: *'Can you deliver the flowers today?' 'I could do it at a push, but it'll cost you extra.'*

○ **give someone the 'push** (*BrE*; *informal*)

1 If you **are given**, or **get**, **the push**, you are dismissed from your job: *It's not easy to prepare yourself mentally for getting another job after you've been given the push.* **2** If you **give** your boyfriend or girlfriend **the push**, you end your relationship with them: *I've given Sam the push, so there. I've got a new boyfriend now.* ♦ *see also* **give someone the boot** ▷BOOT; **give someone the elbow** ▷ELBOW

○ **'push it**

Someone **is pushing it** when they are making a certain person angry by putting pressure on them, or trying to insist that that person does something: *There's no harm in asking, but if he says no, don't push it.*

○ **when push comes to 'shove** or **if push comes to 'shove**

You say **when**, or **if, push comes to shove** when **1** you are talking about what happens, or will happen, if the situation turns into an emergency, or becomes serious and important: *When push came to shove, the lad showed big-match composure.* **2** you are about to say what the reality of a situation is: *But when push came to shove, we knew that the government and the party would get their way.* ♦ *see also* **when the chips are down** ▷CHIPS; **come to the crunch** ▷CRUNCH

put

○ a 'put-down

A **put-down** is something that you say that makes someone appear foolish or stupid, or that criticizes them: *I remember asking John Lennon if those were his own teeth, and he answered, 'Yes. Are those your own spots?' – a good put-down.*

○ hard 'put

You say you would be **hard put** to do something if you would find it difficult or impossible to do: *I used to be good at maths, but I'd be hard put to solve a quadratic equation now.*

○ I wouldn't put it 'past so-and-so

You say that **you wouldn't put** a certain action, usually something bad, **past someone** if you think that they may have done it, considering the kind of person they are: *'I wonder if he stole the money that I left on my desk?' 'I certainly wouldn't put it past him.'*

○ put it 'there (*AmE*; *informal*)

If you tell someone to **put it there**, you are asking them to shake hands with you: *When did you get into town? Put it there!*

○ put one 'over on someone

Someone **puts one over on you** when they tell you a lie or trick you: *Right, son. Tell me what happened, and don't try to put one over on me again.* ♦ *see also* **pull a fast one** ▷PULL; **sell someone a pup** ▷PUP; **take someone for a ride** ▷RIDE; **lie through your teeth** ▷TEETH

○ put 'paid to something (*BrE*)

When something **puts paid to** a certain thing, it prevents that thing from happening: *Our new procedures will soon put paid to any false claims for state benefits.*

putty

○ putty in someone's 'hands

You say that someone is **putty in** a certain person's **hands** if they are easily influenced by that person: *Her father was putty in her hands, would do or get anything she wanted.*

> **Putty** is a soft paste used for fixing glass panes into window frames. You can mould it easily into different shapes by squeezing it.

quart

○ get a quart into a pint 'pot or put a quart into a pint 'pot (*BrE*)

If you say that attempting something is like trying to **get**, or **put**, a **quart into a pint pot**, you mean that it is impossible, especially if you are trying to put a great quantity of something into another thing that cannot hold it: *The fundamental difficulty of all curriculum planning – how to get a quart into a pint pot – still remains to be addressed.*

> A **quart** is a measurement of liquid equal to two pints.

quarters

○ at close 'quarters

Someone or something is **at close quarters** when they are in a position very near you: *The soldier was skilled in all-round weaponry, able to fight at a distance and at close quarters.*

question

○ pop the 'question

You **pop the question** when you ask someone to marry you: *I think her boyfriend might pop the question this weekend.*

○ without 'question

Something is the case **without question** if there is absolutely no doubt about it: *Staffing levels and costs are, without question, too high and must be reduced.* ♦ *see also* **beyond any shadow of doubt** or **without any shadow of doubt** ▷SHADOW; **sure as eggs is eggs** ▷SURE

questions

○ **no questions 'asked**

When something is done for you **no questions asked**, it is done immediately, without anyone asking you questions, or doubting your honesty: *If, after examining your first issue, you are not 100% satisfied, we'll send you a complete refund with no questions asked.*

queue

○ **jump the 'queue** (*BrE*)

Someone **jumps the queue** when, rather than standing at the end of a line of people who are waiting for something [= a queue], they stand between two people who are already there; you also **jump the queue** when you are given help or allowed to do something before other people who have been waiting longer than you: *I don't want to have to wait until I'm homeless before I go for help; I don't want to jump the queue – it should be done on a fair system.*

> The British have a reputation for standing politely in a queue when several people are waiting for something. It is considered very rude to take your place in the middle [= **jump the queue**] when you arrive, rather than standing at the end, behind the last person in the line.

quiet

○ **on the 'quiet**

You do something **on the quiet** when you do it secretly: *He drinks at times; of course, on the quiet, after Gran's safely in bed.*

quits

○ **be 'quits with someone**

You **are quits with someone** when you do not owe them anything and they do not owe you anything any more: *If I pay for the drinks, we'll be quits, okay?* ♦ see also **fair and square** ▷FAIR

○ **call it 'quits**

1 You **call it quits** when you agree with someone that neither person owes the other anything: *'But the rest – forget it. Take this and we'll call it quits.' He handed me the cheque.* **2** (*AmE*) You **call it quits** when you end a love rela-

tionship: *Diane and I finally called it quits.* **3** (*AmE*) You **call it quits** when you stop working for the day: *It's 4 o'clock. Let's call it quits.*

race

○ **a race against 'time**

You are involved in **a race against time** if you are hurrying to do something or finish something important in a limited period of time: *Three more were likely to explode. It was a race against time. There were thousands of people to alert and evacuate.*

rack

○ **go to rack and 'ruin**

1 A place **is going to rack and ruin** if it is getting into a bad state because no-one is looking after it or doing the repairs which are needed: *The house is much too big for her and it's been going steadily to rack and ruin for years.* **2** A person **is going to rack and ruin** if they are destroying their life or their health by behaving in a certain way: *He's gone to rack and ruin since he started drinking.*

rag

○ **like a red rag to a 'bull**

You say that something, such as a remark, is **like a red rag to a bull** if it is likely to make a certain person angry: *'Don't ever let me see you with her again,' she concluded. Saying this to me was like holding a red rag to a bull.*

○ **lose your 'rag** (*BrE*)

You say that a person **has lost their rag** when they suddenly lose their patience and show how angry they are: *Last year he lost his rag in a pub down in Kent and started smashing glasses.* ♦

see also **go off at the deep end** ▷END; **blow a fuse** ▷FUSE; **let fly** ▷LET; **blow or flip your lid** ▷LID; **do your nut** ▷NUT; **fly into a rage** ▷RAGE; **hit the roof** ▷ ROOF; **blow your stack** ▷STACK; **lose your temper** ▷TEMPER; **blow your top** ▷ TOP; **throw a wobbly** ▷WOBBLY

rage

○ **fly into a 'rage**

When a person **flies into a rage**, they suddenly lose control of themselves and become wild with anger: *She must be feeling guilty, because she flies into a rage every time I mention it.* ♦ *see also* **go off at the deep end** ▷END; **blow a fuse** ▷FUSE; **let fly** ▷LET; **blow or flip your lid** ▷LID; **do your nut** ▷NUT; **lose your rag** ▷RAG; **hit the roof** ▷ ROOF; **blow your stack** ▷STACK; **lose your temper** ▷TEMPER; **blow your top** ▷ TOP; **throw a wobbly** ▷WOBBLY

rails

○ **go off the 'rails**

You say that a person or organization **has gone off the rails** if they have stopped behaving sensibly, and have begun behaving in a wild, immoral, or slightly mad way: *I cannot stay within a party which I believe has ideologically gone off the rails.*

rain (*see also* rains)

○ **come rain or 'shine**

You do something regularly **come rain or shine** if nothing ever stops you from doing it: *Every morning at 5am, come rain or shine, James leaves his South Croydon home on his morning run.*

○ **take a 'rain check** (*AmE*)

You say that you will **take a rain check** on a certain activity if you are refusing an invitation to do it just now, but expressing a desire to do it some time in the future: *'Do you want to go to the beach?' 'I can't today, but can I take a rain check on it?'*

rainbows

○ **chase 'rainbows**

You say that someone **is chasing rainbows** if they are wishing or hoping for something that they will probably never get: *I had no ambition to become a 'star'. I certainly couldn't afford to*

waste petrol chasing rainbows as far as Leeds and back. ♦ *see also* **build castles in the air** ▷CASTLES

rains

○ **it never rains but it 'pours**

If someone says '**it never rains but it pours**', they mean **1** that unlucky things often seem to happen all at the same time: *My day was bad enough, and then poor old Gran broke her leg. It never rains but it pours.* **2** that it is common, after a long period of bad luck, for so many opportunities to present themselves at once, that you cannot possibly manage to take advantage of them all: *I'd have liked to have done more work with them, but, as ever, it never rains but it pours – I already had three sessions booked.*

ranks

○ **close 'ranks**

People in a group **close ranks** when they become more dependent on one another and less open to people who do not belong to their group, in order to defend themselves: *Scientists working on the project closed ranks, and no data was made available.*

> When the soldiers in an army **close ranks**, they move closer together so that it is more difficult to get past them.

○ **rise through the 'ranks**

A person **rises through the ranks** of an organization if they start at a low level in that organization and move up over a period of time to reach a position of importance: *He started his career as an auditor and had risen through the ranks of the Finance Ministry.*

rant

○ **rant and 'rave**

A person who **is ranting and raving** is shouting or complaining about something, repeating the same things over and over again because they are so angry: *I don't care how much you rant and rave. I've made my decision and it's final.*

rap

○ **a bum 'rap** (*AmE*; *informal*)

A **bum rap** is a false criminal charge: *Al went to prison on a bum rap.*

rat

○ **give someone a rap over the 'knuckles**

You **give someone a rap over the knuckles** when you criticize them sharply for doing something which you disapprove of: *His boss had given him a rap over the knuckles when he arrived late again.* ♦ see also **haul someone over the coals** ▷COALS

○ **take the 'rap**

Someone **takes the rap**, or **takes the rap for something**, when they take the blame and are punished, often for something which they did not do: *I know it would save our reputation, but I'm sorry, I don't want him to take the rap for something he didn't do.*

rat

○ **smell a 'rat** (*informal*)

You say you can **smell a rat** if you have a feeling that something is not as it should be, but is wrong or bad: *I smelt a rat when he said he was working late, so I went down to the office to check he was there.*

rate

○ **at 'any rate**

You use **at any rate 1** when you are adding something to correct what you have just said and to make it more accurate: *Teenagers, or at any rate the majority of them, are aware that it's important to get qualifications.* **2** when you are making a general statement containing the most important details of what you have just said: *I don't know if he's vegetarian or not. At any rate, he's coming, so you should check with him.*

○ **at a rate of 'knots** (*BrE*)

You are doing something **at a rate of knots** if you are doing it quickly: *We're progressing at a great rate of knots at the moment.*

The speed of a boat or aeroplane is measured in knots, or nautical miles.

○ **at 'this rate**

At this rate means 'if what is happening now continues to happen for some time': *Where's he got to? At this rate we'll miss the train.*

ray

○ **a ray of 'hope**

You say that there is **a ray of hope** when a situation is bad, but there is still a small chance that you will get the result you are hoping for: *Any ray of hope the prisoners had of escaping was lost when a plan of their escape route was found.*

read

○ **take something as 'read** (*BrE*)

You **take something as read** when you accept that it is the case, even though it has not been proven or checked, because you consider it to be certain or obvious: *We need to have it ratified by the Board. But you can take it as read that you have the contract.*

ready

○ **at the 'ready**

You have something **at the ready** when you are ready to use it if or when it becomes necessary: *Make sure you have a piece of paper and a pencil at the ready to note down the secret number.*

real

○ **for 'real**

1 Something that happens **for real** is really happening, as opposed to being an idea or a practice situation: *Army drills are good training, but nothing can prepare you for combat when it's for real.* **2** Something that is **for real** is true or serious, and not a joke: *If you pretend to be ill all the time, nobody will believe you when you get sick for real.*

reaper

○ **the grim 'reaper**

If people talk about **the grim reaper**, they mean death.

The grim reaper is a skeleton holding a scythe [= a curved knife with a long handle for cutting grass], an image which was often used as a symbol of death.

rear

○ **bring up the 'rear**

The person who **is bringing up the rear** is the last one in a line of people moving together: *Right, can we have Jamie leading the way, please, and I'll bring up the rear.*

reason

○ **it stands to 'reason**

If someone says '**it stands to reason**', they mean that something is obviously the case: *It stands to reason that they should want a formal apology for the way they were treated.*

○ **ours is not to reason 'why**

If someone says '**ours is not to reason why**', they mean **1** that people who are not considered important enough to be asked their opinion are supposed to accept the strange or stupid decisions which influential people often make: *That new road bridge is just going to increase the amount of traffic in the city centre, but I suppose ours is not to reason why.* **2** that they would perhaps rather not know the answer to a particular question, or that it is not their business to know: *Curious – they don't usually dispense £20 notes. Still, mine not to reason why.*

> Notice that '**ours**' may be replaced by '**mine**', '**yours**', '**hers**', etc.

○ **within 'reason**

Within reason means within the limits of what most people would consider sensible or acceptable: *I'll get you whatever you want for your birthday ... well, anything within reason.*

record

○ **for the 'record or just for the 'record**

You say you are telling people something **for the record** or **just for the record**, when you want people to know something, so there can be no misunderstanding about it: *Let me say for the record that I was at no point aware of the seriousness of my actions.*

○ **off the 'record**

If you tell someone that what you are saying is **off the record**, or **strictly off the record**, you mean that you do not want them to tell anyone else or make the information public: *Off the record, detectives refer to the growing number of burglaries as one of Britain's few growth industries.*

○ **on 'record**

You use '**on record**' **1** as a way of talking about what someone has said publicly, so that others know about it and can prove that it was said: *He would never have made such remarks if he had realized they were going down on record.* **2** when you are talking about information that you keep, so you may look at it or refer to it in the future: *The original promise was to allow enough information to be placed on record for the public to know who was breaking the law.* **3** when you are talking about the highest or lowest standards or levels anyone has ever recorded: *Fort William had the hottest summer on record that year.*

○ **set the 'record straight or put the 'record straight**

You **set**, or **put**, **the record straight** when you tell the truth about something in order to correct people's false beliefs or ideas: *May I put the record straight on one point? I never claimed that nuclear power was safe, only that it was safer than the alternatives.*

red

○ **in the 'red**

Your bank account is **in the red** if you have spent more money than you have, and you therefore owe the bank money: *I was just a few pence in the red. A simple phone call from the bank would have saved me all this fuss and expense.* ♦ *see also* **in the black** ▷BLACK

> In accountancy, it is customary to write entries on the debit side of a ledger in red ink, and until recently, if you owed your bank a sum of money, that sum appeared in red on your bank statement.

refusal

○ **first re'fusal**

You give someone **first refusal** if you offer them the chance to buy a certain thing from you before you offer it to anyone else: *He's given me first refusal on that boat he's selling.*

regular

○ **regular as 'clockwork**

Something which is as **regular as clockwork** happens with perfect regularity: *Miss Abberley used to give me these chocolates, you see, Christmas and Easter, regular as clockwork.*

rein

○ **free 'rein** or **a free 'rein**

You give someone **free rein** or **a free rein** when you allow them complete freedom to do what they want, or to make their own decisions: *I can't remember a time when he said, 'Don't play that; play this.' He'd always give you free rein.*

○ **keep a tight 'rein on**

You **are keeping a tight rein on** something or someone if you are controlling or limiting them firmly: *If we are to keep the level of taxation down, it is essential to keep a tight rein on public spending.*

relief

○ **on re'lief** (*AmE*)

A person who is **on relief** is receiving government benefits, usually because they are poor or unemployed: *He lost his job but was too proud to go on relief.*

remains

○ **it remains to be 'seen**

You say that **it remains to be seen** whether something will happen if you are avoiding making any judgement on the possibility of that thing happening: *It remains to be seen how far the structural changes will result in a 'cultural' change within the NHS.*

repair

○ **beyond re'pair**

1 A thing which is **beyond repair** is in such bad condition that it cannot possibly be repaired: *There was little furniture, for most was stored in Switzerland, and the few pieces that remained had been damaged beyond repair.* **2** A situation or relationship is **beyond repair** if it is in such a bad state, as a result of recent events, that it can never become happy and stable again: *The friendship seems beyond repair. Suspicion is a soul-destroying evil. Trust, like respect, takes a long time to establish.* ♦ *see also* **the worse for wear** ▷WEAR

resort

○ **as a last re'sort**

You do something **as a last resort** when you do it only because all other methods or approaches have failed: *As a last resort, I tried mouth-to-mouth*

again. Seconds later, Ben suddenly started spluttering and coughing – he was going to be all right!

respects

○ **pay your last re'spects**

If people talk about **paying their last respects** to someone who has recently died, they mean the act of going to their funeral or visiting the place where they are buried.

rest

○ **come to 'rest**

Something **comes to rest** when it stops moving: *The crow circled the house and came to rest on one of the chimney pots.*

○ **give it a 'rest**

You tell someone to **give it a rest** when you want them to stop doing or saying something which is annoying you: *'Why don't you buy some new clothes? You're such a mess.' 'Oh give it a rest, mum.'* ♦ *see also* **give me a break** ▷BREAK; **knock it off** ▷KNOCK

○ **lay someone to 'rest** (*formal*)

You **are laying someone** who has died **to rest** when you respectfully bury their body: *John Smith was laid to rest on the holy island of Iona.*

○ **lay something to 'rest**

You **lay something** such as a problem or worry **to rest** when you are finally able to forget about it as a result of a certain change in the situation: *If we just received some compensation, we could lay the whole affair to rest.*

○ **rest as'sured**

You say that someone can **rest assured of something**, or **rest assured** that something will happen, if you are promising them that thing will happen: *We know Italy as only Italians can, and you can rest assured that our staff are experts in their chosen field – Italian holidays.*

retreat

○ **beat a re'treat** or **beat a hasty re'-treat**

You **beat a retreat**, or **beat a hasty retreat**, when you run away from someone or something unpleasant: *He beat a hasty retreat when he saw me coming, but it wasn't hasty enough.*

returns

○ many happy re'turns

You say '**many happy returns**' to someone on their birthday to wish them a happy birthday: *'It's my birthday on Monday.' 'Oh, I didn't know. Many happy returns for Monday, then.'*

rhyme

○ without rhyme or 'reason

Something that is **without rhyme or reason** does not make sense, or follow a logical pattern: *Three men attacked Joe – and we've been trying to figure out a motive. There's neither rhyme nor reason for it.*

ribbons

○ cut to 'ribbons or torn to 'ribbons

1 If a thin material of some kind has been **cut**, or **torn**, **to ribbons**, it has been badly damaged by cutting or tearing: *His knee was badly injured and his jeans were cut to ribbons.* **2** You say that people or things have been **cut**, or **torn**, **to ribbons** if they have been badly damaged or destroyed: *Like fellow EEC members, the Republic has seen its economy torn to ribbons by recession.*

riddance

○ good 'riddance

You say '**good riddance**' when you are glad that you have got rid of something or someone: *I've finally managed to sell that old car of mine, and good riddance to it.*

ride

○ along for the 'ride

You say you are coming **along for the ride** when you join a person or group of people simply out of interest, not to take part yourself in what they are doing: *Watching them line up, it was clear they wanted to win. They were not along for the ride.*

> In its base sense, to go **along for the ride** means to travel with someone who is going somewhere, for no purpose other than to enjoy the journey and see somewhere new.

○ let something 'ride

You **are letting something ride** when you decide not to do anything yet to change a certain situation: *David was*

making a conscious decision to become famous. He always did it for a while and then just let it ride to see what happened.

○ take someone for a 'ride (*informal*)

You say that someone **has taken you for a ride** if they have cheated or deceived you in some way: *He told you this piece of junk was worth £100? Looks like you've been taken for a ride, mate.* ♦ *see also* **pull a fast one** ▷PULL; **sell someone a pup** ▷PUP; **put one over on someone** ▷PUT; **lie through your teeth** ▷TEETH

> In American criminals' slang, to **take someone for a ride** used to mean to kill them, because murders were often committed in a moving car, in order to attract as little outside attention as possible.

riding

○ riding 'high

Someone is **riding high** when they are having a period of great success: *The members of the band were riding high after their sell-out tour of America.*

> The moon is **riding high** when it is high up in the sky.

right

○ do 'right by someone

You **do right by someone** if you manage to provide them with all the good things you think they deserve: *You mustn't get upset when I buy you things. I just want to do right by you, that's all.*

○ in the 'right

You are **in the right** if what you are doing is morally or legally right: *He has threatened to take me to court, but he won't because he knows I'm in the right.*

○ in your own 'right

You have a position or claim **in your own right** if it is yours because of your own ability or qualifications, independently of the ability or qualifications of the people you know: *Rodin's mistress Camille Claudel was an excellent sculptress in her own right.*

○ right as 'rain

Someone who is feeling as **right as**

rain is feeling perfectly well again after a period when they were not so well. ♦ *see also* **fit as a fiddle** ▷FIT

○ **right, left and 'centre**
Things which are **right, left and centre** can be seen everywhere around you: *There were people screaming and panicking right, left and centre.*

In team games such as football and hockey, a team is divided into three sections, **right, left and centre**, so that the whole field can be covered effectively.

○ **right 'on**
People or ideas are **right on** if they are socially aware and express fashionable and broad-minded views: *This new magazine is so right on. It discusses all of the environmental issues of the day.*

○ **a 'right one** (*BrE*)
You say that someone is **a right one** if they are, or if you think they are going to be, difficult to cope with: *That kid's only six and he's already uncontrollable. He'll be a right one when he gets older.*

This expression is usually only said in private, when the person in question is absent, but sometimes people say it about someone who is present, as a joke.

○ **right you 'are**
People say **'right you are'** to show that they have heard and that they will do what someone has asked: *'Can you deliver my groceries to me?' 'Right you are, then. I'll drop them in this afternoon.'*

○ **too 'right** (*informal*)
You say **'too right'** when you completely agree with what someone has just said: *'You look a bit tired.' 'Too right. I've been up all night.'* ♦ *see also* **that's just it** ▷JUST; **just so** ▷JUST

ring (*see also* **rings**)
○ **have a familiar 'ring**
If something you hear **has a familiar ring**, you think you recognize it but you are not sure from where: *Is he an actor or something? His name has a familiar ring.*

ringer
○ **a dead 'ringer for someone**
A person is **a dead ringer for someone** if they look exactly like them: *Their candidate is Peter Maughan, said to be a dead ringer for opera singer Pavarotti.*

In American English, a **ringer** is a good horse which has been entered for a race under the name of another horse which looks similar but which is not so good. This sense of **ringer** probably comes from an earlier sense, meaning a person sent to vote illegally in a district where he or she is not allowed to vote.

rings
○ **run 'rings round**
You **run rings round** someone when you make them feel embarrassed by doing things which they have no power to prevent, by defeating them easily, or by showing that you are much better than them: *She has no discipline. The kids in her class run rings round her.* □ *'So tell me, are you nervous about the big fight?' 'No man. I reckon I can run rings round him.'*

rise
○ **get a 'rise out of someone**
If someone is trying to **get a rise out of you**, they are trying to make you angry: *Ignore her. She's just trying to get a rise out of you.*

risk
○ **run the 'risk of**
You **are running the risk of** some undesirable event when this event is likely to result from your actions: *Investing in shares can be very profitable, but of course you run the risk of losing the whole lot.*

road
○ **get out of my 'road** or **get out of the 'road** (*BrE*; *informal*)
You say **'get out of my road'**, or **'get out of the road'**, when you are rudely telling someone to move because, in their present position they are blocking your way or preventing you from doing something: *This box of vegetables is heavy and I'm about to drop it if you don't get out of my road.*

○ **hit the 'road**

You say it is time to **hit the road** when you have decided to leave the place you are in, and start travelling: *I'm not really a party-goer, so I just popped my head in to bid my good nights, and hit the road home about 1am.*

○ **off the 'road**

If your car is **off the road**, you cannot use it until it has been repaired: *My car's been off the road since April. I just can't afford to get it fixed.*

○ **on the road to 'such-and-such**

You are **on the road to** a certain thing if your situation is developing towards that thing: *Little Laura has responded positively to the treatment, and is well on the road to recovery.*

○ **one for the 'road**

A person has **one for the road** when they take one last alcoholic drink before leaving the place they are in: *George Carter dipped his hand into his pocket and brought out some small silver. 'One for the road then, Jack?'*

rock (*see also* **rocks**)

○ **between a 'rock and a hard place**

Someone who is **between a rock and a hard place** is in a difficult situation, or has a difficult decision to make: *I had to decide whether to commute or work for less money at home. I was caught between a rock and a hard place.*

○ **hit rock 'bottom**

1 When something such as a quantity or value **hits rock bottom**, it reaches the lowest possible level: *Thousands of shop staff face the sack as sales hit rock bottom, bosses warned yesterday.* **2** When a person **hits rock bottom**, they have reached such a bad mental or physical state that they feel things could not get any worse: *I had been depressed for a while, but a few months after mother's death I hit rock bottom.*

rocker

○ **off your 'rocker**

You say that someone is **off their rocker** if you think that they are completely mad or stupid: *You agreed to babysit for him on your day off? You must be off your rocker.* ♦ *see also* **be bananas** ▷BANANAS; **off your trolley** ▷TROLLEY

> The two curved pieces of wood on the bottom of a rocking chair are called the **rocker**, and if the chair comes **off its rocker**, it is broken.

rocks

○ **on the 'rocks**

1 A marriage or other relationship is **on the rocks** when the people involved are unhappy with each other and are maybe thinking about separating: *By this time, our marriage was on the rocks and Lorna had started drinking heavily.* **2** You serve a strong alcoholic drink **on the rocks** when you serve it poured into a glass on top of ice: *A Scotch on the rocks, please.* [= Scotch whisky with ice] **3** A business is **on the rocks** if it is in a state of great financial difficulty and will almost certainly have to stop trading if it cannot obtain money from somewhere: *The company looked to be on the rocks in late 1991, but made a remarkable recovery the following year.*

rod

○ **make a rod for your own 'back** (*BrE*)

You say that someone is **making a rod for their own back** if, by their own actions, they are making unnecessary problems for themselves: *By agreeing to take on too much work you're just making a rod for your own back.* ♦ *see also* **your own worst enemy** ▷ENEMY; **make a meal of something** ▷MEAL

> This expression comes from the medieval image of the person who provides a stick so that someone else can beat them with it.

roll

○ **on a 'roll**

1 You say you are **on a roll** if you are having a period of good luck: *The Meteors are on a roll – yesterday against the Solihull Dodgers they had their fifth successive win.* **2** You are also **on a roll** if you are doing something fast and enthusiastically, and may be unwilling to stop: *He was on a roll as soon as he started talking about politics and almost impossible to stop.*

rolling

○ **'rolling in it**

You say that someone is **rolling in it** if they have got a lot of money: *With five top 40 hits, you might think 'Take That' are rolling in it.*

Rome

○ **fiddle while Rome 'burns**

You say that someone **is fiddling while Rome burns** if they are doing nothing or spending time enjoying themselves, when they should be trying to help in a difficult or dangerous situation: *The Government, rather than address environmental issues, is content to fiddle while Rome burns.*

> The Roman Emperor Nero is said to have **fiddled** [= played the violin] while the city of Rome was burning. However, since the violin was only invented in the 16th century, the reference is more likely to be to an early instrument such as a lyre or a viol, if indeed the story is true at all.

○ **Rome wasn't built in a 'day**

If someone says '**Rome wasn't built in a day**', they mean that it takes time to change things or to make progress, and that you should not get discouraged just because it is taking longer than you had expected: *'The shop's been open six months and it still hasn't made a profit.' 'Rome wasn't built in a day, you know.'*

○ **when in Rome, do as the 'Romans do**

If someone says about a particular situation '**when in Rome, do as the Romans do**', they mean that it is better to adapt to the habits of the foreign culture you are in, rather than trying to hold on to your own familiar ways: *Gazza knows that when in Rome, do as the Romans do – so he got into the spirit with some impressive hand waving.*

> It is common for journalists to use this idiom when they are writing about a subject relating to Rome, or Italy in general. But the expression can be used to refer to any foreign culture. People often just say '**when in Rome ...**' as a way of resigning themselves to doing something that they would not normally do in their own country or environment.

roof

○ **go through the 'roof**

An amount that **goes through the roof** increases quickly to a high level: *The price of coffee has gone through the roof recently.*

○ **hit the 'roof**

Someone **hits the roof** when they lose their temper and start shouting: *The foreman had naturally hit the roof over the loss of thirty minutes' production.* ♦ *see also* **go off at the deep end** ▷END; **blow a fuse** ▷FUSE; **let fly** ▷LET; **blow** or **flip your lid** ▷LID; **do your nut** ▷NUT; **lose your rag** ▷RAG; **fly into a rage** ▷ RAGE; **blow your stack** ▷STACK; **lose your temper** ▷TEMPER; **blow your top** ▷ TOP; **throw a wobbly** ▷WOBBLY

room

○ **no room to swing a 'cat**

You say that there is **no room to swing a cat** if there is not enough space to do things, or to feel comfortable, in the place you are referring to: *I would call it a cupboard, but they called it a study. No room to swing a cat.*

> The word **cat** here refers to a cat-o'-nine-tails, a type of whip with nine leather 'tails', each of which had a knot at the end.

○ **room for im'provement**

You say that there is **room for improvement** in something if it is not yet as good as you expected or would wish: *Once there is a recognition that there is room for improvement there comes the task of developing a determination to bring about change.*

roost

○ **rule the 'roost**

The person who **rules the roost** is in charge and controls everyone else: *After their mother died in 1890, the eldest daughter ruled the roost.*

root

○ **take 'root**

Something such as an idea **takes root** when it establishes itself or starts to grow in strength: *If a negative thought is about to enter your mind, try to become aware of it before it has had time to take root in your unconscious.*

> A plant **takes root** somewhere when its roots get strong and it starts to grow in that place.

rope

○ **give someone enough rope to 'hang themselves**
You **are giving someone enough rope to hang themselves** when, instead of accusing them of something immediately, you let them continue what they are doing in the hope that they will act even more foolishly and prove more obviously what you already know: *Kellard believes in the quiet approach: give enough rope. He would be the same in his interrogation room: no violence, no threats.*

> There are a lot of possible variants to this idiom. You can say, for example, 'Given enough rope, she would hang herself', or 'They'll give him just enough rope to hang himself'. Notice also, that you can shorten the idiom to 'give 'em enough rope' or 'give enough rope', as in the above example.

ropes

○ **know the 'ropes**
You **know the ropes** if you have a good idea, based on experience, of what needs to be done in a particular situation or for a particular job: *'He's got a good crew with him, hasn't he?' Carys said. 'George's lads know the ropes, they'll guide your Tom all right.'*

○ **show someone the 'ropes**
You **show someone the ropes** when you help them and show them what to do, because you are experienced in a situation or job which is new to them: *This is Laura. She'll be helping you out and showing you the ropes for your first month.*

roses

○ **coming up 'roses**
Things are **coming up roses** for a certain person when that person is having a period of good luck during which everything seems to be turning out perfectly for them: *She was going to marry a rising Minister, successful career, everything coming up roses.*

rot

○ **the rot sets 'in** (*BrE*)
The moment when **the rot sets in** is the moment in a situation when things start to go so badly wrong that it is difficult or impossible to put them right: *The first proof that the rot had set in at the bank was the full disclosure of its profits and reserves in 1969.*

rough

○ **take the rough with the 'smooth**
You **are taking the rough with the smooth** when you make yourself accept the bad things that happen by remembering that life cannot be easy all the time: *Relationships go up and down. You've got to learn to take the rough with the smooth.*

rounds

○ **do the 'rounds** (*BrE*) or **make the rounds** (*AmE*)
1 You **do the rounds**, or **make the rounds**, when you spend a short period staying somewhere and visiting all the usual places, or going to see all the people you know there: *'What are your plans for Christmas?' 'We'll probably spend a few days doing the rounds back home.'* **2** You say that an illness **is doing the rounds**, or **making the rounds**, if a lot of people in a particular area are getting it: *'I think I've got some kind of stomach bug.' 'Yes. There's one doing the rounds just now.'* **3** A joke or a rumour **is doing the rounds**, or **making the rounds**, if a lot of people are telling it to each other at a particular time: *There was a rumour doing the rounds a few weeks ago that one of the big supermarket chains was on the point of phasing out its organic food lines.*

> A doctor **does**, or **makes**, **the rounds** when he or she goes to visit patients in a hospital.

rub

○ **rub it 'in** (*informal*)
You say that someone is **rubbing it in**

when they keep reminding you of something that you find unpleasant or embarrassing, and are trying to forget: 'But how many of these wonderfully high-paid jobs have you been offered over the past eighteen months? None.' 'There's no need to rub it in. You don't know how difficult it is.'

○ **there lies the 'rub or there's the 'rub** (*old*)

If someone says '**there lies the rub**' or '**there's the rub**', they mean that the thing which has just been mentioned is the difficulty which is at the centre of a problem: *Finally, the reader will find chapters on finance and time-management. But there lies the rub. Will busy managers contemplate reading such a large amount of material?*

In the past, the word '**rub**' referred to any kind of hindrance or difficulty. Now, the word remains only in this idiom. In Shakespeare's *Hamlet*, III i, the hero considers killing himself, thinking being dead might be pleasant, just like sleeping. But he decides against suicide when he remembers what bad dreams people have when they are asleep, saying, 'To sleep! perchance to dream: – ay, **there's the rub**'.

rule

○ **as a 'rule**

As a rule means 'generally' or 'usually': *I don't eat sweets as a rule.*

○ **a rule of 'thumb**

A rule of thumb is a measurement or general rule which is a good guide and easy to remember, although it may not be quite accurate: *You can expect to spend one third of your income on accommodation, as a general rule of thumb.*

In its original sense, **a rule of thumb** is a way of measuring using the width or length of your thumb as a guide.

run (*see also* running)

○ **the general 'run of something** or **the usual 'run of something**

The **general**, or **the usual**, **run of something** is the usual kind or mix-

ture: *This happy pessimism is a far more compelling element than the cheerful man-gets-girl conclusion of the general run of romance-adventures.*

○ **give someone a 'run for their money**

You **give someone a run for their money** when you make it difficult for your competitor or enemy to beat you, although you realize that you will probably have to admit defeat in the end: '*I don't pretend that this will ever be a Labour seat, but at least we can force the opposition to work harder, give them a run for their money,' he said.*

In horse-racing, if a horse gives the people who have a bet on it **a run for their money**, it runs fast and tries hard to win the race, even though it does not manage to win in the end.

○ **have a 'run-in with someone**

You **have a run-in with someone** when you have an argument with them, usually about something practical such as bad behaviour or unsatisfactory work: '*We have had our run-ins in the past, but that's all behind us now. Barry has always been the best man for the job.'*

○ **in the 'long run**

You think about something **in the long run** when you consider its more permanent effects: *You may not like the idea of studying for another year, but it'll be worth it in the long run.*

○ **in the 'short run**

You think about something **in the short run** when you consider its immediate effects: *In the short run we may see some improvement, but services will deteriorate in the longer term.*

○ **on the 'run**

A person who is **on the run** has escaped from an enemy, the authorities, or the police: *A prisoner was on the run last night after giving his guards the slip.*

○ **run a'mok**

A person or group of people **run amok** when they start acting in a wild and violent way: *I forced an entry to find the raiders had ran amok inside, hurling bricks through the wooden huts and smashing window frames.*

○ **run before you can 'walk**

Someone who is trying to **run before they can walk** is trying to progress too quickly in a new skill or activity, moving on to the difficult stages before they are able to do the easy things correctly: *The first lesson was not to run before you can walk.'It was a mistake to try to develop the business too fast,' says one of the founders.*

○ **run 'short of something**

You **are running short of something**, such as food, time, money or patience when you do not have much of it left: *He was running short of petrol and that route offered him the chance to find a petrol station along the way.*

runaround

○ **give someone the 'runaround**

1 A person or organization **gives you the runaround** when they keep sending you to someone else for help that they could have provided themselves: *A man living in Glasgow claims he has been 'given the runaround' by the legal system.*

rung

○ **the lowest rung of the 'ladder** or **the bottom rung of the 'ladder**

You are at **the lowest**, or **the bottom**, **rung of the ladder** when you are at the first stage in a certain system or organization, and it will take a long time or a lot of work for you to reach the more advanced stages: *When most people of her age are just setting their first steps on the bottom rung of life's ladder, she is already Radio One's most successful female disc jockey.*

○ **the top rung of the 'ladder**

You are at **the top rung of the ladder** when you have reached the most advanced level in a certain system or organization: *She can't work towards a promotion, because she's already at the top rung of the ladder.*

runner

○ **do a 'runner** (*BrE*)

Someone **does a runner** when they leave a person or place without warning anyone, probably because they have done something illegal and do not want to be caught: *He still hasn't come back from the bank. You don't think he'd do a runner with my cash, do you?*

running

○ **in the 'running**

You say you are **in the running** when you have a chance of winning: *I didn't do well in the last round, but I'm still in the running for the cup.*

○ **out of the 'running**

You are **out of the running** when you have no chance of winning: *He only got a B-minus, which puts him out of the running for a distinction.*

○ **up and 'running**

An activity or process that is **up and running** is actually happening, as opposed to being in the planning stages: *We can start working out how to pay back our debts, now that the business is finally up and running.*

rut

○ **in a 'rut**

You say you are **in a rut** when you are dissatisfied with your life because it has become boring and repetitive: *With a wardrobe comprising jeans and sweatshirts and a hairstyle that hadn't changed in ten years, Julia felt in a rut.*

sack

○ **get the 'sack** or **give someone the 'sack**

You **are given the sack**, or you **get the sack**, when your employer dismisses you from your job: *'I've been given the sack,' Leith told her shakily, and, over coffee, gave her a blow-by-blow account of his argument with the boss.* ♦ see also **give someone the boot** ▷BOOT

The **sack** was the bag that workmen carried their tools in. When they were dismissed, they had to take their bag and go and look for work elsewhere.

○ **hit the 'sack** (*informal*)
You **hit the sack** when you go to bed: *Then he left and I hit the sack. Your English beer's a bit strong for me.*

sadness *see* **Idioms study** page 74

safety

○ **safety in 'numbers**
If you say **'there's safety in numbers'**, you mean that it is fairly safe to do something, even if it seems to be dangerous, if a number of people are doing it together: *If either of you should get into difficulties, help will be at hand. Remember – there's safety in numbers.*

said (*see also* **say**)

○ **enough 'said**
Enough said, used after a statement, means 'and of course we all know about that': *Questioned on his views Lord White tried to backtrack. 'I'm beginning to sound like a right-wing lunatic.' Enough said.*

This expression is often used when you are talking about something you find ridiculous or extreme in some way, but which you do not want to comment on directly.

○ **no sooner said than 'done**
No sooner said than done emphasizes how quickly a particular task was carried out: *When asked what he wanted for his birthday, he said a visit to the lock factory. No sooner said than done.*

○ **when all's said and 'done**
You use **when all's said and done** to summarize a situation, having considered all the facts: *But when all's said and done, we've still got to work out how to pay for it.*

sailing

○ **plain 'sailing**
When you describe a task as **plain sailing**, you mean that it is straightforward and easy to do: *It is not always plain sailing. There are difficulties which may need to be overcome.* ♦ *see also* **downhill all the way** ▷WAY

sake

○ **for the sake of 'argument**
People assume something **for the sake of argument** when they treat it as true in order to discuss something that depends on its being true: *Let us say, for the sake of argument, that the plotter and the assassin are one and the same person.*

salt

○ **rub salt into the 'wound**
You **rub salt into the wound** when you do or say something that adds to the discomfort or distress that someone is already feeling: *The older painter was shocked by this reply and Pollock, sensing this, rubbed salt into the wound by adding: 'Your theories don't interest me!'*

Salt was traditionally used by sailors as an antiseptic. It caused great pain when applied to an already painful injury.

○ **the salt of the 'earth**
If you refer to other people or to another person as **the salt of the earth**, you consider them to be worthy of respect because you can always depend on them: *Most of the urban population see rural areas as being the backbone of society, the salt of the earth.*

○ **take with a pinch of 'salt**
You **take something with a pinch of salt** if you do not take it too seriously because you have doubts about whether it is true: *She's got a very vivid imagination – take what she says with a pinch of salt.*

○ **worth your 'salt**
A person who is **worth his** or **her salt** is competent and worthy of respect: *Any lawyer worth his salt will tell the suspect in no uncertain terms to make no statement to the police under any circumstances.*

same

○ **if it's all the same to 'you**
You add **'if it's all the same to you'** after a statement about what you intend to do, as a way of making sure that the other person doesn't mind you doing it: *I think I'd like just a small*

whisky now, Mr Dalgliesh, if it's all the same to you.

sandbag

○ **'sandbag someone** (*AmE; informal*)

1 You **sandbag someone** when you force them to do something: *Don't let him sandbag you into volunteering.* **2** If you **sandbag** an opponent, you deceive them by pretending to be weak or inferior: *Jack sandbagged Joe into betting more on their next card game.*

Saturday

○ **Saturday night 'special** (*AmE; informal*)

A **Saturday night special** is a small cheap gun that is easy to obtain: *Both men were killed with the same weapon: a Saturday night special.*

> The name comes from the frequent use of such guns in crimes on Saturday nights.

sauce

○ **what's sauce for the goose is sauce for the 'gander**

If you say **'what's sauce for the goose is sauce for the gander'**, you mean that if something is good for one person, then it is also good enough for someone else, who may in fact believe themselves to be in a superior or more advantageous position: *And remember, what's sauce for the goose is sauce for the gander; if your wife is much richer than you, and you get divorced, you're the one who could benefit financially.*

sausage

○ **not a 'sausage** (*BrE; informal, humorous*)

Not a sausage means 'nothing at all': *'Did you manage to get any work done?' 'Not a sausage.'*

say (*see also* **said**)

○ **I'll say 'this for so-and-so** or **I'll say 'this for such-and-such**

You say **'I'll say this for so-and-so'**, or **'I'll say this for such-and-such'** when you want to state a quality you admire in someone, despite having just criticized them for something: *I did not agree one bit with his speech, but I will say this for him: at least he has political integrity.*

○ **needless to 'say** or **it goes without 'saying that**

Needless to say means 'naturally' or 'of course': *We spent the rest of the weekend with my grandparents. Needless to say, we ate far too much.*

○ **never say 'die**

Never say die means 'don't give up or admit defeat': *Billy was an enthusiastic player, full of pep and fight, with the 'never say die' attitude that supporters love to see.* ♦ *see also* **keep at it** ▷KEEP

○ **say no 'more**

People use **'say no more'** to show that it is not necessary to explain something further because the meaning is clear from what has been said already: *She said her husband's been late home every night this week. Say no more.*

○ **say 'when** (*informal*)

You tell someone to **say when** if you want them to tell you when to stop pouring them something to drink, or giving them something to eat.

○ **what would you say to 'such-and-such?** (*informal*)

You ask someone **what they would say to** a certain thing as a way of inviting them somewhere, or offering them something: *What would you say to another little drink before you go?*

○ **you can say 'that again!** (*informal*)

You can say that again! means 'you're absolutely right!': *'Is he in trouble?' 'You can say that again!'*

○ **you don't 'say!** (*informal*)

You use **'you don't say!'** to express surprise, or mock surprise, at something you are told.

scales

○ **tip the 'scales** or **tilt the 'scales** or **turn the 'scales**

If a factor or circumstance **tips**, or **tilts**, or **turns**, **the scales** in favour of a certain decision, it is the one that causes that decision to be made: *The conquest of the north decisively tilted the scales in Franco's favour.*

> **Scales** are a device for weighing things. Something that tips, tilts, or turns, the scales is slightly heavier than the weights on the other side.

says

○ **what so-and-so says 'goes**

If you say that **what** a certain person **says goes**, you mean that you have to do what they say: *If he says it's wrong, then of course it must be. I'm only the nurse. What he says goes.*

scarce

○ **make yourself 'scarce**

You **make yourself scarce** when you leave quickly, usually to avoid trouble or embarrassment: *If you know what's good for you, you'll make yourself scarce before you wake the whole house.*

scene

○ **not your 'scene** (*informal*)

Something that you describe as **not your scene** is not the sort of thing that you like or enjoy: *I don't really want to go myself. Musicals aren't my scene.*

○ **quit the 'scene** (*AmE; informal*)

1 If you **quit the scene**, you leave: *Veronica quit the scene before I could explain.* **2** Someone who has **quit the scene** has died: *Murray changed his will the day before he quit the scene.*

○ **set the 'scene**

You **set the scene** when you describe the situation in which an event took place: *Let's first set the scene. The sunset over a deserted beach. A single white sail on an azure-blue sea.*

scent

○ **throw someone off the 'scent**

You **throw someone off the scent** when you give them wrong or confusing information, so that they will not find the person or thing they are looking for: *He deliberately employed equations that nobody understood to throw them off the scent.*

A **scent** is a natural smell that is given off by people and animals, which can be detected by other animals.

scheme

○ **the 'scheme of things**

When someone refers to **the scheme of things**, they are referring to the way the world seems to be organized: *All his life he had wondered what his place was in the scheme of things.*

school

○ **of the 'old school**

Someone who is described as being **of the old school** follows traditional customs and has old-fashioned habits: *Lord Carrington, an aristocrat of the old school, became Foreign Secretary.*

○ **the old school 'tie** (*BrE*)

The old school tie refers to the habits of some upper class men, especially that of giving jobs to other men with similar backgrounds, or who went to the same school as they did: *The old school tie network was a recipe for disaster. It just doesn't produce a rich enough mixture of ability needed in a political party.*

In Britain, many schools have their own uniform, which includes a tie of a particular colour and design. Some people, who went to very prestigious schools, continue to wear their **old school tie**, as a matter of pride, and also so that they may be recognized by others who went to the same school as they did.

○ **the school of hard 'knocks**

If you say that you went to **the school of hard knocks**, you mean that a lot of what you have learnt about life has come from painful experience: *He certainly came from the school of hard knocks. But he wasn't bitter.* ♦ *see also* **the school of life** ▷SCHOOL

○ **the school of 'life**

If you say that you went to **the school of life**, you mean that a lot of what you have learnt about life has been through experience, rather than from studying: *Although I have no formal training, my experience is drawn from 'the school of life', having come through divorce, and the death of my son and partner.* ♦ *see also* **the school of hard knocks** ▷SCHOOL

science

○ **blind someone with 'science**

Someone **blinds you with science** when they use a lot of technical words to explain something, sometimes deliberately, so that you cannot understand their argument: *There is a technical difference between the two kinds of econo-*

*my, but I don't want to blind you with
science.*

score

○ **on that 'score**

On that score means 'concerning that'
or 'with regard to that': *Don't worry on
that score; everything's under control.*

○ **settle a 'score** or **settle old 'scores**

People **settle a score**, or **settle old
scores**, when they take some action to
settle grudges or grievances that they
have had for a long time against the
other people concerned.

scorn

○ **pour 'scorn on**

If you **pour scorn on** someone or
something, you criticize them severely
and contemptuously: *Did you have one
of those teachers who would pour scorn
on you if you made a spelling mistake?*

scrap

○ **on the 'scrap heap**

Someone or something is **on the scrap
heap** when they are discarded or rejected because they are no longer useful: *Because of these training schemes
they would be better educated and would
not be thrown on the scrap heap.*

scratch

○ **from 'scratch**

You start, or do, something **from
scratch**, when you start it from the
very beginning: *Students have the possibility of learning another language in-
tensively from scratch in the first year.*

The **scratch** used to be the starting
line which was scratched on the
ground to show where a race would
start.

○ **up to 'scratch**

If someone or something is, or comes,
up to scratch, they meet or reach the
required or expected standard: *Our
particular role in training is to make
sure the standard of teaching in every
centre is up to scratch.*

screw

○ **have a 'screw loose** (*informal*)

Someone who **has got a screw loose** is
a bit mad: *Normally I'd hesitate to believe her story because she does seem to
have a screw loose, but it does corre-*

spond to the others. ♦ *see also* **out to
lunch** ▷LUNCH

sea

○ **all at 'sea** or **at sea**

If you are **all at sea**, or **at sea**, you are
in a completely disorganized state or
have no idea what to do next: *The next
Lincoln attack swept United away. They
were all at sea as Matthews took aim and
fired in goal number two.*

seams

○ **bursting at the 'seams**

A thing or a place that **is bursting at
the seams** is very full, or so full that
it appears to be, or actually is, about
to break: *What with the festival and
everything, all the hotels are bursting at
the seams, but we'll do our best for you.*

A **seam**, here, is the join between two
pieces of material, where they are
sewn together.

○ **fall apart at the 'seams** or **come apart
at the 'seams**

Someone or something **falls**, or
comes, **apart at the seams** when they
become useless, ruined, or unable to remain in control: *I fell apart at the seams
– I was in tears all the time, and my doctor put me on pills.*

See note above.

search

○ **search 'me** (*informal*)

Search me means 'I have no idea':
*'Who's Minister for the Environment?'
'Search me.'*

seat

○ **flying by the seat of your 'pants**

Someone who **is flying by the seat of
their pants** is trying to achieve something by using instinct, luck, and not
much skill: *What is the Government up
to? Alas, it is flying by the seat of its
pants. This student loans scheme has de-
generated into open shambles.*

○ **have a 'seat** or **take a 'seat**

You say '**have a seat**', or '**take a seat**',
to someone when you are inviting them
to sit down.

○ **in the 'driving seat**

Someone who is **in the driving seat** is

running, or in control of something, such as a business: *It was the reappearance of Harold Wilson in the driving seat of government which prompted this.*

○ **in the 'hot seat**
You are **in the hot seat** if you are in a difficult position where you are responsible for dealing with awkward questions, criticisms, etc: *They will give the Prime Minister a warm welcome, but they will also put him in the hot seat because of mass unemployment, homelessness and general misery.*

○ **on the edge of your 'seat**
You are **on the edge of your seat** if you are excited, anxious or nervous about what might happen next: *This is a movie which insists you sit on the edge of your seat while skulls are cleaved and scalps lifted by the score.*

○ **a ringside 'seat**
If you have **a ringside seat**, you are in the best position to see something happen: *I'll try to get you a ringside seat for any special occasions, and generally help in any way I can.*

> **Ringside**, here, refers to the area round the edge of a boxing ring.

○ **take a back 'seat**
You **take a back seat** when you take on a less important role than before: *He bowed out, dropping hints that in future he would be taking a back seat in politics.*

see (*see also* seen)

○ **see 'so-and-so coming** (*informal*)
If you say that someone **saw you coming**, you mean that they took advantage of you: *He charged us twenty quid for a little piece of plastic. Saw us coming, that's for sure.*

○ **see 'red**
If you say that something makes you **see red**, you mean that it makes you very angry: *But she was not the only one who was losing her cool. Matilda was also beginning to see red.*

seed

○ **go to 'seed** or **run to 'seed**
If a person has **gone**, or **run**, **to seed**, they have let themselves get untidy, fat or unhealthy because they have not

paid enough attention to themselves: *She looked middle-aged, overdressed, a show-girl gone to seed.*

> When some edible plants produce seeds after flowering, it is no longer possible to eat them.

○ **sow the seeds of**
You **sow the seeds of** a particular thing when you start a process that will develop into something important: *The scheme will overpay some lawyers and underpay others, and that may sow the seeds of mis'trust between client and solicitor.*

seen

○ **have to be seen to be be'lieved**
Something that **has to be seen to be believed** is incredible or ridiculous: *The amount of paperwork surrounding events such as this has to be seen to be believed.* ♦ *see also* **beyond belief** ▷BELIEF

○ **wouldn't be seen 'dead** (*informal*)
You say that you **wouldn't be seen dead** doing something if you would never do it because you think it is stupid, ridiculous or embarrassing: *I wouldn't be seen dead in a hat like that. I'm not 19 any more, you know.*

senses

○ **come to your 'senses**
You **come to your senses** when you start behaving sensibly after a period of foolishness; someone or something **brings you to your senses** when they cause you to do this: *I had to lose a good woman before I came to my senses. But I did kick the drug.*

○ **take leave of your 'senses**
People say that you **have taken leave of your senses** when you do something crazy: *She tugged his arm furiously. 'Let me go! This minute! Have you taken leave of your senses?'*

serve

○ **serve someone 'right**
If you say, in reference to someone's misfortune, that it **serves them right**, you mean that they deserve it: *'He's been sick.' 'Serves him right for eating so much cake.'*

shadow

○ **beyond any shadow of 'doubt** or **without any shadow of 'doubt**

Something that is the case **beyond**, or **without**, **any shadow of doubt** is definitely the case, without any doubt at all: *Tonight, she knew without any shadow of doubt that he was lying to her.* ♦ *see also* **without question** ▷QUESTION; **sure as eggs is eggs** ▷SURE

shake

○ **give someone a fair 'shake** (*AmE; informal*)

If you **give someone a fair shake**, you treat them fairly and equally: *I don't want to win the contract just because I'm his brother. I just want a fair shake.*

shakes

○ **in two 'shakes** (*informal*)

In two shakes means 'immediately': *If I thought you'd gone telling the story all over town, I'd have you out of my house in two shakes.*

shame

○ **a crying 'shame**

If you describe something as **a crying shame** you mean that it is a very great shame: *I think it would be a crying shame if the country pub disappeared, but they need more customers to survive.*

shape

○ **knock into 'shape** or **lick into 'shape**

You **knock**, or **lick**, someone or something **into shape**, when you improve them, make them more organized, or more efficient: *'Don't worry, ma'am,' he laughed. 'We'll soon lick him into shape.'*

○ **in 'shape**

If you are **in shape**, you are physically fit and healthy.

○ **out of 'shape**

You are **out of shape** when you are not as fit and healthy as you can be.

○ **take 'shape**

Something **takes shape** when it takes on a definite or recognizable form: *Now a new line of research is taking shape in the US to combat toxic chemicals.*

shave

○ **a close 'shave**

You have **a close shave** when you just manage to avoid having an accident: *Good gracious, that was a close shave,* *I'll have to sit down for a minute.* ♦ *see also* **close call** ▷CALL; **close** or **near thing** ▷THING

sheep

○ **count 'sheep**

You **count sheep** when, unable to sleep, you imagine an endless number of sheep, jumping over a fence; counting them is supposed to help you fall asleep: *Dougal closed his eyes and tried counting sheep.*

○ **may as well be hung for a sheep as a 'lamb**

If someone says that they **may as well be hung for a sheep as a lamb**, they mean that if you are going to do something wrong, you might as well do something really bad which will benefit you even more.

Stealing a lamb used to be punishable by death, so it was worth stealing something bigger, because the punishment could not be any worse.

sheet

○ **a clean 'sheet** (*BrE*)

You start with **a clean sheet** when you disregard any faults or mistakes you have made in the past, which may be to your disadvantage, and begin again: *It is rarely, if ever, possible to start with a clean sheet.* ♦ *see also* **a clean slate** ▷SLATE

shelf

○ **on the 'shelf**

1 Something that is put **on the shelf** is postponed, or put aside for a time. **2** (*BrE*) If you say that someone, especially a woman, has been left **on the shelf**, you mean that they no longer have the opportunity to marry because they are now too old: *In those days, spinsterhood was seen as a mark of personal inadequacy, and I, as they probably all realized, was being left on the shelf.* **3** (*AmE*) You say someone is **on the shelf** if they are not taking part in social events: *Ann has been on the shelf since her husband died.*

The idea of a single woman being **left on the shelf** is rather an old-fashioned one now, but single women sometimes use the idiom jokingly to speak about themselves.

shell

○ **come out of your 'shell**

You **come out of your shell** when you become more confident and less shy; you **bring someone out of their shell** if you help them to be able to do this: *At university I came out of my shell. I actually talked to my fellow students.*

shellacking

○ **a she'llacking** (*AmE*; *informal*)

1 A **shellacking** is a beating: *Tim finally decided he'd had enough, and gave the bully a real shellacking.* **2** A **shellacking** is also a bad defeat: *The 12-0 defeat was the worst shellacking the team had ever had.*

shine

○ **take a 'shine to someone**

Someone **takes a shine to you** when they decide very quickly that they like you: *I think he took quite a shine to you.*

ship

○ **run a tight 'ship**

Someone who **runs a tight ship** is in control of an efficient, well-run organization: *We've run a very tight ship and we feel now is the time to increase the manager's budget.*

○ **when your 'ship comes in**

If you say that you will be able to do something **when your ship comes in**, you mean that you will be able to do it when you are rich: *The house needs a lot of work, perhaps we'll be able to do it one day, when our ship comes in.*

ships

○ **like ships that pass in the 'night**

You describe people as being **like ships that pass in the night** if they meet each other by chance, once, or several times, but never really get a chance to talk to each other.

shirt

○ **have the shirt off someone's 'back**

Someone who **would have the shirt off your back**, is prepared to cheat you financially, without any feelings of guilt: *I'd watch out for those loan companies – they'll have the shirt off your back if you're not careful.*

○ **keep your 'shirt on**

If you say '**keep your shirt on**' to someone, you are telling them rather rudely, to calm down, and not to become so angry or excited: *All right, all right, keep your shirt on! I'll be ready to go out soon.*

shoes

○ **fill someone's 'shoes**

You **fill someone's shoes** when you successfully replace them in their function: *And if you're to try and fill your mother's shoes, you'll need all the reminding I can give you.*

○ **in 'so-and-so's shoes**

If you say that you would behave in a particular way if you were **in** a certain person's **shoes**, you mean that you would act in that way if you were in their situation: *She really was making his life a misery. If I'd been in his shoes, I'd have lost my patience weeks ago.*

○ **put yourself in 'such-and-such's shoes**

You **put yourself in** a certain person's **shoes** when you imagine how they must feel under the circumstances: *She felt sorry for him. 'Please,' she said coaxingly. 'Put yourself in his shoes.'* ♦ *see also* **put yourself in such-and-such's place** ▷PLACE

shop

○ **all 'over the shop** (*BrE*; *informal*)

If things are **all over the shop**, they are scattered everywhere or in many places; if you, or your behaviour is **all over the shop**, you are behaving in a disorganized, inconsistent way: *In between, Ballesteros was, for much of the time, all over the shop.*

○ **shut up 'shop**

If a business **shuts up shop**, it stops trading, either at the end of a working day, or permanently: *But as shopping habits changed many traders were forced to shut up shop and move out blaming recession, traffic restrictions and fewer bus routes.*

○ **talk 'shop**

People **talk shop** when they discuss their professional concerns when they are away from the workplace: *'Don't tell me that you two are talking shop,' Andrew said. 'Don't you ever stop?'*

short

○ **be short of**

You **are short of** something if you do not have enough of it: *We're a bit short of 'milk. Could you get some?*

○ **short and 'sweet**

Something that is described as **short and sweet** is shorter than expected, often pleasantly so: *I think I've got five minutes, so I'll keep it fairly short and sweet.*

shot

○ **be shot of** (*BrE*)

You **are shot of** someone or something if you have got rid of them, or if they are not there any more to bother you: *I bet you're glad to be shot of those ex'ams.*

○ **call the 'shots**

If a particular person **calls the shots**, they are the person who gives the orders or is in charge: *Mother is in charge: she is the boss and she calls the shots.* ♦ *see also* **call the tune** ▷TUNE

○ **have a 'shot at something** or **take a 'shot at something**

You **have a shot at something**, or **take a shot at something**, when you try to do it: *I'm not very good at cooking, but I'm willing to take a shot at it.*

○ **like a 'shot**

If you do something **like a shot**, you do it extremely quickly without hesitating: *As soon as she heard about the accident she was down the hospital like a shot.* ♦ *see also* **like a dose of salts** ▷DOSE

○ **a shot in the 'arm**

If something that is failing or faltering is given **a shot in the arm**, it is given something which has the effect of reviving its performance: *The $25 billion will be used to create jobs and generally give the economy a shot in the arm.*

○ **a shot in the 'dark**

A **shot in the dark** is a wild guess which may or may not prove to be right: *Every appointment seems to be an outrageous shot in the dark.*

shotgun

○ **ride 'shotgun** (*AmE; informal*)

You **ride shotgun** in a car when you are the passenger in the front seat: *Bill drove, Sue sat in the back with the kids, and I rode shotgun.*

shoulder

○ **give someone the cold 'shoulder**

Someone **gives you the cold shoulder** when they act in an unfriendly way towards you, perhaps by refusing to speak to you: *Will they remember me? What will they say to me when I come back home? Will they give me the cold shoulder?*

○ **put your shoulder to the 'wheel**

You **put your shoulder to the wheel** when you begin to make a great effort or to work very hard: *I want you to put your shoulder to the wheel if necessary. You ready for it?* ♦ *see also* **get cracking** ▷CRACKING

○ **a shoulder to 'cry on**

You give someone who is upset **a shoulder to cry on** when you give them sympathy, and encourage them to feel better: *I felt very inadequate but at least I was a shoulder to cry on.*

○ **straight from the 'shoulder**

You speak **straight from the shoulder** when you speak frankly and forcefully: *Sometimes he spoke straight from the shoulder and sometimes in puzzles and parables.*

show

○ **get the show on the 'road**

You **get the show on the road** when you begin doing what you have planned: *Thanks, Jim. Now let's get this show on the road.*

○ **just goes to 'show**

If you say '**just goes to show**', you mean that things are not always as we expect them to be: *'And they seemed like such a happy couple.' 'Well, just goes to show.'*

shreds

○ **tear to 'shreds** or **rip to 'shreds**

You **tear**, or **rip**, someone or something **to shreds** when you criticize them severely: *In a 'serious' election dealing with economic issues their manifestos would be quickly torn to shreds.* ♦ *see also* **pick holes in** ▷HOLES

shut

○ **'shut it** or **shut 'up** (*informal, offensive*)

'**Shut it**' or '**shut up**' is a very rude way of telling someone to be quiet. ♦ *see also* **shut your mouth** ▷MOUTH

side (*see also* **sides**)

○ **get on the wrong 'side of someone**
You **get on the wrong side of someone** when you do something that makes them displeased with you: *You'll be okay if you don't get on the wrong side of Mr Forbes – he can be pretty ruthless if he doesn't like you.*

○ **give someone the rough side of your 'tongue** (*BrE*)
You **give someone the rough side of your tongue** when you criticize them severely and angrily: *She's likely to receive a piece of my mind, the rough side of my tongue and my boot up her backside.* ♦ *see also* **send someone away with a flea in their ear** ▷FLEA; **give someone hell** ▷HELL; **give someone a piece of your mind** ▷PIECE; **tear someone off a strip** ▷STRIP

○ **keep on the right 'side of someone**
You try to **keep on the right side of someone** by doing whatever pleases them, and avoiding annoying them: *If you manage to keep on the right side of old MacGregor, you'll do well.*

○ **know which side your 'bread is buttered**
Someone who **knows which side their bread is buttered** knows exactly how to behave in order to get the greatest financial benefit: *The employees know which side their bread is buttered. They look around this area, they see the factories that have opened in the past few years.*

○ **laugh on the other side of your 'face**
You say that someone **will be laughing on the other side of their face** if you think that they will not be so pleased with themselves when they discover the unpleasant consequences of a certain thing they have done: *You wait, I'll get you and then you'll be laughing on the other side of your face!*

○ **look on the 'bright side**
You **look on the bright side** when you concentrate on the positive aspects of a situation, rather than the unpleasant ones: *Come on, look on the bright side – at least you won't have to move away from home now.* ♦ *see also* **count your blessings** ▷BLESSINGS; **thankful for small mercies** ▷MERCIES

○ **on the 'such-and-such side**
Something that is **on the large**, or **small**, or **narrow**, etc, **side**, is a bit too large, small, or narrow: *Have you got the next size up? These are a bit on the small side.*

○ **on the 'safe side**
You do something in order to be **on the safe side** if you do it as a precaution: *'There's a train that goes at about half-nine, I think.' 'OK, we'll meet at half-eight just to be on the safe side.'*

○ **on someone's 'side**
Someone who is **on your side** supports you against your opponents: *Look, don't you understand? We're on your side! We want to help you!*

○ **the other side of the 'coin**
The other side of the coin is the opposite argument or view: *One must look at the other side of the coin. There has been a good reduction in the number of strikes; we must give the Government credit where it is due.*

○ **see the 'funny side of something**
You **see the funny side of something** if you are able to laugh about it: *It's all rather embarrassing for us, but I think we'll see the funny side in the morning.* ♦ *see also* **see the joke** ▷JOKE

○ **take 'sides** or **take someone's 'side**
You **take sides**, or **take someone's side**, when you support one person or group against another in a conflict or argument: *The counsellor cannot afford to take sides, but should instead aim to help the whole family face up to the problems they are experiencing.*

> This idiom is most frequently used with a negative form, or with a verb suggesting reluctance. Typical verbs and expressions found preceding it are 'refuse to', 'rather not', 'don't want to', 'would have to', and 'would be forced to'.

sides

○ **split your 'sides**
You **split your sides** when you laugh very long and loudly: *And whatever were you up to? It looked like some amazing mime game. I nearly split my sides.*

sight

○ **at first 'sight**

If something appears in a particular way **at first sight**, it appears that way to begin with, before it has been studied or considered more closely: *At first sight, you might think this machine is new and sophisticated, but in fact it's just another cheap gimmick.*

○ **know by 'sight**

You **know someone by sight** if you recognize them, but have never met them personally: *She knew him well by sight but she had never spoken with him before.*

○ **lose 'sight of**

You **lose sight of** someone or something when you can no longer see them; you lose sight of an aim or target when you are diverted from it: *Why are we doing all this? What do we want to achieve? If you lose sight of that, all the attention to detail in the world is not a great deal of use.*

○ **out of sight out of 'mind**

If you say that something is **out of sight out of mind**, you mean that because you do not see it, you do not think about it: *I don't worry about them when I'm away from home – I suppose it's a case of 'out of sight out of mind'.*

○ **a sight for 'sore eyes**

A sight for sore eyes is a very welcome sight: *The mighty Cairngorm Mountains are a sight for sore eyes in any rambler's book.*

sights

○ **lower your 'sights**

You **lower your sights** when you make your aims less ambitious than before: *I once had ideas of sailing around the world, but work got in the way, and I had to lower my sights.*

○ **set your 'sights on**

You **set your sights on** someone or something when you decide that you will try to achieve it: *Few jobs are easy to get these days and, if you have set your sights on advertising, it must be worth extra effort.* ♦ *see also* **set your heart on** ▷HEART

sink

○ **sink or 'swim**

You describe something as a case of **sink or swim** if the people involved have been left to try to succeed by their own efforts at the risk of suffering complete failure: *That first week was an ordeal. She had been thrown in at the deep end and it was a case of sink or swim.* ♦ *see also* **in at the deep end** ▷END

sitting

○ **be sitting 'pretty**

You **are sitting pretty** if you are rich, successful, or in a pleasant situation: *I'm sitting pretty in a nice house and you're left teaching a lot of nasty little children the ABC.*

situation

○ **no-'win situation**

A **no-win situation** is one in which whatever you do, the result will be unpleasant: *'I was effectively put in a no-win situation – there was nothing else I could do,' he said.*

○ **sticky situ'ation**

A **sticky situation** is one which may cause you embarrassment or difficulties: *I am extremely grateful to them for getting me out of a sticky situation.*

sixes

○ **at sixes and 'sevens**

If someone is **at sixes and sevens**, they are in a state of total disorder or confusion: *I'm all at sixes and sevens. I really don't know what I'm saying.*

size

○ **cut someone down to 'size**

You **cut someone down to size** when you do something that will make them realize that they are not as important as they think they are: *Some of the older boys will probably think you need cutting down to size.*

○ **try something for 'size** (*BrE*)

You tell someone to **try** a particular thing **for size** when you want to see what they think of it: *You may think you're quite good at solving mental problems. If so, try this one for size.*

skates

○ **get your 'skates on** or **put your 'skates on** (*BrE*)

If someone tells you to **get**, or **put**, **your skates on**, they are telling you to hurry up: *We'd better get our skates on if we're going to be there on time.*

skeletons

○ '**skeletons in the cupboard** (*BrE*) or '**skeletons in the closet** (*AmE*)

Skeletons in the cupboard, or **in the closet**, are shameful secrets relating to someone's past: *Nothing's going to be hidden, no skeletons in the cupboard, no dark secrets, everything out in the open.*

> This idiom is variable. For example, you may find **his** or **her** in the place of **the**, or **skeleton** (singular), rather than **skeletons**.

skids

○ **put the** '**skids on** (*AmE*)

If you **put the skids on** someone or something, you slow them down or cause them to fail: *Doris wanted to become an actress, but her parents put the skids on that.*

skin

○ **by the skin of your** '**teeth**

You manage to do something **by the skin of your teeth** when you only just manage to do it: *Consolation came with the Indiana result. He won, but only by the skin of his teeth.*

○ **get under someone's** '**skin**

When someone or something **gets under your skin**, they **1** annoy and upset you very much: *It was the sheer effrontery, the excessive assurance of them which got under my skin.* **2** cause you to feel a strong passion or attraction for them: *I know we haven't known each other long, but you've got under my skin like no other woman I've ever met.*

○ **jump out of your** '**skin**

If you say that someone or something made you **jump out of your skin**, you mean that they startled or surprised you very much: *Do you have to make me jump out of my skin like that every time you come in?*

○ **no skin off** '**your nose**

If you say that something is **no skin off your nose**, you mean that it does not cause you the slightest concern or nuisance: *Why should you worry what my mother says about you? It's no skin off your nose, is it?*

○ **save your** '**own skin**

Someone does something to **save their own skin** when they do it to protect themselves from harm or danger, especially when doing this causes them to neglect someone else's safety or feelings: *He is intent only on saving his own skin. Sarah's feelings and the consequences for her are not considered.*

sky

○ **the sky's the** '**limit**

If you say '**the sky's the limit**', you mean that there is no upper limit to the amount of money that may be spent, or the things that may be achieved: *There's so much potential in this business – the sky's the limit.*

slap

○ **a slap in the** '**face**

A **slap in the face** is a rude or insulting rejection or refusal: *A failure by government to recognize this situation will be a cruel slap in the face to an arts world that has done so much to adapt to the market economy of the 1980s.*

○ **a slap on the** '**wrist**

A **slap on the wrist** is a gentle punishment or mild warning: *They usually get little more than a slap on the wrist and most know they can get away with it unchallenged.*

slate

○ **a clean** '**slate**

You start with **a clean slate** when you disregard any faults or mistakes you have made in the past, which may be to your disadvantage, and begin again: *You'll be starting with a completely clean slate; there are no existing possessions that might prove difficult to accommodate.* ♦ *see also* **a clean sheet** ▷SHEET

○ **put something on the** '**slate** (*BrE*)

You **put something on the slate** when you postpone paying for it, and the supplier records the amount that you owe: *Could you put that one on the slate for me? I haven't got any cash on me just now.*

> A **slate** is a thin layer of dark grey rock that was used in the past for writing on.

sledgehammer

○ **a sledgehammer to crack a** '**nut**

If you say that someone is using **a sled-**

gehammer to crack a nut, you mean that they are putting too much effort into trying to solve a relatively minor problem: *These measures could quite justifiably be regarded as something of a sledgehammer to crack a very small nut, since they are intended to deal with a problem the existence of which is almost totally unproven.*

> A **sledgehammer** is a large heavy hammer used for breaking rocks.

sleep

○ **not lose 'sleep over**
If you tell someone **not to lose any sleep over** something, you mean that it is not worth worrying about: *He described Joe Kinnear's attack on his side as 'rubbish' and says he won't lose any sleep over his comments.*

○ **put to 'sleep**
Vets **put** animals **to sleep** when they kill them painlessly by injecting them with a lethal dose of a drug.

○ **'sleep on it**
If you tell someone to **sleep on it**, you mean that they should delay making a particular decision until the following morning: *It was clear to those around Mrs Thatcher that, although she said she would sleep on it, she was virtually certain to resign.*

sleeve

○ **have something up your 'sleeve**
If you **have something up your sleeve**, you have an idea or plan that you are keeping secret from other people, which you may use at some later time: *He does not look like a prime minister with a secret agenda up his sleeve.*

○ **laugh up your 'sleeve**
Someone **is laughing up their sleeve** when they are feeling secretly very pleased with themselves for having successfully deceived someone: *I trusted him, and all the time he was laughing up his sleeve.*

slice

○ **a slice of the 'action**
You get **a slice of the action** when you have the opportunity to get involved in a particular activity: *If you want a slice of the action tickets may still be avail-*

able. ♦ *see also* **a piece of the action** ▷PIECE; **a slice of the cake** ▷SLICE

○ **a slice of the 'cake**
Your **slice of the cake** is your share of something, such as money or profits: *If the BBC started to take advertising, the commercial TV companies would see their slice of the cake get smaller.* ♦ *see also* **a piece of the action** ▷PIECE; **a slice of the action** ▷ SLICE

○ **a slice of 'life**
You describe a story, a play, or a film as **a slice of life** if it closely resembles or represents real life: *He claimed that he had encouraged the movie industry to take 'the slice of life' as its subject-matter.*

slip

○ **give someone the 'pink slip** (*AmE*)
If you **give someone the pink slip**, you inform them that they are being dismissed from their job: *As soon as the company was sold, half of us got the pink slip.*

> Notices of dismissal were once often pink because of the carbon paper used.

○ **give someone the 'slip** or (*AmE*; *informal*) **give someone the 'shake**
You **give someone the slip**, or **the shake**, when you succeed in escaping from them: *I decided to give the authorities the slip, and went through the bathroom window of the hotel.* ♦ *see also* **make a break** ▷BREAK

○ **slip of the 'tongue**
A **slip of the tongue** is a small mistake you make when speaking: *'The most painful ...' He paused, corrected a slip of the tongue, and went on, 'The most painless way is for us to keep out of each other's way until you can leave.'*

slope

○ **the slippery 'slope** (*BrE*)
You are on **the slippery slope** if you have started doing something which reputedly leads to failure, ruin or self-destruction: *'Having another drink is the worst thing for a hangover and could put you on the slippery slope to alcoholism,' warns the magazine.*

sly

○ **on the 'sly**
You do something **on the sly** when you

do it secretly: *The more anyone told me not to do a thing, the more I tried to do it. So we continued to meet on the sly.*

smack

○ **smack-'dab** (*AmE*; *informal*) or **smack-'bang** (*BrE*; *informal*)

'**Smack-dab**' or '**smack-bang**' means 'exactly': *The tree fell smack-bang in the middle of my garden.* ◻ *His words were smack-dab on the mark.*

smile

○ **wipe the 'smile off someone's face**

Someone or something that **wipes the smile off your face** makes you feel suddenly foolish or regretful, when you had just been feeling very pleased with yourself: *Robyn glared; how she longed to wipe that infuriating smile off his face!*

smoke

○ **go up in 'smoke**

A plan **goes up in smoke** when it is completely ruined or comes to nothing: *We haven't worked all these months to have it go up in smoke now.*

○ **no smoke without a 'fire**

If you say that there's **no smoke without a fire**, you mean that if a lot of people are saying that something has happened, there must be at least a little truth in it: *In general, people tended not to believe them. But the 'no smoke without fire' theory remained in people's minds.*

snail

○ **at a 'snail's pace**

Someone or something that progresses **at a snail's pace** progresses very slowly: *They worked at a snail's pace in that place – I don't know how they ever managed to compete with other firms.*

A **snail** is a small animal, with a soft body and a shell, which moves very slowly.

snake

○ **a snake in the 'grass**

If you describe someone as **a snake in the grass**, you mean that they cannot be trusted: *She knew what she was doing, that snake in the grass, that viper! And I daresay she thinks she's suc-*

ceeded. ◆ *see also* **a wolf in sheep's clothing** ▷WOLF

snap

○ **snap 'out of it**

If you tell someone to **snap out of it**, you mean that they should take control of themselves and stop feeling sorry for themselves, or stop behaving foolishly: *I was miserable for weeks – couldn't snap out of it. It was dreadful.* ◆ *see also* **pull yourself together** ▷PULL

snappy

○ **make it 'snappy** (*informal*)

If you tell someone to do something 'and **make it snappy**', you mean, impatiently, that they should do it very quickly: *He broke off as his phone rang. 'Hello. Is that you again? Make it snappy – I have important visitors.'*

sneeze

○ **not to be 'sneezed at**

Something that is **not to be sneezed at** should not be disregarded or dismissed as being of little value: *They'll take her on because of the money. And she'll get all I have, which isn't to be sneezed at.* ◆ *see also* **not to be sniffed at** ▷SNIFFED

sniffed

○ **not to be 'sniffed at**

Something that is **not to be sniffed at** should not be disregarded or dismissed as being of little value: *We worked very hard, and we're very pleased. £7 million is not to be sniffed at.* ◆ *see also* **not to be sneezed at** ▷SNEEZED

snow

○ **a 'snow job** (*AmE*; *informal*)

A snow job is an act of deception or persuasion that includes flattery: *Caroline wanted a better job, but her boss spent two hours telling her how much the office depended on her. It was a real snow job.*

snuff

○ **'snuff it** (*informal*)

Someone **snuffs it** when they die: *If I'm going to snuff it, I'd rather snuff it with a pint in my hand than carrot juice.* ◆ *see also* **kick the bucket** ▷BUCKET; **cash in your chips** ▷ CHIPS; **pop your clogs** ▷CLOGS; **bite the dust** ▷DUST; **give up the ghost** ▷GHOST

soapbox

○ get on your 'soapbox

You **get on your soapbox** when you give your opinions loudly and forcefully: *Last week the Prime Minister, on his soapbox, was being heckled by a young man carrying a banner.*

> A **soapbox** is a small platform that someone stands on when they are making a speech in public.

sock

○ put a 'sock in it (*BrE*; *informal*)

If someone tells you to **put a sock in it**, they are saying, rudely, that they want you to be quiet: *Put a sock in it, will you? You've caused enough trouble today.*

socks

○ pull your 'socks up

If someone says you should **pull your socks up**, they mean that you should make an effort to do better than you have been doing recently: *If we don't pull our socks up and actually start working, then it could happen to us as well.*

sold

○ 'sold on something

If you are **sold on** a particular idea, you are extremely enthusiastic about it or convinced by it: *I get the impression they're not altogether sold on the idea.*

something

○ have 'got something there

If you say to someone '**you've got something there**', you mean that they have made an interesting observation.

○ a little 'something

A little something is a gift: *We've bought you a little something to say thank you for everything you've done.*

○ something 'else (*informal*)

Something else means 'special' or 'incredible': *That car of his really is something else – have you had a ride in it yet?*

song

○ for a 'song

Something that goes, or is sold, **for a song**, is sold at a price much lower than its real worth: *Contrary to all expectations, the painting went for a song at Sotheby's last week.*

○ make a song and 'dance

You **make a song and dance** about something when you make a lot of unnecessary fuss about it: *There's no need to make a song and dance of it. Just convey the basic facts.*

sorrows

○ drown your 'sorrows

People **drown their sorrows** when they drink alcohol in order to forget their problems: *With the first results of the exams due on Thursday night, you may be in the mood to celebrate or drown your sorrows.* ♦ *see also* **hit the bottle** ▷BOTTLE

sort

○ nothing of the 'sort

'**Nothing of the sort**' is an emphatic negative which means 'not at all the thing just mentioned': *I smiled in a way that was meant to signify interest in this excursion, but Carla could see that it showed nothing of the sort.* ♦ *see also* **nothing of the kind** ▷KIND

○ sort of

You use **sort of** when giving a rough description or idea of something: *I feel sort of 'funny when I look at those photos.* ♦ *see also* **kind of** ▷KIND

sorts

○ it takes 'all sorts

If you say '**it takes all sorts**', you mean that you can't expect everyone to like the same things as you, even if you cannot understand why they do or like certain things: *They've gone on a fishing honeymoon. Not my idea of romance – takes all sorts.*

○ of 'sorts

Something you describe as a certain thing **of sorts** is not a very good or very typical one of its kind: *This chapter is therefore an invitation of sorts – an invitation to pause before plunging into the issues that follow.* ♦ *see also* **of a kind** ▷KIND

○ out of 'sorts

You are **out of sorts** if you are not feeling very well: *He's seemed a bit out of sorts these past few days. It's probably nothing.* ♦ *see also* **below** or **not up to par** ▷PAR; **under the weather** ▷WEATHER

soul

○ bare your 'soul

You **bare your soul** when you tell someone your deepest feelings: *I don't know what it is about you, Miss Abbott, but you make me want to bare my soul to you.*

The **soul** is the part of a person that is believed to consist of personality, emotions and intellect.

○ sell your soul to the 'devil

You **sell your soul to the devil** when you do something immoral or illegal in order to get something you want: *We were wondering if her essays were all her own work. She's sent them up to a London publisher. Do you think she's sold her soul to the devil?*

sound

○ sound as a 'bell

Something that is as **sound as a bell** is undamaged and in very good condition: *It's twenty five years old, but it's sound as a bell – take it for a drive.* ♦ *see also* in mint condition ▷CONDITION

soup

○ in the 'soup

You are **in the soup** if you are in trouble or difficulties: *Democracy must be seen to work, or else we're all in the soup.* ♦ *see also* up the creek without a paddle *or* up the creek ▷CREEK; out of your depth ▷DEPTH; in a tight spot ▷SPOT; in deep water ▷WATER; in hot water ▷WATER

sour

○ turn 'sour

If a situation **turns sour** it becomes less enjoyable: *But as time went by the marriage turned sour.*

Milk that has turned **sour** has an unpleasant taste because it is no longer fresh.

spade

○ call a spade a 'spade

Someone who **calls a spade a spade** speaks plainly without trying to make things seem better than they really are: *Let's call a spade a spade. The answer is no.*

A **spade** is a long-handled digging tool with a broad metal blade that you push into the ground with your foot.

spanner

○ put a 'spanner in the works (*BrE*)

You **put a spanner in the works** when you spoil a plan or activity by introducing an obstacle which prevents it from progressing: *No, something always comes along and puts a spanner in the works and that upsets everybody.* ♦ *see also* put a spoke in someone's wheel ▷SPOKE

A **spanner** is a tool with one or two specially shaped ends which fit around a nut or bolt which can then be turned with the handle.

spare

○ go 'spare (*BrE*)

You **go spare** when you become very angry: *Old Stevenson would go spare if he knew what we'd done to his precious library.*

sparks

○ sparks 'fly

Sparks fly when people become very angry with each other: *I know he made the sparks fly sometimes in council committees but most of that was good humoured.*

speak

○ speak for it'self

Something **speaks for itself** if it has an obvious meaning or significance and does not need to be explained: *Her success speaks for itself.*

○ speak too 'soon

You **speak too soon** when you say something optimistic and then find out that it is not the case: *I don't want to speak too soon, but I think I've been fairly consistent this season.* ♦ *see also* tempt providence ▷PROVIDENCE

○ to 'speak of

Nothing, or no-one, **to speak of** means nothing, or no-one, of any size or importance: *'Have you got a decent resource library?' 'Well, nothing to speak of really.'*

spectacle

○ make a 'spectacle of yourself

If someone **makes a spectacle of themselves** they do something foolish or ridiculous that makes them the focus of attention: *She couldn't get on the bicycle – she was too worried that she might fall off and make a spectacle of herself.*

speed

○ at breakneck 'speed

You do something, such as drive, **at breakneck speed**, when you do it very fast: *There speaks the man who drove us here at such breakneck speed that I began to take pity on his poor Ferrari's engine.* ♦ *see also* **at a rate of knots** ▷RATE

spikes

○ hang up your 'spikes (*AmE*)

If someone, especially an athlete, **hangs up their spikes**, they retire: *Boston's best first baseman was hanging up his spikes.* □ *'Writers', he warned, 'can never hang up their spikes.'*

> The term comes from the fact that athletes' shoes have spikes to grip the ground.

spirit

○ enter into the 'spirit of

You **enter into the spirit of** an occasion when you get involved in the general atmosphere or feeling created by the people present: *Mr and Mrs Lewis entered into the spirit of the occasion but I thought I could see some sadness in Mrs Lewis's eyes.* ♦ *see also* **let your hair down** ▷HAIR

spoke

○ put a spoke in someone's 'wheel (*BrE*)

You **put a spoke in someone's wheel** when you make problems and difficulties for them: *'They'll put a spoke in our wheel,' Lionel said. 'If they know what we're planning, they can out-manoeuvre us.'* ♦ *see also* **put a spanner in the works** ▷SPANNER

spoon

○ born with a silver 'spoon in your mouth

If you say that someone was **born with a silver spoon in their mouth**, you mean that they have had a privileged, comfortable and sheltered upbringing: *She thinks that we have absolutely no understanding of anybody ordinary because we were born with a silver spoon in our mouths.*

spot (*see also* spots)

○ have a 'soft spot for someone

You **have a soft spot for someone** if you, maybe privately, feel affection for them: *Dad had a soft spot for Auntie Nellie and perhaps Mum had something to be jealous about.* ♦ *see also* **have a crush on someone** ▷CRUSH

○ in a tight 'spot

You are **in a tight spot** if you are in a difficult position: *You're in a tight spot. If you refuse to co-operate I can force you to pay me the money you owe me.* ♦ *see also* **up the creek without a paddle** or **up the creek** ▷CREEK; **out of your depth** ▷DEPTH; **in the soup** ▷SOUP; **in deep water** ▷WATER; **in hot water** ▷WATER

○ on the 'spot

1 If you do something **on the spot** you do it immediately: *She preferred to make corrections on the spot.* **2** If you are **on the spot** when something happens, you are at the scene: *Companies appear to rely on the perceptions of their own managers on the spot, with a loyalty to head office.* **3** If someone puts you **on the spot**, they put you in a difficult position, especially one that forces you to take action or make a response when you would rather not: *Such a development would certainly put the directors on the spot.*

○ rooted to the 'spot

You are **rooted to the spot** if you are so terrified or shocked that you cannot move your legs: *Her feet seemed to be rooted to the spot as she saw the pram with baby Donald in it disappear over the bank.*

○ spot 'on (*BrE*)

'Spot on' means **1** absolutely accurate: *He was spot on when he described the car as 'quite simply a revelation.'* **2** excellent or exactly what was required: *You look marvellous. Spot on. Can I get you a drink?* ♦ *see also* **bang on** ▷BANG ON

spots

○ knock 'spots off (*BrE*)

If one person or thing **knocks spots off** another, they are very much better than that other person or thing: *The policy review certainly knocks spots off anything attempted by the Conservatives in the run-up to the 1979 election.*

spout

○ up the 'spout (*BrE*; *informal*)

Something that is **up the spout** is useless, ruined or damaged: *I'm doing this on a PC but for some reason the function keys are all up the spout.*

spread

○ spread yourself 'thin or spread yourself 'too thin

You **spread yourself thin** or **spread yourself too thin** when you try to do too many things: *Martha spread herself thin when she joined every club in the area.*

spur

○ on the spur of the 'moment

If you do something **on the spur of the moment**, you suddenly decide to do it on an impulse: *We all buy things on the spur of the moment – this is what the retail trade calls an 'impulse buy'. It means a purchase that hasn't been planned in advance.*

square

○ back to square 'one

If you have to go **back to square one**, you have to go back to the place or position that you started from originally, with no progress being made; you are **back at square one** if you are in this position: *One drink, and you find yourself back at square one.*

○ 'square yourself with someone (*AmE*)

You **square yourself with someone** when you correct a wrong that you have done to them or apologize for it: *I was glad I was able to square myself with Dad before he died.*

stab

○ have a 'stab at or make a 'stab at

If you **have**, or **make**, **a stab at** something, you try to do it: *Why don't you have a stab at it? You've got nothing to lose.*

stable

○ shut the stable door after the horse has 'bolted

If someone **shuts the stable door after the horse has bolted**, they take measures to prevent something from happening when it has already happened, and it is too late: *To lock up young car thieves is another example of shutting the stable door after the horse has bolted.*

> This idiom has many variations, such as **close**, **slam**, or **bolt**, **the stable door after the horse has fled** (or **bolted**). Sometimes it is shortened to 'it's a case of shutting the stable door', or even 'it's a stable-door situation'.

stack

○ blow your 'stack

If you **blow your stack** you become very angry: *Can't you have a reasonable discussion without blowing your stack every five minutes?* ♦ *see also* **go off at the deep end** ▷END; **blow a fuse** ▷FUSE; **let fly** ▷LET; **blow** or **flip your lid** ▷LID; **do your nut** ▷NUT; **lose your rag** ▷RAG; **fly into a rage** ▷ RAGE; **hit the roof** ▷ROOF; **lose your temper** ▷TEMPER; **blow your top** ▷ TOP; **throw a wobbly** ▷WOBBLY

stage

○ the stage is 'set

If **the stage is set** for something to take place, the circumstances indicate that it will happen: *These imbalances threaten the welfare of younger generations and of society as a whole – the stage is set for a profound confrontation.*

stake

○ 'stake someone to something (*AmE*)

You **stake someone to something** when you provide them with it, usually as a loan: *I'll stake you to a meal.*

stakes

○ raise the 'stakes

You **raise the stakes** when you increase the reward that you or others are competing for: *Mr Major raised the stakes in the final phase of the election campaign last night.*

A **stake** here, refers to a sum of money risked in betting.

○ **up 'stakes** or (*AmE*) **pull up 'stakes**
You **up stakes**, or **pull up stakes**, when you leave home and move on to another place: *You don't imagine we can simply walk out of here, do you – up stakes and toddle off back to the world of boiled cabbage and beds with sheets?*

'**Stakes**' here refers to the pegs which support a tent. You take them up when you are ready to move your tent to another place.

stand

○ **make a 'stand** or **take a 'stand**
You **make a stand** against something or **take a stand** on something when you state your position on some issue and prepare to defend it.

○ **stand cor'rected**
You say '**I stand corrected**' when someone points out that you have made a mistake and you accept that they are right: *Sorry people, I stand corrected, the game is on Tuesday night, not Thursday.*

○ **stand up and be 'counted**
If people have to, or decide to, **stand up and be counted**, they feel it is necessary to make their opinions known, even if doing so is going to cause problems: *I'm a Socialist, I am proud to be a Socialist, so I will stand up and be counted.*

○ **take the 'stand** (*AmE*)
You **take the stand** when you give evidence in a law court: *The defence said their client would not take the stand.*

stars

○ **reach for the 'stars**
You **reach for the stars** when you are very ambitious: *This was her chance to be her own boss, to stand up and reach out for the stars.*

○ **see 'stars**
You **see stars** when you see flashes of light in front of your eyes after you have knocked your head hard against something: *With the blow on his head, Anton saw stars.*

starters

○ **for 'starters**
You say that something is the case **for starters** when that point is the beginning of a list of complaints or arguments: *Here's a couple of his weak points, just for starters. He's unreliable and he's totally irresponsible.* ♦ *see also* **for a kick-off** ▷KICK

state

○ **in a 'state**
Someone who is **in a state** is nervous, anxious or upset: *She's in a terrible state and she won't let them give her sedatives because of the baby.*

stead

○ **stand in good 'stead**
Something **stands you in good stead** for a future activity if it prepares you well for it: *Conran is convinced, too, that his experience of manufacturing in the early days has stood him in good stead as head of a retailing company.*

steam

○ **let off 'steam**
People **let off steam** when they do something that has the effect of releasing the anger or energy that has built up inside them: *He doesn't mean to get at you personally. It's just that he wants to let off steam, and you're the only person he can lose his temper with.* ♦ *see also* **get something out of your system** ▷SYSTEM

○ **run out of 'steam**
If something **runs out of steam**, it loses its energy or momentum: *Yes, I write short stories when I feel I've run out of steam on the novels.*

○ **under your own 'steam**
If you get somewhere **under your own steam**, you get there by your own efforts: *Ask them if they can make it under their own steam on Saturday or whether they'll need a lift.*

steer

○ **a bum 'steer** (*AmE*; *informal*)
You give someone **a bum steer** when you give them false information or wrong instructions: *She told me he lived on Wilson Street, but that was a bum steer.*

step

○ **mind your 'step** or **watch your 'step**

If you **mind**, or **watch**, **your step**, you proceed with caution, taking care not to anger or offend others: *You better watch your step from now on. You've already upset the management.*

○ **a step at a 'time** or **one step at a 'time**

If something is done **a**, or **one**, **step at a time** it is done gradually: *Changes must be made one step at a time, each step being an improvement on the preceding one.*

○ **a step 'forwards** or (*AmE*) **a step 'forward**

A **step forwards**, or **forward**, is an advance made in a task or process: *The success of his operating systems took Mr Gates another giant step forwards.*

○ **one step 'forward, two steps 'back**

A situation is a case of **one step forward, two steps back**, when, despite all attempts to progress, you still find yourself in a worse position than you were in when you started: *It is no good signing up a new member and then losing two others. That's one step forward, two steps back.*

○ **step by 'step**

If something is done **step by step**, it is done gradually: *She stressed that talk of a reunited Germany was 'going much too fast. You have to take these things step by step.'*

○ **a step in the right di'rection**

You take **a step in the right direction** when you do something that brings you nearer to your goal: *The MP called the move 'a major step in the right direction'.*

○ **'step on it**

If you tell someone to **step on it**, you mean that they should hurry up: *The Corporal and I shouted at the Sergeant to step on it, as the explosions were getting closer.*

In driving, you **'step on it'** when you press your foot down on the accelerator to make the car go faster.

steps

○ **take 'steps**

If you **take steps** to do something, you take the necessary action to ensure that something is done: *The Government considered the need to take steps to improve public order.*

stick

○ **give someone 'stick** (*BrE*)

You **give someone stick** when you tease or criticize someone for not doing something properly: *I had to win, or the rest of the boys would have given me stick, particularly Linford.*

○ **in a cleft 'stick** (*BrE*)

You are **in a cleft stick** when you have to choose between two very important and difficult matters: *So it's a cleft stick. And it's very difficult to make a final decision.* ♦ *see also* **in two minds** ▷MINDS

sticks

○ **out in the 'sticks**

A place that is **out in the sticks** is a long way from any big towns or public facilities: *Living out in the sticks, I can't afford to lose my driving licence.* ♦ *see also* **the back of beyond** ▷BACK; **in the middle of nowhere** ▷MIDDLE; **off the beaten track** ▷TRACK; **out of the way** ▷WAY

sting

○ **a 'sting in the tail** (*BrE*)

If something such as a set of circumstances has **a sting in the**, or **in its**, **tail**, it has a part or consequence that is unexpectedly unpleasant or harmful: *The budget certainly had a sting in its tail, with an increase in fuel charges.*

An insect's or other creature's **sting** is a sharp part that can pierce skin and inject poison.

○ **take the 'sting out of**

If something **takes the sting out of** an unpleasant event or situation, it makes it slightly less painful or easier to accept: *The company took the sting out of a halved dividend by saying it thought the figures were the low point in its fortunes and the only way to go was up.*

stink

○ **cause a 'stink** or **kick up a 'stink**

If someone **causes**, or **kicks up**, a **stink**, they make a fuss by complaining loudly: *The decision was finally changed, but only after he had kicked up a stink.*

stir

○ **cause a 'stir** or **create a 'stir**

If something **causes**, or **creates**, a **stir**, it causes or creates an excited re-action: *Microsoft recently caused quite a stir in computer circles by announcing that it is using real people to test its products.*

stitch

○ **not have a stitch 'on**

When you **do not have a stitch on**, you are completely naked: *One hot day I remember leaving our clothes along the river bank and swimming without a stitch on.*

stitches

○ **in 'stitches**

You are **in stitches** if you are helpless with laughter; someone has you **in stitches** if they cause you to be help-less with laughter: *I thought the film was excellent. It had me in stitches a lot of the time and definitely wasn't just for the kids.*

stomach

○ **not have the 'stomach for**

If you say that you **do not have the stomach for** something, you mean you do not have enough courage or determination to do it or face it: *He found he no longer had the energy, the stomach for getting on.*

○ **sick to the 'stomach**

Something that makes you **sick to the stomach** disgusts you: *Cara stared at it, unbelieving. She felt sick to the stomach.*

stone

○ **carved in 'stone**

Something such as a rule or regulation that is **carved in stone** is strict, and cannot be altered: *The rules aren't carved in stone – they're just there to guide you.* ♦ *see also* **set in** or **written on tablets of stone** ▷TABLETS

This idiom is commonly used in the ne-gative, as in the above example.

○ **leave no stone un'turned**

If you **leave no stone unturned**, you search for something in every possible place: *We shall leave no stone unturned in our search for the culprit.*

○ **a 'stone's throw**

Something that is **a stone's throw** away is very near: *I'm really happy with my new flat. It's got a great view and the station's just a stone's throw away.* ♦ *see also* **in** or **within spitting distance** ▷DISTANCE; **on your doorstep** ▷DOOR-STEP

stools

○ **fall between two 'stools**

Something you do **falls between two stools** when it fails because you have tried to fulfil two aims, and have been unsuccessful with both, perhaps because you could not decide which one to focus on: *The film's attempt to combine social comment with an escapist action movie format cause it to fall heavily between two stools.*

stop

○ **come to a full 'stop** (*BrE*)

Something that **has come to a full stop** has come to an end: *Will the com-pany come to a full stop? Probably not, even though the next couple of years will be tough.*

In British English, a **full stop** is the punctuation mark (.) which indicates the end of a sentence.

○ **stop at 'nothing**

Someone who will **stop at nothing** is willing to do anything, however im-moral, to get what they want: *He was a coolly calculating, ruthless man who would stop at nothing to get where or what he wanted.* ♦ *see also* **at any price** ▷PRICE

stops

○ **pull out all the 'stops**

You **pull out all the stops** when you act with as much energy, determina-tion or emotion as possible: *The staff pulled out all the stops to ensure patients had a magical day.* ♦ *see also* **take the bull by the horns** ▷ BULL; **grasp the nettle** ▷NETTLE

The **stops** here, refer to the devices on an organ, which, when pulled out, en-able you to play the instrument as loudly as possible.

store

○ **in 'store**
Something that is **in store** is coming in the future: *We have some great music in store for you on tonight's show.*

○ **lay great 'store by** or **set great 'store by** or **put great 'store by**
If you **lay**, **set** or **put great store by** something, you value that thing highly: *The market economy must lay great store by individual responsibility.*

storm

○ **a storm in a 'teacup** (*BrE*) or **a tempest in a 'teapot** (*AmE*)
If you describe a situation as **a storm in a teacup**, or **a tempest in a teapot**, you mean that a great deal of fuss is being made over an unimportant matter: *This disagreement between the different schools of thought is just a storm in an academic teacup.* ♦ *see also* **make a mountain out of a molehill**
▷MOUNTAIN

○ **take by 'storm**
A performer or performance **takes a place by storm** when they gain rapid and widespread popularity: *Carol took the local Theatre Royal by storm.*

○ **weather the 'storm**
You **weather the storm** when you survive in a difficult time: *Their vigorous reshaping programme last year helped the company weather the storm slightly better than some of its rivals.*

story

○ **the same old 'story**
You use **the same old story** to refer to an unpleasant or undesirable situation that happens again and again: *And every winter it was the same old story, everyone was short of work again.*

straight

○ **on the straight and 'narrow**
Someone who is **on the straight and narrow** is living their life in a moral and principled way, especially after a period of criminal, immoral or unacceptable behaviour: *Many returned to the straight and narrow as the result of his firm but compassionate influence.*

○ **straight as an 'arrow** or **straight as a 'die**
Something that is as **straight as an arrow**, or **straight as a die**, is very straight; someone who is as **straight as an arrow**, or **die**, is very honest: *A wall goes down from the road straight as a die to East Gill.* □ *The other friend, who also decided to become a lawyer, was as straight as an arrow.*

○ **'straight up¹** (*BrE*; *informal, slang*)
'Straight up' is used to emphasize that what you have just said is true: *'They gave us all this free.' 'No.' 'Yeah, straight up – they were closing down – throwing loads of stuff away.'*

○ **'straight up²** (*AmE*)
If you drink a cocktail without ice, you drink it **straight up**: *I'll have a bloody Mary, straight up.*

straw

○ **draw the short 'straw** or **get the short 'straw**
You **draw**, or **get**, **the short straw** when you are given the least pleasant task to do, or when you are chosen to do something that no-one wants to do: *I drew the short straw and could not drink as I had to drive us all home.*

○ **the last 'straw** or **the final 'straw**
You say that something is **the last**, or **final**, **straw** when it is the last in a whole series of disagreeable events and is the one that makes you feel that you cannot tolerate any more: *The final straw was when the government put up the price of rice yet again.* ♦ *see also* **the straw that broke the camel's back**
▷STRAW

○ **the straw that broke the camel's 'back**
You describe something as **the straw that broke the camel's back** if it is the last in a series of disagreeable events, and is the one that makes the person or thing involved finally break down: *In fact, the proposed mass redundancy in and around the mining industry was probably the straw that broke the camel's back for the British people.* ♦ *see also* **the last** or **final straw**
▷STRAW

Straw is the dried cut stalks of corn and other crops, used as food and bedding for cattle.

straws

○ **clutch at 'straws** or **grasp at 'straws**
You **clutch**, or **grasp**, **at straws** when you try, in desperation, to get out of a difficult situation by means that are unlikely to succeed: *She was in love with him, a sort of frantic grasping at straws, in love with the idea of love.*

> Someone who is drowning or falling is likely to try to hold on to anything, however useless, to try and save themselves.

streak

○ **on a winning 'streak**
You are **on a winning streak** if you are enjoying a series of successes: *Michael picked up his cards and studied them carefully. He was on a winning streak tonight.*

street

○ **up someone's 'street**
Something that is **up your street** is just the sort of thing that you like: *You like travelling. The assignment should be right up your street.*

> This idiom is very often preceded by 'right', which gives it emphasis.

streets

○ **on the 'streets**
Someone who is **on the streets** is homeless: *Tenants who refuse to accept leases are given notice to quit and find themselves on the streets.*

○ **'streets ahead**
You say that something is **streets ahead** of others when it is much more advanced or much better than they are: *The Scandinavian countries are already streets ahead in the area of alternative energy production.*

strength

○ **give me 'strength**
People say **'give me strength'** when they feel that they cannot tolerate a situation any more: *He moaned aloud and rolled his eyes to the ceiling. 'Give me strength,' he yelled.*

○ **go from strength to 'strength**
People or things **go from strength to strength** when they keep improving or becoming more successful: *For several years the business went from strength to strength.*

○ **on the strength of**
You do something **on the strength of** some circumstance or experience when the circumstance or experience persuades you to do it: *McNeill signed Jack for £650,000, largely on the strength of 'video evidence.*

stretch

○ **at a 'stretch**
You do something for a certain length of time **at a stretch** when you do it continuously throughout that period: *They can't expect you to work for more than five hours at a stretch.*

○ **by no stretch of the imagi'nation**
Something that can **by no stretch of the imagination** be described in some way cannot possibly be described in that way: *Carl could, by no stretch of the imagination, ever be called good-looking.*

stride

○ **get into your 'stride** or *(AmE)* **hit your stride** or **reach your stride**
You **get into your stride**, or **hit your stride**, or **reach your stride**, when you begin to work or do something well or effectively: *I've had to cut back a little recently, but I'm hoping to get back into my stride really soon.*

strikes

○ **have two 'strikes against you** *(AmE; informal)*
Someone who has **two strikes against them** has a big disadvantage: *Harry already had two strikes against him because of his time in prison.*

string

○ **another string to your 'bow** or **a second string to your 'bow**
You have **another**, or **a second**, **string to your bow** if you have another ability or skill apart from your main occupation, which will give you a second chance if you lose your job, for example: *He decided to take the degree so he would have another string to his bow.*

strings

○ **hold the 'purse strings**
The person who **holds the purse**

strings in an organization or group is the one who is in charge of looking after the money, and deciding how it will be spent: *Colleges will now be responsible for managing their own budgets but the Government will hold the purse strings.*

○ **pull 'strings** or (*AmE*) **pull 'wires**

If you **pull strings**, or **pull wires**, you use your influence or your friendly relationships with influential people in order to get something done: *He's one of the managers. He can pull strings for you.*

○ **no strings at'tached**

If a situation or proposal comes with **no strings attached**, it has no undesirable conditions or limitations: *And there's no strings attached to the sponsorship that I received. I didn't have to stay with the company after I finished studying.*

strip

○ **tear someone 'off a strip** (*BrE*)

You **tear someone off a strip** when you tell them off angrily: *Don't just tear them off a strip. Explain why what they are doing is wrong.* ♦ *see also* **send someone away with a flea in their ear** ▷FLEA; **give someone hell** ▷HELL; **give someone a piece of your mind** ▷PIECE; **give someone the rough side of your tongue** ▷SIDE

stuff

○ **know your 'stuff**

Someone who **knows their stuff** has a thorough knowledge of their subject: *We've used him in the past on a few projects. He's a good man and knows his stuff.* ♦ *see also* **know your onions** ▷ONIONS

stuffing

○ **knock the 'stuffing out of**

If someone or something **knocks the stuffing out of** a person or thing, it takes away their strength or power and makes them weak and feeble: *Mike Spence's death at Indy in 1968 knocked the stuffing out of me.*

stump

○ **up a 'stump** (*AmE*; *informal*)

If you are **up a stump**, you have a difficult choice to make and do not know

what to do: *I liked both candidates, so that left me up a stump.*

stupidity *see* **Idioms study** page 81

style

○ **cramp someone's 'style**

Someone or something that **cramps your style** stops you behaving as freely as you would like: *He looked over at the crutches with an expression of deep distaste.'I try not to let them cramp my style.'*

○ **do something in 'style**

You **do something in style** when you do it the most expensive or elegant way: *Buy this new garden furniture and relax in the sun in style.*

sublime

○ **from the sublime to the ri'diculous**

You say that something goes **from the sublime to the ridiculous** if it starts off well, but quickly becomes laughable or very bad: *Constructed layer by layer, Ostrowski's paintings range from the sublime to the ridiculous, presenting many paradoxes in the process.*

success *see* **Idioms study** page 180

suit

○ **follow 'suit**

If someone does something and you **follow suit**, you do the same thing as they have done: *When West Germany raised its interest rate last week, Britain was forced to follow suit.* ♦ *see also* **take a leaf out of someone's book** ▷LEAF

In a card game, you **follow suit** when you play a card of the same suit (diamonds, hearts, clubs or spades) as the player before you.

sure

○ **sure as eggs is 'eggs** (*BrE*)

You say that something is the case **sure as eggs is eggs** if you want to emphasize that you know for certain that it is the case: *She'll wait up for us. Sure as eggs is eggs. You know what she's like.* ♦ *see also* **without question** ▷QUESTION; **beyond any shadow of doubt** or **without any shadow of doubt** ▷SHADOW

○ **sure 'thing** (*informal*)

Sure thing means 'yes, of course': *'Can you find the phone number?' 'Sure thing. I'll check the Yellow Pages.'*

IDIOMS*study*   success

The next time you write or talk about **success** you might try to use some of the following idioms. (Remember you can see how to use each idiom correctly by looking at its entry, which you can find under the word printed in heavy type.)

being successful

go with a **bang**	make the **grade**	be **riding** high
make it **big**	**make** it	come up, or turn up,
sweep the **board**	hit the **mark**	**trumps**
carry it off	make your **mark**	go up in the **world**
(pass) with flying	make a **name** for	be on the **up** and up
colours	yourself or make	have the **world** at
carry the **day**	your **name**	your feet
go the **distance**	come into your **own**	
fall on your **feet**	go **places**	

winning

get the **better** of	wipe the **floor** with	run **rings** round
someone	someone	someone
beat someone hollow	make **mincemeat** of	be on a winning
beat someone **hands**	someone	**streak**
down	pip someone at the	make a clean **sweep**
win **hands** down	**post**	come out on **top**

surface

○ scratch the 'surface

You **scratch the surface** when you only deal with the superficial elements of something: *So far, research has done no more than scratch the surface of this potentially important topic.*

surprise *see* **Idioms study** page 181

swear

○ swear 'blind (*BrE*)

You **swear blind** that something is the case when you say firmly and for certain that it is true, even though other people have their doubts: *He used to swear blind he saw his mother standing at the end of the bed.*

sweat

○ 'no sweat (*informal*)

'No sweat' is a very informal way of saying that something is not a problem for you: *I just returned from an exhibition and wrote a 6,000 word report in one burst in my hotel room. No sweat.*

sweep

○ make a clean 'sweep

You **make a clean sweep** in a series of contests when you win them all: *But he failed to achieve a clean sweep of the end-of-season awards.*

sweetness

○ all sweetness and 'light

If you say that someone is **all sweetness and light**, you mean that they are behaving in an insincerely friendly and pleasant manner: *We've talked several times. He's been all sweetness and light, promised nothing and done nothing.*

IDIOMS*study*

surprise

The next time you write or talk about **surprise** you might try to use some of the following idioms. (Remember you can see how to use each idiom correctly by looking at its entry, which you can find under the word printed in heavy type.)

being surprised

not believe your **ears**
jump out of your **skin**

you could hear a **pin** drop

things people say when they're surprised

you're **joking**
you're **kidding**
that's **news** to me

you don't **say**!
wonders will never cease
of all **things**

surprising

out of the **blue**
a **bolt** from the blue
beyond **belief**
too **good** to be true

a **new** one on you
none other than so-and-so
have to be **seen** to be believed

swing

○ go with a 'swing (*BrE*)
An event that **goes with a swing** is very successful and enjoyed by the people present.

○ in full 'swing
If something is **in full swing**, it is at its liveliest or most active stage: *The holiday season begins to get into full swing as our schools close.*

swoop

○ in one fell 'swoop
A number of things are dealt with or done **in one fell swoop** when they are all dealt with or done at one time rather than gradually or in stages: *You are likely to suffer from headaches, lethargy and so on, if you try and cut the stimulants out in one fell swoop.*

sympathy

○ come out in 'sympathy with
You **come out in sympathy with** another person or group of people

when you do the same thing as them in order to demonstrate your support for them: *Dockers everywhere came out in sympathy. Strikes were announced throughout the country.*

system

○ all systems 'go
'All systems go!' means 'let's go!'; if a project is **all systems go**, it is just starting, on a large and ambitious scale: *Blue skies and sunshine reigned supreme and it was all systems go for a great airshow.*

○ get something out of your 'system
When you have been feeling anger, sorrow, or frustration, and you manage to **get it out of your system**, you succeed in getting rid of that feeling by expressing it openly: *Don't be afraid to cry; it's the best way to get it out of your system.*

T

○ **to a 'T**
To a T means 'perfectly': *Mmm-mmm. This beef is done to a T.* ♦ *see also* **done to a turn** ▷ TURN

tab (*see also* **tabs**)

○ **pick up the 'tab**
You **pick up the tab** when you pay the bill: *We will pick up the tab for your hotel.*

table

○ **drink someone under the 'table**
You say you can **drink someone under the table** if you can drink a lot more alcohol than they can before getting completely drunk: *He was 24, highly intelligent, and could drink Malc under the table.*

○ **under the 'table**
Something that is done **under the table** is done secretly, rather than publicly or officially: *Do you think he is working under the same conditions as everybody else? Everybody keeps quiet but under the table he's making money.*

tables

○ **turn the 'tables**
You **turn the tables**, or **turn the tables on someone**, in a competitive situation, when you remove the advantage from one person or people, and take the advantage yourself: *'You're just mad now because I turned the tables on you.' 'I'm mad because you told me all those lies!'* ♦ *see also* **the boot is on the other foot** ▷ BOOT

tablets

○ **set in tablets of 'stone** or **written on tablets of 'stone**
A belief or principle is **set in**, or **written on**, **tablets of stone** if it is fixed and cannot be changed: *The existing programmes will not stand still, set in tablets of stone, but must improve and evolve to meet business needs.* ♦ *see also* **carved in stone** ▷ STONE

> This idiom commonly occurs in the negative form, as in the above examples. Other variants include '**cast** in tablets of stone', and '**engraved** on tablets of stone'.

tabs

○ **keep 'tabs on**
You **keep tabs on** someone or something when you watch them closely so that you know exactly what they are doing and where they are: *Make sure you keep tabs on the books you lend to people, otherwise you may never get them back.*

tack

○ **a different 'tack**
1 If someone goes off on **a different tack**, they start talking about something which is not directly connected with the subject of your discussion: *'You're different. You're not at all ordinary. In fact,' said Owen, his mind beginning to go off on a different tack, 'you're altogether extraordinary.'* **2** If someone tries **a different tack**, they try a different way of dealing with a situation or problem, because their previous method was unsuccessful: *If he doesn't respond to criticism, try a different tack. Encouragement works better in some cases.* ♦ *see also* **fly off at a tangent** or **go off at a tangent** ▷ TANGENT

tacks

○ **get down to brass 'tacks**
Two or more people **get down to brass tacks** when they start discussing the exact details of something: *Then they got down to brass tacks: how old was he? Was he married? How did he make his money?*

> '**Brass tacks**' comes from the Cockney rhyming slang for 'facts'.

tail

○ **have your 'tail between your legs**
Someone **has got their tail between their legs** when they feel or look

ashamed and embarrassed; if they **go off with their tail between their legs**, they go away feeling or looking like this: *We took her in when she came back from London with her tail between her legs, and we fed her and gave her a roof over her head.*

○ on someone's 'tail

You are **on someone's tail** if you are following close behind them: *I only realized that I had been breaking the speed limit when I saw the police car on my tail.*

○ the tail is wagging the 'dog

You say that **the tail is wagging the dog** if a small and unimportant part of the situation that someone is in has started controlling their actions and decisions, when it should in fact be that person's actions and decisions that control the situation: *It sounds like a recipe for feeble government, with the tail wagging the dog.*

take (*see also* **taken** and **takes**)

○ you can't take so-and-so 'anywhere (*often humorous*)

1 You say that **you can't take** a certain person **anywhere** if they always behave badly or embarrass you in public: *Please help as we can't take her anywhere, she just goes mad!* **2** '**I can't take you**, or **him**, or **her**, **anywhere**' is also a humorous comment made about the unsocial behaviour of the person you are with: *You must excuse John's terrible jokes. I can't take him anywhere.*

taken

○ be 'taken with

You **are taken with** someone or something when you find that you like them: *I'm quite taken with your cousin. What did you say her name was?* ♦ *see also* **have a thing about** ▷THING

takes

○ takes one to 'know one (*informal, insulting*)

If someone says '**takes one to know one**' as a response to an insult or criticism, they are returning the insult or criticism by suggesting that you can only recognize faults in them if you are guilty of those faults yourself: *'I'm working with bloody amateurs here!' 'Takes one to know one.'*

tale

○ live to tell the 'tale

Someone who **lives to tell the tale** manages to escape alive from a dangerous situation and is therefore able to describe what happened: *In order to survive the jungle and live to tell the tale it is important not only to have good companions, but also to have the best available equipment.*

talk (*see also* **talking**)

○ all 'talk

You say that someone is **all talk** if you do not believe that they will really do what they say: *Politicians were the least respected group: 'They're all talk. They always break their promises.'*

○ 'you're a fine one to talk or 'you can talk or 'you can't talk

If you say '**you're a fine one to talk**', or '**you can talk**', or '**you can't talk**' to someone who has been criticizing someone else for some fault, you mean that they have the same fault themselves: *'Your trouble is you've been watching too much crime on telly.' Nev was a fine one to talk. He watched TV for at least five hours a day.*

talking

○ now you're 'talking (*informal*)

You say '**now you're talking**' to someone who is at last making a suggestion or an offer that interests you: *'If you don't want to be my employee, how about becoming a partner in the business?' 'Now you're talking.'*

tangent

○ fly off at a 'tangent or go off at a 'tangent

You **fly**, or **go**, **off at a tangent** when you begin to think, talk about, or do something unrelated to the original subject: *So I leave what I was going to do, go off at a tangent and do something totally different. So, you know, it never gets dull, which is good.* ♦ *see also* **a different tack** ▷TACK

If you are swinging an object in a circle around a central point, and then you let go of it, it will **fly**, or **go**, **off at a tangent**, moving in a straight line away from the circle.

tantrum

○ throw a 'tantrum

Someone, especially a child, **throws a tantrum** when they become violently angry about something relatively unimportant: *Thomas kicked his legs. He went red in the face. He yelled.'He doesn't usually throw tantrums,' Ashley said ruefully.*

tap

○ on 'tap

Something which is **on tap** is ready to be used as soon as it is needed: *How useful it must be, she thought, to have all this information on tap.*

Beer is **on tap** if it is served straight from the barrel into the glass through a tap, rather than being kept in bottles.

target

○ on 'target

You are **on target** when you are working at the correct rate and will finish or achieve something on time: *Employees and shareholders will be pleased to hear that mid-year sales figures were on target.*

○ a sitting 'target

You describe a person or thing as **a sitting target** if they are a likely victim for some attack because they obviously have no way of defending themselves: *Anyone who is driving a hire-car in Los Angeles will be seen as a sitting target by muggers.*

In hunting, an animal which is sitting still can be shot more easily than if it is running.

task

○ take someone to 'task

The people in authority **take someone to task** when they criticize that person strongly for what they have done and demand to hear an explanation: *I refuse to be taken to task over a decision which was made without my knowledge.*

taste

○ give someone a taste of their own 'medicine

You give someone **a taste of their own medicine** when you punish them by giving them the same bad treatment that they have given you, or someone else: *Tired of the humiliation my husband's affairs imposed on me, I decided to give him a taste of his own medicine.*

♦ see also **pay someone back with interest** ▷INTEREST

○ leave a bad 'taste in your mouth or leave a bitter 'taste in your mouth

Something **leaves a bad taste in your mouth** when you feel uncomfortable or unpleasant after it has happened: *She had known the fear of being rejected, and it left a bitter taste in her mouth. Why couldn't he love her?*

○ no accounting for 'taste

You say that there is **no accounting for taste** when you are surprised that someone likes a certain person or thing, because you find that person or thing worthless: *I just don't know what she sees in that dreadful guy. Still, I suppose there's no accounting for taste.*

tatters

○ in 'tatters

1 Clothes that are **in tatters** are badly torn: *His hair was matted and his clothes were in tatters.* **2** Something that is **in tatters** has been destroyed: *A year at teacher training college had left my confidence in tatters.*

teach

○ teach someone a 'thing or two

You **teach someone a thing or two** when you **1** are able to give them advice, perhaps unexpectedly: *The amateur can so often teach the professionals a thing or two.* **2** punish them because you think they need to be less proud or selfish: *I've overheard the Headmaster saying he would like to teach me a thing or two.*

tears

○ bored to 'tears

You are **bored to tears** when you are very bored: *I stuck it for about a year and then moved on to another. The move was really just a change for change's sake – I was simply bored to tears by it all.*

teeth

○ armed to the 'teeth

People are **armed to the teeth** if they are carrying a lot of weapons or other equipment which will be useful in a particular situation: *We were already armed to the teeth with mountaineering equipment.*

○ **fed up to the back 'teeth with** (*BrE*)
You are **fed up to the back teeth with** someone or something if you have been patient with them for long enough and you feel unwilling to give them any more of your time or energy: *Smaller practitioners are fed up to the back teeth with all forms of regulation, and audit regulation in particular.*

○ **get your 'teeth into**
You **get your teeth into** an activity when you get involved and start working hard and enthusiastically on it: *He was a bit slow at first, but he's working much better now he's got his teeth into the project.*

○ **grit your 'teeth**
1 You **grit your teeth** if you press them together tightly so that you can, for example, bear pain more easily: *I watched him grit his teeth and try not to scream as I removed the shrapnel from his shoulder.* **2** You **grit your teeth** when you prepare yourself mentally for some unpleasant experience: *It wasn't going to be fun, but I decided to grit my teeth and get on with it.*

○ **lie through your 'teeth**
Someone who **is lying through**, or **in their teeth** is telling you something which is completely untrue: *'Don't worry, Lavender, you'll soon catch up,' Miss Honey said, lying through her teeth.* ♦ *see also* **pull a fast one** ▷PULL; **sell someone a pup** ▷PUP; **put one over on someone** ▷PUT; **take someone for a ride** ▷RIDE

○ **set someone's 'teeth on edge**
Something such as a noise **sets your teeth on edge** if it is so unpleasant that you find it difficult to bear: *The chalk scraped across the blackboard, setting my teeth on edge.*

teething

○ **'teething troubles**
If people talk about **teething troubles**, they mean the problems which a project or activity often have when they are just starting and are not yet firmly established or working per-

fectly: *There were an awful lot of teething troubles in the first year or so, but it is working very well.*

When babies are teething [= getting their first teeth], they are often in pain and cry a lot.

tell

○ **'tell me about it** (*informal*)
You say **'tell me about it'** when you want to indicate that you also have the problem that has just been mentioned: *'I always end up spending more money than I expect on holiday.' 'Tell me about it.'*

○ **tell you 'what** (*informal*)
You say **'tell you what'** as a way of introducing a suggestion or offer: *Tell you what. Why don't I get us both a nice cake to cheer us up?*

○ **you never can 'tell**
If someone says **'you never can tell'**, they mean that, even if something is unlikely, it may still surprise you by happening: *It is difficult to foresee any end to this task in the immediate future, but then you never can tell.*

telling

○ **you're telling 'me** (*informal*)
You say **'you're telling me'** to express emphatic agreement: *'Phew, that was a lucky escape.' 'You're telling me.'*

Sometimes this idiom is shortened to 'telling me'.

temper

○ **keep your 'temper**
You **are keeping your temper** if you are managing to control yourself and avoid getting angry: *The children were doing their best to annoy him, but somehow he managed to keep his temper.*

○ **lose your 'temper**
You **lose your temper** when you suddenly get angry and start shouting or behaving violently: *I didn't mean to lose my temper. I'm sorry.* ♦ *see also* **go off at the deep end** ▷END; **blow a fuse** ▷FUSE; **let fly** ▷LET; **blow** or **flip your lid** ▷LID; **do your nut** ▷NUT; **lose your rag** ▷RAG; **fly into a rage** ▷ RAGE; **hit the roof** ▷ROOF; **blow your stack**

▷STACK; **blow your top** ▷ TOP; **throw a wobbly** ▷WOBBLY

ten
○ **ten to 'one** (*BrE*)
You say that it is **ten to one** that something will happen if you think that thing is almost certain to happen: *Find out what other parents think. Ten to one you'll find that they hate the idea too.*

terms
○ **come to 'terms with something**
You **come to terms with something** such as a personal problem or difficulty when you learn to live with it and accept it: *It's a terrible illness, but she seems to have come to terms with it.* □ *She is still having difficulty coming to terms with her husband's death.*

○ **in no uncertain 'terms**
You give your opinion, usually a disapproving one, **in no uncertain terms** when you express it strongly: *I told him in no uncertain terms what I thought of his behaviour.*

○ **on bad 'terms**
Two people are **on bad terms** when they are angry with each other, and also may not be speaking to each other: *You can't work well if you're on bad terms with your colleagues.*

○ **on 'speaking terms**
1 Two people who are **on speaking terms** know each other well enough to speak to each other when they meet in the street, for example: *I feel very isolated from everything around me, and I'm not on speaking terms with any of the neighbours yet.* **2** You also say that two people who have had an argument are **on speaking terms** if they are no longer angry with each other, although they may not yet be behaving in a very friendly manner towards each other: *Daisy nearly made a rude remark, but stopped herself because it was so good to be on speaking terms again.* **3** Two people who are not, or who are barely, **on speaking terms** are so angry with each other that they do not want to speak to each other: *The problem is there's no point my going over there. Suzie hates me – we were barely on speaking terms the week before she left.*

test
○ **stand the test of 'time**
Something which **stands the test of time** shows its strength by lasting for a long period of time: *Their relationship has stood the test of time.* □ *The wit and wisdom of Oscar Wilde has stood the test of time.*

that
○ **just like 'that**
If you do something **just like that**, you do it immediately and without any more thought or discussion: *That boy learns amazingly quickly. I only had to show him once and he did it himself, just like that.*

○ **that's more 'like it**
You say **'that's more like it'** when you are satisfied with a change that has just been made: *I'll turn down the music and light some candles. Ah, that's more like it.*

○ **that's 'that**
You use **'that's that'** to say there is no more to be said or done about a certain thing: *You are not going to the party and that's that.* ♦ *see also* **that's flat** ▷FLAT; **no two ways about it** ▷WAYS

them
○ **them and 'us**
You use the expression **'them and us'** to describe a relationship in which two groups feel that they are on opposing sides, rather than working together: *Try not to see the employer/employee relationship in terms of 'them and us'.*

there
○ **not all 'there** (*informal, insulting*)
If you describe someone as **not all there**, you mean that they think slowly, probably because they are not very intelligent: *She's very sweet, but she's not quite all there, is she?*

○ **so 'there** (*informal*)
'So there' is used to emphasize a defiant or obstinate statement: *I'm going and you can't stop me, so there!*

○ **there and 'then or then and 'there**
Someone does something **there and then**, or **then and there**, if they do it as an immediate and decisive reaction to something: *I went to see the flat and*

told the landlord there and then that I'd take it.

○ **there you 'are** or **there you 'go** *(informal)*

You say '**there you are**' or, informally, '**there you go**' **1** when you are giving something to someone: *'Could I have that dictionary, please?' 'There you are.'* **2** to close your remarks about a situation you have described, that is unsatisfactory but has to be accepted: *I was made redundant after only six months in the job. But there you go, that's just how things are.* **3** You use '**there you are**' to point out that you were right about something: *'I should never have trusted that woman with my money.' 'There you are, what did I tell you?'*

thick

○ **in the 'thick of something**

1 You are **in the thick of something** if you are very busy with it: *She didn't have time to talk because she was in the thick of her wedding preparations.* **2** You are also **in the thick of something** if you are at the point where the greatest amount of activity is taking place: *in the thick of the fight.*

○ **thick as 'thieves**

Two or more people who are as **thick as thieves** are very close friends.

○ **thick as two short 'planks** *(BrE)*

Someone who is described as being as **thick as two short planks** is not at all intelligent.

○ **thick and 'fast**

Things happen, or come, **thick and fast** if they happen or come quickly and in great numbers: *Viewers' letters have been coming in thick and fast.*

○ **through thick and 'thin**

You do something **through thick and thin** if you continue to do it no matter what happens and despite any difficulties: *We've been friends since we were kids, and have always stuck together through thick and thin.*

thing *(see also **things**)*

○ **another 'thing** or **another thing alto'gether**

You say that something is **another thing**, or **another thing altogether**, if your opinion about that thing is very different from your opinion of the

situation referred to before: *Time off work for illness is one thing. It's another thing altogether to take time off for a hangover.*

○ **the best thing since sliced 'bread**

You say that someone or something is **the best thing since sliced bread** if you have a very high opinion of them, and you wonder how you managed without them before they appeared: *The Maastricht Treaty is not necessarily the best thing since sliced bread, there are problems with it.*

○ **a close 'thing** or **a near 'thing** *(BrE)*

1 The result of a competition is **a close thing** or **a near thing** if the winner only won by a small amount: *The judges all agree that it was a close thing, but we have finally agreed on a winner.* **2** A **close thing** or **a near thing** is also a situation in which you only just manage to avoid an accident: *It was a near thing, I tell you. The weight fell on the stage – missed me and the lads by inches.* □ *We were all roped together, so we got him out, but it was a close thing. He could easily have drowned.* ♦ *see also* **close call** ▷CALL; **close shave** ▷SHAVE

○ **do the right 'thing**

You **do the right thing** when you act wisely or honourably: *I think you should do the right thing and hand the money in to the police.*

○ **do your own 'thing**

You **do your own thing** when you do what you want to do, rather than what other people prefer to do: *I've never been on a package tour. I prefer to do my own thing when I'm on holiday.*

○ **have a 'thing about**

You **have a thing about** someone or something **1** if they make you nervous: *She's had a thing about rats ever since she had them in her house one winter.* **2** if you like or dislike them to an unusual degree: *I think she's got a bit of a thing about that guy Oliver.* ♦ *see also* **be taken with** ▷TAKEN

○ **it all comes to the same 'thing** or **it all amounts to the same 'thing** or **it all boils down to the same 'thing**

You say '**it all comes**, or **it all amounts**, or **it all boils down**, to the

same thing' if you consider that there is no real difference between the things which have been mentioned: *Whether you're given the sack or made redundant, it all amounts to the same thing – you're jobless.*

When you heat a liquid for a period of time, it boils down to a smaller quantity of stronger liquid, containing all the essential flavours.

○ **just the 'thing** or **the very 'thing**
You describe something as **just the thing**, or **the very thing** if it is exactly what you need: *A pair of sheepskin slippers. They'll be just the thing for the cold winter evenings.*

○ **make a big 'thing of something** (*informal*)
People **make a big thing of something** if they treat it as important: *My family has never made a big thing of Christmas.*

○ **neither one thing nor the 'other**
Something is **neither one thing nor the other** if it fits no exact description because it is a mixture of two different things: *The ceasefire hasn't brought peace, just a tense situation which is neither one thing nor the other.*

○ **no bad 'thing**
If you say that something is **no bad thing**, you mean it is beneficial, despite what people may think: *What it lacks is sophistication and complexity, which is no bad thing, in my view. It sets out to do one job, and it does it well.*

○ **not the done 'thing**
If something is **not the done thing**, it is not socially acceptable: *You mustn't ask people how much they earn. It's just not the done thing here.*

○ **on to a good 'thing** (*informal*)
You are **on to a good thing** when you have discovered a way of obtaining something, especially money or profit, relatively easily: *She only married him for his money. She knew she was on to a good thing.*

○ **one thing after an'other**
You say it has been **one thing after another** if a lot of unexpected things have been happening which have all

needed your attention: *I haven't had five minutes to relax all day. It's just been one thing after another.*

○ **one thing leads to an'other**
If you say **one thing led to another** you mean that there was a series of events in which one small event caused the next, and so on, finally leading to the result you mention: *I don't want him to come to my flat because, as you know, one thing leads to another and we would probably end up in bed.*

People often use this expression to avoid giving details of a series of events which might shock or offend people, especially when the incident involves matters related to sex. They may say 'One thing led to another ...' leaving you to use your imagination about what happened next.

○ **the real 'thing**
The real thing is a real example of something, as opposed to something which is similar: *Frozen pizzas are all right, but they are nowhere near as delicious as the real thing.*

○ **sure 'thing** (*informal*)
If someone says **'sure thing'** when they are asked to do something, they are agreeing to do that thing: *'Can we finish up here?' she asked. Candy nodded slowly. 'Sure thing. Go and take some time off.'*

This phrase is used more often in American English than in British English.

○ **the thing 'is**
You use **'the thing is'** 1 to introduce an explanation: *I'm sorry I didn't get the work done on time. The thing is, my mother's been ill.* 2 before describing a difficult problem which is the reason why you aren't able or willing to do something: *He wants me to marry him. The thing is, I'm not sure I love him enough.*

○ **too much of a good 'thing**
If someone says that you can have **too much of a good thing**, they mean that, even if you usually enjoy something, you will not continue to enjoy it

if you have or do it too much: *I'll go off pasta if we have it every night. You can have too much of a good thing, you know.*

> This expression is often used in a humorous or sarcastic way when someone is talking about something which they didn't like to begin with, for example: *Watching you play football once a week is enough. A woman can have too much of a good thing.*

o **what with one thing and a'nother**
You use '**what with one thing and another**' to show that there are several reasons for something, without saying what they are: *I meant to get that work done, but what with one thing and another I never got round to it.*

things

o **all good things come to an 'end**
People say '**all good things come to an end**' when they are sad, but accepting of the fact, that something they have enjoyed doing is now finished.

o **all things being 'equal** or **all other things being 'equal**
All things, or **all other things, being equal** means 'unless anything unexpected happens,' or 'if other facts, after having been considered, make no difference': *Research has shown that, all other things being equal, the person who exercises regularly performs better in tests requiring mental agility.*

o **how are 'things?** (*informal*)
You say '**how are things?**' when you are asking someone to tell you how they are, or about their situation: *'So, how are things at work?' 'Fine.'*

o **just one of those 'things**
If you say a certain event or situation is **just one of those things** you mean **1** that it could not have been prevented: *'You must have been so disappointed to lose your job.' 'Well, I suppose it's just one of those things.'* **2** that it is difficult to explain: *I don't know why I love him. I guess it's just one of those things.* ♦ *see also* **chalk it up to experience** ▷EX-PERIENCE

o **of all 'things**
You use '**of all things**' to express your surprise at the fact that a particular

thing is the case: *He's lost interest in sailing and has taken up knitting, of all things.*

think

o **have another think 'coming** (*informal*)
If you say that someone **has got another think coming**, you are saying with annoyance that they are wrong to expect a certain thing, because it is not going to happen: *If he thinks he's going to kiss me he's got another think coming, she decided firmly.*

o **think a'gain**
Someone advises you to **think again** about doing something if they think you would be wrong to do it: *If you expect to be waited on hand and foot, think again.*

o **think 'better of**
You **think better of** doing something which you had intended to do when you change your mind and decide not to do it: *I opened my mouth to protest, but thought better of it.*

o **think 'nothing of**
1 You **think nothing of** something, or of doing something, if you consider it quite normal or usual: *In my youth, I used to think nothing of cycling 100 miles in a day.* **2** If you have noticed something strange or different about a situation, but fail to recognize its importance, you say that you **thought nothing of it**: *I had been feeling a little sick, but had thought nothing 'of it.*

o **'think straight**
You say that you **are not thinking straight** when you are unable to organize your thoughts as well as you usually do: *I'm sorry about some of the things I said. I wasn't thinking straight.*

o **think 'twice**
You **think twice** about doing something when you take time to consider whether or not it is right or sensible before doing it: *I didn't think twice about giving him my address.* □ *Think twice before you exchange your company pension for a private one.*

thorn

o **a 'thorn in your side** or **a 'thorn in your flesh**
You describe someone or something as **a thorn in your side**, or **a thorn in**

your flesh, if they continually annoy or bother you: *Despite attempts to reduce the budgets of various councils, local authority finances remained a thorn in the flesh of the Government.*

> The expression **a thorn in the flesh** comes from the Bible (2 Corinthians 12:7).

thoughts

○ **collect your 'thoughts** or **gather your 'thoughts**
You are **collecting**, or **gathering**, **your thoughts** when you become calmer and consider things more carefully: *I needed a bit of time alone to gather my thoughts.*

○ **on 'second thoughts** (*BrE*) or **on second 'thought** (*AmE*)
You use '**on second thoughts**', or '**on second thought**', to show that you have changed your mind about the thing you have just said: *Could you make sure this goes off in the last post, please? No, on second thoughts, could you get a courier? It's quite urgent.*

thread

○ **hang by a 'thread**
If you say something **is hanging by a thread**, you mean there is uncertainty about whether it will succeed, or continue to exist: *Peace is hanging by a thread this week as negotiations run into serious difficulties.* ❑ *She was devastated by the news of Liz and Owen's terrible accident – and the knowledge that their lives were hanging by a thread.*

> In Greek legend, the sword above Damocles' head was hanging by a single hair, and was therefore likely to fall and kill Damocles at any moment. This story may be the origin of the expression '**hang by a thread**'.

○ **lose the 'thread**
You **lose the thread** of something such as a story, or of what you are saying, if you find that you are no longer able to follow the logic of the ideas within it: *If you do not make notes you will quickly lose the thread of the ideas with which you are trying to come to terms.*

throat

○ **jump down someone's 'throat**
A person **jumps down your throat** when they answer you in an angry and unreasonable way without giving you a chance to finish what you are saying: *'I was about to say, before you jumped down my throat, if your plans need altering in any way ...' 'I won't allow them to be altered!'*

○ **ram something down someone's 'throat**
Someone **is ramming something down your throat** when they express strong opinions and try to force you to agree with them: *I'm quite capable of making up my own mind on subjects like vegetarianism. I don't want it rammed down my throat.*

> To **ram** something into a place means 'to push it there with great force'.

○ **stick in your 'throat**
1 Something **sticks in your throat** if you find it difficult to accept: *Imagine promising to love, honour and obey some man! 'Obey' would stick in my throat.* **2** If words **stick in your throat**, you try to say something without success, usually because of the strong emotions which you are feeling: *I longed to call out to him to help me, but his name stuck in my throat.*

throats

○ **at each other's 'throats**
Two or more people or groups are **at each other's throats** if they are fighting or arguing violently: *How can we hope to reach an agreement with the two main parties constantly at each other's throats?* ♦ *see also* **fight like cat and dog** ▷CAT

> When two dogs are fighting, they often bite each other's throats because a bite to the throat can cause severe injury.

thumb

○ **stick out like a sore 'thumb**
Someone or something **sticks out like a sore thumb** if they are noticeable because they are so different from the things or people around them: *If every-*

one else is in jeans and I wear this suit, I'm going to stick out like a sore thumb.

thumbs

o **all thumbs** *see* **all fingers and thumbs**
  ▷FINGERS

o **the thumbs-'down** (*informal*)
  1 You give someone **the thumbs-down** when you clench your fist, or fists, and point one thumb, or both thumbs, towards the ground in order to show that you are unhappy about something: *'How did your exam go?' I asked. She pouted and gave me the thumbs-down.* **2** Someone gives something such as a plan or idea **the thumbs-down** when they decide not to give their approval to it: *American and British reviewers gave the film a thumbs-down when it was released at the end of 1972.*

> In Roman times, when one of two gladiators in a fight had won, the spectators had to vote on whether or not he should kill his opponent. They made gestures similar to our **thumbs-up** sign if they wanted his opponent to live, and to our **thumbs-down** sign if they wanted him to die.

o **the thumbs-'up** (*informal*)
  1 You give someone **the thumbs-up**, or **a thumbs-up sign**, when you clench your fist, or fists, and point one thumb, or both thumbs, up as a sign of encouragement, or to show that everything is fine: *Give me the thumbs-up when you're ready.* **2** You give something such as a plan or idea **the thumbs-up** when you approve of it: *We're waiting for the official thumbs-up before we start work.*

> See note at **the thumbs-down**.

o **twiddle your 'thumbs**
  You say you **are twiddling your thumbs** if you are waiting for something, with nothing else to do to keep you busy: *The last few months had been very quiet. 'We've been sitting around twiddling our thumbs for some time ,' he said.* ♦ *see also* **at a loose end** ▷END

> Although it is traditionally a sign of inactivity or boredom, it is rare to see a person actually **twiddling their**

thumbs [= holding their hands with the fingers locked together, and moving the thumbs in circles round each other].

thunder

o **steal someone's 'thunder**
  Someone **steals your thunder** if they take people's attention away from something that you are about to do or say, usually by doing or saying it first: *The Minister had planned a speech of thanks himself during a visit to Stoke Mandeville Hospital, but five-year-old Adis Avdic stole his thunder.*

> In the 17th century, the playwright John Dennis invented a machine to create the effect of thunder for one of his plays, but the idea was copied by his rivals and used in another play.

tick

o **in a 'tick** (*BrE*; *informal*)
  In a tick means 'in a moment': *Could you just wait here? I'll be back in a tick.*

> It takes a very short time for a clock to **tick** once.

o **what makes so-and-so 'tick**
  If you talk about **what makes** a certain person **tick**, you mean the thing or things that make that person behave in the way they do: *Nicholson insists that everything he does on screen is in some way autobiographical, helping us to understand what makes him tick.*

ticks

o **in two 'ticks** (*BrE*; *informal*)
  In two ticks means 'in a moment': *Hang on. I'll be with you in two ticks.*

> See note at **in a tick**.

tide

o **go against the 'tide** or **swim against the 'tide**
  You **go**, or **swim**, **against the tide** when you ignore what everyone else thinks or is doing, and continue with your own activities: *Despite condemnation, the Government continues to swim against the tide of public opinion.*

tightrope

○ **walk a 'tightrope**

You **are walking a tightrope**, or **walking a tightrope between** two things, if you are trying to maintain a balance between those things, but there is a high risk that you will fail: *Parents of allergic children have to walk a tightrope – on the one hand they need to warn their child about things to avoid, but on the other hand they must not make the child over-anxious.*

In a circus, the **tightrope** is a thin rope which is stretched tightly between two points high above the ground, and which acrobats walk across. Another name for the tightrope is the 'high wire'.

time (*see also* times)

○ **all in good 'time**

If you say that something will be dealt with **all in good time**, you mean that it will certainly be dealt with, but since there is no need to rush, not immediately: *'I appreciate the importance of your discovery, but why don't you go to the police?' 'All in good time.'*

○ **be ahead of your 'time**

Someone, such as an artist or thinker, who **is ahead of their time** has ideas that other people do not understand the importance of until much later: *Coleridge was in many ways far ahead of his time in his understanding of the unconscious mind, pre-dating Freud.*

○ **buy 'time**

Someone who **is buying time** is making excuses or finding ways to delay a certain event: *Such unreasonable demands are the company's attempt to buy time before coming to a decision.*

○ **do 'time** or **serve 'time**

Someone who **is doing time**, or **serving time**, is in prison: *He admits his crimes openly, and is not afraid to do time for them.*

○ **for the time 'being**

For the time being refers to the present situation, with the suggestion that a change will soon come or be needed: *The ceasefire seems to be holding for the time being.*

○ **from time to 'time**

Something that happens **from time to time** happens probably with some regularity, but not often: *He would phone me from time to time, just to check that I was okay.*

○ **give someone a hard 'time** (*informal*)

If someone **is giving you a hard time**, they are speaking to you in a critical and unkind way: *'You never do a single bit of housework.' 'Come on, honey. Don't give me a hard time.'*

○ **have no 'time for**

You **have no time for** someone or something if you dislike them or disapprove of them: *A lot of people seem to admire the Prime Minister, although I personally have very little time for him.*

○ **have the time of your 'life**

A person who **is having the time of their life** is enjoying themselves a lot: *From what I hear they're both having the time of their lives! My father has been buying Margaret a designer wardrobe and escorting her to all the best restaurants and clubs.* ♦ *see also* **have a ball** ▷BALL; **live it up** ▷LIVE

○ **have 'time on your hands**

You **have time on your hands** if you are bored because you have a lot of time and no special plans for how to use it: *I can't see the sense in leaving all the work to you, when I have so much time on my hands.*

○ **have time on your 'side** or **time is on your 'side**

You say you **have time on your side** if you have enough time to do something, even though that thing might take a long time: *It's going to be a massive job, but the good thing is we've got time on our side.*

○ **in good 'time**

You arrive **in good time** for an event if you arrive well before it is supposed to start: *We arrived in good time, and went for a coffee.*

○ **in no time at 'all**

Something that is done **in no time at all** is done very quickly: *The make-up artist worked quickly, and in no time at all I found myself transformed.*

○ **in your own 'time**

1 You do something **in your own time**

if you choose to use your free time to do it: *I studied French and German at school, and Italian in my own time.* **2** You do something **in your own time** if you do it at the speed which is natural to you: *Don't be tempted to rush. Just answer the questions in your own time.*

○ **kill 'time**

You **are killing time** when you find something to do to use up the time and stop you getting bored, for example during a period of waiting: *He had to meet Martin at four o'clock and he had to kill time till then.*

○ **live on borrowed 'time**

1 A person **is living on borrowed time** when they live longer than is expected or is thought likely: *They've told her she's had three years more than she should've had, she's living on borrowed time.* **2** You also say that someone **is living on borrowed time**, or **is on borrowed time**, if they are still accepted as a member of a group, but are likely to be rejected very soon: *The Government is living on borrowed time. Party leaders have lost the confidence of markets, their Euro-partners and their own people.*

○ **make up for lost 'time**

A person who **is making up for lost time** is trying to gain as much experience of a particular activity as possible, or working particularly hard at something, because in the past they have not managed to do it: *He may not have travelled much as a young man, but he has now made up for lost time. 'Whenever I have a week off, I try and visit a new city in Europe.'*

○ **next to 'no time**

It takes **next to no time** to do something if that thing can be done very quickly: *'Thanks for mending my bike.' 'That's okay. I did it in next to no time.'*

○ **no time to 'lose**

You say that there is **no time to lose** when the situation is so urgent that you will have to act immediately and as fast as possible: *Come on, there's no time to lose. We've got about quarter of an hour before the bomb goes off.*

○ **not before 'time** (*BrE*)

You say that something that has hap-

pened was **not before time** if you think that it should have happened sooner or earlier: *I received my copy today. Not before time, I may add, since I needed it for a meeting tomorrow.*

○ **play for 'time**

You **are playing for time** when you delay something such as an action or a decision, while trying not to show that you are unsure of yourself: *He had feared being confronted with an unexpected decision like this. He needed to play for time. 'I scarcely know what to say. You've obviously been very ... busy.'*

○ **time and tide wait for no 'man**

If someone says '**time and tide wait for no man**', they mean that life moves on without waiting for people to make decisions or plans, and that you must therefore take opportunities when you can: *The drinking session that followed stretched until 4am; the players disproving the theory that time and tide wait for no man.*

○ **time's 'up**

If someone says to you '**time's up**', they mean that the time allowed for something, for example answering the questions in an exam, is finished: *Okay time's up. You can stop now please.*

○ **time will 'tell**

If you say '**time will tell**', you mean that it will not be known for some time whether things are working out as you hope: *There's no reason why, with a bit of luck, they shouldn't make a full recovery. Time will tell.*

times

○ **fall on hard 'times**

You say that a person who previously had no financial problems **has fallen on hard times** if their luck has changed and they have become poor: *He was a man of noble birth, whose family had fallen on hard times.*

○ **for old 'times' sake**

You do something **for old times' sake** when you do it because it reminds you of the people and things you were involved with in the past: *We met for a drink, more for old times' sake than any other reason.*

○ **move with the 'times**

A person or organization **is moving**

with the times when they change and develop in order to fit in with social changes, for example in fashions or people's opinions: *The Church faces certain decline unless it can begin to move with the times and attract more young people.*

tip

○ **on the tip of someone's 'tongue**

Something such as a name is **on the tip of your tongue** when, although you know it, you cannot quite remember it: *'I don't mean Carole Lombard, do I?' said Jannie. 'No, no. The name's on the tip of my tongue.'*

○ **the tip of the 'iceberg**

If you say that something, such as a problem you are dealing with, is just **the tip of the iceberg**, you mean that it is just a small part of something much bigger, most of which is still waiting to be discovered or dealt with: *The 50 drug-related deaths which have been documented are probably only the tip of the iceberg.*

> Only about one ninth of the total mass of an iceberg shows above sea level. The rest of it is hidden under the water.

tissue

○ **a tissue of 'lies**

A story that someone tells, especially a complicated one, is **a tissue of lies** if it is completely false: *I would rather not hear what she has to say since I imagine it is a tissue of lies, of excuses and complaints.*

toes

○ **be on your 'toes**

You say that someone **is on their toes** if they are ready and prepared for action: *The boss is coming round today, so you'd better be on your toes.*

○ **keep someone on their 'toes**

Something such as a possible event **keeps someone on their toes** if it prevents them from getting lazy and makes them perform as well as they can: *Leisure studies, interests and hobbies will keep you on your toes so if you're a couch potato or telly addict you'd better change your ways.*

○ **tread on someone's 'toes** or **step on someone's 'toes**

You **tread**, or **step**, **on someone's toes** if you do something to offend them, especially by trying to do something that they themselves are responsible for: *She will have to discover where she can be most useful at the hospital, without treading on anyone else's toes.*

toll

○ **take its 'toll**

Something **takes its toll** when it begins to have an effect and to cause problems or suffering: *Forty months of non-stop work on one project was beginning to take its toll.*

tomorrow

○ **like there's no to'morrow** or **as if there's no 'tomorrow**

Someone who is doing something **like**, or **as if**, **there's no tomorrow** is doing it in a wild and irresponsible way, without thinking about the future results of their actions: *They were knocking back drinks as if there was no tomorrow.*

ton

○ **like a ton of 'bricks**

You come down on someone **like a ton of bricks** if you speak to them angrily or punish them severely: *She thinks a lot of you, you know. I made the mistake of criticizing you and she came down on me like a ton of bricks.*

tongue (see also tongues)

○ **bite your 'tongue**

You **bite your tongue** when you want to say something but you stop yourself, because you feel that it would not be wise: *I wanted to tell her that I despised her, but I bit my tongue.*

○ **find your 'tongue**

You **find your tongue** when you finally manage to speak after a time during which the strength of your feelings has made you unable to say anything: *Somehow she found her tongue and shakily voiced her only fear.*

○ **have your tongue in your 'cheek**

You do or say something with your **tongue in your cheek** if the way in which you do it shows that you mean something different from, or even the opposite of, what your actions or words suggest: *Benet, who wrote 'Bury my heart at Wounded Knee' may have had his tongue firmly planted in his cheek, but there is something rather wonderful about American place names.*

○ **lose your 'tongue**

If you ask someone, especially a child, if they **have lost their tongue**, you are asking why they are not answering your question, or why they are so quiet: *Tell me who is responsible for this. What's the matter, lad? Have you lost your tongue?*

○ **trip off the 'tongue**

A name or word that **trips off the tongue** is one that is easy to pronounce: *This place is called Efailnewydd, a name that doesn't exactly trip off the tongue, unless you're a Welsh speaker.*

tongues

○ **start 'tongues wagging** or **set 'tongues wagging**

An event or situation **starts**, or **sets**, **tongues wagging** when people start gossiping about it: *Having a boyfriend who is young enough to be your son can still set tongues wagging.*

tooth (see also teeth)

○ **fight tooth and 'nail**

You **fight tooth and nail** if you do everything you can to make something happen, or to prevent something from happening: *I'll fight tooth and nail to keep the school open.*

○ **long in the 'tooth**

If you say that a person or animal is **long in the tooth**, you mean that they are old: *He's a bit long in the tooth to be starting a new career now.* ♦ *see also* **over the hill** ▷HILL; **past it** ▷PAST

> It is possible to tell the age of a horse by looking at its teeth. In general, the older the horse is, the longer its teeth will be.

top

○ **at the top of your 'voice**

You say something **at the top of your voice** when you say it as loudly as you can: *He was shouting at the top of his voice into the microphone but nobody could hear a word because someone had cut the amplifier cable.*

○ **blow your 'top**

Someone **blows their top** when they get very angry and lose their temper or start shouting: *Graeme is more volatile and likely to blow his top if his demands aren't met.* ♦ *see also* **go off at the deep end** ▷END; **blow a fuse** ▷FUSE; **let fly** ▷LET; **blow** or **flip your lid** ▷LID; **do your nut** ▷NUT; **lose your rag** ▷RAG; **fly into a rage** ▷ RAGE; **hit the roof** ▷ROOF; **blow your stack** ▷STACK; **lose your temper** ▷ TEMPER; **throw a wobbly** ▷WOBBLY

○ **come out on 'top**

You **come out on top** when **1** you succeed after a period of difficulty: *It was the best match I have ever played in and proof that the underdog can sometimes come out on top.* **2** results show that you have performed best in a competition, election, match, etc: *League tables of exam results published today are being roundly condemned – even by some of those schools which came out on top.*

○ **from top to 'bottom**

From top to bottom means from the highest to the lowest point, or completely: *The building was shaken from top to bottom by the blast.*

○ **from top to 'toe**

'**From top to toe**' means 'all over the body', or 'completely' in reference to someone's appearance: *Beautifully coordinated from top to toe, he wore a soft wool coat that matched his eyes.*

○ **let something get on 'top of you**

You **let something**, usually a problem, **get on top of you** when you allow yourself to get so upset about it that you lose the ability to deal with it effectively: *I know you're going through a lot of stress at work, but you mustn't let it get on top of you.*

○ **off the top of your 'head**

1 If someone makes a statement **off the top of their head**, they are relying on their own knowledge or experience, rather than referring to notes or reference books: *I gave a short talk off the top of my head.* **2** If you tell someone that you cannot give them a particular piece of information **off the top of your head**, you mean that you do not know it, and will need to find it for them, in a book, for example: *We'll come back to you with the precise details. I just can't say off the top of my head.*

○ **on 'top of something**

Someone who is, keeps, or gets, **on top of something** such as their work has it well organized and under control: *It's a relief to feel I'm on top of all my paperwork at last.*

○ **over the 'top¹** (*BrE*)

You describe something as **over the top** if it is so extreme that it is unacceptable; you **go over the top** if you act in an unacceptably extreme way: *Her behaviour last night was over the top.* □ *It's nice to have some Christmas decorations, but they've just gone over the top.*

The abbreviation **OTT** ('oh-tee-'tee) is often used in place of this expression.

○ **over the 'top²** (*AmE*)

A campaign to raise money goes **over the top** when it raises more money than people had hoped it would: *We went over the top with the last $500.*

○ **sleep like a 'top**

You say that you **slept like a top** if you had a good, peaceful sleep with no interruptions: *The bed in the hotel room was warm and comfortable and I slept like a top.* ♦ *see also* **sleep like a log** ▷LOG

○ **to top it 'all**

When you mention one last misfortune in a list of unfortunate events, you can introduce it with the expression '**to top it all**': *On hearing the news, her boyfriend promptly leaves her and her father has a fatal heart attack. To top it all her mother rejects her.* ♦ *see also* **to make matters worse** ▷MATTERS; **what is more** ▷WHAT

torn

○ **'torn between**

You say you are **torn between** one thing and another when you must choose one or the other but the choice is difficult because whichever one you choose you will feel unsure whether you have done the right thing: *I was torn between my feelings of loyalty and my duty to tell the truth.*

toss

○ **argue the 'toss** (*BrE*)

A person **argues the toss** when they openly disagree with what has been said or decided: *He grunted, 'Please yourself.' He had better things to do than argue the toss.*

○ **not give a 'toss** or **not care a 'toss** (*BrE; informal*)

If someone does **not give**, or does **not care**, **a toss** about something, they do not care at all about it: *Out on the motorway he let rip. He either wasn't a local or he didn't give a toss about the video cameras mounted every couple of miles along the motorway to catch the speeders.* ♦ *see also* **not care** or **give a hoot** or **two hoots** ▷HOOT; **not give a monkey's** ▷MONKEY'S; **not care** or **give tuppence** ▷TUPPENCE

touch

○ **in 'touch**

1 You get **in touch** with someone when you contact them by writing or telephoning; you are, keep, or stay, **in touch** with them if you meet, telephone, or write to each other regularly: *Get in touch and tell me your new address when you know it.* **2** You are **in touch** with a subject or situation if you have all the most up-to-date information about it, or if you are paying careful attention to it: *I try to keep in touch with the latest medical developments.*

○ **lose 'touch**

1 You **lose touch** with someone when you meet and contact each other less and less often, until you do not contact each other at all: *We used to write to each other, but over the past few years we've lost touch.* **2** You **lose touch** with a subject or situation when you don't keep your knowledge of it up to date: *It's easy to lose touch with what's going on in the fast-moving world of computers.*

○ **out of 'touch**

You are **out of touch** with a subject or situation if you do not have up-to-date information about it, or are not paying careful enough attention to it: *'I'm a bit out of touch with this modern medicine,' Kate Maybury admitted. 'Does that mean she's cured?'*

○ **touch and 'go**

Something is **touch and go** when it is just as likely to turn out badly as it is to turn out well: *It was touch and go for a while after the operation, but her condition is now much more stable.*

tough

○ **tough as old 'boots**

1 Something that is as **tough as old boots** is very tough: *Do you remember that steak I had there? It was tough as old boots.* **2** Someone who is as **tough as old boots** has a lot of determination and is not sensitive or easy to hurt emotionally: *Beneath her frail exterior, Kylie is as tough as old boots.*

towel

○ **throw in the 'towel**

When a person **throws in the towel**, they are giving up and admitting defeat: *The likelihood is that governments pursuing these policies will be forced by recession and rising unemployment to throw in the towel.*

In boxing, **throwing in the towel** is a sign that the boxer accepts defeat.

town

○ **go to 'town on something** (*informal*)

You **go to town on something** if you spend a lot of money on it or make a great effort in preparing it: *There wasn't much to drink at the party, but she had certainly gone to town on the buffet.* ◆ *see also* **push the boat out** ▷BOAT; **go to great lengths** ▷LENGTHS; **go out of your way** ▷WAY

○ **paint the 'town red**

When people **paint the town red**, they go out for a wild evening of pleasure which probably involves a lot of drinking and dancing: *The Noufara is an ideal meeting place to have cocktails before painting the town red.*

traces

○ **kick over the 'traces**

You say that someone **is kicking over the traces** if they are refusing to respect authority in the way that they used to: *You start the weekend wanting to kick over the traces of convention and conformity. In fact, you're out to shock.*

The **traces** are the long strips of leather which join a cart or other horse-drawn vehicle to the harness of the horse which is pulling it. If a horse kicks over the traces, its leg passes over these strips, and the horse becomes difficult to control.

track

○ **keep 'track of**

You **keep track of** someone or something if you make sure you know where they are, what they are doing, or what is happening to them: *While the organizers did their best to keep track of all those who attended the conference, the list below is not complete.*

○ **lose 'track of**

You **lose track of** someone or something if you do not know where they are, what they are doing, or what is happening to them any more; you **lose track of** time when you do not know what time it is any more: *We wanted to invite the Collins twins, but everyone who knew them seems to have lost track of them.*

○ **off the beaten 'track**

A place is **off the beaten track** when it is far away from main roads, public services and centres of population: *I'd like to try and arrive before it gets dark. It's a bit off the beaten track and I don't want to get lost.* ◆ *see also* **the back of beyond** ▷BACK; **in the middle of nowhere** ▷MIDDLE; **out in the sticks** ▷STICKS; **out of the way** ▷WAY

○ **on the right 'track**

You are **on the right track** if you are thinking or acting in a way which will result in you being successful or finding the correct answer: *If he wants to make me angry, he's on the right track.*

tracks

○ **make 'tracks** (*informal*)

You **make tracks** when you leave a place: *Come on, Jen. Shall we make tracks?*

○ **stop dead in your 'tracks**

Someone who is walking or moving forwards **stops dead in their tracks** when they stop suddenly and remain standing in the same position: *There* *was a feeling of high spirits in the air. And then she saw them. She stopped dead in her tracks. Her mouth fell open.*

trail

○ **blaze a 'trail**

If a person or organization **blazes a trail**, they lead or show the way towards something new: *After years of quiet research, the company is blazing a trail in the development of an AIDS cure.*

○ **hot on the 'trail**

You are **hot on the trail**, or **hot on the trail of** someone or something, when you have almost succeeded in catching them: *Police are hot on the trail of the burglar who stole a CD player and sentimental items from a local couple's house last night.*

train

○ **train of 'thought**

Your **train of thought** is a connected series of thoughts: *I didn't want to interrupt your train of thought.*

treat

○ **go down a 'treat** (*BrE*)

You say that a person or thing **goes down a treat** if they are greatly appreciated by everyone: *Her lively and helpful attitude went down a treat with the tourists.*

tree

○ **bark up the wrong 'tree** (*informal*)

You say that someone **is barking up the wrong tree** if they have the wrong idea about something: *We've been barking up the wrong tree all along. How could we have been so stupid?*

○ **be out of your 'tree** (*informal*)

If you say that someone **is out of their tree** you mean they are mad or crazy, or that they are drunk or acting strangely because they have taken drugs: *You've decided to join the Foreign Legion? You must be out of your tree.*

trick

○ **do the 'trick**

Something **does the trick** when it does what you want or need it to do: *Don't call the plumber, I'll fix it with a piece of old cloth. There, that should do the trick.* ♦ *see also* **do the job** ▷ JOB

○ **every trick in the 'book**

You say that someone is using **every**

trick in the book if they are using a wide range of methods to try and achieve the result they want: *That child will try every trick in the book to avoid going to school.*

○ **a trick of the 'trade**

If people talk about **a trick of the trade**, they mean one of the ways of being successful in the particular activity they are referring to: *Monthly meetings will provide a forum for teachers to meet and swap tricks of the trade.*

trigger

○ **'trigger-happy**

Someone who is **trigger-happy** is too willing or likely to use guns or violence: *How can we be expected to negotiate with a bunch of trigger-happy terrorists?*

trimmings

○ **all the 'trimmings**

You say that a particular dish comes with **all the trimmings** if it is served with all the vegetables and sauces that are traditionally eaten with it: *I used to look forward to Sundays. We always had roast beef with all the trimmings.*

trooper

○ **swear like a 'trooper**

Someone who **swears like a trooper** uses a lot of shocking swear-words: *She looks so sweet and innocent, but she swears like a trooper.*

trolley

○ **be off your 'trolley** (*informal*)

If you say that someone **is off their trolley**, you mean that they are mad or crazy: *'I'll gather some seaweed and make soup with it.' 'Do you know something? You're off your trolley.'* ♦ *see also* **be bananas** ▷ BANANAS; **off your rocker** ▷ ROCKER

trot

○ **on the 'trot**

You do a series of things **on the trot** when you do them one after the other: *I'm quite looking forward to staying in tonight. Three nights out on the trot has just about finished me off.*

trouble

○ **borrow 'trouble** (*AmE*)

You **borrow trouble** when you create

problems for yourself: *If you start arguing religion with Frank, you're borrowing trouble.*

trousers

○ **catch someone with their 'trousers down**

When you **catch someone with their trousers down**, you put them in an embarrassing situation by doing something which they do not expect, or discovering something which they would have preferred to keep a secret: *By combining different topics in his questions, the examiner caught a few students with their trousers down.* ♦ see also **catch someone red-handed** ▷CATCH; **catch someone at it** ▷CATCH

○ **wear the 'trousers** (*BrE*) or **wear the 'pants** (*AmE*)

The person who **wears the trousers**, or **wears the pants**, in a relationship, is the one who makes the decisions: *I'd like to take a bet on it that she wears the trousers in that marriage.*

trumpet

○ **blow your own 'trumpet** (*BrE*) or **blow your own horn** (*AmE*)

You **blow your own trumpet**, or **blow your own horn**, when you talk in a proud way about yourself and your achievements: *Unashamedly blowing his own trumpet, he said he was doing a far better job than his predecessor.*

trumps

○ **come up 'trumps** or **turn up 'trumps** (*BrE*)

You **come**, or **turn**, **up trumps** when you behave or do your work successfully under difficult circumstances, especially when people do not expect you to do so: *And to think I doubted your commitment! You've come up trumps, Derek. I'm proud of you.*

In card games, a **trump card** is a card which scores more points than a higher card of another suit, because it belongs to a particular suit which was chosen as 'trumps' before the game started. You 'turn up trumps' when you win a game unexpectedly by showing the other players that you were holding a trump card.

trust

○ **not trust someone as far as you could 'throw them** (*informal*)

If you say that you would **not trust someone as far as you could throw them**, you mean that you do not trust them at all: *You can believe him if you like. But personally, I wouldn't trust him as far as I could throw him.*

○ **trust 'so-and-so** (*informal*)

If you say, in reference to something foolish that someone has done, '**trust them**', or '**trust them to do that**', you mean it is typical of them to do such a thing: *'Did you hear that Billy's been arrested for nude sunbathing in Hyde Park?' 'Oh, trust him.'*

truth

○ **to tell you the 'truth**

You say '**to tell you the truth**' to correct somebody when you think they have over-estimated your experience: *'What do you think of Martin Amis?' 'To tell you the truth, I haven't read anything of his.'*

○ **truth will 'out**

If someone says '**truth will out**', they mean that it is impossible to hide the truth about something for ever: *It may take time, but we will find out who was responsible for this. Truth will out, as they say.*

tune

○ **call the 'tune**

If a certain person **is calling the tune**, they have control over a situation: *Six countries will be represented, but the US envoy will be calling the tune in next month's peace talks.* ♦ see also **call the shots** ▷SHOT

○ **change your 'tune**

Someone **changes their tune** if they express a completely different opinion from the opinion they held before: *'You've certainly changed your tune, anyway,' Peter went on, 'I thought you were intent on warning me against her. Now it seems you rather approve of my choice.'*

You often use this idiom to show that you are suspicious of someone's reasons for changing their opinion so radically.

○ **in 'tune with**

You are **in tune with** other people or things if you are able to understand and fit in with them, rather than opposing them: *Primitive human beings were much more in tune with nature than we are now.*

○ **to the tune of 'such-and-such** (*informal*)

To the tune of a particular large amount means having that amount as a total: *He demanded fees to the tune of ten million dollars.*

tuppence

○ **not give 'tuppence** or **not care 'tuppence** (*BrE; informal, rather old*)

If someone does **not give tuppence** about something, or does **not care tuppence** about it, they do not care at all about it: *How could he treat her like this? Clearly he didn't love her, he didn't care tuppence for her! Damn the man.* ♦ *see also* **not care** or **give a hoot** or **two hoots** ▷HOOT; **not give a monkey's** ▷MONKEY'S; **not give** or **care a toss** ▷TOSS

turn

○ **done to a 'turn**

You say that food is **done to a turn** if it is cooked to exactly the right degree: *This is delicious. The beef is done to a turn.* ♦ *see also* **to a T** ▷T

○ **have a 'funny turn** (*BrE; informal*)

If a person or animal **has a funny turn**, their behaviour suddenly changes and they act strangely for a short period of time: *'Tell me how you feel when you have these funny turns,' he said.'I get very dizzy,' she replied.*

○ **speak out of 'turn** or **talk out of 'turn**

You **speak**, or **talk**, **out of turn** when you say something which is considered to be unsuitable for the situation you are in: *I'd better be careful not to speak out of turn if he's going to be there.*

○ **take a turn for the 'better**

If the state of a person or thing **takes a turn for the better**, it suddenly improves: *At last, I had a job interview. Things seemed to be taking a turn for the better.*

○ **take a turn for the 'worse**

If the state of a person or thing **takes a turn for the worse**, it becomes suddenly worse: *The vet said that Caspar had taken a turn for the worse overnight, and had died early in the morning.*

○ **a 'turn-up for the books** or a **'turn-up for the book** (*BrE*)

An event can be described as **a turn-up for the books**, or **a turn-up for the book**, if it is a surprise: *Fancy you being in New York too. What a turn-up for the books!*

turns

○ **whatever turns you 'on** (*informal*)

If you say **'whatever turns you on'**, you are remarking in a humorous way that the activity which has just been mentioned may be enjoyed by certain people, but that you would not like it: *'He collects railway time-tables.' 'Whatever turns you on, I suppose.'*

twinkling

○ **in the twinkling of an 'eye**

In the twinkling of an eye means 'in a moment' or 'immediately': *She'd come to perform a routine task, and virtually in the twinkling of an eye, her entire life had been turned upside-down.* ♦ *see also* **in the blink of an eye** ▷BLINK

twist

○ **round the 'twist** (*BrE; informal*)

If you say that someone is **round the twist**, you mean you think they are mad: *There was talk that Albert was round the twist. Especially since his old mother died.* ♦ *see also* **round the bend** ▷BEND

two

○ **put two and two to'gether**

You **put two and two together** if you judge correctly what is happening in a certain situation from the clues or signals which you have noticed: *After a while, I started putting two and two together and wondering if perhaps Richard's disappearance might have had something to do with them.*

If you say that someone **has put two and two together and got five**, you mean that that person has made an incorrect judgement of a certain situation, by taking certain facts as proof of something which is not really the case.

○ **that makes 'two of us** (*informal*)
If you say **'that makes two of us'**, you mean that you are in the same situation as the person who is speaking to you: *'I cannot stand that man.' 'Yeah, well that makes two of us.'*

ugly

○ **as ugly as 'sin**
Someone or something that is **as ugly as sin** is very ugly: *Whereas James had been referred to by more than one gossip columnist as a sex symbol, Leo, bless him, was as ugly as sin.*

unstuck

○ **come un'stuck**
You **come unstuck** when you fail to achieve the result you are aiming for: *These companies have moved into an area which they are ill-equipped to deal with, and have come unstuck.*

up

○ **not up to 'such-and-such**
You say you are **not up to** a certain activity when you feel too tired to do it, or think you cannot do it for some reason: *I don't feel up to going out tonight. I think I'll have to cancel it.*

○ **on the up and 'up** (*BrE*)
Something that is **on the up and up** is improving all the time or becoming increasingly successful: *Production is on the up and up.*

○ **up a'gainst it**
You are **up against it** when you have a difficulty or challenge to face: *But when you are really up against it there are times when the only way to win is by a little crafty reinterpretation of the rules.* ♦ see also **the cards are stacked against someone** ▷ CARDS

○ **up and a'bout** or (*AmE*) **up and 'around**
Someone who is **up and about**, or **up and around**, is out of bed, and can get on with their tasks: *Because there was no pressing urgency to be up and about he lay for a little, considering the day ahead.*

○ **up-and-'coming**
Someone who is described as an **up-and-coming** star, artist, designer, etc, is one who is becoming successful or well-known: *Up-and-coming executives use a period of employment with a multinational as a form of training in the methods and values of big business.*

○ **up and 'down**
A situation that is **up and down** is not very stable or predictable: *Things have been a bit up and down since Christmas, but we're confident things will improve this summer.*

○ **up and 'go**
You **up and go** when you decide to leave a place: *He just upped and went off with that posh woman.*

○ **up-to-the-'minute**
Something that is **up-to-the-minute** is the most recent of its kind; someone who is **up-to-the-minute** has all the most recent knowledge about something: *They took her to Vidal Sassoon's salon so that her hair could be cut in an up-to-the-minute style.* □ *You can use the Internet to get up-to-the-minute information.*

○ **'up to something** or **up to no 'good**
You say someone is **up to something**, or **up to no good**, if you think they are doing something secret or dishonest: *I'm sure he's up to something; every time I go into his office he hurriedly puts the phone down.*

○ **up to 'you**
If you say **'it's up to you'** to someone, you mean that they must, or may, make a particular decision: *You know what I think about it, but it's up to you now.*

○ **well 'up on something**
You are **well up on** a particular subject if you have a lot of knowledge about it: *Is that a pterodactyl? I'm not very well up on dinosaurs.*

upright

○ **bolt 'upright**

You are **bolt upright** if you are sitting or standing in a very straight, rigid way, possibly because you are afraid, anxious or shocked: *They all sat bolt upright in their seats, in business suits and ties, and remained silent.*

> 'He or she **sat bolt upright**' can mean that the person moved into that position, or that they were already in that position.

ups

○ **ups and 'downs**

Something goes through a series of **ups and downs** when it goes through alternating periods of success and failure: *I have to try and accept it. Life is full of ups and downs and I know that there are going to be bad times to go with the good ones.* ♦ *see also* **ebb and flow** ▷ EBB

uptake

○ **quick on the 'uptake**

Someone who is **quick on the uptake** is quick to understand or realize something: *I thought it would be obvious to you; you are usually very quick on the uptake.*

○ **slow on the 'uptake**

Someone who is **slow on the uptake** is slow to understand or realize something: *In fact I've had to conclude that I am generally rather slow on the uptake.*

use

○ **a 'fat lot of use**

Something that is angrily described as **a fat lot of use** is of no help at all to a situation: *Well, that's a fat lot of use. I thought she was supposed to be available at all times.*

○ **it's no use doing 'such-and-such**

You say that **it's no use doing** a particular thing if doing it would not help the situation: *We don't think the product is right yet, so there is no use marketing it just now.*

○ **no use to man nor 'beast**

Something that is **no use to man nor beast** is useless: *I advise you to take some such steps yourself. Otherwise, my dear fellow, you will soon be of no use to man nor beast.*

○ **what's the use of**

You ask '**what's the use of**' doing a certain thing when you cannot see why it is necessary to do it: *What's the use of having a car if you never 'drive it?*

usual

○ **as per 'usual**

You say that something has happened **as per usual**, if it happens more regularly or more often than you would like: *When he came back he was drunk as per usual. So my mother calmly said, 'I'm not opening the door to you now or ever.'*

utmost

○ **do your 'utmost**

You **do your utmost** to achieve something when you try as hard as you can to achieve it: *He promised them that he would do his utmost to find their son and deliver him safe from harm.*

variety

○ **variety is the spice of 'life**

If someone says '**variety is the spice of life**', they mean that we need change sometimes, even if it causes problems, because it makes life more interesting: *For him, variety is indeed the spice of life and he revels in his constant changes of pace, environment and attitude.* □ *Oh, yes, I'm fine. It all adds variety. You know what they say – the spice of life, and all that.*

> Note how the idiom is shortened in the second example. People often do this with proverbs, sometimes adding an expression like 'and all that', or 'as they say'.

veil

○ **draw a 'veil over something**

You **draw a veil over** a particular action or state when you ignore it, decide to forget it, or pretend that it did not happen: *'Let's draw a veil over yesterday,'* he said. *'It won't happen again.'*

vengeance

○ **with a 'vengeance**

You do something **with a vengeance** when you do it in a determined, intensive way: *Mark was now speaking out with a vengeance. For the first time in his life he was free from corporate restraints, to say what he really thought.*

vent

○ **give full 'vent to**

You **give full vent to** your feelings when you express them freely: *He moved away from the house before stopping and giving full vent to his fury.*

ventured

○ **nothing ventured nothing 'gained**

If someone says **'nothing ventured nothing gained'**, they mean that if you never try anything, you will never achieve anything: *However, 'nothing ventured nothing gained', and you only improve at something by doing it.*

verge

○ **on the verge of 'such-and-such**

Someone or something is **on the verge of** doing a particular thing when they are likely to be doing it very soon: *At that time, the company was on the verge of bankruptcy.*

vessels

○ **empty vessels make most 'noise** (*BrE*)

If someone says **'empty vessels make most noise'**, they mean that the people who are talking or shouting most are likely to be those who know the least about the subject in question.

A **vessel** is a container.

view

○ **colour someone's 'view of**

Someone or something **colours your view of** someone or something when they cause you to see it in a less attractive way: *His overwrought state of mind colours his view of the world around him, and he is no longer able to distinguish between imagination and reality.*

○ **in view of 'such-and-such**

You make a decision **in view of** certain circumstances when those circumstances influence your decision: *In view of the current situation, I think we should postpone our trip until a later date.*

○ **take a dim view of 'such-and-such**

You **take a dim view of** someone else's actions if you do not approve of them: *As a keen amateur astronomer I take a dim view of being mistaken for a fortune teller.*

○ **with a view to**

You do something **with a view to** a certain purpose when you do it for that purpose: *They're taking me on for a trial period with a view to possibly employing me long term at a later 'date.*

○ **with something in 'view**

You do something **with** a certain purpose **in view** if you do it for that purpose: *He wrote on various subjects, all of them with one aim in view, namely to keep his name before the public.*

violet

○ **no shrinking 'violet**

Someone who is described as **no shrinking violet** is an exhibitionist: *Julie T Wallace has never been a shrinking violet – which is probably just as well, as it would be almost impossible for her to fade quietly into the background.*

virtue

○ **by virtue of** (*formal*)

You can use **by virtue of** to explain why something is true or is the case: *Once permitted and enabled (chiefly by virtue of legal aid) to petition for divorce, women have done so in ever-increasing numbers.*

visit

○ **a flying 'visit** (*BrE*)

You pay someone **a flying visit** when you call in to see them for a short time: *Lynch may make a flying visit to the French festival but he's a busy man, preparing three new films.*

voice

○ **give voice to**
You **give voice to** your feelings or opinions when you express them openly: *He paused as if to collect himself, allowing the crowd to give voice to their frustrations and 'feelings.*

○ **in good 'voice**
You are **in good 'voice** if, when you sing, you sing well: *The girl singer was in good voice by the pool, singing some sentimental Spanish favourites.*

○ **make your 'voice heard**
You **make your voice heard** when you make sure that people know about your opinions: *If you oppose this development then make your voice heard.*

○ **raise your 'voice**
You **raise your voice** if you begin to speak more loudly: *She raised her voice over the noise of the children playing around her.*

○ **with one 'voice**
People speak **with one voice** when they are united in expressing the same opinion: *The important thing is that we present our proposals with one voice.*

volumes

○ **speak 'volumes**
An action that **speaks volumes** is very easy to interpret, even though the person in question has not expressed their feelings explicitly in words: *She remained silent, but the look on her face spoke volumes.*

wagon

○ **on the 'wagon**
Someone who is **on the wagon** has decided not to drink any alcohol for a period of time, often because they have

been an alcoholic, or because they have been drinking too much: *I offered him a drink out of courtesy. He said 'No thanks, I'm on the wagon now.'*

wait

○ **just you 'wait**
You say to someone **'just you wait'** when you are giving them a warning or threatening them: *'Just you wait,' he said, 'I'll get you.'*

○ **wait and 'see**
You say **'wait and see'** to people to tell them to be patient about something, and not get anxious unnecessarily: *'What have you got in that box?' 'Wait and see.'*

wake

○ **in the wake of 'such-and-such**
One thing follows **in the wake of** another if it is caused by the other: *In the wake of the killings the Government was overthrown.*

> The **wake** of a ship or aircraft is the line of disturbed water or air left by it.

walk

○ **from every walk of 'life** or **from all walks of 'life**
If you talk about people **from every walk**, or **all walks**, **of life**, you mean 'all kinds of people' or 'people from many different professions and backgrounds': *You get people from all walks of life coming into a psychiatrist's consulting rooms. Princes, professors, and plumbers.*

○ **walk all 'over someone**
If someone **walks all over you** they treat you without respect, especially when you have already helped them or trusted them in some way: *Don't let him get away with it! It's your house after all! Don't let him walk all over you!*

○ **'walk it** (*BrE*; *informal*)
If someone says, referring to a test or competition, for example, that you **will walk it**, they mean that you will easily pass or win it: *Come on, don't worry. After all the work you've done, you'll walk it.*

wall

○ **drive someone up the 'wall**
Someone or something **drives you up**

the wall when they annoy you intensely, and make you feel very angry and frustrated: *Most teenagers drive their parents up the wall.*

○ **go to the 'wall**

An organization, such as a company, that **goes to the wall** is ruined financially: *It would be a tragic loss to theatre if such an important organization were to go to the wall.*

○ **off-the-'wall**

Something that is **off-the-wall** is strange and unusual: *No idea was too off-the-wall, no scheme too madcap. He was going to have fun.*

walls

○ **climb the 'walls**

You say that you **are climbing the walls** if you are intensely angry, frustrated or in pain: *A nightmare of pain. A period of almost literally climbing the walls.*

wand

○ **wave a magic 'wand**

You say that you can't **wave a magic wand**, or that so-and-so thinks you can **wave a magic wand**, if you are unable to immediately produce something that someone wants: *I cannot wave a magic wand and change everything around. But I will plan ahead.*

> A **magic wand** is a thin rod that magicians or fairies are said to wave in order to perform magic.

wane

○ **on the 'wane**

Something that is **on the wane** is getting smaller or weaker: *The party's popularity is on the wane.*

want

○ **have someone right where you 'want them**

You say that you **have someone right where you want them** if you have so much influence over them that you can persuade them to do what you want: *I can't believe we were so stupid. They've got us right where they want us now.* ♦ *see also* **have someone wrapped round your little finger** ▷FINGER; **have someone eating out of your hand** ▷HAND; **have someone eating**

out of the palm of your hand ▷PALM; have someone in your pocket ▷POCKET

warpath

○ **on the 'warpath**

Someone who is **on the warpath** is in an angry mood, and is looking for the person who caused them to feel that way: *The last thing he needed was an outraged husband on the warpath.*

wars

○ **in the 'wars** (*BrE*)

You say that someone has been, or is, **in the wars** if they have been injured: *Another international player in the wars was Worcestershire's Graham Dilley, who underwent an operation on his left ankle at the end of April.*

warts

○ **warts and 'all**

Something that is presented to you **warts and all** has not been edited, censored or cleaned up in an attempt to make it more superficially attractive: *Our philosophy is an absolute open door policy where people can look at everything, warts and all.*

> **Warts** are little hard lumps that grow on your skin, especially on your face or the backs of your hands.

wash

○ **come out in the 'wash**

If you say that a particular problem will **come out in the wash**, you mean that it will work out satisfactorily in the end: *He promised that the story of his stormy relationship with Flashman would 'all come out in the wash'.*

○ **not 'wash**

If you say that a particular explanation or excuse **doesn't**, or **won't**, **wash** with someone, you mean that they will not be convinced by it: *It does no good to say there is not as much crime there as in Chicago or Sydney. That does not wash. Crime has doubled since 1979.*

waste

○ **go to 'waste**

Something **goes to waste** when it is not used and has to be thrown away: *'Eat up,' Isabel said, 'we cannot afford to let things go to waste.'*

○ **waste not 'want not**

If someone says **waste not want not**, they mean that if you do not waste things, you will be less likely to find yourself in need of anything later: *'Eat up now,' Dad said. 'Waste not, want not.'*

○ **waste of 'space**

If you describe someone as a **waste of space**, you mean, very disrespectfully, that they are worthless: *So if you're going to tell somebody they're a waste of space, you should at least tell them why.*

watch

○ **'watch it**

You say '**watch it!**' to someone to warn them to be careful, or as a threat.

○ **watch 'out**

You say '**watch out!**' to someone to warn them that they are likely to be hit by a moving object if they do not move very quickly.

water

○ **a lot of water has passed under the 'bridge since then** or **a lot of water has flowed under the 'bridge since then**

If someone says '**a lot of water has passed**, or **flowed**, **under the bridge since then**', they mean that a lot of things have happened since the time mentioned, and that the situation is different now: *A lot of water has flowed under the bridge since we lifted the trophy in 1992.*

○ **hold 'water**

An argument that **holds water** is one that you can find no mistakes in, or that you can prove: *This argument just does not hold water. The whole system was ill-conceived from the outset.*

○ **in deep 'water**

You are **in deep water** when you are in trouble, danger, or difficulty: *Suddenly Sophie found she was in deep water. It would be foolish to appear evasive.* ♦ *see also* **up the creek without a paddle** or **up the creek** ▷CREEK; **out of your depth** ▷DEPTH; **in the soup** ▷SOUP; **in a tight spot** ▷SPOT; **in hot water** ▷WATER

○ **in hot 'water**

You are **in hot water** if you are in trouble. ♦ *see also* **up the creek without a paddle** or **up the creek** ▷CREEK; **out**

of your depth ▷DEPTH; **in the soup** ▷SOUP; **in a tight spot** ▷SPOT; **in deep water** ▷WATER

○ **like water off a duck's 'back**

You say that someone's reaction to something is **like water of a duck's back**, if that person is not at all surprised or bothered by it: *It was like water off a duck's back to Nick, but I'm sure it upset Paul.*

○ **test the 'water** or **test the 'waters**

You **test the water** when you try something out tentatively before committing yourself to it: *Why do so many of us feel the need to test the water first? Is a period of living together any indication of how the marriage will fare?*

○ **water under the 'bridge**

If you say about something unpleasant '**it's water under the bridge**' or '**that's all water under the bridge now**', you mean that you want to forget about the things mentioned because they happened in the past and the situation is different now: *'Look,' he went on hurriedly, 'It's all water under the bridge; you don't want to hear it.'*

waters

○ **muddy the 'waters**

Someone **muddies the waters** when they cause confusion in a situation which had been clear up until that point: *Those who can pay but refuse to do so muddy the waters and make it more difficult for local councils to adopt collection policies.*

○ **still waters run 'deep**

If someone says '**still waters run deep**' they mean that reserved, quiet people often have deep feelings or a lot of knowledge about a subject: *It is said that 'still waters run deep'. I for one could never penetrate his thoughts, could never really feel comfortable with him.*

Compare this idiom with: 'empty vessels make most noise' (at **vessels**).

---

wavelength

○ **on the same 'wavelength**

Two people who are **on the same wavelength** understand each other well and tend to have similar opinions about things: *I must confess I don't think*

I was on the same wavelength as the Prime Minister from the start.

waves

○ **make 'waves**

Someone who **makes waves** causes trouble, or spoils a comfortable situation: *Outspoken people are often the ones who make waves and achieve something.* ♦ *see also* **rock the boat** ▷BOAT

way

○ **by the 'way**

You use **by the way** to introduce a point that you want to mention while you remember it, though it may not be relevant to the present subject: *Yes, I saw him yesterday. By the way, are you going to be at home tonight?*

○ **downhill all the 'way** (*BrE*)

1 You say that it's **downhill all the way** with reference to a job or task when all the hard work has been done and the difficulties have been dealt with: *Two-nil up at home against moderate opposition – it would have been downhill all the way for most teams.* **2** You also say that it's **downhill all the way** when a situation gets worse from a certain point in time onwards: *I launched into a career as a journalist and for my health it became downhill all the way. I drank a bottle of scotch a day.* ♦ *see also* **plain sailing** ▷SAILING

○ **every which 'way** (*AmE*)

'**Every which way**' means 'in many directions': *Eddie dropped his piggy bank and the pennies went every which way.*

○ **go all the 'way**

1 To '**go all the way**' is to have sex, as opposed to just kissing and touching, etc: *You mean, you want to make love to her? Go all the way? Some of the girls allow petting on a date, but I don't know anyone who's actually done it.* **2** To '**go all the way**' is also to complete something you have started: *I haven't toured for a few years now, apart from the World Cup and I made that an exception because I felt we could go all the way.*

○ **go back a long 'way**

Two people **go back a long way** if they have known each other for a long time: *Oh yes, we go back a long way. I could tell you a few things about old Charlie here.*

○ **go down the wrong 'way**

Food **goes down the wrong way** when it gets stuck in your throat and makes you choke.

○ **go out of your 'way**

You **go out of your way** to do something when you make a particular effort, or disrupt your plans, in order to be able to do it: *They really went out of their way to give us a good time.* ♦ *see also* **push the boat out** ▷BOAT; **go to great lengths** ▷LENGTHS; **go to town on something** ▷TOWN

○ **go your own 'way**

Someone who **goes their own way** does what they want without considering others: *She is simply a normal balanced youngster who knows her own mind and goes her own way.*

○ **have a 'way with such-and-such**

Someone who **has a way with** a certain kind of thing or person is good at dealing with them: *He's always had a way with children – he'll be a great primary school teacher.*

○ **have a 'way with you**

Someone who **has a way with them** has an attractive manner and is good at impressing people: *He's a handsome man, oh yes, brown and glossy, with a light in his eye, and a smile on his lips and a way with him.*

○ **in a bad 'way**

Someone or something that is **in a bad way** is in a poor condition: *Poor girl, she was in a bad way. The doctor gave her some pills, and she's asleep now.*

○ **in a big 'way**

You do something **in a big way** when you do it on a large scale: *Looks like they're going in to electronic publishing in a big way.*

○ **lead the 'way**

You **lead the way** somewhere when you guide someone there: *She led the way through the undergrowth to the spot where the body was lying.*

○ **learn the 'hard way**

You **learn the hard way** when you realize your mistake through experience, after having ignored someone's advice which would have enabled you to avoid making it: *There is a trick in making privatizations a success, something that the*

UK Government has had to learn the hard way.

○ **learn your way a'round**

You **learn your way around** when you accustom yourself to your new surroundings or duties: *When you've learnt your way around you'll be able to start enjoying yourself a bit more.*

○ **look the other 'way**

You **look the other way** when you pretend not to notice something: *Next time you see that kind of thing going on, don't just look the other way, do something about it.*

○ **make way for**

You **make way for** someone or something when you move aside to give them space: *You should make way for the people getting off the bus before you try to get on.*

○ **no 'way** (*informal*)

You answer '**no way**' to a suggestion or proposal when you consider it unacceptable or impossible: *'Are you going to the concert?' 'No way. It's not worth £20.'*

○ **'one way or another**

One way or another means 'in some way': *Don't worry, we'll get there one way or another.*

○ **out of someone's 'way**

You keep **out of someone's way** when you try to avoid meeting them: *I try to keep out of his way when he's in one of those moods.*

○ **out of the 'way**

1 A job that is **out of the way** is finished: *When I've got this paperwork out of the way I'll be able to enjoy myself a bit more.* **2** A place that is **out of the way** is a long distance from any main roads or public facilities: *It's a bit out of the way – I suppose we'll have to take the car.* ♦ *see also* **the back of beyond** ▷BACK; **in the middle of nowhere** ▷MIDDLE; **out in the sticks** ▷STICKS; **off the beaten track** ▷TRACK

○ **pave the way for**

Someone or something **paves the way for** something to happen if it makes it easy or possible for that thing to happen: *In a case which could pave the way for other people living near Sellafield to bring similar claims, the couple are suing British Nuclear Fuels.*

○ **pay your 'way**

You **pay your way** when you pay your own debts and living expenses as distinct from being dependent on someone else: *And incidentally, I always pay my way, whoever I'm with. Tonight will obviously be no exception.*

○ **rub someone up the wrong 'way**

You **rub someone up the wrong way** when you do or say something that annoys them: *Here she was, creeping around her own house like a burglar, trying to avoid a man who rubbed her up the wrong way.* ♦ *see also* **drive someone round the bend** ▷BEND; **get someone's goat** ▷GOAT; **get on someone's nerves** ▷NERVES; **get up someone's nose** ▷NOSE; **get on someone's wick** ▷WICK

○ **take the 'easy way out**

A person who has to decide between a number of possible actions **takes the easy way out** when they choose the one which is easiest or involves the least effort: *Because of her pain and the stiffness, the easy way out is to stay in her chair, but May is determined not to let pain master her.* ♦ *see also* **the soft option** ▷OPTION

○ **that's the way the cookie 'crumbles**

If someone says '**that's the way the cookie crumbles**', they mean that unpleasant things happen sometimes in life, and that we must accept them: *Hey, that's the way the cookie crumbles; you can't always win you know.*

○ **under 'way**

A project is **under way** when it has begun: *Plans are under way for a new bridge across to the mainland.*

ways

○ **can't have it 'both ways**

If someone says '**you can't have it both ways**', they mean that you should not expect to benefit from two situations, since each excludes the possibility of the other: *Listen, John, you can't have it both ways. There's no point in us meeting again until you've reached a decision.*

○ **change your 'ways** or **mend your 'ways**

You **change**, or **mend**, **your ways** when you start taking your responsibilities seriously after a period of unacceptable or irresponsible behaviour: *I really do think you're going to have to mend your ways very considerably if you're to succeed in this job.* ♦ *see also* **turn over a new leaf** ▷LEAF

○ **in more ways than 'one**
You say '**in more ways than one**' when you use an expression which is appropriate in both its literal, and its figurative or idiomatic, sense: *He celebrated his home debut with his first goal – he used his head in more ways than one.* [= he scored the goal with his head, and he used his intelligence].

○ **no two ways a'bout it**
If you say that there are **no two ways about it**, you mean that you refuse to discuss something any further because you have made your final decision: *I'm afraid there are no two ways about it; you're not going.* ♦ *see also* **that's flat** ▷FLAT; **that's that** ▷THAT

○ **set in your 'ways**
Someone who is **set in their ways** has been doing things in the same way for a long time and is reluctant to change: *A period of sharing your home is sometimes healthy, because it teaches you to be more adaptable and stops you from becoming too set in your ways.*

wayside

○ **fall by the 'wayside**
Someone or something **falls by the wayside** when they fail in what they are trying to do, or get neglected and forgotten about: *One source of solace to the US team must be the rate at which the UK's best players are falling by the wayside.*

wear

○ **the worse for 'wear**
Someone or something that is **the worse for wear** is in a poor state through too much activity, too much alcohol, or too much use: *A few minutes later, feeling decidedly the worse for wear after the last Armagnac had been downed, Mark moved unsteadily into the lift.* ♦ *see also* **have seen better days** ▷DAYS

weather

○ **keep a 'weather eye on**
You **keep a weather eye on** someone

or something if you remain alert and watchful: *Every three months we will send you a statement. This lets you keep a weather eye on your finances.*

○ **make heavy 'weather of** (*BrE*)
You say that someone **is making heavy weather of** something if you think they are making unnecessarily slow and difficult progress with it: *They made heavy weather of the opening sections, completely robbing the music of any momentum or atmosphere.*

○ **under the 'weather**
You are **under the weather** when you are not as healthy or well as you usually are: *Your own ability will vary. You will have off days when you are tired or a bit under the weather.* ♦ *see also* **below** or **not up to par** ▷PAR; **out of sorts** ▷SORTS

weight

○ **carry 'weight**
Someone or something that **carries weight** has an important influence on others: *You do not just want someone whose opinion is going to carry weight but someone who is also going to provide persuasive evidence.*

○ **a 'weight off your mind**
If you say that something is **a weight off your mind**, you mean that you are relieved: *There is nothing wrong with you, nothing that a rest cannot cure. There, is that not good news? A weight off your mind?* ♦ *see also* **a load off your mind** ▷LOAD

○ **pull your 'weight**
You **pull your weight** when you do your full share of work, for example, in a team or group: *I can't tolerate incompetent, unreliable labour. If you're going to stay out your time here, you'll have to pull your weight.*

○ **take the 'weight off your feet**
You **take the weight off your feet** when you sit down for a rest: *Come in and take the weight off your feet. You look tired out.*

○ **throw your 'weight about**
Someone **throws their weight about** when they give orders to other people in an unnecessarily rude way: *Do not use the opportunity of promotion to throw your weight about.*

○ **worth your weight in 'gold**

Someone or something that is **worth their weight in gold** is very useful or helpful: *This is where experienced help is worth its weight in gold, since the correct set-up can only be established by an expert.*

well

○ **all well and 'good** or **all very 'well**

Something that is **all well and good**, or **all very well**, is apparently satisfactory: *Exercises in a room were all very well, but they were no substitute for running every day.*

> **All well and good** and **all very well** are usually followed by 'but ...'.

○ **just as 'well**

If you say that it is **just as well** that something has happened, you mean that you are pleased or feel lucky that it has happened, because you have been able to benefit from it: *It's just as well I didn't go in to work today, or I wouldn't have been in when you called.*

○ **well 'off**

1 You are **well off for** something when you have plenty of it. **2** Someone who is **well off** has plenty of money: *He would be well off now. As an ex-minister there was no doubt he would be able to pick up numerous lucrative directorships.* **3** You are **well off** when you are in a situation that you ought to be contented with: *Some people don't know when they're well off.*

whale

○ **a 'whale of a time**

You have **a whale of a time** when you enjoy yourself thoroughly: *She'd been on the floor for nearly every dance, and was having a whale of a time meeting lots of new people.*

what

○ **what is 'more**

You say '**what is more**', when you are about to mention a final argument which supports a particular point you have made: *I have been fortunate to find a career that I love and, what is more, get paid reasonably for it.* ♦ *see also* **to make matters worse** ▷MATTERS; **to top it all** ▷TOP

wheat

○ **separate the wheat from the 'chaff** or **sort out the wheat from the 'chaff**

You **separate**, or **sort out**, **the wheat from the chaff** when you decide what is valuable and what is worthless: *In theory this filtering system should sort out the wheat from the chaff.* ♦ *see also* **separate** or **sort out the men from the boys** ▷MEN

wheel

○ **behind the 'wheel**

The person who is **behind the wheel** in a car is the driver: *With a sigh of relief, she got behind the wheel. She turned the ignition key. Nothing happened.*

○ **wheel and 'deal**

Someone who **wheels and deals** makes business deals that are clever, but not necessarily honest or moral: *He says that money will be made available for Glenn Hoddle to buy players and he will wheel and deal as he usually does to get the men he wants.*

wheels

○ **oil the 'wheels**

Something that **oils the wheels** of a particular activity makes it work more easily, especially when it involves use of influence or money: *Compliments oil the wheels of life. Even a bit of flattery doesn't go amiss.*

○ **set the 'wheels in motion**

Someone or something **sets the wheels in motion** when they cause an activity to begin: *With the sale of the manor, Jane set the wheels in motion to find somewhere smaller to live.*

while

○ **worth someone's 'while**

If you tell someone whom you have asked to do something that you will make it **worth their while**, you mean that you will pay them to do it, or give them something in return: *'That depends,' he said softly, 'On whether you make it worth my while.' Peter smiled a predatory smile.* ♦ *see also* **for someone's pains** ▷PAINS

whip

○ **crack the 'whip**

Someone who **cracks the whip** uses their power and influence over others in a severe manner: *He has been urging them to crack the whip a bit, arguing that the whole establishment needs reorganization before reforms can be introduced effectively.*

> A **whip** is a long narrow strip of leather, or a narrow rope, attached to a handle, for striking people or animals with.

whisker

○ **within a 'whisker**

You are, or you come, **within a whisker** of something when you are very close to it: *He came within a whisker of losing his job.*

> An animal's **whiskers** are the long coarse hairs growing around its mouth.

whistle

○ **blow the 'whistle**

Someone **blows the whistle** on someone else if they make that person's illegal or deceitful schemes known to the public: *He blew the whistle on safety violations by his drilling company, two months after the Piper Alpha disaster.*

whys

○ **whys and 'wherefores** or (*AmE*) **why and 'wherefore**

The **whys and wherefores**, or **why and wherefore**, of a particular situation are the reasons and explanations behind it: *I want to find the answers to certain whys and wherefores which have puzzled me all my life.*

wick

○ **get on someone's 'wick** (*BrE*)

Someone who **gets on your wick** annoys or irritates you: *Of course I care about you. You just get on my wick at times, that's all.* ♦ *see also* **drive someone round the bend** ▷BEND; **get someone's goat** ▷GOAT; **get on someone's nerves** ▷NERVES; **get up someone's nose** ▷NOSE; **rub someone up the wrong way** ▷WAY

wildfire

○ **spread like 'wildfire**

Something, such as a piece of news, a rumour, or disease **spreads like wildfire** when it spreads very fast: *The news of his marriage spread like wildfire.*

will

○ **at 'will**

You can do something **at will** if you can do it whenever, and however, you want to: *I'd love to be able to spend vast amounts of money at will.*

○ **where there's a will there's a 'way**

If someone says '**where there's a will there's a way**', they mean that if you want something strongly enough, you will find a way of getting or achieving it.

○ **with the best will in the 'world**

If you say that **with the best will in the world** you cannot manage something, you mean that however much you would like to be able to do it, it is impossible: *With the best will in the world we can't allow you to do that.*

wind

○ **get 'wind of**

You **get wind of** something when you hear about it: *By February the local press had got wind of the affair.*

○ **get the 'wind up** or **have the 'wind up** (*informal*)

You **get**, or **have**, **the wind up** when you get anxious or alarmed; you **put the wind up** someone when you make them anxious or alarmed: *It was his mental state which put the wind up the hospital staff.*

○ **it's an ill 'wind** or **it's an ill wind that blows nobody any 'good**

If someone says '**it's an ill wind**', or '**it's an ill wind that blows nobody any good**', they mean that some good has come of an apparent misfortune: *However, it was an ill wind and some did profit by it, namely the undertakers.*

○ **sail close to the 'wind**

Someone who **is sailing close to the wind** is taking a big risk, by being close to breaking a law or social rule: *He'd been sailing close to the wind for years and everything was just about to blow up in his face.*

> If a boat sails too closely towards the direction from which the wind is blowing, it is likely to turn over.

○ **take the wind out of someone's 'sails**

You **take the wind out of someone's sails** when you make them suddenly lose belief in what they are doing or saying, especially when they felt very strongly about it before: *Wouldn't it take the wind out of his sails more thoroughly if she seemed indifferent rather than angry?*

wine

○ **wine and 'dine**

You **wine and dine** when you have, or go out for, a lot of expensive meals; you **wine and dine someone** when you take them out for expensive meals: *Tony bursts into a plush restaurant where Sharon is being wined and dined by a romantic Italian rival for her affections.*

wing

○ **under someone's 'wing**

You are **under someone's wing** if you are under their protection or guidance; someone **takes you under their wing** if they decide to protect or guide you: *Hattie had the wonderful ability of taking people under her wing. She was mum, sister – everything to all of us.*

wings

○ **clip someone's 'wings**

You **clip someone's wings** when you take away from them the power to do something: *Her nose wrinkled with distaste. 'Actually I've decided against having children – they clip your wings.'*

People sometimes clip birds' wings to stop them from flying away.

○ **spread your 'wings**

You **spread your wings** when you try to carry out your plans for yourself, rather than under someone else's guidance: *If you're interested in doing business with people who encourage you to spread your wings, why not make a date to come and see us?*

○ **wait in the 'wings**

You **are waiting in the wings** if you are waiting in readiness, for example to take over someone's job: *Waiting in the wings, there was a young colleague of his. Charles wanted his protégé in and I happened to be in the way.*

The **wings**, here, are the areas at each side of a stage in a theatre, where performers wait to enter, hidden from the audience.

wink

○ **not get a wink of 'sleep** or **not sleep a 'wink**

You **don't get a wink of sleep**, or you **don't sleep a wink**, when you do not go to sleep at all: *'Holiday!' he stormed. 'That was no holiday. I didn't get a wink of sleep.'*

winner

○ **on to a 'winner**

You are **on to a winner** if you have found a person or situation that is likely to ensure you success: *He's not going to give up that easily. He knows when he's on to a winner.*

wire

○ **down to the 'wire** (*AmE*)

If something goes **down to the wire**, it continues until the last possible moment: *Sue had to study down to the wire to finish her schoolwork on time.*

wires

○ **get your 'wires crossed**

People **get their wires crossed** when they misunderstand each other: *We have to talk. Somewhere along the way we seem to have got our wires crossed.*

wish

○ **wouldn't wish such-and-such on 'anyone**

If you say that you **would not wish** some bad experience **on anyone**, you mean that it is so unpleasant that no-one should have to suffer it: *I wouldn't wish this flu on anyone.*

with

○ **'with it**

1 You are **with it** when you are concentrating on, or paying attention to, what is happening around you: *Sorry, I'm not really with it today. What did you say?* **2** (*rather old*) Someone who is **with it** is fashionable: *I always used to wish my parents were a bit more with it.*

wits

○ **at your wits' 'end**

You are **at your wits' end** when you cannot think how to deal with a problem and are in despair about it: *I don't know how I'm going to pay the rent this month. I'm at my wits' end.* ♦ *see also* **at the end of your tether** ▷END

> Your **wits** are your ability to think fast in a difficult situation.

○ **collect your 'wits** or **gather your 'wits**

You **collect**, or **gather, your wits** when you try to think calmly: *Eva gathered her wits together. She must concentrate hard so she could report in full detail when she got back.*

○ **have your 'wits about you** or **keep your 'wits about you**

You **have**, or **are keeping, your wits about you** when you are constantly prepared to deal with dangers and difficulties: *For this kind of interview you need all your wits about you, which means being well prepared and getting a good night's sleep beforehand.*

○ **pit your 'wits**

You **pit your wits** against someone when you compete with them in a trial of intelligence: *Here's your chance to pit your wits against the world champions.*

○ **scared out of your 'wits**

You are **scared out of your wits** when you are terrified: *Frightened? I was scared out of my wits, and that's the truth.*

wobbly

○ **throw a 'wobbly** (*BrE*; *informal*)

Someone **throws a wobbly** when they suddenly become very angry about something: *It's no good trying to work with someone who throws a wobbly every time something goes wrong.* ♦ *see also* **go off at the deep end** ▷END; **blow a fuse** ▷FUSE; **let fly** ▷LET; **blow** or **flip your lid** ▷LID; **do your nut** ▷NUT; **lose your rag** ▷RAG; **fly into a rage** ▷ RAGE; **hit the roof** ▷ROOF; **blow your stack** ▷STACK; **lose your temper** ▷ TEMPER; **blow your top** ▷TOP

wolf

○ **cry 'wolf**

You **cry wolf** when you regularly ask for help or give people warning of an imaginary fear, so that when you really do need help, or when there is a real danger, people no longer believe you: *He nearly said, 'My wife is ill,' but he had cried wolf too often.*

○ **keep the 'wolf from the door**

If you do something to **keep the wolf from the door**, you do it in order to keep away poverty or hunger: *I work part-time in a library, just to pay the mortgage and keep the wolf from the door. Really, I'm a writer.*

○ **a wolf in sheep's 'clothing**

Someone who is described as **a wolf in sheep's clothing** is a dangerous or cruel person who appears to be gentle and harmless: *The murderer was a really first-grade monster. A beast. A raving wolf in sheep's clothing.* ♦ *see also* **a snake in the grass** ▷SNAKE

wonder

○ **little 'wonder** or **no 'wonder** or **small 'wonder**

If you say that it is **little**, or **no**, or **small**, **wonder** that something is the case, you mean that it is not surprising that it is: *The number of cases of skin cancer has more than doubled to at least 3,000. Small wonder that doctors are calling for the return of the parasol.*

wonders

○ **do 'wonders** or **work 'wonders**

Someone or something **does**, or **works**, **wonders** if they achieve marvellous results: *Have some of this, it works wonders for indigestion.*

○ **wonders will never 'cease**

If someone says '**wonders will never cease**' they mean, humorously, or sarcastically, that they are pleasantly surprised because they didn't expect the person in question would do or achieve something in particular, or the thing in question would happen: *I can't believe it! Wonders will never cease. How did you manage it?*

wood

○ **can't see the wood for the 'trees** (*BrE*) or **can't see the woods for the 'trees** (*AmE*)

If you say that someone **can't see the wood, or the woods, for the trees**, you mean that they are so concerned with detail that they cannot see the obvious or general point: *One of the main features of people under stress is that* very often they can't see the wood for the trees.

○ **touch 'wood**

You superstitiously say '**touch wood!**', sometimes touching something wooden at the same time, when you have just said that things are all right, and you do not want them to go wrong: *I look on life with a great deal of optimism, and touch wood, I've been fairly lucky in my life.*

woodwork

○ **come out of the 'woodwork** or **crawl out of the 'woodwork**

People and things that **come**, or **crawl**, **out of the woodwork** make themselves known after having been hidden for a long time: *All sorts of secrets started crawling out of the woodwork after a few drinks.*

wool

○ **pull the 'wool over someone's eyes**

You **pull the wool over someone's eyes** when you deliberately deceive or trick them: *I'm not stupid. You can't pull the wool over my eyes like that. I'm not so easily fooled, oh no.*

word

○ **as good as your 'word**

Someone who is **as good as their word** keeps a promise: *She had always promised her schoolfriend a room when she got her own apartment. She was as good as her word.* ♦ *see also* **true to your word** ▷WORD

○ **by word of 'mouth**

You receive information **by word of mouth** when you hear it from people, rather than read it or hear it on radio or television: *Such events succeeded in attracting large audiences via word of mouth invitations.*

○ **a dirty 'word**

If you say that such-and-such is **a dirty word** for a particular person or group of people, you mean that they do not like the particular person or thing mentioned, and that they may react badly if you mention them: *In most serious artists' studios, from Paris to New York, prettiness was indeed a dirty word.*

○ **from the word 'go**

Something that has been the case **from the word go**, has been so since the beginning: *The marriage was doomed from the word go, although I didn't realize this until it was all over.*

○ **get a word in 'edgeways** or (*AmE*) **get a word in 'edgewise**

You **can't get a word in edgeways**, or **edgewise**, when someone else is talking so much that you cannot get a chance to speak: *Whenever Barker was allowed to get a word in edgeways, it was obvious that he would be fascinating if only Hamilton would remain silent long enough for him to do so.*

○ **give your 'word**

You **give your word** when you make a promise: *Francis, you promised! That was part of the deal! You gave your word, and now you're telling me it's not on.*

○ **go back on your 'word**

You **go back on your word** when you do not do something that you said, or promised you would do: *All sorts of doubts clouded my mind. What if the dealer had a cash-in-hand offer from someone else and went back on his word?*

○ **have the last 'word**

You **have the last word** in an argument when you make the final remark: *You always have to have the last word, don't you? Can't you just let it rest?*

○ **not breathe a 'word**

If you say that you will **not breathe a word**, you mean that you will not tell a particular secret to anyone: *Do you promise not to breathe a word to anyone?*

○ **not have a good word to 'say about**

Someone who **does not have a good word to say about** a certain person or thing does not like them, and considers that they have a lot of faults: *His wife definitely was aware of the relationship and never had a good word to say about Mary.*

○ **put in a good 'word**

You **put in a good word** for someone when you speak about them to someone influential in a way that gives a good impression of them: *Because he put in a good word for her, Ruth was given the job without references.*

○ **say the 'word**

If you tell someone to '**say the word**', or '**just say the word**', you mean that they should tell you as soon as they need your help, advice, etc: *What would you like now? Cereal? Toast? Fruit? Just say the word.*

○ **spread the 'word**

You **spread the word** when you make sure that as many people as possible know about a particular thing: *I'd like you to spread the word around and tell people about my new shop and the things they can buy here.*

○ **take someone at their 'word**

You **take someone at their word** when you accept what they say as being true without checking that it is so: *The problem is whether to take a politician at his word when he is publicly declaring a desire for greater friendship and understanding with these people.*

○ **take my 'word for it**

You say to someone '**take my word for it**' when you want them to know that what you are saying is true, and that they should trust you: *There are things I can't tell you guys, you'll just have to take my word for it.*

○ **there's many a true word spoken in 'jest**

If someone says '**there's many a true word spoken in jest**', they mean that a lot of jokes people make actually have a basis in truth.

○ **true to your 'word**

You are **true to your word** when you do what you say you will do, or keep a promise: *'Now Felix, if you stand there I shall lash out at the next off ball and knock you down.' Felix did not move and true to his word the batsman knocked him down.* ♦ *see also* **as good as your word** ▷WORD

○ **word for 'word**

1 You repeat something **word for word** when you say the exact words that you heard: *When she recounted word for word the interview she had had with Moran they exploded into wild laughter.*
2 You translate **word for word** when you translate into words that correspond exactly with those in the original language: *They recognize that it is inadequate and sometimes completely misleading to translate the text word for word.*

○ **a word in someone's 'ear**

You have **a word in someone's ear** when you tell them something secretly, or when you tell them something that you think they ought to know: *I wonder if I could just have a word in your ear before we continue with the next point.*

words

○ **eat your 'words** or (*BrE*) **swallow your 'words**

You have to **eat**, or **swallow**, **your words** when you are forced to admit that something you said before was wrong: *I'm not what he thinks and he'll have to eat his words.*

○ **have 'words with someone**

You **have words**, or **have words with someone**, when you have an angry argument with them: *You know. I was in a bad mood, and he kept pestering me, so we had words.*

○ **put words into someone's 'mouth**

Someone who **puts words into your mouth** states that you have said something that you have not said, or suggests that you are about to say something that you have no intention of saying: *I did not say that about you! Don't you dare put words into my mouth!*

○ **take the words out of someone's 'mouth**

Someone who **takes the words out of your mouth** says exactly what you were intending to say.

○ **words 'fail me**

You say '**words fail me**' when you are so surprised, overwhelmed or annoyed that you cannot express yourself: *I cannot tolerate incompetence. And as for you, Fiona, words fail me.*

work *see also* **Idioms study** page 216

○ **all work and no 'play**

When people talk about '**all work and no play**', or say '**all work and no play makes Jack a dull boy**' they mean that too much working and not enough enjoyment leads to inefficiency, and may make you bored, or boring: *It seems that all work and no play, even in the workplace, makes not only for a dull boy, but also one that is not as efficient.*

IDIOMS *study* work

The next time you write or talk about **work** you might try to use some of the following idioms. (Remember you can see how to use each idiom correctly by looking at its entry, which you can find under the word printed in heavy type.)

being busy

up to your **eyeballs**
up to your **eyes**

have your **hands** full
up to your **neck**

working very hard

burn the **candle** at both ends
work like a **dog**
(do) the **donkey** work
work your **fingers** to the bone
work your **guts** out

keep your **nose** to the grindstone
put your **shoulder** to the wheel
all **work** and no play

○ **do someone's 'dirty work**
You **do someone's dirty work** when you do the unpleasant jobs that they do not want to do, especially when it involves explaining or apologizing for mistakes, or telling people things that they will not like hearing: *They asked me to protest to get them off the hook. I told them to do their own dirty work.*

○ **have your 'work cut out**
You **have your work cut out** when you face a challenging task: *The leaders had their work cut out keeping the group together, and one or both had to remain at the back to motivate the slower ones.*

○ **make light 'work of something**
You **make light work of** a task when you do it very quickly and efficiently: *Make light work of cooking with the help of this electronic food processor.*

works

○ **in the 'works** (*AmE*)
Something that is **in the works** is being planned or is already underway: *Don't worry. Your salary request is in the works.*

○ **shoot the 'works** (*AmE*; *informal*)
If you **shoot the works**, you do or use everything: *Let's shoot the works and*

dance all night. □ *Garry put all of his money on the roulette table and said, 'Shoot the works!'*

> The term comes from shooting (throwing) dice.

world

○ **dead to the 'world**
You are **dead to the world** if you are very deeply asleep: *I hadn't realized how tired I was till I saw that bed. Ten minutes later I was dead to the world.*

○ **do you a 'world of good**
Something that **does you a world of good** makes you feel much better: *Everyone should spend a week somewhere like this once a year. It does you a world of good.*

○ **go 'up in the world**
You **go up in the world** if you are successful: *John's gone up in the world since he left school. I hear he's a merchant banker in the City now.*

○ **have the 'world at your feet**
Someone who **has the world at their feet** is very successful and admired by many people: *You've got the world at your feet, everything you've ever wanted, and look at you. You're still unhappy.*

○ **in a world of your 'own**
Someone who is **in a world of their own** is detached from everyday life, and preoccupied with their own thoughts: *Never mind. The old man evidently lived in a world of his own; it's pointless blaming him.*

○ **mean the 'world to someone**
Someone **means the world to you** if you are very fond of them, or if you love them very much; something **means the world to you** if it is very important to you: *She means the world to me. That's why I've got to try, even though it looks hopeless.*

○ **out of this 'world**
Something that is **out of this world** is marvellous, or excellent: *The food and the service there is out of this world.*

○ **think the 'world of**
You **think the world of** someone if you love or admire them greatly: *Lee thinks the world of that dog.*

○ **the world is your 'oyster**
If someone says **'the world is your oyster'**, they mean that all opportunities in life are open to you.

> Some oysters have pearls inside them, and are therefore seen as a symbol of wealth and opportunity.

○ **a 'world of difference**
There is **a world of difference** between things if they are entirely different: *There is a world of difference between ham that has been sliced from the bone and the prepackaged stuff.*

worlds

○ **the best of 'both worlds**
You get **the best of both worlds** when you can enjoy two things that cannot usually be enjoyed together: *Working and looking after children part-time gives me the best of both worlds.* ♦ *see also* **the grass is always greener on the other side of the fence** ▷GRASS; **have your cake and eat it** ▷CAKE

○ **'worlds apart**
Things that are **worlds apart** are entirely different: *The Chinese food you get here and the food you get in China are worlds apart.* ♦ *see also* **poles apart** ▷POLES

worm

○ **a worm's eye 'view**
A **worm's eye view** is the way someone who is closely involved in something sees it: *Those accepted for training at Sotheby's will get a one year worm's-eye view of the company in three or more departments and they will be paid £9,500.*

> This idiom is derived from the more common 'bird's eye view', meaning a good view, especially from above. Worms live in the earth, and so 'view' things from the inside.

○ **the worm has 'turned**
If you say that **the worm has turned**, you mean that someone who has suffered over a long period of time has decided not to tolerate an unpleasant situation any longer: *Ever since I came here, you have treated me like dirt! Well, the worm has turned, madam!*

worst

○ **if the worst comes to the 'worst** or (*AmE*) **if worst comes to worst**
You say that something may happen **if the worst comes to the worst**, or **if worst comes to worst**, if you think it may happen if things develop in the most unfavourable way: *Look, if the worst comes to the worst and you really can't contact us, we'll just have to come looking for you.*

wounds

○ **lick your 'wounds**
You say that someone **is licking their wounds** when they are comforting themselves after something painful or disappointing has happened to them, especially if you do not feel a great amount of sympathy for them: *They met when Sarah was still licking her wounds after her romance with the Duke of Westminster had ended.*

> When an animal has been injured, it licks its wounds in order to help them heal.

wraps

○ **keep under 'wraps**
You **keep something under wraps** when you keep it hidden or secret: *All*

this has to be kept under wraps. You've signed the Official Secrets Act.

wringer

○ **put someone through the 'wringer**

You **put someone through the wringer** when you ask them difficult questions in order to find out if they are doing their job properly: *Barry Fry wants to put Stan Flashman through the wringer by forcing him to account for yesterday's decision to sack him as manager.*

> A **wringer** is a device that squeezes water out of wet cloth.

wrongs

○ **two wrongs don't make a 'right**

If someone says '**two wrongs don't make a right**', they mean that it is foolish to think that just because someone has hurt or angered you, that you should do the same to them in return: *I do not think there is any punishment in this world that would fit what they have done. My instinct would be to do the same to them, but two wrongs don't make a right.*

> In this idiom, telling a long exaggerated story is likened to drawing out and twisting fibres.

year

○ **since the year 'dot** (*BrE*)

Something that has been happening **since the year dot** has been happening since the beginning, or ever since you can remember: *Scientists have been involved in war since the year dot.*

young

○ **you're only young 'once**

If someone says '**you're only young once**', they mean that you have to take advantage of being young, because there are some things you won't be able to do any more when you are older: *'Oh, I don't know.' Vi pursed her lips. 'You're only young once. May as well enjoy yourself.'* ♦ *see also* **seize the day** ▷DAY

○ **go the whole nine 'yards** (*AmE*)

If you **go the whole nine yards**, you go to the limit, or do everything you can: *I only planned to start the campaign for him, but then I went the whole nine yards.*

yarn

○ **spin a 'yarn**

Someone **spins a yarn** when they tell you a story, usually with a great degree of exaggeration: *He spun me some yarn about coming face to face with a shark.*

zonkers

○ **go 'zonkers** (*AmE; informal*)

You **go zonkers** when you act in a foolish or irrational manner: *Dan went zonkers when they said he'd failed the exam.*